HEGELIAN/WHITEHEADIAN PERSPECTIVES

Darrel E. Christensen

Lanham • New York • London

B
2948
.C49
1988

Copyright © 1989 by

University Press of America,® **Inc.**

4720 Boston Way
Lanham, MD 20706

3 Henrietta Street
London WC2E 8LU England

All rights reserved

Printed in the United States of America

British Cataloging in Publication Information Available

Library of Congress Cataloging-in-Publication Data

Christensen, Darrel E.
Hegelian/Whiteheadian perspectives / Darrel E. Christensen.
p. cm.
Includes bibliographical references and indexes.
1. Hegel, Georg Wilhelm Friedrich, 1770–1831. 2. Whitehead,
Alfred North, 1861–1947. I. Title.
B2948.C49   1988
190—dc 19   88–17251 CIP
ISBN 0–8191–7078–X (alk. paper)
ISBN 0–8191–7079–8 (pbk. : alk. paper)

All University Press of America books are produced on acid-free paper.
The paper used in this publication meets the minimum requirements of American
National Standard for Information Sciences—Permanence of Paper for Printed
Library Materials, ANSI Z39.48–1984.

Assistance with the composition costs
in connection with the preparation of this volume
was provided by
the Elna M. Ellis Trust Fund of San Marino, California.

Acknowledgements of Permissions to Reprint

Our thanks are due the following publishers for permission to reprint:

2,294 words from Alfred North Whitehead, *Process and Reality*, are reprinted by permission of The Macmillan Publishing Co.

661 words from Alfred North Whitehead, *Science and the Modern World* are reprinted by permission of the Macmillan Publishing Co. (for rights in the United States and Canada) and the Cambridge University Press (for rights in the remainder of the world).

1,509 words from Karl R. Popper, *Objective Knowledge* are reprinted by permission of the Clarendon Press.

1,092 words from Charles Sanders Peirce, *Collected Papers* are reprinted by permission of the Harvard University Press.

Quotations from two works by Henry Nelson Wieman – *Man's Ultimate Commitment* (355 words) and *The Source of Human Good* (922 words) are by permission of the Southern Illinois University Press.

Quotations from Henry Nelson Wieman, *Religious Experience and Scientific Method* (437 words) are by permission of Laura M. Wieman and The Southern Illinois University Press.

Quotations from Wm. Desmond, *Art and the Absolute. A Study of Hegel's Aesthetic* (317 words); Donald Phillip Verene, *Hegel's Recollection: A Study of Images in the Phenomenology of Spirit* (681 words); and George R. Lucas, jr. (Ed.), *Hegel and Whitehead* (364 words) are reprinted by permission of the State University of New York Press.

568 words from Josef Simon, "The Categories in the 'Habitual' and in the 'Speculative' Proposition: Observations on Hegel's Concept of Science", translated by Gunther Heilbrunn, are reprinted by permission of Wilhelm Braumüller of Vienna and Stuttgart, the publisher of the original German edition, and the Pennsylvania State University Press, which published the translation in *Contemporary German Philosophy*, Vol. 2.

423 words from Dorothy Emmett, *The Nature of Metaphysical Thinking* are reprinted by permission of the author.

Quotations from Philip Wheelwright, *Metaphor and Reality* (453 words) are reprinted by permission of the Indiana University Press.

A quotation (86 words) and a figure (on p. 299 following) drawn from Darrel E. Christensen, *The Search for Concreteness: Reflections on Hegel and Whitehead* are reprinted by permission of the Associated University Presses.

Dedicated to my two grandsons,

Jeremy and Ryan Baugh

Destined to live in a technology-dominated society,
may they one day live
in a land that is humanized by philosophy.

TABLE OF CONTENTS

Table of Contents vii
Abbreviations of More Frequently Cited Sources. ix
Preface xi

A Strategy with Hegel

I. *On Rendering Hegel's Truth which is the (Concretely Actual) Whole Adequate and Tolerable.* 1

Some Aspects of a Hegelian/Whiteheadian Synthesis

II. *On Rendering Whitehead's "Complete Fact" Complete: Aspects of a Constructive Critique of Whitehead from a Somewhat Hegelian Perspective* 23

III. *Can the Contrasts Constitutive of an 'Actual Occasion of Experience' Be Specified in their Concrete Particularity? Aspects of a Somewhat Hegelian Critique of Whitehead* 45

IV. *Whitehead's 'Prehension' and Hegel's 'Mediation': Parallel Dynamical Concepts at the Service of Different Methodologies* 71

The Perspective on Peirce

V. *A Hegelian Critique of Peirce* 101
VI. *Was Hegel 'According to Peirce' the Great Vindicator of Pragmaticism?* 115

The Perspective on Popper

VII. *A Hegelian Critique of Popper's Theory of Objective Knowledge* 123

The Perspective on Wieman

VIII. *Henry Nelson Wieman and the Critical Tradition* 155

The Perspective on Language

IX.	*The Social Character of Concrete Language*	171
X.	*How is it that a (Concrete) Fact Can Speak for Itself? Process Phenomenology as an Alternative of Philosophical Empiricism*	189
XI.	*Recollection, Image, and Metaphor in Hegel's Phenomenology of Spirit*	201
XII.	*Hypothetical and Actual Perspectives on Metaphor From a Hegelian Point of View*	227
	Appendix: *Metaphor and the Analogia Entis of St. Thomas Aquinas*	260

Some Additional Perspectives

XIII.	*Cultural Relativity as an Aspect of Absolute Truth: A Neo-Hegelian/Whiteheadian Construal of the Relationship Between Society and Truth*	277
XIV.	*The Whole that is the Context of Meaning*	301
XV.	*On the Moderation of Scepticism; First Philosophy and the Particular Sciences*	309

Usages	329
Index of Terms	331
Index of Names	337

ABBREVIATIONS OF FREQUENTLY CITED SOURCES

G. F. W. Hegel

Einleitung — *Einleitung in die Geschichte der Philosophie,* ed. by Johannes Hoffmeister (Hamburg: Felix Meiner, 1940).
Logik/Logic — *Wissenschaft der Logik,* Ed. by Georg Lasson, in two volumes (Hamburg: Meiner, 1934)); or *Hegel's Science of Logic,* trans. A. V. Miller (London: George Allen & Unwin Ltd., 1969).
Phän./Phen. — *Phänomenologie des Geistes,* Hoffmeister Ed. (Hamburg: Meiner, 1952); or *Phenomenology of Mind,* trans. J. B. Baillie (New York: Macmillan, 1955).
Phil. of Hist. — *The Philosophy of History,* trans. J. Sibree (New York: Dover Publications, 1956).

Alfred North Whitehead

AI *Adventures of Ideas* (New York: Macmillan, 1933).
MT *Modes of Thought* (New York: Macmillan, 1938).
PR *Process and Reality,* corrected edition prepared by David R. Griffin and Donald W. Sherburne (New York: The Free Press, 1978).
SMW *Science and the Modern World* (New York: Macmillan, 1926).

Charles Saunders Peirce

CP *The Collected Papers of Charles Saunders Peirce.*

Karl R. Popper

OK *Objective Knowledge: An Evolutionary Approach* (Oxford: Clarendon Press, 1972).
SB *The Self and its Brain: An Argument for Interactionism,* coauthored with John C. Eccles (Munich: Springer International, 1977), Part I (authored by Popper).

Henry Nelson Wieman

See page 170 at the end of Chapter VIII.

Other Essays by the Author Involved with the Same Basic Problematic:

CHSS "Can Hegel's Concept of Self-evidence be Salvaged?" Presented to the 5th bi-annual meeting of the Hegel Society of America, Oct. 12-14, 1978, Pennsylvania State University, *Idealistic Studies,* Vol. XIV, No. 2 (May, 1984).

KWdT "Eine Hegelisch/Whiteheadsche Kritik an Whiteheads dipolarem Theismus", prepared for the Conference on "Naturphilosophie und natürliche Theologie bei Alfred N. Whitehead", sponsored by the

Schweizerischen Philosophischen Gesellschaft und die Schweizerischen Arbeitskreis für ethische Forschung, , held Sept. 2-5, 1987, in Sigriswil. It is anticipated that the contributions to this meeting will be published in book form, possibly as a supplement to *Studia Philosophica*.

LHW "George R. Lucas, Jr., *Two Views of Freedom in Process Thought: A Study of Hegel and Whitehead*", *CLEO*, Vol. 13, No. 4 (1983).

RAtP "On Rescuing the Hegelian Absolute through Whitehead's Perishing", prepared for the XVII. World Congress of Philosophy, 21-27 Aug., 1983, in Montréal, Canada, and published with the proceedings of the Congress.

SC *The Search for Concreteness: Reflections on Hegel and Whitehead*, containing Book I, *Hegel and the Concrete: A Somewhat Whiteheadian Perspective,* and Book II, *Whitehead and the Concrete: A Somewhat Hegelian Perspective.* (Cranburg, New Jersey: Susquehanna University Press through Associated University Presses, 1986).

TCMM "A Throb of Creation and the Making of Meaning; Toward a Neo-Hegelian/Whiteheadian Concept of Meaning", presented to the Conference on "The Meaning of Life — The Meaning of History", held in Warsaw, Aug., 24-28, 1981, under the sponsorship of the Polish Academy of Sciences, *Dialectics and Humanism,* Vol. VIII, No. 3 (1981, Summer).

PREFACE

Rather than *Hegelian/Whiteheadian Perspectives*, this collection of essays might well have been entitled *A Hegelian/Whiteheadian Perspective.* This would have served to emphasize that it is *a single* systematic perspective that is working itself out within several variant contexts.

The collection might also quite properly have been entitled *Perspectives Beyond Hegel and Whitehead*, which would have served to emphasize that a reconstruction is under way that in some ways takes me beyond what most informed readers will recognize as a merely Hegelian or merely Whiteheadian Problematic.

I owe the following brief summary to the thoughtful reader of an earlier form of this *Collection,* to whom I wish to express my thanks, even though his name is unknown to me:

> The goal of this *Book* is to develop a critical phenomenology which unites the Hegelian notion of self-evidence (holism, circularity, presuppositionlessness) with the Whiteheadian notion of the perishing of all actual occasions. This is to provide the core for first philosophy which in turn is to be carefully distinguished from both the sciences and the philosophy of science, or more generally speaking, *Wissenschaftstheorie.* This phenomenological first philosophy is then applied to the interpretation and critique of various individuals (Peirce, Popper, and Wieman) and philosophical issues (the philosophy of language, cultural relativity, skepticism). The essays are quite loosely related to each other and have as their unifying thread the theory just mentioned.

The statement is helpful, and generally accurate as far as it goes. This is except for seeming to include the particular sciences under *Wissenschaftstheorie*, which does not correspond to my usage and, indeed, strikes me as odd. Also, it would reflect my intentions more accurately if it were made clear in the final sentence that I do not subsume phenomenology under theory. The point proves absolutely crucial to the defense of the status that I claim for Hegelian self-evidence.

To this most general account I would add the five paragraphs following in this section, which, however, the reader may safely pass over or merely scan at this point, seeing that they can serve equally well as a retrospective overview, after the essays have been read, at which point they will doubtless be more readily understood.

A dominating motif of the *Collection* is the developing and relating of the sphere of concrete actuality, grasped as such in a lived occasion construed in a Hegelian manner in its self-evidence, on the one hand, and the sphere of hypothetical thinking and of potentialities, construed in a manner reminiscent of Whitehead, as theory, on the other, as two distinct spheres that require explication by very different methods if each is to retain its authentic character and unnecessary confusion is to be averted. This is because concrete actuality grasped *a priori* as such, although this grasping takes place within the lived occasion — the occasion having already actualized what of its envisioned future could be actualized — is ever on the fringe of being **retrospective**. This grasp, moreover, can be recapitulated in the sense of being set forth in linear language for the understanding only through a **retrospective** (secondary) reflection. Hypothetical thinking, by way of contrast, being always oriented toward an unrealized future, is **prospective** rather than retrospective. What results is a duality of perspectives — let us call these the concretely actual perspective (the sphere of concrete fact), and the hypothetically potential perspective (the sphere of theory). The two perspectives are understood to follow one another alternately in temporal succession, the latter being derivative from the former upon the perishing of the occasion. That we do not directly perceive this alternation is attributed to the fact that death in the sense of "my own death" is something of which we can never be conscious. What we are normally conscious of is merely(!) change, and on the present analysis this is found to be constituted by alterations from one completely determined self-evident occasion to another, hypothetical thinking — the alternating phase, which turns out to be that by which possibilities may be introduced through secondary reflection — bridging the peaks between occasions climaxing in achieved coherence.

That the described alternation in temporal succession resists being mediated to a unity of accents within an inclusive identity in Hegelian fashion, following the present theory, is owing to the fact that the sphere of concrete fact consists exclusively of internal relations and the sphere of theory consists exclusively of contingent relations (this latter being subject to change and manipulation), which may be arbitrarily internal or external or mixed. The upshot is that it is only from a hypothetical perspective, such as that assumed by Whitehead, that one may tell a likely story about external relations being rendered internal, this being a story of such a sort that it can never be known to be true or false, knowledge here being essentially Hegelian, i.e., not belief in theory that has somehow been warranted but the knowledge of a lived occasion grasped *a priori* in its self-evidence. It would seem to make no sense from an actual perspective to inquire as to what could be prior to what is grasped *a priori,* unless perhaps to occasion a response in the form of belief in the capability of theoretical reason to prepare possibilities for actualization or of faith in the Divine Transcendence.

I wish just here to introduce the consideration that concrete actuality, being grasped *a priori,* is not, and indeed cannot conceivably be, itself the (subject-)object of a search. This is to say, wherever there is consciousness and a world present for consciousness, the occasion is already present as sufficiently explicit to render possible, at least in principle, a phenomenological account of its being grasped *a priori* as such. Thus in my *The Search for Concreteness: Reflections on Hegel and Whitehead* (hereafter SC), the term "search", insofar as it pertains not only to Whitehead but to either Hegel's or my own view, as well, contains an initial ambiguity, which I later clear up: given the *a priori* status of concrete actuality grasped as such, it is the search for **an appropriate philosophical explication** of concreteness that can only, in the final analysis, be in view.

It is being presupposed in the foregoing that the accounts of Hegel and Whitehead as they stand simply do not serve the same objective nor do they operate at the same level. They have, in fact, little in common, as I have endeavored to show, especially in my SC. This is with the result that even when pains are taken to develop analogues that may with plausibility be viewed as complementary — the aim of the reconstruction of method for first philosophy that I have adumbrated in SC and am further developing within the present context — these are systematically related only by temporal succession. The systematic relation that I develop between the two perspectives, regarded from a Hegelian point of view, may thus at first glance appear to be of a sufficiently weak sort to render at least understandable that Giacomo Rinaldi, in a review the same *Work* which I am informed is to appear in *Idealistic Studies,* should have been led to doubt that I have found them to be systematically related at all. In this connection, it is to be acknowledged that relations that are merely external are not known, but remain no more than theory, a point the profound importance of which might easily escape a Whiteheadian, I suppose, or indeed any philosopher who proposes to regard truth as warranted belief. The necessity of regarding the two perspectives as alternants, notwithstanding, should not be permitted to prevent us from noting the parallelism of their basic structures, owing to the fact that *both exhibit, and indeed are constituted by, precisely the same discriminations.* In this sense the hypothetical perspective — regardless of what hypothetical speculations may have been introduced into it through the manipulation of symbols — ever bears within it as its most basic stratum a shadow image of the system of internally related discriminations that were priorly constitutive of the actual perspective from which it was derived. In SC, I label this parallelism, approached from the side of Whitehead, "the isomorphism of actualized contrasts and the form of potential order" (See SC, Figure 4, p. 383 and context). Indeed, the very completeness of this parallelism has tempted many a casual thinker to lump both perspectives off as equally hypothetical or to entirely overlook this very fundamental discrimination between the living and the dead. The close parallelism of structure between these two realms should not, however, be permitted to tempt us to conflate or confuse the radically different methods that are applicable in the explication of the two realms.

A concern in all of this is to salvage the core of the Hegelian account of concrete actuality as grasped *a priori* by setting this within a context in which hypothetical reason is also accorded a clearly defined role, the specification of which is undertaken in such a way that this is not subject to being confused with the role of actual reason. A hedge is thus built against certain errors and excesses that at least have seemed to many interpreters to be present within Hegel's conceptuality, as for example a determination that renders the explication of novelty or of further change problematical.

This cursory overview is intended only for purposes of general orientation. It will almost inevitably give rise to more questions than it answers. Some of these, at least, will be addressed in the essays that follow. It admittedly renders prominent the more theoretical aspect of my reconstruction at the expense of the exposition of its phenomenological base. The justification of these aspects must ultimately be sought by reference to its measure, namely concrete actuality grasped as such in the reader's own lived occasions, for which no mere theory can be substituted. The bias to which I call attention is justified by the fact that the balance will be shifted somewhat toward the explication and illustration of the method pertaining to the phenomenological base in the essays that immediately follow.

My dominant intention in extending my critique to various individuals and themes within the present volume has been to open new avenues of approach to my reconstruction of method for first philosophy to readers whose interests may not be centered in either

Hegel or Whitehead in a very special way. The present essays, excepting the first four, which in this respect serve an introductory function, are less an account of my appropriations from Hegel and Whitehead than an application of my reconstruction of method that has previously been initially developed through such appropriations. For a generally more comprehensive account of my appropriations from Hegel and Whitehead, respectively, the reader is advised to turn to my SC, seeing that I have seen no need to duplicate this here. Although the first four essays here serve an introductory function in the sense indicated, so that the reader who has accorded SC a reasonably careful reading might find the remainder of the essays understandable apart from having first read these, each develops some one or more themes more comprehensively than I found possible or plausible within the larger *Work*.

Since the various essays introduce themselves, I shall by way of further introduction of substantive content limit myself to calling special attention to two characteristics of my appropriation of Hegel that are here presupposed and presented in summary form. This is especially appropriate here at the beginning, seeing that I find Hegel's method to provide the foundation for that of Whitehead and not the reverse.¹ If we would understand Whitehead's method of

---

¹ *Late Addendum*: With respect to this issue I take a position somewhat different than that of Errol E. Harris, in "The Contemporary Significance of Hegel and Whitehead", in George R. Lucas, Jr. (Ed.), *Hegel and Whitehead: Contemporary Perspectives on Systematic Philosophy* [Albany: SUNY Press, 1986]) . Harris there proposes that

> [t]he most common reason we are given for the impossibility of returning to a system like Hegel's is its incompatibility with the outlook and attitude established by contemporary science. The advance of modern science and technology, Professor Charles Taylor has told us, has burst the bonds of the Hegelian system and has shattered the ideals and illusions of nineteenth-century Romanticism. Nobody could make similar allegations about Whitehead, whose metaphysic is intimately and intricately bound up with contemporary scientific and mathematical concepts. (p. 17)

Harris draws a close parallel between the thought of Hegel and that of Whitehead for the purpose of making Taylor's strictures less formidable. Were one to read this article apart from having any acquaintance with his previous work, one might reasonably conclude that the program he has in view is to bring us to appreciate Whitehead anew and, if the parallels hold, Hegel, as well — at least insofar as what he has to teach us lies in close proximity to Whitehead's conceptuality — will be brought into a new relevance by association.

I find that the parallels to which Harris directs our attention — often with penetrating insight — are generally there to be observed, if they are not always as close as he wishes us to believe. On this account I heartily recommend this article to anyone interested in the Hegel-Whitehead relation, which brings into a systematic unity much that its author has said in passing allusions scattered through several major works. This is even though the apologetic approach that he here takes to Hegel capitalizes on similarities in such a way that it is inclined to maximize them and to ignore, or pass ever so lightly over, differences of the sort to which I shall be calling attention, some of which Harris has been less disposed to overlook within other contexts. The over-all effect is a tendency to level Hegel to Whitehead. In taking this approach, Harris has assisted us to see that Hegel is much less a victim of the scientific revolution than Taylor supposes, and this is evidently still needed in some quarters. As one who, unlike Harris, does not see the foundations of metaphysics as being clearly visible in the natural sciences (to paraphrase the title of his *The Foundations of Metaphysics in Science* (New York: Humanities Press, 1965), so much as a task that has to be approached by a method that is quite different than, and in need of being strictly distinguished from, that most commonly practiced by the particular sciences, I find it necessary to render explicit contrasts between the two systems. What especially emerges out of this contrast is that Hegel's method is by no means as proximate to that of the particular (especially natural) sciences as is that of Whitehead, and that we have no reason for concluding that this works out to his disadvantage.

I shall now render this suggestion more specific in terms of the focus that I shall be developing. If one maintains the Hegel inspired notion that first philosophy has as one of its tasks the analysis-resynthesis of consciousness (including self-consciousness, as well as the world as concretely present for self-consciousness) as it manifests itself in living occasions, as I shall be proposing, this task seems not to be subservient to any of the particular sciences. This is to say, in any historical situation there is consciousness and a phenomenology of that consciousness, quite apart from the presence or non-presence, the practice or non-practice, of any of the particular sciences. This is not to deny that particular sciences, where there are such, will likely have contributed to the make-up of the discriminations that are constitutive of an occasion of the type that is of interest, but to recognize that it is consciousness itself and the world for consciousness that is the subject-object of inquiry and not such sciences (or theories) as may have contributed to its determination. This is to assume that the particular sciences presuppose consciousness and its world, or better, concrete actuality grasped *a priori* as such irrespective of what theories they may construe, by appealing to a hypothetico-deductive model, as being most adequate to explain this, the phenomenology of the given being **uneinholbar.** This is to say, as grasped from an internal (actual) perspective, it is ever prior in such a way that it can never be overtaken by hypothetical speculations.

I would not propose that the force of Hegel's *Methodenlehre* in its entirety can be assimilated to an account along the lines of the foregoing. The position I might hope to defend is that the phenomenology of consciousness is not only a fitting introduction to this *Methodenlehre,* but, as an account of what constitutes knowledge in some given time and place, an indispensible aspect of it, as well.

The foregoing will I believe be adequately suggestive of its source of inspiration in Hegel. What is to be noted here is a procedure that can free first philosophy from the particular sciences in a strategic sense and to a strategic degree. I find nothing remotely resembling any of this in Whitehead. Furthermore, I am able to see no compelling reason why first philosophy should be nothing more than, or even principally, general theories of the sort that operate within the context of the hypothetico-deductive method, distinguished only from "scientific theories" by the supposed range of their generality having been somehow expanded, as Whitehead would have it. The situation seems much more to be one in which the sort of procedure toward which Hegel points us can lay the groundwork for adventures of hypothetical speculations of the sort Whitehead encourages.

Anyone who has read either Harris's *Nature, Mind, and Modern Science* (New York: Macmillan, 1954), especially chap. XII, "Hegel", or his *An Interpretation of the Logic of Hegel* (Lanham/New York/London: University Press of America, 1983), will know that he is by no means always reacting to Taylor nor does he always treat Hegel in the apologetic manner that I have described. These sources remain well worth reading and seem to me to represent more adequate and balanced scholarship. In addition, I wish to note that I have learned much from Harris, whose forthright, and at the time courageous, critique of empiricism within the same *Work* I have taken with special seriousness. Moreover, his philosophy of biology has contributed significantly to our sense that there are natural scientists today

generalization we must *priorly* grasp concrete actuality in a way that Hegel can strategically assist us to understand. There is nothing arbitrary about this and the order is not reversable.

In the first place, the appropriation here reflected is holistic. *If we begin the consideration of Hegel by laughing a single fundamental notion out of court before the hearing, as it were, the conduct of the retrial will prove to be largely a waste of time, as it so often has in the past, because nothing that remains will make very much sense.* In Hegel's dictum, "The Truth is the whole" would seem to lie an implicit guideline for the appropriation of his systematic philosophy that might be expressed: *The Truth of Hegel is the whole of Hegel.* To understand Hegel's system holistically, i.e., *as a system*, forbids, e.g., the picking and choosing that overlooks or deemphasizes such "problematical" notions as the identity of the real and the rational, perhaps in the interest merely of avoiding a position that might seem "extreme", in preference for understanding both aspects in a manner commensurate with this identity. In like manner it forbids the maintenance of an embarrassed silence about Hegel's claim to have accorded to the concretely actual a concretely specific account in its own native form, shrinking dialectic to the conveniently understood form of a pattern of dialogue or argumentation external to actuality rather than constitutive of it, in a manner that reflects understandings that are common coin today, to leave us with the comfortable sense that, after all, Hegel was somehow groping toward insights we have by now more securely grasped. It will then be obvious, as well, that a holistic understanding forbids regarding absolute knowledge as pertaining to some kind of theory of the sort that a skeptical age believes to be the end of inquiry and all that there is to be "known", rather than to concrete actuality. This can amount to the absurd portrayal of Hegelian speculation as a kind of *rumination about* actuality, roughly parallel to the speculative production of

who extend themselves to be aware of what their theories presuppose, which presuppositions can lend themselves to being understood in terms of metaphysical models to which one can appropriately appeal. I suspect that it is with respect to the method by which first philosophy is supposed to assimilate from the theories of the particular sciences that I may be least in agreement with him. With respect to this issue of method, I find Hegel and Whitehead to be poles apart — an issue that Harris sometimes, as in the article first cited, seems not to make enough of. Also see my "der universelle Systemgedanke bei Errol Harris", *Wiener Jahrbuch für Philosophie 1975, Band 7*. Even so, in the final analysis the difference between us may consist more in a lack of patience on my part with philosophers who seem unable to grasp the violence that has been done all things human by an excessive and one-sided preoccupation with "the advance of modern science and technology" to the point of assuming that there is no other option than the hypothetico-deductive method also for first philosophy. If so, it is owing in part to his patience that I may hope that my lack of patience is not untimely.

theories within the framework of the hypothetico-deductive method (except, perhaps, for being entirely removed from the strictures of science!), rather than in terms of an attempt to render a strictly phenomenological account of a function and an activity of reason found *in fact* to have gone into the mediated constitution of actuality [the Truth that is the whole (the occasion that is presently actual)]. My intent has been to shun all such consciously or unconsciously pursued "strategies", which seem to me to be too much in evidence today, in the belief that it is the systematic whole of his conceptuality which lends whatever meaning we may expect to find in any part (even as the whole derives its meaning, in turn, from the parts) and that can provide us with clues as to how we must advance beyond him *if* this is to be found possible. Commensurate with this intent, my intention has been to take up some of Hegel's most radical claims *in context* (and this even though it is not possible within a small volume of essays to more than suggest the context) and to see what, *by a certain reconception,* and apart from potentially endless interpretative debate of a sort that would be found of interest only to a few specialists, these might be made to contribute in confrontation with competing philosophical orientations. In this way I hope to have rendered more available than might otherwise have proven possible something of **the import** of Hegel's work, viewed from a certain perspective, that tends to be lost sight of in such debate, and the assimilation of which, especially outside of his own language community, would seem barely to have begun. This has been in the belief that there **is no way around** Hegel's work, which stands at the threshold of the nineteenth century, and that there is in fact no way into twentieth century philosophy except across this threshold into the nineteenth. It seems to me to have become progressively clearer in recent decades that no one gains legitimate entrance **philosophically** (*wissenschaftstheoretische* considerations just here aside) into the twentieth century except by taking deliberate and careful account of him. This same approach will serve the ultimate purpose of providing a context within which also Whitehead's quite different method may be found to fill a rightful role, a consideration that will receive progressively more attention once the more Hegelian foundations for this have been laid, if in a way that bears also the imprint of Whitehead's conceptuality.

The English language tradition in philosophy has proven itself particularly intransigent to the impact of Hegel. If we pass over the "British Hegelians," who can hardly be counted entirely blameless in the matter, then especially from Russell and Moore to the present this intransigency has been especially in evidence as a veritable Hegel renaissance has arisen during the past three decades to set it off by providing a vivid contrast. The result is a dialogue that is now above ground and being carried forward in the spirit of open confrontation on many fronts. These essays are a partial record of this confrontation. If the aspects of Whitehead's work with which we are herein principally to be concerned have been far from a center stage attraction, Whitehead scholarship is not in need of anything comparable by way of a radical "about-face".

In the pursuit of the holistic approach I too may very well have neglected some aspects of the philosophy either of Hegel or of Whitehead that will be accorded status by another interpreter. In this regard it would be absurd to pretend that any single appropriation of either conceptuality could be exhaustive. I may perhaps with some right claim to have accorded principal attention to various themes in each that no appropriation can totally overlook. In addition, the reader may be assured that nothing has been left out of the account *merely because it might seem extreme, obstruse, or far-fetched* to some (perhaps all too) common sense or other. In the case of Hegel, it is precisely the building stones which past builders have most frequently rejected or passed over in embarrassed silence that are characteristically counted as indispensible to the largely methodology oriented reconception here undertaken. Thus the concept of knowledge grasped *a priori* is accepted forthrightly, and a context for this notion is sought, without too much regard as to how far this might prove to have taken us beyond Hegel, that is intended to assist the reader to see it in what I take to be its native obviousness. Insofar as what results is found in some way to be reflected also in Hegel, the thoughtful reader will discern that this is a Hegel who, in moving beyond theory, in some sense anticipated Heidegger.

This concludes my remarks on holism. I wish, secondly, to call special attention to the method-oriented character of my appropriations from both philosophers. For a complex of reasons growing out of my critique of Hegel, and in view of the requirements of a philosophy of concreteness, which this appropriation is intended to serve, what I derive from each falls primarily on the side of method. This follows inevitably from the standpoint that the self-creation of every concretely actual occasion is both new and complete, a notion the development of which is importantly influenced by Whitehead, and that its analysis and reconstitution (or resynthesis) after the fact should be pursued with the ideal in view of achieving a commensurate completeness.

With regard to his method, as I have made especially clear in Essay V, §1, I place Hegel within the "post-Kantian critical" tradition. This is worthy of note, because most American Whiteheadians with whose work I am familiar tend to the view that, being a "speculative philosopher", he represents, with Whitehead, a reversion to a pre-Kantian — and in this sense pre-critical — mode of thought. Hegel is of course a speculative philosopher, but with the crucial distinction that "speculative" for him does not refer principally to hypothetical speculation, as it has for so many philosophers of the modern period, but to *actual* speculation. Actual speculation has *already* contributed crucially to the constitution of the lived truth that is the whole before its make-up is subjected to analysis and reported.[2] That not a few Whiteheadians should have missed this point is not surprising in view of the fact that the actuality of Hegelian speculation has seldom come over very well into Hegel scholarship in the English language. The issue is crucial, and it need not, therefore, be supposed strange that Essay VIII, "Henry Nelson Wieman and the Critical Tradition" was written as much with reference to Hegel as to Kant, the concern here being integral with that of the remainder of the *Collection*.

Explicit reference to a very few passages in Hegel's works actually forms part of a strategy for giving more weight to selective appropriation and reconception than to interpretation, even though the two are not strictly separable. I take it to be a hermeneutically sound principle that appropriation precedes, or is a necessary stage within, interpretation, even in the case in which appropriation is not what gets written up. In the present collection of papers, however, it is appropriation that takes center stage. This is to say, it is an interpretation that is oriented toward a perspective **somewhat distanced both from Hegel and from Whitehead**, that is by stages and within differing contexts broadened and deepened. On this account, the

---

[2] The point is intimately bound up with the fact that Hegel's Begriff is grasped *a priori*. If we neglect this consideration we end up attributing to him the view that concreteness is somehow worked up out of abstractions, perhaps in the manner of an American pragmatist. Nothing, I propose, could be further removed from the historical Hegel (see Essay IV and V), to depart from whom with respect to this issue is to risk a flirtation with an intellectual hybris of a more flagrant sort than any with which Hegel, approached from the present perspective, can properly be charged. This is a consideration that can readily elude interpreters who approach him with insufficient orientation in the development of German idealism from Kant to Hegel. In my "Kant and Hegel", *Review of Metaphysics*, vol. XL, No. 158 (Dec., 1986), I have approached this issue from the side of recent Kant scholarship.

images of these thinkers that emerge in these papers invites an interpretative effort to discover more precisely than I could here undertake to what extent they share the perspective herein developed. Even what I am inclined to label departures from Hegel or Whitehead in order to realize what I take to have been the most fundamental intentions of one or the other are to be understood as a part of a strategy for cutting short interpretative debate not germane to my purpose.

Essay XI constitutes the only exception to the above paragraph, in that here I initially make Hegel interpretation my principal concern. Subsequently, and especially in the last few pages, I bring the results of the inquiry into relation to my reconstruction.

Excepting Chapter X, the essays that make up this collection were all written during the period of nearly twelve years during which I was at work on SC. This was from early 1974 until the fall of 1985, when the final composition and incorporation of late addenda was completed, the conclusion of a final systematic revision having preceded this by a year and a half. These were for the most part completed between 1978 and 1983, when, with "Whitehead's 'Prehension' and Hegel's 'Mediation': Parallel Dynamical Concepts at the Service of Different Methodologies" (*Review of Metaphysics*, Vol. XXXVIII, No. 2), I concluded my series of essays explicitly treating the Hegel-Whitehead relation, excepting late editorial revisions while seeing some of this work through the press. The first four chapters of the present volume are representative of this series, which was to count as important background for subsequent work in which I range more widely and which is represented somewhat more prominently within the present collection. This series also included SC, and three additional shorter essays within the list of "Other Essays by the Author Involved with the Same Basic Problematic", to follow, namely CHSS, RAtP, and TCMM. The final essay, Chapter XV, might also with plausability be included within this group, even though it is more explicitly problem oriented, and deals somewhat less explicitly with either Hegel or Whitehead. This is in part because it was written earlier than most of the other shorter essays, and in part because it reflects the sorting out of a problem area that importantly determined the intelligible aim of the entire series.

Following the first four essays, the Hegelian/Whiteheadian synthesis is brought to bear and further elaborated within a variety of contexts, now in some degree freed from its principal sources. Thus, Chapters V and VI are devoted to the critique of Peirce. Chapter VII sets forth a critique and a strategy for the appropriation of the work of Karl Popper. Chapter VIII contains a critique of Henry Nelson Wieman. Following, chapters IX through XII pertain to language. The last two members of this group are devoted to the concept of metaphor. Especially where the influence of the empiricist tradition has been most strongly felt, this concept has been very problematical and unstable. I have undertaken to provide a formulation that will prove to be more durable. The appendix to Chapter XII might well have been listed as a separate paper were it not for the fact that in its present form it can in no sense stand alone. In addition to extending my treatment of metaphor and analogy, it serves secondarily to open my Hegelian/Whiteheadian perspective out upon the philosophy of religion, especially as pertaining to the doctrine of God. In chapters XIII and XIV I take up certain characteristically Marxist themes. In the concluding Chapter XIII, already mentioned in passing, I concentrate upon the issue of scepticism as it pertains to the division of labor between first philosophy, second philosophy, and the particular sciences together with the theory of science (*Wissenschaftstheorie*).

The order of the essays in the *Collection* is not the order in which they were completed. A couple of additional comments thereto pertaining may prove useful. The essays presented in chapters II, III, and IX were completed first, and the one in Chapter I shortly thereafter. The one in Chapter IV was completed early in 1983, this having been the last of my series of essays explicitly devoted to the Hegel/Whitehead relation. It may interest some readers that those presented in XIII and XIV were completed somewhat earlier than the first of the series on language. Members of the latter series were prepared in the order in which they are here presented, the first two in 1982, except for Part II of the first one, which was added in 1983. The latter two were prepared successively during 1986, except that the Appendix to the last one was completed early in 1987.

Each of the essays is intended to stand on its own, in the sense that it may be read as a systematic unit. This is although the full bibliographical information on a reference work, once given in the list of abbreviations of frequently cited sources, or in the notes, is generally not repeated. In addition, they all provide more inclusive context, each for the others. This broader context plays a more important role in some cases than in others. Thus, e.g., Chapter VII, my critique of Popper's theory of objective knowledge, goes much farther than it might have had I not been presupposing the first four essays. Accordingly, it will be found too dense for most readers who have not first read a good deal of what has gone before, either my SC or within the present *Volume*. This is even if attention has been paid to the notes, which, in this as in other essays within the *Collection* appear under the text and contain remarks that are sometimes presupposed in the text that follows. Chapter IX, Part II, Chapter XIII and XV, as well, are likely to be found excessively dense if read ahead of the four "introductory" essays or SC.

These exceptions being noted, the rendering of each chapter a *relatively* autonomous essay has of course been at the price of some repetition, especially seeing that, in order to make the systematic unity of my Hegelian/Whiteheadian perspective more apparent, I have based my interpretations upon comparatively few passages and references, to certain of which I return again and again. The reader will be more patient with me on this account if, upon comparing more or less parallel passages, he or she discovers that what at first may appear to be *sheer* repetition will almost always be found, upon closer inspection, to occasion the introduction of some dimensions of the problematic not previously taken up. If there is a case of overlapping themes that an observing reader might regret, this is in the second of the two papers pertaining to Ch. S. Peirce, which takes up Chapter VI. I have found no way readily to remedy this, however, and, in any case, the essay is quite short and it will, I believe, be found to make its own point. It has on these accounts seemed preferable to leave it essentially in its original form, determined by the occasion for which it was prepared.

Of the fifteen essays, all but four appear here for the first time in print. These take up chapters II, III, IV, and V. This is excepting Chapter XII, an earlier form of which was distributed to the membership of *Félag áhugammanna um heimspeki* (the Icelandic Society for Philosophy). Of the essays that have previously appeared, only II and IV have had a substantial circulation within the English-language sector. I have included these, notwithstanding, because of the strategic place they fill within the *Collection*.

I wish to thank *Idealistic Studies* for permitting "On Rendering Whitehead's 'Complete Fact' Complete..." to appear again in this *Collection*. I wish to thank Wilhelm Braumüller for permitting the republication of "Can the Contrasts Constitutive of an 'Actual Occasion of Experience' be Specified in their Concrete Particularity?...", following upon its original appearance in Herta Nagl-Docekal (Ed.), *Überlieferung und Aufgabe: Festschrift für Erich Heintel zu 70. Geburtstag*. The *Review of Metaphysics* has my thanks for permitting "Whitehead's 'Prehension' and Hegel's 'Mediation': Parallel Dynamical Concepts at the Service of Different Methodologies" to appear again here. I wish to thank *The Owl of Minerva* for permitting "A Hegelian Critique of Peirce" to reappear in this *Collection*.

Revisions in the texts of essays reprinted in this *Volume* have been for the most part very minor, and merely stylistic. The notes have undergone more extensive revisions, some having been shortened to take advantage of the opportunity for cross references afforded by this form of publication, and a few additional notes having been added. It has seemed preferable to renumber them on this account, although in the final editorial revision irregular numbers, such as "8a" have again been introduced, this time to indicate to the reader that a late addendum is to follow. Where there has been a late addition to an already existing note, this is labeled "**Late Addendum:**". A late addendum constitutes an afterthought, frequently to relate to something in the recent literature. I have intended to meet my responsibilities to relate what I am doing to other contributions to the literature of philosophy principally through footnotes. In a few cases the desire to do some measure of justice to the systematic character of the position to which I am relating has led me to include a single note of some length in preference to a series of shorter notes. The reader will judge whether the gain in terms of coherent representation of the positions discussed compensates for what may on occasion be felt to be an undue interruption of the continuity of the text.

Most of the essays appearing here in print for the first time have been presented publicly at some time or others. Also in the revision of these essays for the present context I have not deviated far from the pattern that I have just described.

I shall close this Preface with some remarks evoked by a friendly critic, who proposed the following:

> Since the theory is presented as an explicitly phenomenological one it invites comparison with work in the phenomenological tradition that derives from Husserl. Much of what I understand to be going on strikes me as very similar in essential content to themes to be found in Merleau-Ponty and Husserl's own *Crisis,* and to a lesser degree in central themes in Heidegger and Gadamer.

It being assumed that I grasp the occasion in which I live as "the truth that is the whole", when it comes to explicating for another this that I myself perceive with more or less explicitness in its all-at-onceness, and for certain purposes — i.e., the projection of new possibilities — even to myself, I must procede in a linear fashion, this being one of the conspicuous ways in which I am marked as mortal, i.e., a temporal being. Commensurate with this status, I have found it necessary to establish priorities and an order for the projected fulfillment of various tasks from the outset. Already in my SC these priorities were set, where I acknowledged that "it is inevitable that any critique of Hegel deserving of the name must grasp in thought the time subsequent to that within which he worked" (SC 231). In saying this, I had in view the persons above named and others. Despite the fact that I was constructing an intrinsically historical dialogue between two historical traditions, however, priorities required that, excepting a few incidental references (including several to Heidegger and Gadamer), I put off the task of setting the results of this dialogue within a larger historical perspective to another occasion (SC, 249). This was owing in part to the intricacy of the two conceptualities that I was relating and to the need to document my appropriations and interpretations within the respective contexts of Hegel scholarship and Whitehead scholarship at the same time that I fulfilled the documentary demands in showing how I arrived at the reconstruction of method in first philosophy that I was proposing with reference to both.

The work in which I hope to set the reconstruction that I adumbrated within SC, within this larger historical context of the history of philosophy, especially since Hegel's time, I now plan to entitle, *Phenomenology: The Path to Knowledge*. In the present *Collection I am not yet undertaking this task*. Rather, the position is here undergoing further development at the same time that I am laying further background for it. Acknowledging my limitations with regard to my critics suggestion, providing a few additional bits of historical context here may compensate in a general way.

It may be found of interest to note that my concept of concrete language — to which I herein give appreciable attention, especially in Essays IX through XII — will be found readily to lend itself to being viewed as a corrective to Heidegger, who as a result of what I can only regard as a colossal methodological blunder construed philosophy to end up in poetry. What he was led to call poetry I am disposed to subsume principally under the normatively literal, this is to say, concrete, language, the explication of which in occasions typical of a relevant epoch is the principal task of first philosophy. This amounts to an outright rejection of his disposition, which so far as I have noticed he never made fully explicit, to permit conventional language to function in this role and thus to become a kind of prison, until renewed by poetry, for the human beings who use it. By shifting things around, I have managed to avert the implied creation of this prison and a commensurate distortion and denial of essential aspects of what I find to be human rationality.

I find the felt want of references to Husserl on the part of my critic to be more especially worthy of a reply. It is true of course that Husserl shares the use of the term "Phänomenologie" with Hegel, even though in his usage it stands for very different methods, procedures, and results. Moreover, Husserl develops his phenomenology as though Hegel had never lived and, so far as I am able to recall, without so much as a reference to him. Even so, there is certainly a parallel to be observed between Hegel's emphasis upon the necessary status both of subjectivity and objectivity in knowledge, on the one hand, and Husserl's *Welterfahrendes Leben*, which, as in the case of Hegel's Begriff, is equally subjective and objective. Some other parallels that may seem deserving of note are perhaps more readily discernable between my reconstruction and Husserl than between Hegel and Husserl. Among these would be the concept of *Evidenz* that is centrally thematic for Husserl and what I call "Hegelian self-evidence" — my way of rendering Hegel's "Selbstgewißheit der Vernunft". Out of the nest of issues that constitute Hegel's relatively undeveloped concept of time I have shown how we may derive a time/temporality discrimination which I was subsequently reminded shares with Husserl the attribution to time of the status of being prior to temporality, which is derived. (Consult SC, the Index, under "time/temporality".) Closely associated with this discrimination in my reconstruction is the notion that the particular sciences have their origin in concreteness, which might for this purpose faintly resemble Husserl's *Lebenswelt,* and arise through abstraction. Thus philosophy, insofar as it presents us with this origin, is the science of the final foundation, i.e., Husserl's "die letzt-begründende Wissenschaft". This latter is a claim that Heidegger gave up and that I have reclaimed, not deliberately, but as an afterthought, my thoughts at the time not having been upon Husserl at all. This along with the other parallels with Husserl that I have noted has resulted much less from deliberate appropriation than from the fact that we to some considerable extent are making reference in common to the "same" or a similar actuality, and from the fact that one lives within an intellectual climate that he has influenced. They have for the most part first been observed retrospectively, however, largely through the prompting of others. It seems to me that it would be an error to conclude from such parallels as I have mentioned that the phenomenology that I am advocating is in any very fundamental way Husserlian. We seem here to be faced with the choice of emphasizing relatively superficial points of commonality, on the one hand, or the to my thinking far more fundamental differences that exist between the Hegelian and Husserlian types of phenomenology, on the other.

I am here reminded of Leonard Nelson's utterance to the effect that all great philosophers affirm the same basic truths, and that what distinguishes them is their different ways to these shared truths. If we take this tack, certain conclusions shared by Hegel and Husserl are no indication of a significant commonality in the substance of their philosophies, which consists much more in their paths to these truths. Also to be noted is that Self-evidence or *Evidenz* is no invention of philosophers, whose task it should be to explicate its basis, but first and foremost a characteristic of lived occasions. In the case of Hegel, it is dialectic that is here to be understood, and not merely as a method to be externally applied but more fundamentally as the being/becoming of concrete actuality itself. The "logic" of Hegelian type phenomenology, which I have characterized as the logic of discrimination, is what is here of interest. I placed the term "logic" in quotes because once one acknowledges the uniqueness of every actual occasion at the same time that one insists that a dialectical account should exhaustively account for its radical particularity, as I do, one has sacrificed the possibility of a Hegelian type logic, assumed to be universally constitutive of all occasions.[3] Notwithstanding this sacrifice, I wish to point to the type of structure

---

[3] Having noted that it is the logic of Hegelian type phenomenology that has been of special interest here, I should observe that my concept of Hegelian phenomenology is by no means drawn exclusively from Hegel's *Phänomenologie des Geistes*. It draws no less upon the phenomenological dimension of the *System* itself, to which he came to regard his *Phän.* as an introduction. This will be evident, e. g., to anyone who takes the trouble to observe the differences between my concept of actual time, drawing upon the *System*, and that which is rendered prominent at the close of the *Phän.*, where spirit appears in time just so long as it does not grasp its pure Begriff (*Phän.*, p. 558: or *Phen.*, p. 800). Indeed in Hegel's *Phän.* to be in time is to be in a kind of fallen state, somewhat proximate to what I would call temporality, to be strictly distinguished from the concretely lived (space-)time, more concretely expressed as space(nature)-time(history) being mediated within a lived occasion.

That my concept of phenomenology draws upon Hegel's *System* as a whole has as an additional outworking that it is not a phenomenology of mind or spirit (*Geist*) alone that is in view. Commensurate with my emphasis upon Hegel's method as an explication of the mediation of the ideal and the real, phenomenology in my usage embraces the natural order and all that is counted "real" no less than the "ideal" aspect. This is consistent with what I understand his concept of concrete universality to import, namely that the whole is implicated within every (concretely universal) aspect of the fully determined Begriff in-and-for-itself. Thus each aspect of the duality in question — the ideal and the real — being an accent within an identity inclusive of both, *the real (and thus nature) is ultimately no less inclusive of the ideal than is the ideal inclusive of the real.* Each, indeed, consists ultimately in relations ([being-]mediated), these being inclusive of relations to the other. Thus, where, e.g., G. Gentile develops his actual idealism from Hegelian beginnings, the position I propose might more adequately be characterized in terms of the actual ideal/real. If idealism is to be characterized as an acknowledgement that there is no actuality in which the deter-

presumed to be constitutive of all occasions, however varied this may prove to be in constitutive discriminations that are self-determining in accordance with this principle. I am able to recall nothing even remotely resembling this structure in Husserl's phenomenology, nor anything that seems even to approach what I perceive to be its "critical" capabilities.[4]

mination of the subject is not a necessary aspect, then my position is unproblematically idealistic. No doubt G. Rinaldi had something like this in view in so characterizing it in a review to appear in *Idealistic Studies* which he has thoughtfully shared with me. It should nonetheless be borne in mind that we have here to do with a form of idealism with a very much lower profile than that of Gentile, equally open to the full force of such realistic sensibilities as can find any basis at all in concrete fact. It is thus to be decisively distinguished from that of Gentile (between whose work and mine Rinaldi has called my attention to several arresting parallels) and in a way that has fairly wide reaching ramifications. Accordingly, I can more readily speak of nature as actual than can Gentile, who discovers nature to be in mind but appears to have failed to discover mind in nature (see *The Theory of Mind as Pure Act*, trans. by H. Wildon Carr [London: Macmillan, 1922], pp. 18ff, 52, 200, 248f. 256f, 259) and feel that when I have done so with proper qualification, this is also true to Hegel's most basic intent.

[4] There are several themes that I might enter upon by way of specifying what is here in view as "critical" capabilities intrinsic to Hegelian-type phenomenology. Perhaps it will suffice to mention one to which I am unable to perceive anything at all similar in Husserl. I have in view Hegelian negation or its affirmative counterpart, the mediation (*Vermittlung*) of sublated (*aufgehobenen*) aspects. This is the dynamical and processural principle by which concrete discriminations constitutive of concrete actuality come to be within the organic wholeness achieved in actual speculation, the polar aspects of which lend themselves to abstraction after the concrete fact. This is wherever there is human consciousness and thus knowing. I here emphasize the possibility provided us by a Hegelian type phenomenology of tracing our conceptuality to the mediation of its particular constitutive discriminations, many of which lend themselves to plausible representation within specific types (Essay III). The following remarks by Giacomo Rinaldi in "Intentionality and Dialectical Reason" (*The Monist*, Vol. 69, No. 4 [Oct., 1986]), although cast in somewhat variant terminology, may here be found relevant:

> In accordance...with the identification, carried out in [[Husserl's]]...*Logische Untersuchungen,* of *a priori* concept with a merely **abstract universal,** an only 'possible' ideality, the phenomenological-transcendental analysis of the constitution of experience's intentional objects does not concern any **real act** of transcendental subjectivity, but only its merely 'possible', abstractly 'ideal' form (p. 576).

The intended contrast with Hegel, whose focus is upon **concrete universality** and the **real act**, is made clear. Rinaldi additionally remarks:

> If, now, we come back to the scholastic and phenomenological concepts of intentionality, it immediately appears evident that, in the last resort, both of them do coincide with that of Hegel's 'finite understanding'. Their raising to original and absolute essence of any human knowledge whatever thus amounts to nothing more nor less than **undue denial** of the possibility and necessity of the ***finite intellect's*** 'sublation' (*Aufhebung*) into the superior sphere of *dialectical* and *speculative* reason. The insuperable contradictions that radically compromise the coherence and validity of both scholastic and phenomenological epistemologies, then, are but the unavoidable consequence of their essentially **antidialectical** and **antispeculative** orientation. (pp. 581)

In conclusion I would observe that these two types of phenomenology appear to be so fundamentally different that a fairly ponderous volume might be required to relate my reconstruction of method for first philosophy to Husserlian phenomenology in a way that could prove really satisfying, were this to be considered worthwhile. I would remind the reader that the term has been in steady usage within the Hegelian tradition since a century before Husserl did his work. Perhaps there is a task here that should be undertaken, all in good time, if not by me then by another. If so, it might well be deserving of a separate treatment.

The case is quite different with reference to Heidegger's concept of "being-toward-death". Although I was principally and initially drawing upon Whitehead's concept of the perishing of an actual occasion, the direction of my development of the idea of death within the context of a Hegelianized actual occasion was with an eye to Heidegger, with whom I share the association of death with the projection of distinctly human possibilities. This would have to be the case because I view it as associated not only with possibilities pertaining directly to concretely actual occasions — i.e., occasions constitutive of human beings — but with possibilities in nature supposed to enter into the concrescence of events that lie outside of such occasions, as well. Also to be noted is that Heidegger was not talking about the death of an actual occasion (of any sort) but about death in a more conventional sense. Heidegger's concept of death is so well known and the connection so readily perceived that I had supposed it not necessary to label it, especially since, for reasons already explained, I found it inappropriate to take note here of much that distinguishes my position from his with respect to this notion.

I have received one additional suggestion from a reader that I would like to pass on with a comment. It was suggested that I begin the *Collection* with what here appears as essays IX and XII rather than with the present order. I will concede that a reader with more interest in the philosophy of language than in Hegelian "logic" might well prefer to read the section on language (now Essays IX — XII) first. In spite of this, I do not recommend that suggested order for most readers, because the first four essays listed are more systematically invested with the task of introducing what the reader should eventually see to be foundational for the fullest comprehension of the others, namely the "logic" of Hegelian type phenomenology, appropriated in a way not entirely anticipated by Hegel himself and set in relief through contrast with Whitehead's method of generalization. Especially these initial papers are quite condensed, owing to the fact that each was initially written to introduce a systematic conceptuality that was in important respects new and that yielded grudgingly to a partial exposition. All the more on this account they should be accorded a close reading. Also the reader who has previously read my SC would do well not to pass over Essay IV, seeing that its theme counts importantly here and there is nothing closely suggestive of its working out in the previous larger *Work*.

I have intended throughout to write for the reader whose time is limited, but bearing in mind Thomas Carlyle's dictum in "Goethe's Helena",

> *...if time is precious,*
> *no book that will not improve by repeated reading*
> *deserves to be read at all.*

I should not close this Preface apart from expressing my thanks to Sonja Rethy for her often painstaking efforts in the copy-editing. Nor would I close without acknowledging, with gratitude, the fact that I could share many of the concerns that are developed within these papers with my wife, Renate (Gruber) Christensen, over the decade and more during which they have been in preparation.

Salzburg, August, 1987

I

ON RENDERING HEGEL'S TRUTH WHICH IS THE (CONCRETELY ACTUAL) WHOLE ADEQUATE AND TOLERABLE*

> "... the Absolute alone is true
> ... the True is alone absolute."
> (Intro. to the *Phen.*)

1. Introduction

This essay will tend to indicate, so far as it reaches, that truth is a whole which actualizes itself, climaxing in a concretely integral and completely coherent system, which upon achieving its climax perishes. For the purposes of first philosophy, this is most appropriately conceived as a unty and wholeness of discriminations, these having ontological as well as epistemological significance. A philosophy of the concretely actual whole which is the truth calls attention to the propensity native to thought as such to grasp successive concrete wholes, each as multiply discriminated, or perhaps it is preferable to say, as being discriminated, prior to the abstraction of discriminations and discriminated elements and aspects subsequent to their perishing.

Thought in this its native function is understood, following Hegel's conception of the philosophical proposition — every proposition insofar as it is concrete — as an accent within an identity of thought and actuality. This is a discriminated identity, the mediation of the the poles of which is achieved concretely within each concretely actual occasion. I adapt the term "concretely actual *occasion*" from Whitehead,[1] as a device for pointing to the emphasis within Hegel's philosophy upon concrete individuality, the highest realization of

---

*Presented to the Graduate/Staff Colloquium sponsored by the Dep't of Philosophy of Trinity College, University of Dublin on March 7, 1980.

[1] For Alfred North Whitehead's exposition of the concept of an actual occasion, see *Process and Reality* (hereafter PR), corrected edition by David Ray Griffin and Donald W. Sherburne (New York: The Free Press, 1978).

objective spirit. The concept of climaxing and perishing is taken primarily from Whitehead, and where I, following Hegel, refer to discriminations, Whitehead up to a point referred to contrast. Whereas Whitehead's actual occasion that climaxes in the achievement of full concrescence and perishes in principle could not contain its own understanding, interpreting subject, and hence in principle could not be self-evident, I understand these notions to be applicable to a concept of self-evidence adapted from Hegel's presuppositionlessness, which he expressed affirmatively as "the self-certainty of reason". Following this application, an actuality (or one of its sub-identities or sub-facts *within its context*) is self-evident when and only when its constitutive discriminations are adequate to its explication — which, when the matter is spelled out, comes to mean, when it is self-explicating. What I am especially interested to show, however, and what so far as I know no one before me has attempted, is that a necessary connection exists between self-evident truth as presented in our ordinary perceptual-conceptual-intentional experience (to designate some principal dimensions of the whole which is the truth) and perishing.

The episodic, climactic character of truth, and of the concretely actual which is the truth, together with the timely perishing of both aspects as they attain their true character in and as fact, preserves the contextual character of truth while at the same time saving it from becoming intolerable through inflation. These features of truth appear today not merely to be reflected in theories within the particular sciences and the theory of science as such (*Wissenschaftstheorie*), but to be required by the character of self-evidence itself that we natively attribute to *concrete* facts. I shall herein be concerned to approach this matter from the standpoint of the character inherent to self-evidence, as such, which falls to first philosophy. This approach, insofar as it can be made to stand free of the shadow land of theory, appears in any case to be the more reliable indicator.

This is the inside (actual) approach to an actual occasion, implicated with the possibility of the analysis-synthesis[2] of its constitutive discriminations in its — and their — own native form, to be contrast-

---

[2] My use of the term "analysis-synthesis" is intended to reflect a taking account of the consideration that in their philosophical usage, neither half of this hyphenated term can ultimately stand alone. Each is an accent within an identity of meaning inclusive of both, as every Hegelian, apart from awaiting Quine's deliberations in the matter, which led him to a similar conclusion, should know. Neither can analysis ultimately yield any truth, in the sense in which that term is here being employed, apart from a complementary synthesis. The analysis of a term with a view to discovering the generic discrimination it contains must be followed by an experimental synthesis of its constituents. This may lead to the discovery of its similiarity to a discrimination in concretion, or even contribute to such a concretion.

ed with the external (hypothetical) view. In pointing to the possibility of an external perspective ever being actualized in fact, I shall not intend to depreciate hypothetical thinking as such but to cast it in its proper role: the preparation of possibilities for actualization. It will be seen that, since no one could even possibly have stepped outside of that some one occasion which at any instant constitutes him and his world, relations held to obtain *between* occasions must of necessity be hypothetical, i.e., theory. As such, they must be imaged in such poor metaphors as lie at hand, e.g., Whitehead's "inheritances." Such relations may, however, be rendered internal to an actual occasion, and thus be concretely actualized. After all, history as an interrelated series of past occasions is actualized in the actual occasion which presently constitutes me and my world as discriminated aspects. This fact might be taken as a basis for construing that relations *between* occasions are in a way no less factual than relations internal to the occasion that is now actual.

The standpoint here reflected, however, is that the character which must be attributed to self-evident truth (as a system of internal relations) for it to function as such must be accorded *absolute priority*. *Even as theories have truth as their touchstone and ought to be subordinate to truth, so their characterization ought to be subordinate to, and in conformity with, the characterization demanded by truth. To render Hegel's concrete truth which is the whole certainly tolerable, then, by rendering it a throb of actuality that arises, completes itself and perishes, renders it no less absolute, in its season.*

2. The Philosophical Proposition

It was Hegel who laid down as a basic methodological principle that the subject and predicate of a philosophical or speculative proposition (*Satz*, which may be translated either proposition or judgment, within different contexts) are each accents within an identity of meaning inclusive of both.[3] This is by going beyond the habitual

---

[3] "Formell kann das Gesagte so ausgedrückt werden, daß die Natur das Urteils oder Satzes überhaupt, die den Unterschied des Subjekts und Prädikats in sich schließt, durch den spekulativen Satz zerstört wird, und der identische Satz, zu dem der erstere wird, den Gegenstoß zu jenem Verhältnisse enthält. — Dieser Konflikt der Form eines Satzes überhaupt und der sie zerstörenden Einheit des Begriffs ist dem ähnlich, der im Rhythmus zwischen dem Metrum und dem Akzente stattfindet. Der Rhythmus resultiert aus der schwebenden Mitte und Vereinigung beider. So soll auch im philosophisches Satze die Identität des Subjekts und Prädikats den Unterschied derselben, den die Form des Satzes ausdrückt, nicht vernichten, sondern ihre Einheit [soll] als eine Harmonie hervorgehen. Die Form des Satzes ist die Erscheinung des bestimmten Sinnes oder Akzent, der seine Erfüllung unterscheidet..." *Phän.*, p. 51; or *Phen.*, p. 120.

Late Addendum: I have quoted from Hegel's initial introduction, within the works of his maturity, of his concept of the speculative or philosophical proposition. This is a con-

distinction between the two to the discovery of the process of how knowledge comes to be. From the perspective of how knowledge comes to be it is of course possible to account for the arising of habitual distinctions such as are contained in common language and set forth in dictionaries.

cept to which he recurs again and again, and which is also a prominent feature of his *Logik* (his principal statement of method). Moreover, it may be found illustrated in any major phase of his mature writings. That the subject and predicate of a speculative or philosophical proposition (or judgment) for Hegel are mediated to become accents within an identity inclusive of both says, among other things, that they are determined or discriminated out of a whole. The synthesis of the two terms, if you will, is not something arrived at by addition, as though they were priorly actual rather than merely components in an ordinary language and thus nothing more than abstract potentials (see Essays IX and X). What is given is a whole, which in the *Phän.* is the whole that is consciousness (along with the world for consciousness that determines it to be what it is). This whole is discriminated, and is indeed grasped as discriminated (see SC, chap. I. In my reconception, I propose that it is *being* discriminated.) In discrimination the inclusiveness of the whole by each of the two terms becomes explicit. In other words, the terms are all *internally related*, and all are at least implicit within any one. Thus a single philosophical proposition may be seen accurately to image, at least up to a point, Hegel's Begriff as a unity of internal relations, seeing that this is nothing other than concrete actuality, grasped as such, i.e., as the multiply discriminated identity that it is.

I am convinced that many erroneous understandings of Hegel may be averted by giving sufficient attention to this most basic concept. Consider, for example, Robert C. Neville's proposal, in "Hegel and Whitehead on Totality" (in, George R. Lucas, Jr. (Ed.), *Hegel and Whitehead: Contemporary Perspectives on Systematic Philosophy* (Albany: SUNY Press, 1986), that Hegel's conception of totality is problematical.

> [I]nfinite reason is a totality by virtue of being a third term which interrelates its determinate contents. The third term is determined either because its contents are determinate or because of its own character. But the contents cannot be fully determinate without the new contribution of the third term. How is the third term's contribution determinate? Not by virtue of its contents, and so by virtue of contrasting with what is external to it. But if something is external, the third term is no totality in the required respects. (pp. 90f)

For the purpose of evaluating Neville's case, consider his "first term" to be the subject of a philosophical proposition in Hegel's sense and his second term the predicate. His third term will then be the explicit identity of the discriminated aspects. I might call into question each of several phases of the complex argument that Neville recapitulates in the statement above quoted. From the present perspective, however, the fact that what he calls the "third term" is conceived as external to the first two terms suffices to show us that his argument, although it is perhaps not to be faulted within the framework that it presupposes, does not pertain to Hegel. For Hegel the "second term" (moment) is implicit within the first and the "third term" (or what we may regard as the synthesis — which is here what counts as crucial) is implicit within both the "first" and the "second". To anyone who has observed that Hegel's Begeiff is grasped *a priori*, all of this will be obvious, so that it does not need to be spelled out piecemeal, since in this case it is entirely present (to whatever degree only inexplicitly) in every term and aspect (precisely what concrete universality entails).

The ultimate reference of Hegel's dialectic is to the Begriff as a system of internal relations. Every authentically philosophical proposition illustrates this by itself being an internally related trinity of terms. If we grant that Hegel sometimes wrote propositions in language that does not qualify as philosophical by his own criterion, or at least not unproblematically, this, it seems to me, cannot suffice to render Neville's critique fitting, which

The Philosophical Proposition 5

In considering further the distinction between such concretely particular meanings as those which philosophical propositions yield and ordinary abstract meanings, I can for the present purposes do no better than to cite the example of a philosophical proposition provided by Josef Simon.

---

nonetheless, if cogent, would need to be shown to pertain wherever the dialectical form of the philosophical proposition (or judgment) is to be found. Seeing that philosophical propositions in Hegel's sense are definitely not to be regarded as propositions in an ordinary language, most of which qualifies quite well as being merely language of the understanding, I judge this to be precisely where it will not be found cogent. Neville errs with respect to what I take to be one of the very most basic and elementary points of Hegel interpretation. One might even argue that this is not an issue of interpretation at all, seeing that it falls much more under the category of now well-established signposts for finding the ballpark where Hegel's kind of game is played than under that of playing rules.

To state the issue in another way, Neville's reflection is carried on as though it were to pertain only to what Hegel considers to be the level of the understanding (*Verstand*), which considers things as they are externally related, and which is therefore totally unsuitable to the presentation of the sort of relations that he proposes to be discussing, which in Hegel are invariably internal. It is by virtue of this trait of being internal that they portray for us concrete actuality and not merely hypothetical ideas about what might be. He is indeed commenting on Hegel as though his were the sort of philosophy that one might expect to encounter in the pages of the New Series of *The Journal of Speculative Philosophy*, for which expression of the American pioneer spirit speculative philosophy is "always tentative", i.e., purely hypothetical, in character.

Although I find reason to be confident that Neville's critique of Hegel cannot be made to stand up, I am much more impressed by what he affirms than by what he denies, i.e., by the reconstruction that he adumbrates following. This is although I am disinclined to regard such an adventure of ideas as sufficient in itself to constitute a first philosophy. By virtue of the kind of status that this procedure implies for hypothetical thinking within the framework of the hypothetico-deductive method, I find it to fall more naturally under the category of a theory of science (*Wissenschaftstheorie*), although one that seems to lend itself to being qualified as second philosophy (see Essay II, §6, Essay IX, §15, and SC, pp. 439-44, "The Primary and Secondary Tasks of Philosophy"). The qualification would consist in one's being able to share concretely and persuasively (see esp. Essays IX and X) the concreteness adequate to found such an adventure of ideas, which I regard as the more basic task of first philosophy.

I cannot here undertake to summarize Neville's constructive position, which I nonetheless commend to the reader. Especially persons knowledgeable of it may find the following excerpt from a letter of mine to W. Welten S. J., dated 13. IV. 1986 of interest.

> If only the *ontological status* that he [[Neville]] wishes to accord to vagueness were denied, I could accept with enthusiasm everything he says in his reconstructive remarks. If the exception is allowed, he says rather precisely how I view the matter *from a theoretical (hypothetical) perspective*. What I wish to insist upon is that such a view of vagueness belongs to the sphere of the hypothetical, and needs grounding in a concrete actuality grasped as such, this grasp being conceptualized philosophically for what it is. The possibilities out of which an occasion is concretized may be vague, and vagueness will always cling to a representation of these and indeed even to a re-resentation of what is actualized. I wish to maintain that the occasion grasped as the actuality it is is nonetheless concretely present in all respects, even with respect to such detailed aspects as are only implicitly specified in the grasping.

If my concern for detail in the account of concreteness exceeds that of Hegel in a direction inspired, in part, by Whitehead — a consideration which contributes to my sense of the importance of vagueness in hypothetical thinking — the position reflected in the foregoing quotation seems in other respects to be proximate to Hegel's conceptuality.

It may not be amiss to introduce an example, not in Hegel's text, of a possible meaningful statement uttered in some situation or other and in some context, perhaps a descriptive one. In "this table is round", the subject-concept "table" does not mean something which, as a basis underlying the determination, could accept "accidents". What is meant is that this certain round table has not fortuitously *taken on* the property "round", but rather exists only in this shape. Further, the predicate does not signify a property which could "belong to" other objects as well. Only in a mathematical judgment could the "universal round" of a geometrical circle, constructed in pure intuition — that is, a concept that is to be constructed and not one *necessarily to be exemplified* — be intended, and only here could this constructed figure be the "basis" of the determination round, since in this case the free *action* of constructing is itself as "pure capactiy" the "basis" of the various properties of figures. In this mathematical possibility, the categorial forms must synthesize an appropriate conceptual material, namely, concepts that have been constructed, with no reference made to an external, individual, real object. This possibility finally accounts for the form of the proposition, which "involves" the (fixed) "distinction between subject and predicate"[4] and thus refers to fixed meanings. In language, which is concerned with existent things, however, it is not the case that quiescent and passive "meanings" are linked together in a purely formal way. Rather, it happens that the subject with which a certain predicate is linked determines, on the basis of its meaning, that of the predicate, and the predicate determines the meaning of the subject.... According to Hegel, the "object"... "manifests itself as its development".[5]

Here, with one additional quotation, a basis will be provided for the consideration of the philosophical proposition:

---

[4] *Phän.*, p. 49; or *Phen.*, p. 118.

[5] "Die Kategorien im 'gewöhnlichen' und im 'spekulativen' Satz", *Wiener Jahrbuch für Philosophie 1970*, pp. 9-37 (hereafter KgsS). See pp. 23f. The quoted passage is taken from the translation of this article (CHSP) by Gunther Heilbrunn in *Contemporary German Philosophy*, Vol. 2 (University Park, Penn.: The Pennsylvania State University Press, 1983). For the final quotation within the citation, see *Phän.*, p. 49; or *Phen.*, p. 118. I have given attention to the developmental and cumulative import of dialectic, referred to here and following, in "Die Phänomenologische Methode Hegels und das Unbewußte", in, *Wiener Jahrbuch für Philosophie*, Vol. VI (1973), pp. 178-207. See also "Hegel and a Philosophical Doctrine of God for Theism", *Indian Philosophical Quarterly*, Vol. V, No. 4 (1978), pp. 521-58.

Late Addendum: While Hegel, both in the *Phän.* and in his *Philosophy of Absolute Spirit*, sets out to render an account of the universal individual, I have endeavored in the reconstruction under way to set the methodological basis for providing a dialectical account of the idiosyncrasies, as well, that distinguish persons and individuals from one another. In part on this account I do not ordinarily make reference to *spekulativen Sätzen* as categories, which might suggest to some a degree of stability or finality that is not wanted. I prefer as an alternative to make reference to generic types and to make allowance for the possibility of variations within any given type from one occasion to another. My intent is to achieve a greater consistency in the treatment of the mutual determination of universality and particularity each by the other than does Hegel.

The proposition ought to express what the truth is, in its essential nature subject. As such truth is the dialectical movement, the self-producing course of activity, advancing and returning into itself.[6]

Such terms as "determines", "action", "development", and "movement" in the foregoing passages are indicative of the emphasis upon the mediation *process* as that which is actual in a philosophical proposition. The following additional points are to be especially noted as implicated in these passages: (1) The philosophical proposition functions in the determination of *original* and *concrete*, that is, *concretely particular*, meanings. (2) The subject and predicate of such a proposition (or judgment) at once come to be determined (and indeed in their concrete specificity *come to be*[7]), and *to be discriminated (unterschieden)*. (3) These concretely discriminated aspects are neither abstractable from this concrete discrimination, nor is the discrimination abstractable from them. As concrete, then, a particular discrimination and its mutually determined and mutually dependent discriminated aspects are integral. But one can go one step further.

Any particular discrimination is integral as well with other discriminations constitutive of any particular concrete identity. If this latter point is perhaps less than completely documented by what I have said thus far, it will be suggested by "the object manifests itself in its development" if this assertion leads us to think of further determinations to be unfolded and more positively, perhaps, by the example of "roundness" which leaves one to consider that the table referred to, to be what it is, must surely possess other attributes as well.

Certainly Hegel's system, regarded in its entirety, can leave no doubt but that any particular identity is multiply discriminated or, otherwise said, that any particular identity is constituted by a multiplicity of discriminations.[8] The system of philosophical propositions, viewed in respect to the foregoing, indeed represents an attempt to explicate all of the discriminations constitutive of any particular

---

[6] *Phän.*, p. 53; or *Phen.*, p. 123.

[7] When Hegel's dialectic and the philosophical propositions that constitute dialectic are properly understood as not merely constitutive of thought but of actuality as well, the two — thought and actuality — being accents within an identity inclusive of both, it will be clear that the subject and predicate are actualized in their concrete specificity at the same time that they come to be discriminated. The immanent character of Hegel's dialectic, and for that matter of his proposition, within nature — a notion which has its parallel in Whitehead, who in effect made consciousness an unessential feature of (some) propositions — can be rendered clear from his statements of method.

[8] For Hegel's dialectical definition of *Unterschied*, of which *Unterscheidung*, which I am translating "discrimination", is a derivative, see his dialectic of identity and difference, *Logik*, II, pp. 26-40; or *Logic*, pp. 411-31.

identity, regarded in its completeness.⁹ This attempt exhibited a mistake in that different identities are not, or at least not evidently, constituted by precisely the same totality of discriminations and because, one particular discrimination, for example, space(nature)-time (history),¹⁰ actualized through mediation in one occasion will not be the same space-time actualized in another. This is a fact which must come into evidence (1) whenever the pluralistic dimension of Hegel's thought is rendered explicit, and (2) where critical principles,¹¹ which, if the concept of "the truth is the whole" is to be rendered intelligible, requires an exhaustive explication of the discriminations constitutive of any particular identity, are in force. I shall shortly return to this point.

I previously noted three ways in which the constituent aspects and relations within Hegel's Begriff are integral with one another. Regarded together, these seem to constitute one way, at a certain level of abstractness, of giving an account of concrete universality. This amounts to saying that within the wholeness of relations constituted by Hegel's Begriff (the concrete universal), every part or aspect is implicated in every other so exhaustively that any one implies the whole.¹² This is to say that it plays its role throughout the entire whole and is thus universal throughout the entire whole. For purposes of convenience of reference, I shall in what follows refer to the Begriff as a concretely actual occasion, a term I adapt from White-

---

⁹ The following statement, understood in its context, will go some way toward documenting the point. "Philosophy.... is the process that creates its own moments in its course, and goes through them all; and the whole of this movement constitutes its positive content and its truth", *Phän.*, p. 39; or *Phen.*, p. 105.

¹⁰ "History...is therefore the development of Spirit in *Time*, as Nature is the development of the Idea in *Space*." Hegel, *Philosophy of History*, p. 72.

¹¹ For the initial outline of what I here refer to as "critical principles", see CHSS, 2nd paragraph. The sense of this statement is repeated within the present collection near the beginning of essay VI.
In the Preface to PR, Whitehead wrote, "In the main the philosophy of organism is a recurrence to pre-Kantian modes of thought" (p. xi). Pre-critical thinker that he most fundamentally was, he maintained that the comprehending, interpreting subject of an actual occasion somehow takes up a perspective outside of it, even though the occasion, as self-constituting, includes within itself all that from its perspective is actual. Hegel, in recognition that the self-conscious subject contributes to the constitution of every concrete fact, was constrained to include the discrimination of subject and what presents itself for the subject within Whitehead's "complete fact", in this way rendering it actually complete. Thus he at once made this one of the discriminations constitutive of every actual occasion, and placed the subject within the occasion which it constitutes and which is constitutive of it; the two discriminated aspects functioning throughout the whole, following the sense of his account of concrete universality. See the next essay.

¹² For a more detailed statement on concrete universality in Hegel, see SC, pp. 104, 226, 242ff.

head's usage.¹³

From the consideration that every part or aspect of a concretely actual occasion is implicated in every other it seems necessarily to follow that the explication of the truth that is the whole requires an exhaustive explication of its constitutive discriminations, each in a philosophical proposition.¹⁴ Were it not possible to render an account of its constitutive discriminations, no particular discrimination could be explicated with respect to its relation within the whole to other discriminations and discriminated aspects. It can hardly be surprising, then, that Hegel's claim with reference to the concrete universality of his Begriff is based upon the position that all of the various phases of the development of Spirit can be dialectically traversed and accounted for, which is tantamount to saying that the analysis-synthesis of the discriminations constitutive of a contemporary occasion can be carried through exhaustively.

The presuppositionless character which Hegel attributed to concrete actuality rests also upon his having shown us that a concretely specific explication of a concretely actual occasion, discrimination by discrimination, is feasible. By the presuppositionless character of concrete actuality I mean that characteristic of a concretely actual occasion by virtue of which it may be explicated by the employment of discriminations intrinsic to itself so that a conceptuality need not be brought to this task from elsewhere (as though this were ultimately possible).¹⁵

3. On Rendering Hegel's Truth which is the Whole Adequate

Following a number of years of deliberation on the matter, I have arrived at the conclusion that Hegel saw this matter correctly: a concretely specific explication of a concretely actual occasion is in principle possible.¹⁶ This is if allowance is made for certain considera-

---

[13] This adaptation is to be progressively unfolded throughout the present collection of essays, especially in numbers II and III; and it is treated with greater fullness within SC, especially Book II.

[14] The requirement here adumbrated holds for discriminations construed as completely abstract from one another. Otherwise, the requirement is qualified by the consideration that the import of some discriminations is contained within that of others that are understood more concretely, i.e., within some significant portion of the context of the occasion imaginatively reconstructed through a second reflection.

[15] I have sometimes referred to Hegel's presuppositionlessness as his concept of self-evidence. See CHSS.

[16] I made reference to all discriminations constitutive of an actual occasion being *in principle* explicable in philosophical propositions. This "in principle" ideal may in a particular case be very difficult and perhaps impossible to achieve. Even when allowance is

tions which, in his exuberance over his great new discovery of his philosophical proposition, he did not properly take into account, moving rather too quickly to the conclusion that a certain finite number (ca. 165) of discriminations are exhaustively constitutive of concrete actuality, whether implicitly or explicitly,[17] in every time and place. If one makes adequate allowance (1) for the consideration that not all discriminations are (abstractly) universal to all occasions, as he would seem to have supposed,[18] (2) for the consideration that all occasions are not, or not obviously, constituted by precisely the same totality of discriminations, even when the latter are construed generically, rather than concretely, a simplification which, regarded for what it is, can be very useful, and (3) for the possibility of novel discriminations, no principle seems to pose a fundamental impediment in the way of executing such an analysis-synthesis. The loosening of one or more of these strictures, it may be argued, leads to a somewhat different conception of the whole which is the truth than Hegel proposed. The foundational methodological principle embodied in the philosophical proposition remains unaltered, however, as well as its application with the analysis-synthesis of all of the discriminations constitutive of an actual occasion in view. The changes in conception thus proposed, though far-reaching in their implications, are less fundamental than what is retained.

One of the implications which follows from them is that an analysis-synthesis of concrete actuality now necessarily concerns itself with the self-evidence (presuppositionlessness) of some actual occasion *typical of some relevant epoch*. This is seeing that the analysis-synthesis of a single occasion, such as that which is determinative of me and my world when I glance to the right — certainly a different

made for discriminations which may so far as we know be unique to a particular occasion, however, it is nearly enough achievable so that the concept need suffer no want of clarity on account of practical difficulties which may stand in the way of its ideal execution. See essay III, §8.

[17] He distinguished historical periods from one another by reference to which dialectical stages in the march of Spirit were yet made explicit and which remained only implicit. Pursuing this idea, he has led some readers, at least, to construe that other cultures would advance in lock step through the same series in order, which is to say, discrimination by discrimination, as in his time constituted Germanic culture.

[18] To allude in this manner to all occasions may at first seem strangely *un*-Hegelian, owing to the consideration that in Hegel's *Phän.*, if we set aside his commentary, dialectic for the most part appears to move at a trans-temporal level, *as well as* because he seems to be construing the same discriminations as actual at all times and places. When the latter dogma is challenged, the fall of the first is accompanied by a sigh of relief, because with this the high status which Hegel accorded to individuality in making it the highest achievement of the dialectic can be complemented by lending essential status to those traits by virtue of which a particular individual is unique, which he was in a cramped position to do. For a more detailed treatment of this issue, see SC, pp. 177-85, 419-22.

occasion, all must agree, constituted by a different system of space-time relations, etc., than when I glance to the left — considering the effort required and the fleeting character of a glance, could hardly be justified were it not held in the main to be representative of a relevant epoch. This will usually be a cultural epoch or a (more particular) social-political-ethical development, but it might be a yet shorter epoch, such as the life span from birth to death of a person, or that series of actual occasions which is constitutive of the act of raising my arm. Even with the changes of conception thus proposed (with its implied dimension of radical nominalism), Hegel's system remains the most poignant catalog to date of the wide variety of types of discriminations which such an analysis-synthesis is likely to exhibit: being-nothing, quality-quantity, form-content, structure-function, space (nature)-time (history), subject-substance, lordship-bondage, individual-community, etc.

4. On Rendering Hegel's Truth which is the Whole Tolerable

The innovations I have proposed in the foregoing section were directed toward rendering Hegel's account of an actual occasion adequate, especially with reference to the variety of lived occasions, and in such a way as to render their differences ontologically relevant aspects of truth conceived as something which occurs within, and ultimately is, a coherent whole of philosophical — I would prefer to say *concrete* — propositions. The innovation I now propose against this background is directed toward rendering this truth, in its character of being absolute, tolerable.

The absolute character of Hegel's truth which is the whole consists in its being presuppositionless, whereby its explication requires no discrimination outside of its own concretization. It is thus self-contained and self-constitutive, needing nothing outside of itself to be what it is. If the integral character of a discrimination and what is discriminated are kept in view, it will be clear that an actual occasion contains all that from its perspective is actual, one might say, all that falls within its perceptual-conceptual-intentional horizon.

The problem posed in connection with such an absolute truth has perennially been that, as mediated, i.e., as a completed process of mediation — whereby each member of a pair of discriminated aspects becomes an accent within an identity of meaning inclusive of both, this identity along with its sub-members being multiply discriminated — all of its potentiality has spent itself into concrete actuality. There is then no more freedom in the sense that something different might be done, actualized, or even thought. Moreover, if truth in this completed state persists, it becomes overbearing, effecting its sway in other occasions *ad infinitum,* long after its concreteness has become no more than a remote memory. Perhaps it may even become confused with a kind of transcending vision of the wholeness of the physical universe or a divine vision of a sort such as could only hypothetically be entertained and could not even conceivably be (except perspectivally) within the perceptual-conceptual-intentional horizon of any single occasion of the sort that might be constitutive of a human subject and the world present for such a subject. Especially in view of the variety of occasions (the way of doing full justice to which has now been opened) such an extension of its sway would clearly be illicit, seeing that it is the totality of discriminations which conditions the self-evidence of the truth of, or within, any occasion, and since this totality, in the case of two significantly separated occasions, is likely to be notably different. This difference, moreover, is likely to extend even to occasions which are constituted by the "same" discriminations, generically considered, by virtue of variant concretizations.

The solution to the problem thus posed lies in the simple recognition of what may well seem at once obvious to the ordinary consciousness: Every occasion, upon having achieved the certainty of itself implicated with the totality of its constitutive discriminations in mediation (which *is* self- and world-consciousness), i.e., upon achieving a coherent wholeness and unity of concrescence, perishes. The fact it has become, together with its sub-facts and sub-identities, all concretely universal throughout the occasion, is self-evidently given in each occasion. The discriminations providing the basis for the self-evident truth of the occasion form for the most part the conceptual basis for abstraction and for hypothetical thinking germane to that occasion. Hypothetical thinking survives the occasion — within a successor — after its self-evidence fades. In dissimulation, hypothetical thinking may for a time seem virtually to displace self-evidence. Actually, it does not, so long as there is consciousness.

To meet the issue, then, I propose Whitehead's death of an actual occasion, adapted now to an occasion which includes the discrimination of its comprehending, interpreting subject and its world as present for this subject (along with its discriminated aspects) as one of its constitutive discriminations. This notion is, I think, not without possible parallels in Hegel's thought; I shall note three aspects of his thought which seem to lend themselves to being interpreted as at least pointing in this direction, although these remain relatively undeveloped and to my knowledge no interpreter before me has considered them in anything like the manner I am proposing.

Thus at the conclusions of the *Phen.,* the *Logic,* and the *Philosophy of Absolute Spirit* are to be found what I have called "the anticlimactic passage".[19] At the point at which the wholeness and unity of discriminations constitutive of the Begriff is supposed to have been rendered explicit in these works (as considered in respect to the aim of the particular work[19a]), this whole is portrayed as falling asunder into its disparate phases. Having considered these passages in the sources cited, I wish here only to note, in addition, that this state appears to amount to a regression from reason to the understanding, i.e., from concrete to abstract knowing, suggestive of a parallel to Whitehead's perishing of an actual occasion whereby its resultant data become objective, indeed objectively immortal.[20]

A second possible undeveloped parallel in Hegel to Whitehead's perishing consists in his references to the Golgotha of Absolute Spirit at the very close of the *Phen.*, in which he writes, "Both together, or History (intellectually) comprehended (*begriffen*), form at once the recollection and the Golgotha of Absolute Spirit, the reality, the truth, the certainty of its throne, without which it were lifeless, solitary, and alone".[21] The close connection of the notions of *re*-collection and death is here to be considered in the light of the fact that self-certainty for Hegel is a result of mediation and no mere recollection. If the suggested parallel holds, this is the recollection of what was actual but has now given way to a mere recollection.

A third undeveloped and possible parallel consists in Hegel's concept of the circularity of the dialectic. I quote from the *Logic*, although the concept is anticipated in the *Phen.*

> By reason of the nature of the method which has been demonstrated science is seen to be a circle which returns upon itself, for mediation bends back its end into its beginning or simple ground. Further, this circle is a

---

[19] See "Hegel's Altar to the Known God", *Hegel-Studien*, Beiheft 11 (Bonn: Bouvier Verlag, 1974), pp. 219-30, and "Hegel's Justification of Christianity: Serious or Sophistry?", *The Southern Journal of Philosophy*, Vol. XIV, No. 4 (Winter, 1967-77), pp. 413-30.

[19a] In the *Phän.* (p. 563), e.g., it is explicitly noted that the Begriff enters into consciousness. Thus the account of how consciousness has come to be is completed. In the *Logik* (II, p. 503), there is a completed dialectical circle and a return to the concrete immediacy with which the account began, now grasped, however, in its concretely universal significance.

[20] What is here suggested is that for both thinkers, if I may provisionally attribute the import of the term also to Hegel, "perishing" amounts to the loss of subjective immediacy and a "fall" of actuality into a static condition, but whereas for Whitehead the gain is true objectivity, for Hegel true objectivity (with its necessary component of subjectivity, subject and object being accents within an identity inclusive of both) gives way to something "lifeless" and "merely" objective. In making objectivity as lifeless and static as he did, Whitehead showed himself to be less radical, and with respect to this point, less consistent, in his process orientation than was Hegel.

[21] *Phän.*, p. 581; or *Phen.*, p. 808.

circle of circles...²²

If the passage leaves unanswered what happens to a completed circle [a previous occasion or an aspect of a previous occasion (?)] it seems at least to lend itself to interpretation within a context in which the death of an actual occasion counts as one consideration.

The concept of perishing seems a necessary complement to the concept of self-evidence even though — as it is only proper to acknowledge — it itself (as my own death) can never lend itself to being rendered self-evident. Indeed death, so far as I am able to see, can never be more than a theory, i.e., a part of the structure of expectations that the empiricist tradition since J. S. Mill has referred to as "nature as a permanent possibility of experience" and which has so frequently been confused with knowledge. In assisting us to salvage self-evidence, as Paul Kuntz has helped me to see with greater clarity, perishing assists us to explain how it can be that dualisms of all sorts remain indispensible aspects of philosophy and indeed of actuality,²³ even though each must in some sense be mediated as a condition of our even being able to recognize and to talk about it as such. The problem is at once resolved if these dualisms are mediated within the occasion presently constitutive of me (as subject, i.e., "I") and the world present for me and yet remain to be mediated anew within each successor occasion likewise constitutive (each in series) of me and the world present for me.

5. Possible Objections to Perishing

(1) Experience is continuous, and I experience a world as continuous. If occasions perish, it will be argued, my grasp of actuality would be discontinuous, perhaps even jerkily so; whatever may be the case with actuality, experience is more compatible with a stream of consciousness than with discontinuity.

According precedence to the requirement of an account of self-evident truth, the problematic becomes one of determining whether it is possible to account for the continuity of self and world as I experience them at the same time that I proceed on the basis of a concept of truth as episodic, climactic, and mortal. In reply to this problematic, I submit the following: (a) each of us does ordinarily experience a difference in what is self-evident from one instant to the next. We are not for the most part confronted by what impress us as

---

²² *Logik*, II, pp. 504f; or *Logic*, II, pp. 484f. See also *Phän.*, p. 559; or *Phen.*, p. 801.

²³ See Paul Grimley Kuntz, "The Dualism of Paul Elmer More", *Religious Studies*, 16, pp. 389-411.

absolute discontinuities, it is true. This might in part be due to the consideration that many discriminations, generically considered, remain the "same" through myriads of successive concretizations. Many of the successive concretizations of some one particular generic discrimination undergo little perceptible variation. And there is a substantial group of discriminations, generically considered, that it seems almost necessary to presume to be (abstractly) universal to all occasions, and which it seems plausible to suppose as transcendentally conditioning their possibility. These are all factors pertaining to continuity. (b) Hypothetical thinking, based upon abstracted discriminations from proximate and relevant past occasions, bridges the gap between absolute truth instances. Truth instances fade, flow, and blend into one another. The data of past occasions that have perished, inherited by the presently actual occasion, constitute a record of *change* through succession, i.e., history as actual within the *present (Wirkungsgeschichte)*, which in turn form the basis for hypothesizing the series of occasions that have perished *as past*: memory. My access to the past must be within the present occasion, which contains all that from its perspective is actual. No one has ever (actually) taken up a position outside of that some one occasion that includes him (as subject) and his world. Efforts to do so, like memory itself, inevitably consist in hypothetical thinking. It is a great advantage to us, of course, that memory is hypothetical, in that this renders possible the recreation of the past to render it and the anticipated future, also hypothetical, mutually compatible and complementary.

It is reasonable to conjecture, I think (although theorizing of this sort can hardly be the proper business of first philosophy except as it should find and report it as mediation phenomena or as an inference from such phenomena), that the movement here described has its analogue in the unconscious biological level.

(2) "The grasping of the truth which is the whole is in principle impossible, on which account to speak of its perishing is superfluous". There will always be skeptics to raise this challenge, sometimes in such a spirit as presupposes that the point itself, although inferred, ought to be self-evident. I can only provide some supplementary remarks that invite disinterested interest in an approach by which the claim under discussion can be sustained.

(a) We do experience something as self-evident every waking moment. Moreover, nothing can dissuade us from what presents itself as self-evident. And of what presents itself self-evidently, nothing presents itself as more obvious than discriminations. This amounts to saying that the fact of self-evident truth is what must be accounted for. The way I have proposed that self-evidence is to be conceived can, I believe, be rendered as self-evident as the fact of self-evidence itself: That is, Truth as an accent within an identity inclusive of truth and actuality, the discrimination being continuingly concretized anew.[24] Where an actualized identity of something ideational which I hold to be true with that which it represents is achieved, there is Truth, a correspondence test having been sustained. But this that is true also exhibits itself as conditioned by being within a context of coherence achieved as an episode in which strivings and interest play a role.[25]

(b) The discrimination of subject and object (i.e., the world present merely *for* me), in process of concretization and as such, is an actual aspect of every occasion. The plausibility of the position rests upon the Buberian (as well as Hegelian) position that the I-It relation — the discrimination — is graspable prior to abstraction, even though this grasping is "momentary". Subsequent to being grasped the discriminated aspects fall asunder as lifeless abstractions, the potency of the occasion having spent itself. In this state it exists only as hypothetically entertained "data" of a subsequent occasion, within the earlier phases of its concretization, at first only within its objective pole, rather than knowledge in the proper sense, i.e., knowledge that is *concretely* factual.

(3) It may be objected that, even granting that the self-evidence of an actual occasion is in some non-trivial sense graspable, this self-evidence must necessarily be prior to its explicit analysis-synthesis. Were the proponent of this objection to say no more, he might well be construed to be on the way toward the truth of the matter. Unfortunately, he wishes also to maintain that, the analysis-synthesis of what presents itself as self-evident being exclusively after the fact, this analysis-synthesis is rendered in principle impossible, seeing that the discriminations constitutive of a past occasion under analysis-synthesis are always displaced by others which constitute the fact (and its sub-facts) of the moment. The point that an explicit analysis-syn-

---

[24] A refinement of the proposal that the conception of self-evidence can be rendered as self-evident as self-evidence itself must take systematically into account the fact that the concept of death, which to be existentially meaningful must ultimately refer to "my own death", can never be more than a theory. I can never experience my own death, although I may experience occasions which lead me to anticipate it. More specifically, it must be shown that the self-evidence of the occasion stands free of all theory, including this one, even though we must appeal to this theory to render an account of change. See Essay XI, n. 32, Essay IX.

[25] The correspondence, coherence, and pragmatic theories of truth are in this way all aspects of Hegelian dialectic constituted of philosophical propositions. See "Das Problem der Verifizierbarkeit historischer Dialektik", *Philosophisches Jahrbuch*, 84. Jahrgang (1977), 1. Halbband, pp. 126-34.

thesis of an actual occasion or of even one of its constitutive discriminations is after the fact is well taken. It would be a mistake, however, to conclude the impossibility of such an analysis-synthesis owing to a radical discontinuity between discriminations constitutive of the fact (and its sub-facts) of the moment and discriminations under analysis-synthesis. The difficulty consists in that the foregoing complex objection is flawed by a hidden premise that discriminations *are not known prior to their analysis-synthesis*.[26] Hegel perceived correctly that it is precisely *as discriminated* that concrete actuality lays its claim upon us. It would surely be inconsistent with this conclusion to maintain that individual discriminations — especially such as are at the focal point of an experience — are not perceived prior to their analysis-synthesis. Moreover, if a given particular discrimination is perceived within the context of the occasion of which it is an aspect prior to abstraction, as the occasion perishes and it acquires the status of an abstract entity, there will be no difficulty in perceiving it to be the "same" discrimination that was priorly concrete. In stating the matter thus I am assuming that abstraction is a necessary aspect of an analysis-synthesis of discriminations. Seeing that an analysis-synthesis must take the linear form of language, there seems to be no escaping this conclusion. The further conclusion to which this line of thought decisively points is that such an analysis-synthesis after the fact has as its aim the recapitulation of the mediation process constitutive of each discrimination, and of the unity and wholeness of discriminations, priorly constitutive of the fact. Some such understanding would appear to follow necessarily the attempt to interpret Hegel's dialectic with consistent regard to the consideration that (indubitably) concrete actuality is its outcome.

An additional remark pertains to the case of authentically concrete (spoken) language, the utterance of which involves no explicit analysis-synthesis, or recapitulation of the mediation of discriminations, as though it were after the fact rather than the fact itself, i.e., an accent within an identity of word and fact. Self-evident occasions speak for themselves, and this speech is concrete (thought and spoken) language, the "being mediated" of subjects and predicates in statements.[27] Language being inherently linear, however, it must be acknowledged that the mediations of all of the discriminations con-

---

[26] — or, what comes to the same, prior to their *second* reflection, which is *after the fact*.

[27] See Essay X. The philosophy of language implicated with this view has much in common with that of Renate Christensen, in "On the Problematic of a Philosophy of Language", *International Philosophical Quarterly*, Vol. XVI, No. 1 (1976), pp. 33-47; and with that of Josef Simon, KGsS. Also see my review article, "Erich Heintel, 'Einführung in die Sprachphilosophie'," *Wiener Jahrbuch für Philosophie*, Vol. VI (1973), pp. 433-43.

stitutive of a given occasion cannot be rendered explicit in speech or even to thought all at once. Indeed no more than one subject and predicate (or predicate complex) can be mediated in a single declarative sentence, and one cannot speak quickly enough to render a complete exposition of the discriminations constitutive of any single occasion while it is still actual.[28] On this account certain of the discriminations constitutive, with the one which is mediated, of the self-evidence of the present occasion, although grasped (or being grasped) in thought by the speaker, regarded from the standpoint of a hearer who lacked this context of thought, would need to be somehow conjured up and presupposed. If they are mentally grasped in a manner sufficient to lend conviction to the utterance of the proposition being expressed, their particularity does not thereby come to clear expression. Allowing for a constant shift in propositions and discriminations which do and do not come to overt expression, those which do not being presupposed by the hearer of what is said (the speaker need not, of course, presuppose what he directly knows), we are not, nonetheless, in want of direct access to the mediation process by virtue of which a given occasion is self-evident. The subject and predicate of at least some one proposition may at any time be in the process of being mediated in such a way that this process is an explicit datum of consciousness. Secondly, all of the constitutive discriminations are in principle in view as the open context of the proposition which is an explicit datum of consciousness, even though some will lie at the fringes of awareness, by virtue of having minimal relevance to such decisions as lie at hand. The preceding is not intended to deny that the entire actuality of an actual occasion is grasped as a datum of consciousness — what we all in fact experience. The issue here is what discrimination can be not merely known to be present, but grasped with some explicitness with respect to its subject and predicate in mediation (and not merely as results, perhaps separated off by abstraction from their lived mediation) and with respect to its function within the occasion as a whole.

In the normal course of affairs, presuppositions can stand in for discriminations present but not rendered fully explicit in a present

---

[28] Following the lead of the Whiteheadians, I am assuming here that the duration of an occasion of experience might, on the average, be of the order of 1/10th or 1/20th of a second. Clock time, pertaining as it does to relations between occasions, is, however, hypothetical in character and to be distinguished from the time concretely actualized within an actual occasion, i.e., the time of *becoming*.

The foregoing statement in the text constitutes the indication that discriminations not explicitly expressed are less real or essential to an occasion's being the particular occasion that it is, or that any one of them, generically considered, is in principle forever unaccessible to articulation in other occasions.

occasion or epoch of occasions, so long as a requisite concrete proposition can be elicited upon demand to vouch for them. This is although it seems necessary to maintain that concrete discriminations, by which I mean concrete propositions, must all alike be capable of arising to consciousness apart from any assistance from generic propositions, seeing that it would otherwise be impossible to account for their arising to consciousness in the first place, or for that matter, for the arising of consciousness at all.

6. First Philosophy and the Theory of Science

The foregoing strategy, by the reconciliation of freedom with a completely determined truth which refers to a coherent whole of internal relations, and therefore to a closed system, would appear to set the ontological status of truth upon fundamentally new ground. This is by rendering every new occasion the occasion of a new birth of freedom. I shall content myself just here by noting only one additional ramification. I intended to show that the conception of relations internal and external to that some one actual occasion which at any instant is constitutive both of me and the world present for me provides a trustworthy basis for distinguishing between concrete knowing and hypothetical thinking. I wish now to indicate how this same conception also provides a basis for distinguishing first philosophy from the theory (and theories) of science (*Wissenschaftstheorie*) and from second philosophy.

First philosophy has as its task the analysis-synthesis of discriminations constitutive of concretely actual occasions typical of relevant epochs, its syntheses being set forth in philosophical propositions self-consciously employed as such.[29] Its business, in other words, is the explication in its time and place, and with respect to relevant epochs, of the truth which is the concrete whole.[30] The theory of science has the various theories of the particular sciences as its sub-

---

[29] For the proposition to have relevance for the subject of an actual occasion is for it either to become a fully concretized philosophical proposition in the process of concrescence or to be omitted (through negative prehension) or relegated to negligible emphasis prior to the final phase of this process. In the latter case it remains theory, and, as such, it may serve the process of concrescence as a "lure for feeling" prior to its exclusion. Philosophical propositions serve as lures for feeling *throughout* the process of concrescence, until their potency has spent itself for the hard coin of actuality and the occasion perishes. Whitehead's proposition, by way of contrast, ever remains a "hybrid", transcending any particular concrescence, i.e., it remains in part potentiality unactualized, a "lure for feeling" (PR, pp. 25, 184, 186, 224, 259).

[30] The attempt of the pragmatists to leave the question of absolute truth to a receding future stands in the starkest possible contrast to the program here advocated. See essays V and VI.

ject matter, and interests itself in seeing what follows from these theories and their criticism. When it pursues this task by self-consciously drawing upon conceptions of concrete actuality provided by first philosophy, it serves a mediating role between first philosophy and the particular sciences, which role may appropriately be designated second philosophy. First philosophy, following this conception, is itself a science in the sense that it is practiced in observance of specifiable methodological principles. Certain of its deliverances, especially respecting discriminations which, generically considered and so far as can be determined, recur in every actual occasion, appear to be more stable than are most theories, a matter which up to this time would seem not to have been very well explained, and which in modern times has often gone unnoticed. Even discriminations, generically considered, the concepts of which are relatively stable, however, must give way to changes reflected in their concretizations, in part owing to novelties introduced in other discriminations which must have their effect throughout every other aspect of any particular occasion.[31] On this account no single phase of the work of first philosophy, i.e., the analysis-synthesis of no single discrimination, can with certainty be brought to a final conclusion in the sense of being assuredly adequate to the portrayal of future concretizations. Indeed, for first philosophy to venture *anything at all* about the future, except as the future is fulfilled in a presently actual occasion — *even that it will resemble the past* — would be tantamount to a regress into an *intolerable* kind of truth which is the whole.

That the ideal for first philosophy thus held out is in principle achievable is linked to the consideration that philosophical propositions should reflect no speculations which have not been actualized in fact. This is in marked contrast to the particular sciences, the constitutive theories of which would be completely uninteresting, were they to appear as having been entirely actualized in fact. First philosophy, then, for the most part restricts its attention to concrete facts and their character, and interests itself in theories only insofar as these have been concretized as fact. This is although it may interest itself marginally in theories insofar as they have influenced the formation of discriminations constitutive of what is concretely factual apart from themselves passing into factuality. It thus lays the groundwork for those sciences whose mastery of their respective subject matters requires a certain provisional reliance upon abstract facts. These, then, are *the theoretical sciences* in a not unusual sense of the

---

[31] I have elsewhere developed this notion as "the settlement effect", or the "*Einbettungswirkung*". See Essay VII.

term, the theories of which are necessarily couched in the language of external relations — relations *between* occasions — and which contribute to the bridging and blending of spasmodic instances of absolute actuality and absolute knowing — accents within an inclusive identity — that constitute our existence and that of our universe.

II

ON RENDERING WHITEHEAD'S "COMPLETE FACT" COMPLETE:
ASPECTS OF A CONSTRUCTIVE CRITIQUE OF WHITEHEAD
FROM A SOMEWHAT HEGELIAN PERSPECTIVE*

1. Introduction

Ivor Leclerc, citing the following passage from *Adventures of Ideas* (Chap. IV, sec. VIII), interprets Whitehead's metaphysics as an explication of the concept of an actual entity (or actual occasion) construed as a "complete fact":

> The final problem is to conceive a complete [$τῷ$ $παντελῶς$]¹ fact. We can only form such a conception in terms of fundamental notions concerning

---

* This paper, which was originally carried in *Idealistic Studies*, XII, No. 2 (May, 1982), was initially presented to the staff and graduate students of the Dep't of Philosophy of Emory University, Jan. 9, 1981. I wish to take this opportunity to thank participants in the discussion for their criticisms, and, in particular, Paul Kuntz, with whom I corresponded following, and who assisted me to achieve greater clarity at some points, particularly in the revision of the notes.

¹ Whitehead refers us to Sophist, 248E:
"And, O heavens, can we ever be made to believe that motion and life and soul and mind are not present with perfect being [$τῷ$ $παντελῶς$]? Can we imagine that being is devoid of life and mind, and exists in awful unmeaningness an everlasting fixture?" From *The Dialogues of Plato*, trans. by B. Jowett, in two volumes (New York: Random House, 1937) 14th printing, Vol. II, p. 257; and *Platon, Der Sophist*, Griechisch-Deutsch ed. (Hamburg: Meiner Verlag, 1967), p. 102.

It is suggested that perfect being includes the hierarchy moving from motive to life to soul to mind and is not merely something immovable.

These levels — if in a somewhat different order — might all be made out in the perspective from which Whitehead is to be criticized. This is to say, the notion of completion or perfection here alluded to is suggestive of the more developed and concretely detailed one, the principles of which are to be set forth. This being the case, Whitehead's appeal to the above cited text might be supposed, at least at first glance, to weaken the force of the criticism to follow. That it does not is owing to the consideration that the subject of Whitehead's actual occasion, by virtue of not being self-conscious, does not include the listed attributes in the manner and degree required.

the nature of reality. We are thrown back upon philosophy.[2]

Supplemented by the following four citations from *Process and Reality*, in the second and third of which the term recurs, the passage will suffice to justify my reference, in what is to follow, to Whitehead's actual occasion as a complete fact:

> The philosophy of organism is a cell-theory of actuality. Each ultimate unit of fact is a cell-complex, not analyzable into components with equivalent completeness of actuality (PR 210).

> Actual occasions in their "formal" constitutions are devoid of all indetermination. Potentiality has passed into realization. They are complete and determinate matter of fact, devoid of all indecision (PR 29).

> An actual entity is at once the produce of the efficient past and is also, in Spinoza's phrase, *causa sui*. Every philosophy recognizes, in some form or other, this factor of self-causation, in what it takes to be ultimate actual fact. (PR 150)

> The facts of nature are the actualities [actual occasions]; and the facts into which the actualities are divisible are their prehensions (PR 290).

There would appear to be no more adequate way to define in a single sentence the process of concrescence of Whitehead's actual occasion than by saying that it is a process wherein polarities issue in contrasts and in a single complex contrast. As will be made clearer in what follows, the difference between a polarity and a contrast principally consists in the fact that contrasted aspects or elements are explicitly determined and defined by their relation to one another, which is thus necessary to their being what they are. It is with respect to the particular constituent contrasts of a conscious actual occasion, which Whitehead sometimes called an 'actual occasion of experience', that I wish to consider the issue of completeness. (By the term "actual occasion" I shall generally be referring to such a conscious occasion.) This may seem strange to some, since Whitehead himself would appear never to have attempted to render a concretely specific account of concreteness in respect to constituent contrasts.[3] He left some indications, nevertheless, which lend themselves to being interpreted as suggestions as to some possible candidates for the status of generic contrasts universal to all actual occasions, had he

---

[2] Ivor Leclerc, *Whitehead's Metaphysics* (Bloomington: Indiana University Press, 1958), p. 14.

[3] That the subject contributes to the constitution of a fact may safely be regarded as a central tenet of the tradition of critical philosophy which had its inception with Kant and within which Hegel worked. This notion, which counts importantly in this paper, although not rendered explicit within the statement of method in Essay V, par. 2, in which I indicate what I understand to be most centrally involved in being a critical philosopher in Hegel's sense, is nonetheless implicated by it.

done so. Space/time, physical feeling/conceptual feeling, subject pole/physical pole, the subject of a proposition/the predicate of a proposition are to be listed among these. Moreover, it would require a minimal amount of imagination, in one fell swoop, to add a myriad of others to this list by adding the particular subject and the particular predicate term of each particular proposition which is sufficiently interesting to function effectively as a lure for feeling, and thus to actualize itself as a contrast, within the process of concrescence of an actual occasion.

I propose to show that where this task is taken up it becomes immediately apparent that his complete fact — a designation in keeping, as I wish to maintain, with the requirements of knowledge and science — is not in fact complete. It is not complete for want of at least one constitutive contrast, which may be a complex contrast, and which would be essential to its character of being self-constitutive or self-created. I refer to the contrast between the objective data and the understanding, interpreting subject of an actual occasion. This contrast (together with the contrasted aspects) is essential to the self-constitutive character of an actual occasion because the self-conscious subject contributes essentially to what presents itself as concretely actual in experience: to what is actual *in fact*. This consideration — a hallmark of all philosophers within the critical tradition — is one to which Whitehead, by locating the understanding, interpreting subject in a *subsequent* occasion, was unable to do justice. The making up for this lack points the way toward a critical process philosophy which can assimilate substantial elements of Whitehead's metaphysics by reinterpretation.[4]

---

[4] In acknowledging his philosophy of organism to be in the main "a recurrence to pre-Kantian modes of thought" (PR, p. xi), Whitehead provides a useful clue to the precritical character of his speculative thought.

In the foregoing paragraph in the text I made reference to the contrast between the objective data and the understanding, interpreting subject of an actual occasion as being essential to what is actual in fact. If we express the relation in terms of Hegel's formulation of his concept of a speculative or philosophical proposition, this is to say that each of the two — objective data and the subject — are necessarily mediated to constitute an accent within a(n) (discriminated) identity constitutive of both. To be especially noted just here is that the subject and its objective data being identical as mutually determining each of the other, *they will prove, moreover, to be equally processual in character.*

In connection with this latter point, Harry Kohlsaat Wells, in *Process and Unreality: A Criticism of Method in Whitehead's Philosophy* (New York: King's Crown Press, 1950) rendered a distinctive service to Whitehead scholarship in pointing out that Whitehead, in dividing nature into events and sense objects, accomplished the separation of qualities from passage. Here in view are the qualities possessed in sense awareness, primary qualities, such as size and shape as well as secondary qualities, such as colors and smells. By identifying such qualities with particular (unchanging) eternal objects, he in effect eliminated the problem of dealing with them as processes, in which, e.g., "any concrete instance of a shade

The need for brevity will be served by assuming (1) that science and theory can ultimately be based upon nothing except fact, (2) that it is a central task of philosophy to explicate facts with respect to the self-evidence they natively display, and (3) that to function in

of red is at the same time becoming a *different* shade, and, indeed, in the long run becoming non-red" (pp. 58f).

> [W]hat Whitehead accomplishes through his bifurcation of nature into events and sense-objectivities is the reduction of qualities to static, definable entities which render nature accessible to rational method, where the latter is rooted in the principles of identity and non-contradiction (p. 59).

It is abstract and not concrete identity that is in view. This will certainly be the case if by the latter we are to refer to identities that are contextually determined within something like Hegel's truth which is the whole. The assigning of this status to objects appears to be equivalent to construing them as being unreal. Thus Wells entitles his *Work, Process and Unreality,* which title he proposes as descriptive of what Whitehead actually has under discussion in his *Process and Reality*.

The effect of Well's critique of Whitehead will be softened if, following Hartshorne, we look beyond his concept of eternal objects, to which even he attributed no ontological status, to the occurrences of being *within* becoming, which have such status and which this concept was supposed to assist us to understand. For Whitehead, "[m]ere being is an element within becoming, not becoming within being" (Charles Hartshorne, "Das metaphysische System Whiteheads" (Ernest Wolf-Gazo (Ed.), *Whitehead* [Freiburg/ München: Alber, 1980], p. 40). That abstract objects cannot as such be real finds itself reflected also within the reconstruction of method in progress. Thus they are relegated to the status of potentials which may be hypothetically entertained in the preparation of possibilities for future actualization. What is potential can become actual only as one pole of a mediation in process.

Whitehead once wrote that "in formal logic, a contradiction is a signal of defeat: but in the evolution of real knowledge it marks the first step in progress toward a victory" (SMW, 267). Wells remarks with reference to this utterance that the absolute opposition or "contradiction", between Whitehead's method — which he found to be rooted in the principle of [[abstract]] identity and non-contradiction — and the content to which he attempted to apply it — which, he found to be events in process — can, itself, be a "step in progress toward a victory." Continuing within the Preface to the same *Work* he notes:

> The lesson to be learned is that...a method must be developed which will be adequate to deal with process in its own terms — that is, without attempting to find something static, eternal, and unchanging. This does not mean that there cannot be relative permanences in the form of laws of nature and of thought. But it does mean that such relative permanences must be developed as functional structures within process, not standing over and above it in the form of mechanisms by means of which to rescue traditional method from bankruptcy. (pp. viif)

Wells goes on to note that Whitehead himself might have been led to recognize the contradiction between "traditional method" and process had he consulted Hegel's criticism of formal logic in one of his logic texts. In this case, "recognizing the difficulty, he might have been led further, perhaps partly through Hegel, to develop a new method" (p. viii).

I can only regret that, due to my own neglegance and to contingencies involved in the use of the inter-library loan system through which I have had to obtain access to many English-language sources pertaining to Whitehead, I found access to the *Volume* by Wells to which I have just made reference only after my SC and several other essays explicitly treating the Hegel-Whitehead relation had already appeared. That I am unable to recall or just now to spot a single reference to the *Work* in the literature, including contributions to George R. Lucas, Jr. (Ed.), *Hegel and Whitehead: Contemporary Perpsectives on Systematic*

this way, facts must stand theory-free. Process philosophers should have a special interest in this latter point especially seeing that, once the critical principle that the understanding, interpreting subject contributes essentially to the constitution of facts is acknowledged, their process principle is absolutely essential to rescuing the theory free status of facts. Where this principle is acknowledged, truth cannot be the contextual whole that it self-evidently is without being an organically developing whole, in some cases containing a theoretical component at some stage along the way, in which coherence is actualized, which, being once actualized, however, is 'no longer' impregnated with theory but is *fact*. This fact then perishes to become abstract data.

I shall have the exposition of a single principle in mind as the intelligible aim of the exposition: truth presents itself self-evidently as a coherent unity and wholeness of contrasts in concrescence, i.e., as contrasts being actualized as such, which by virtue of perishing do not become overbearing. So far as I know, no one before me has directed explicit attention to the necessary connection of these two notions — self-evidence and perishing — which appears to have equally fundamental import for process philosophy and for philosophies in the Hegelian tradition. Notions in some sense parallel to the perishing of an actual occasion of experience are relatively weak in Hegel;[5] and in Whitehead what perishes, far from being self-evident, is yet subject to judgment. The necessary connection of these two notions has the import that the periodic spasmodic character of concrescence is an essential condition of such knowledge as in fact presents itself as self-evident. Systems of coherence constituting a so-

---

Philosophy (Albany: Suny Press, 1986) hardly renders my part in the neglect of this small but important *Work* less painful to me. All the more urgently on this account, I wish to commend it as deserving of a wider readership than it has yet had. Especially the reader who is seeking to understand the Hegelian subordination of the traditional concepts of identity and non-contradiction to the principle of holistic organic process — to which I am unable to point to anything at all comparable in Whitehead's conceptuality — will find it rewarding.

Even though my own efforts stand almost totally independent of those of Wells, and even though the issue posed by the Hegelian subordination of the concepts of abstract identity and non-contradiction to organic process ought, it seems to me, to be found less problematical today than it was at the time that he wrote, I would be no less complimented on this account by any disposition on the part of my readers to regard my series of essays on the Hegel-Whitehead relation as a plausible fulfillment of much that Wells had in view in envisioning the new method that Whitehead might have undertaken had he been knowledgeable of Hegel.

[5] I have made reference to three "weak" analogues to Whitehead's perishing in Hegel within Essay 1, §4. Also see SC, Book I, Chap. III, §4, "The 'Continuing' Actuality of the Form of Becoming", pp. 187-84.

ciety of occasions develop themselves in periodic succession, each climaxing in the truth, the whole truth, and nothing but the truth, thus providing the foundation for abstraction, the construction of theories, and error.

2. Contrasts

A more specific characterization of Whitehead's concept of a contrast will set the background for taking up this problematic.

Whitehead's metaphysics is a metaphysics of relations. This in view, his seemingly unobtrusive statement that "What are ordinarily termed 'relations' are abstractions from [[and hence less than]] contrasts" (PR 28) will serve to document the centrality of his concept of contrasts. He devotes a great deal of space in *Process and Reality* to the detailed exposition of various types of contrasts, which, at least for the most part, are supposed to be identifiable in human experience.

In listing contrasts as the eighth and final category of existence, he refers to them as "Modes of Synthesis of Entities in one Prehension or Patterned Entities". To this he adds: "The eighth category includes an indefinite progression of categories, as we proceed from 'contrasts' to 'contrasts of contrasts', and on indefinitely to higher grades of contrasts" (PR 22). This hierarchy of contrasts later in the *Work* becomes a "complex contrast", to which I shall be referring again.

Seeing that a prehension is always a concrete fact of relatedness necessarily involving a subject, the datum prehended, and the 'subjective form' which is how the subject prehends that datum (PR, p. 23), it would appear that to speak of a contrast is an alternative way, with its characteristic emphasis, of referring to a prehension. This would imply that contrasts are formed throughout the various phases of the process of concrescence of an actual occasion, notwithstanding the fact that Whitehead accords them less explicit emphasis in the earlier than in the later phases of concrescence. Christian and others have held a different view, namely, that contrasts are less primary than prehensions.[6] With respect to present considerations, the issue

---

[6] What I have referred to as the "anticlimactic passages" within Hegel's *Phän.*, *Logik*, and VPR are here relevant. See the articles cited in Essay 1, n. 19. Something of the bearing of this theme upon Hegel's concept of God is portrayed in my "Hegel and a Philosophical Doctrine of God for Theism", *Indian Philosophical Quarterly*, Vol. V, No. 4, pp. 521-58.

In the above context and throughout this collection, I have left "Begriff" untranslated (ordinarily in roman print) as a reminder that no English term captures its meaning. This is Hegel's philosophical "concept" of the whole, this being a concept which is at once idea and actuality, these forming a complex contrast. This is to say, idea and actuality are each

does not seem to figure crucially, so long as what I should prefer to refer to as the more primary and the simpler contrasts are construed to be accorded a place within the phase of full concrescence of the occasion through being assimilated within "later" and more complex types of contrasts, particularly within propositions, rather than as such and in simple form. Whitehead's concept of "multiple contrast" — by which he means contrasts within contrasts within contrasts, in what could be shown to be a very Hegelian manner of organization[7] — goes some considerable way, at least, toward showing this to have been his position:

> The term "multiple contrast" will be used when there are or may be more than two elements jointly contrasted, and it is desired to draw attention to the fact. A multiple contrast is analyzable into component dual contrasts. But a multiple contrast is not a mere aggregation of dual contrasts. It is one contrast, over and above its component contrasts. (PR 229)

To be stressed is that contrasts are concretely specific facts of relatedness. Unless specifically referred to as such, they are within Whitehead's usage not generic.

> [T]he real synthesis of two component elements in the objective datum of a feeling must be infected with the individual particularities of each of the relata....A contrast cannot be abstracted from the contrasted relata. (PR 228)

Whitehead's discussion of God and the world as a contrast is highly instructive (see especially PR 348f). His concept of a contrast also comes to full expression in his treatment of propositions, which treatment lends itself to the present context. A proposition enters into experience as the entity forming the datum of a complex feeling derived from the integration of a physical and a conceptual feeling (PR 256). The datum of a conceptual feeling is an eternal object. "[A]n eternal object refers to the purely generic among undetermined actual entities" (PR 256). The data of physical feelings are actual entities.

> The definite set of actual entities involved are called the 'logical subjects' of a proposition'; and the definite set of eternal objects involved are called the 'predicates of the proposition'. The predicates define a potentiality of relatedness for the subjects. The predicates form one complex

---

accents within an identity inclusive of both, this identity being the Begriff. The Begriff is in principle the Absolute Identity, the concrete universal, Absolute Spirit, and, within some contexts, the Holy Spirit. But it is presented at various levels of the dialectic in varying grades of explicitness, its constitutive discriminations in many contexts being only partially explicit.

[7] The term in Hegel which functions in a manner more or less parallel to Whitehead's contrast is "discrimination" (*Unterscheidung*), there being discriminations within the Begriff. Indeed, the Begriff, considered within Whitehead's frame of reference, is a complex contrast.

eternal object: this is 'the complex predicate'. The 'singular' proposition is the potentiality of this complex predicate finding realization in the nexus of reactions between the logical subjects, with assigned stations in the pattern for the various logical subjects. (PR 186)

In another context he notes,

> [T]he physical feeling indicates the logical subjects and provides them respectively with that individual definition necessary to assign the hypothetic status of each in the predicative pattern. The conceptual feeling provides the predicative pattern. Thus in a proposition the logical subjects are reduced to the status of food for a possibility.... they are no longer factors in fact, except for the purpose of their physical indication. Each logical subject becomes a bare "*it*" among actualities, with its assigned hypothetical relevance to the predicate. (PR 258)

With variations in language, we may be seeing here something of a reflection of Hegel's *spekulativen Satz* (speculative judgment or speculative proposition),[8] which may well have entered Whitehead's thought at this particular point through Bradley. The aspect of Hegel's formulation which is here of interest is that the subject and the predicate of a *spekulativen Satz* are mediated to become accents within an identity inclusive of both (*Phän.* 51ff; *Phen.* 120ff). I understand this to be a **discriminated** identity. To employ Whitehead's term, Hegel's discriminated identity of the subject and the predicate is one within which they are contrasted.

The notion of subject and predicate mutually determining each other, each to be exhibited as an accent within an identity comprehensive of both, is perhaps more clearly suggested in the following comment on the nature of consciousness, in which consciousness is the subject and theory is the predicate:

> [T]he admission of ... selected elements of the lure, as felt contraries, primarily generates purpose; it then issues in satisfaction; and satisfaction qualifies the efficient causation. But a felt 'contrary' is consciousness in germ. When the contrasts and identities of such feelings are themselves felt, we have consciousness... Consciousness requires more than the mere entertainment of theory. It is the feeling of the contrast of theory, as *mere* theory, with fact, as *mere* fact. (PR 188)[9]

To be noted in passing is that it is here presupposed that consciousness, although more than entertained theory — that is, judgments

---

[8] Viewed specifically as pertaining to founding judgments of experience, Hegel's *spekulativer Satz*, like Whitehead's proposition, insofar as the latter is actualized within a present occasion, conditions self-consciousness.

[9] One might be tempted to construe, on the basis of this passage, that contrasts are to be discriminated from more primitive prehensions by virtue of being conscious. If Whitehead's concept of perception in the mode of causal efficacy is consistently understood as implying that all prehensions are in principle perceivable, however, this discrimination falls away.

which, in addition to their function as elicitors of feeling, are subject to being true or false — is constituted as such.¹⁰ "Judgment is the decision admitting a proposition into intellectual belief" (PR 187). From the foregoing longer citation, it may be noted that the relation obtaining between subject and predicate in their mutual determination, then, obtains as well between fact and theory as such. The manner in which this dynamic relation works itself out, tending toward a discriminated identity as its final cause (a dominating motif in Hegel's parallel conception) is shown by the following account of the mediation of the subject and predicate poles of a proposition.

> It is evident that the datum of the conceptual feeling reappears as the predicate in the proposition which is the datum of the integral, propositional feeling. In this synthesis the eternal object has suffered elimination of its absolute generality of reference. The datum of the physical feeling has also suffered elimination. For the peculiar objectification of the actual entities, really effected in the physical feeling, is eliminated, except in so far as it is required for the services of the indication. (PR 258)

A proposition may be simply factual. Whitehead designates such a proposition as "conformal". But there are nonconformal propositions, which, when they are admitted into feeling, promote or destroy order.

> When a non-conformal proposition is admitted into feeling the reaction to the datum has resulted in the synthesis of fact with the alternative potentiality of the complex predicate. A novelty has emerged into creation. The novelty may promote or destroy order; it may be good or bad. But it is new, a new type of individual, and not merely a new intensity of individual feeling. (PR 187)

Insofar as this new order is created at once within a single occasion, it becomes, of course, a new fact. Here it is worth noting that propositions, unlike contrasts, are for Whitehead generic — his term is 'general' (PR 186) — in character. In other words, a proposition transcends whatever degree to which it is actualized as a contrasting subject and predicate pattern, thus retaining potential for actualization in other occasions. It retains its theoretical aspect, and is thus "a hybrid between pure potentialities and actualities" (PR 185f).

I wish to note here in passing that when Hegel is consistently understood as a pluralistic personalist must interpret him, his *spekulativer Satz*, like Whitehead's contrast, is not generic or 'general' in character, but mediated in a concretely specific sense within the occasion under consideration.¹¹ This mediation must, of course, be within the context of a total, multiply discriminated identity (analogous to

---

[10] This point pertains to whether, and the sense in which, self-consciousness is of itself inherently rational.

Whitehead's complex contrast), a consideration to be understood in terms of the general import of concrete universality, to which reference is shortly to be made. What is here implicated is that ordinary propositions, in contrast to speculative propositions, are derived by abstraction from what has been mediated (actualized) as fact.

Whitehead assimilates a proposition as actual to a proposition as such, which retains a theoretical dimension and on this account is a "hybrid". When we consider that there may be no shared proposition that is not of this hybrid sort, given the disposition to construe language as inherently a means of communication and as such social, except for the purpose of rendering a concretely specific account of the concretely actual in its own native form, this is useful and commonsensical. For the purpose of his attempt to explicate the concretely actual, however, Hegel correctly perceived the need to refer to a kind of judgement and to a kind of proposition which is purely actual, in which (in the language of Whitehead) the subject and the predicate pattern are rendered commensurable (without residual)[12] and in which (in the language of Hegel) subject and predicate are rendered accents within an identity inclusive of both. If this discriminated identity is interpreted with reference to Hegel's process principle, which receives its dialectical exposition especially in the dialectic of being and becoming (*Logik*, I, 66f; *Logic* 82f), it will become clear that subject and predicate are rendered accents not so much within a discriminated identity as within an identity *being* discriminated. This is to perceive the mediation process to be what is actual in dialectic, and its results, insofar as these are regarded as no longer dynamically a part of this process, as abstractions. I return now to Whitehead's proposition.

The "locus" of a proposition for Whitehead consists of those actual occasions which include its logical subjects (PR 186). "When an actual entity belongs to the locus of a proposition, then conversely the proposition is an element in the lure for feeling of that actual entity" (PR 186). In addition to referring to logical subjects in actual occasions in the plural, Whitehead refers to a single actual entity termed a 'prehending subject' of a proposition, who determines its truth or falsity. The distinction between logical subjects of pro-

---

[11] The Boston and the California Personalists would appear to have been closer to their German sources in respect to this point than were Royce and some others who interpreted Hegel's monism in a simplistic way.

[12] An inconsistency is thus overcome which haunts Whitehead's concept of a proposition. Whitehead's proposition, insofar as it remains merely potential, survives the occasion of which it is a part, which occasion, however, is inconsistently construed to perish precisely because its potentiality has been spent into actuality.

positions and subjects who entertain propositions and judge them to be true or false must be kept clearly in mind.

> In every proposition, as such and without going beyond it, there is complete indeterminateness so far as concerns its own realization in a propositional feeling, and as regards its own truth. The logical subjects are, nevertheless, in fact actual entities which are definite in their realized mutual relatedness. Thus the proposition is in fact true, or false. But its own truth, or its own falsity, is no business of a proposition. That question concerns only a subject entertaining a propositional feeling with that proposition for its datum. Such an actual entity is termed a "prehending subject" of the proposition. (PR 258)

3. A Complete Fact

A principal characteristic of a complete fact is that it is self-constitutive, or self-creating (PR 25). It needs nothing outside of itself to be what it is (becomes). Notwithstanding, Whitehead locates the understanding, interpreting subject of such a "complete" fact in a subsequent actual occasion. In other words, the discrimination (contrast) of the occasion and its understanding, interpreting subject (together with the discriminated aspects) is not internal to the occasion. The subject of the occasion, moreover, as construed by the understanding, interpreting subject (together with the discriminated aspects) is not internal to the occasion. The subject of the occasion, moreover, as construed by the understanding, interpreting subject of a successor occasion, is no longer actual; presumably it is construed as having been a subject merely by analogy to itself, the subject of the successor occasion.[13]

As though thus to underscore the fact that the understanding, interpreting subject is not internal to the occasion, Whitehead allows that an actual occasion [even in its final phase of concrescence (!)] may contain error (PR 168, 180, 262, 271f). This error is, of course, to be judged as such by the understanding, interpreting subject of the successor occasion. Now one may doubtlessly be in error *about* a fact; but it seems curious to say that a fact contains, or *is in,* error. This appears, in fact, to be a contradiction of terms.

From a Hegelian perspective there can be no objection to be raised to the notion of a complete fact so long as it is what it purports itself

---

[13] From a Hegelian standpoint it would seem most natural to consider the abstracted results of an actual occasion following its perishing, not merely as objectively immortal, as for Whitehead — for this surely smacks of a prejudice at least as marked as Plato's belief in the immortality of the soul (when this latter notion is considered with care) — but as equally subjective and objective. The subjective pole of the occasion having spent itself in the "organization" of the data (which on this account can hardly be something "merely" objective), the form of these data, which seems not to vanish entirely upon the perishing of the occasion, might properly be said to constitute its immortality. See Essay III, §4.

to be. Within the Hegelian terminology, the term "absolute" would suggest itself. A fact should then be complete in the sense that it should be absolute. If it may at first seem strange to refer to an absolute fact, consider that characteristic of Hegel's concretely universal Begriff whereby every constitutive discrimination and discriminated aspect is equally essential to the being of the whole. In other words, every discrimination and discriminated aspect is concretely universal throughout the unity and wholeness of the Begriff considered in respect to its self-constitution as a discriminated whole and as a unity and wholeness of discriminations. This can only import that every particular fact and every particular identity which is a component within that particular fact, considered within the whole as its defining context, is equally absolute.[14] It is perfectly plausible on this account to speak of subidentities (and subfacts) within the identity that is the whole, and to regard each as likewise constituted of discriminations (contrasts) and discriminated aspects.

From a Whiteheadian perspective, a fact is purported to be what it is for a subject. From a Hegelian perspective, it must purport itself to be what it is. This role cannot be served by an understanding, interpreting subject not internal to the occasion. To put the matter otherwise, the discrimination between the occasion and its understanding, interpreting subject is one of the discriminations (contrasts) which (along with its concretely discriminated aspects) is constitutive of the occasion. The absoluteness of an absolute fact together with that of all of its subfacts consists precisely in that it contains all of the discriminations needful for its explication. On this account it is self-explicating or self-evident, at least in principle.[15] Hegel's term is not fact but concrete actuality, or Absolute Spirit,[16] and he does not speak of self-evidence, which indeed has no natural counterpart

---

[14] To say that a fact is absolute is to have regard to the totality of relations (and relativities!) which are constitutive of it. Whitehead's 2nd and 3rd categoreal obligations can be made to yield much of the sense of Hegel's concrete universal:

"The Category of Objective Identity. There can be no duplication of any element in the objective datum of the 'satisfaction' of an actual entity, so far as concerns the function of that element in the 'satisfaction'... each element has one self-consistent function, however complex."

"The Category of Objective Diversity. There can be no 'coalescence' of diverse elements in the objective datum of an actual entity, so far as concerns the function of those elements in that satisfaction." (PR, p. 28)

[15] It is true, of course, that in ordinary experience some discriminations are not rendered explicit, presuppositions standing in for them. This may in a given instance be unproblematical, and yield a worthwhile economy of attention, so long as the generic contrasts borne by ordinary (that is, "dead") language approximate sufficiently well what is actually there, and so long as this lies available to recall, in its concrete particularity, upon demand. This economy can proceed some way apart from resulting in a loss of self-evidence per se or a total amnesia, although it introduces distortion.

in German. His term is "presuppositionlessness", and this characteristic of an absolute fact is affirmatively expressed as "the self-certainty of reason". These terminological shifts permit me to focus a Hegelian critique of Whitehead upon those aspects of experience which are most disposed to change radically from one occasion to another; i.e., when I turn my head I experience another here and now and a different here/now contrast than I did a moment previously.

From a Hegelian perspective, Whitehead's "complete fact" falls short of being complete. In a world in which all facts are subject-dependent, no fact can be self-constitutive apart from being self-evident as well. The necessary and sufficient condition of a fact's being self-evident is that it must contain all of the discriminations (contrasts) needful for its (self-) explication. That the discrimination between (the contrast of) the objective pole of an actual occasion and its understanding, interpreting subject is not included within it constitutes a serious flaw in Whitehead's metaphysics,[17] which must in this respect be corrected if it is to be brought into conformity with the requirements of the critical tradition in philosophy, which had its inception in Kant. According to this tradition, the understanding, interpreting, and acting subject contributes to the character of knowledge and of facticity. As an accompaniment of this flaw, Whitehead was unable to affirm that the self-consciousness of an actual occasion, where there is such, contributes essentially to its character, a position of which it is especially difficult to make good ethical sense.

The point I have been making might otherwise be stated in the following way: Whitehead failed to observe that reflection is a contrast, which, together with the reflecting subject and that upon which the subject reflects, must be included within an actual occasion as a condition of its being a complete fact and an organic whole of equally complete subfacts.

---

[16] With the term "Absolute Spirit" are associated some connotations which are not wanted within the present context and which Hegel, by virtue of not having sufficiently developed and emphasized the notion of the perishing of an actual occasion, did not himself separate off precisely enough from such connotations as are here in place. A problem in Hegel's conceptuality to which the death of an actual occasion answers is that of drawing a clearer line of distinction between the concretely actual in its here and now absolute claim upon us at some point within history and Absolute Spirit conceived as transcending all particular perspectives.

[17] James Felt, in "Philosophic Understanding and the Continuity of Becoming", *International Philosophical Quarterly*, Vol. XVIII, No. 4 (Dec., 1978), pp. 375-93, describes Whitehead as having taken up a perspective *outside* of immediate experience (pp. 388ff). Within the same article, in noting, "Bergson makes plainer, I think, how intelligence and intuition differ than he does now they interrelate..." (p. 386), Felt would appear to have brought us to the very threshold of dialectic and the possibility of a critical process philosophy.

In his philosophy, Martin Buber recapitulated that aspect of Hegel's conceptuality which in respect to the act of reflection is here germane, in that he construed the "I" and the "It" to be constituted in a reflexive movement, with which, prior to abstraction, they are integral aspects.[18]

Seeing that there is knowledge and science, and that all knowledge and science are based squarely upon facts, there can be no compromising the character of an absolute fact. Only a fact which can explicate itself, which *can speak for itself,* constitutes an adequate basis for theory. One cannot even render the notion of theory intelligible apart from reference to a fact from which it is discriminated, and to which it stands related in a meaning bestowing contrast. We know concrete facts in their absolute claim upon us from a perspective internal to them before we (in subsequent occasions) construct hypotheses and theories based upon abstractions derived subsequent to their perishing. For failure to observe this, for several generations now many philosophers have been discussing theories without knowing what they are talking about.

It may be argued that the proposed concept of self-evidence can hold even if some of the contrasts constitutive of an actual occasion are inherited, and that therefore Whitehead's fact is sufficiently complete. A difficulty with this view lies in the consideration that inherited contrasts, insofar as they are constituted of abstractions derived from past occasions, tend to be merely generic in character. I say "tend to" because cases of particular contrasts are widely variant. Such as are constituted of physical purposes, for example — the counterpart of Hegel's dialectic of life — are less likely to be altered through abstraction than are complex propositions, such as those pertaining to the level of ethical decisions. To propose that a complete fact in part constituted by merely generic contrasts could speak for itself would amount to proposing that its explication for the understanding, by the employment of a conceptuality given in its generic contrasts, would be a feasible operation. Generic contrasts can never suffice for this role, however, and are very likely to lead us to absurdity through an imagination-fed inflation of our reason.[19]

---

[18] Martin Buber, *I and Thou,* trans. by Ronald Gregor Smith (New York: Schribner's Sons, 1937).

[19] In respect to this matter, Hegel's Begriff has often been falsely understood as though it were supposed to be the wholeness of the physical universe, plus something more, rather than as a wholeness of concretized discriminations (contrasts) together with the discriminated aspects. This is on the one hand because the counterpart in his philosophy to Whitehead's perishing is relatively undeveloped, and, on the other, because, when the matter is stated with reference to present considerations, he failed to perceive the necessary connection between the self-evidence of an absolute fact and its perishing.

They may guide us to concrete contrasts in concrescence which can serve, however, in a manner somewhat analogous to that in which Bergson once proposed that we are able to pursue the two poles of a generic contrast to the point at which they converge upon a single intuition of duration.[20]

There are luminous moments of experience, somewhat special occasions, I think, which it seems are not to be explained by appeal to inheritance of a sort that involves the distorting influence of theory. The birth of consciousness is one of these — it needs no conceptuality brought from elsewhere or from some previous occasion — and we seem to have no reason for restricting this to infancy.

4. The Internal and External Perspectives

In compromising the absoluteness of a fact in the manner considered, Whitehead was led to commit what from the perspective of a critical process philosophy must be regarded as two additional mistakes, which I shall take up in this and the section following, each in turn.

Overlooking the fact of the knowledge of facts and (following the dominant tendency of the pragmatists) mistakenly construing all knowledge as hypothetical or theoretical, he was naturally led to take up an external (and hence hypothetical) perspective upon an actual occasion, in preference to an actual (internal) perspective. [In fact — and this is also in keeping with some aspects of his own teaching — it is in principle impossible that anyone has at any time stood outside of that some one concretely actual occasion which constitutes him (her) and his (her) world at a given instant, seeing that this occasion contains all that from its perspective is actual.] This characteristic of his thought testifies to his primary interests having previously been theories of the sciences. From an external perspective one can, of course, only construct theories for possible concretion, or for concretion in some degree, in future occasions. But the knowledge of their concretion, insofar as this can only come in subsequent occasions, must remain a philosophical problem. Such concretions, in other words, can only be there *for* the subject (as *merely* objective) and not *in and* for it (as equally subjective — with reference to the present, actual subject — and objective).[21]

---

[20] If Bergson has been in possession of a sufficiently seasoned knowledge of Hegel at the time this insight came to him, he might have been on the way toward the discovery of the kind of concept of completeness here in view.

[21] As I have more fully remarked in Essay 5, Whitehead's concept of self-evidence is for the most part taken over from the pragmatists. It is then futuristic in the sense that it pertains to theories the truth of which may be approached asymptotically in a receding future

5. Eternal Objects

Having compromised the absoluteness of a fact, he compensated for this error by introducing the notion of eternal objects to account for how an actual occasion, falling short of being a complete system of internal relations, could yet be known and contain truth.

> The difficulty which arises in respect to internal relations is to explain how any particular truth is possible. In so far as there are internal relations, everything must depend upon everything else. But if this be the case, we cannot know about anything until we know equally everything else. Apparently, therefore, we are under the necessity of saying everything at once. This supposed necessity is palpably untrue. Accordingly it is incumbent on us to explain how there can be internal relations, seeing that we admit finite truths. (SMW 235)

An actual occasion, being constituted by polarities being synthesized into contrasts and in its end phase, by a wholeness and unity of integrated contrasts, is a complete fact. It is a completed system of internal relations, which perspectivally and with selective emphases presents an entire universe. Hence, there is no need to invoke a transcending principle to explain its being what it is. Neither is it necessary to appeal to a conceptuality brought from elsewhere, as, for example, from a traditional language, dependence upon which would imply for the concrete the status of being something merely hypothetical, when in fact, as absolute, it *can speak for itself*.[22] There is nothing more absolute than the first words — or even of the first cry — of an infant. But facts that speak for themselves are not the exclusive property of any particular age group.

Rather than upon eternal objects, the continuities of experience and the intelligibility of the universe, upon which the possibility of intelligible experience rests, are founded upon such contrasts, generi-

---

which in fact never arrives. I say "for the most part": fortunately there are brilliant inconsistencies. Consider, for example, his rare and, so far as I have yet seen, undeveloped utterance: "Understanding, however imperfect, is self-evidence of pattern, so far as it has been discriminated" (MT, pp. 71f). Then there is the isolated and undeveloped characterization of "the poor pragmatist" as an intellectual Hamlet:

"[I]t is hardly an exaggeration to say that the very meaning of truth is pragmatic[!]. But though this statement is *hardly* an exaggeration, still it *is* an exaggeration, for the pragmatic test can never work, unless on some occasion — in the future, or in the present — there is a definite determination of what is true on that occasion. Otherwise the poor pragmatist remains an intellectual Hamlet, perpetually adjourning decision of judgment to some later date." (PR, p. 181)

The present effort, insofar as it pertains to the concept of self-evidence, may be regarded as a development of these two passages, left undeveloped und unaccented within Whitehead's own thought and which stand in an unreconcilable opposition to his dominant dispositions. For my critique of Whitehead's concept of self-evidence, see SC, pp. 371-77.

[22] See Essay 1, n. 27.

cally considered, which it proves plausible to consider to be universal to all occasions of experience, supplemented, perhaps, by such as may be universal only within the epoch under consideration. The range of abstract universality of these contrasts is based upon "observation" and hypothesis, however, and not merely upon what, as constitutive of a present occasion, is concretely actual and hence concretely universal.

As a matter of fact, it does indeed appear to be the case that a considerable number of discriminations remain relatively constant constituents of occasions of experience, in the sense that each is actualized anew in every occasion. With some exceptions, Hegel's system, constituted of roughly 165 discriminated (contrasted) pairs of terms, may serve to illustrate the wide variety of sorts of contrasts which, generically considered (i.e., as abstract types), are constitutive of all occasions of experience. To count for the present purpose, these, regarded as discriminations, must be considered relative to their context within an occasion of experience also constituted by variant and perhaps novel contrasts. This is to say, they must be considered as actual, or as being actualized, rather than as merely generic. Such relatively "constant" discriminations (in the sense that they are ever concretized anew) are adequate to account for the possibility of self-consciousness and of actuality, for the continuity from one occasion to another, and hence for the intelligibility of the universe.[23] Were there no other way in which to take account of the differences between occasions of experience than these alone render possible, however, we could not satisfactorily explain change, novelty, individuality, and creativity — traditionally problem areas for philosophy in the Hegelian tradition.

When we come to consider contrasts with respect to their range of abstract universality, their universality throughout the totality of actual occasions, four types are readily identifiable. Universal contrasts, and contrasts which have a range of universality restricted to one or more epochs or types of epochs of occasions of varying lengths, have been mentioned. There are additionally entirely novel contrasts, which need not be sharply distinguished from concretized variations on generic contrasts (mutations), that enjoy a range of universality and assist us to account for emergent novelty. A fourth type consists in contrasts of the sort that normally occur once and only once within an epoch of the type they help to define, and the effects of one such, following a single concretion, may be inherited throughout the

---

[23] To render this statement entirely intelligible, I should need to make an extended reference to history as actual within a present occasion, a theme I have developed within the final chap. of SC, the final section.

society of occasions constitutive of this epoch. A series of such contrasts is definitive of the life cycle from birth to death of members of a species. An example of the latter is Hegel's Lordship and Bondage, which functions in this manner within several types of epochs of varying ranges of inclusiveness. Considered with respect to the life cycle of a human individual from birth to death, for example, it typically occurs in late puberty but may in exceptional cases be forestalled to early manhood, the effect sufficing to be inherited throughout the life cycle following.

6. The Two Roles of Philosophy

Given the situation that no one has ever stepped outside of that some one actual occasion constitutive of him (or her) and his (or her) world at a given instant, the possibility of hypothetically taking up an external perspective upon a plurality of actual occasions must lie residual in the manner in which the causal past is actual within a present occasion. "Inheritances" from past occasions are taken up with a sufficient degree of integrity to suggest the idea of each as an entity in relation to other entities of the same general type. Seeing that the language being employed (just here note especially the term "inheritance") belongs to the hypothetical perspective we are attempting to justify, however, we are posed with a problem. Such remarks as I can make here can only serve to ameliorate this problem.

The interplay of the inner and outer perspectives strongly suggests two distinct roles for philosophy. There is *first* philosophy which, by the analysis-synthesis of the specific contrasts constitutive of a typal actual occasion belonging to a relevant present cultural epoch, presents us with the concrete conceptuality and a language at least proximate to the literal language of present fact from an inner (actual) perspective. Second philosophy as a theory of the particular sciences (*Wissenschaftstheorie*), by having this conceptuality, arrived at by strict adherence to critical principles, as its point of reference, by abstraction and reconstruction (in cooperation with the particular sciences) goes about the business of rendering a critique of theories and of forging new theories.[23a]

[23a] As pertaining to the division of labor that I have suggested for first and second philosophy, drawing upon antecedents in Hegel and Whitehead, respectively, it seems worth noting that the accounts of the two philosophers simply do not serve the same objective nor do they operate at the same level. They have, in fact, little in common, as I have endeavored to show, *so that even when pains are taken to develop analogues that may with plausibility be viewed as complementary — the aim of the reconstruction of method for first philosophy that I adumbrated in SC and am further developing within the present context — these are systematically related only by temporal succession.* The systematic relation that I develop between the two perspectives, regarded from a Hegelian point of view, is thus of a

The role I have indicated for first philosophy is an ideal to be approximated. That this ideal is not, perhaps, to be perfectly attained is not owing to any want of self-evidence in our knowledge of facts, however, but to difficulties which lie in the way of a complete exposition of the contrasts which constitute any given occasion of experience under analysis-synthesis. It is only such a complete exposition,[24] also of contrasts which are only implicit, which can lay bare the concrete universality of the function of every part throughout the occasion and the totality of conditions of its self-evidence. A special difficulty, e.g., lies in the way of discerning novel contrasts, in which case there is no generic contrast to draw our attention to the type of relation to be discerned in its concrete particularity. In the case of such, works of art may play a decisive role.

This ideal appears in any case to be nearly enough attainable so as to render the idea of its complete attainment clear, and to justify the exposition of this concept as an adequate account of how conscious-

---

weak enough sort to render at least understandable that Giacomo Rinaldi, in a review of the same *Work* which I am informed is to appear in *Idealistic Studies*, should have been led to doubt that I had found them to be systematically related at all. In this connection, it is to be acknowledged that relations that are merely external are not known, but remain no more than theory, a point the profound importance of which might easily escape a Whiteheadian, I suppose, or indeed any philosopher who proposes to regard truth as warranted belief.

There appears to be no way to make Whitehead's external (hypothetical) perspective in the explication of a lived occasion serve as a natural introduction to Hegel's internal (actual) perspective to parallel the way in which one may move quite naturally from Hegel's internal (actual) perspective to Whitehead's external (hypothetical) perspective. Thus, on the one hand, the way from the hypothetical to the actual perspective is forever blocked by the fact that an occasion is grasped *a priori* for the concrete actuality that it is and thus in complete independence of any supposed antecedents that we might be inclined hypothetically and from a temporally subsequent perspective to suppose as having perhaps preconditioned the concrete fact that it was. This is a barrier that no theory can possibly overcome, and it would amount to an intellectual hybris on behalf of theoretical reason to suppose otherwise. On the other hand, the way from concrete to abstract being/thought is ever being traversed anew in the lived occasion and in our subsequent second reflection upon it after the fact, a consideration that may be attested to by anyone who achieves the least awareness of his own reflective processes. The result of the indicated asymmetry, is that by following what I have proposed to be the substance of Hegel's phenomenological method we may be provided with an excellent foundation for, and point of access to, the sort of adventures of ideas with which Whitehead's interest is taken up. Whitehead's hypothetical type speculations, far from providing an equally suitable point of access to Hegel's concretely actual speculations, regarded apart from a compatible phenomenological base, can serve principally to point to an endless series of other possible hypothetical speculations — the world of seeming being in principle of unlimited complexity — all more or less equally distanced from the (even following his own account in itself unknowable!) concreteness of the lived occasion.

[24] Essay III, immediately following, will take up the problematic of rendering a complete account of concreteness, a theme to which I later return in Essay IX, Part II, pp. 183-87.

ness can arise unconditioned by anything other than discriminations internal to itself, thereby explicating its self-evident character.

7. Conclusion

In conclusion, the following eight effects seem principally to issue from rendering Whitehead's incomplete fact complete. These are intended to constitute a profile of what must be involved in rendering process philosophy amenable to critical principles.

(1) Whitehead's predominantly external perspective upon an actual occasion is displaced by a phenomenological analysis-synthesis from an internal (actual) perspective of an actual occasion typical of some present and relevant historical epoch under consideration. Far from being rendered superfluous, however, the external perspective now becomes a model as to how we prepare possibilities (theories) for possible concrescence in future occasions. It is true, of course, that in a theoretical civilization we can move from theory to fact as a shadow can serve as a sign of light. *The fundamental direction of movement, nonetheless, is from fact to theory.*[25]

In addition to serving as a model of how we prepare possibilities for possible concretion, Whitehead's external conceptuality may suggest roughly what the function of the various *Wissenschaftstheorien*, second philosophy, might be, were they to be framed by the employment of a conceptuality derived exclusively by the analysis-synthesis of concreteness (i.e., of a typal occasion from a relevant and present cultural epoch) from an *actual* perspective.

(2) Seeing that an actual occasion, as absolute, is a complete system of internal relations, the concept of eternal objects, excepting a single function taken on by a hypothetical structure of expectations,

---

[25] Since this assertion has posed a stumbling block to some, it may be helpful to note that what is being affirmed includes the perhaps trivial assertion that consciousness (and the world present for consciousness) is prior to any theory whatsoever. The self-grasping of a completed truth which is the whole is here counted as a condition of consciousness as such, regardless of how many discriminations within that whole may as yet be implicit only. Thus, for example, what might be shown, although, due to the intricacy of Hegel's thought, a volume might need to be dedicated to this purpose, is that also for him knowledge and actuality occur *only* as the truth which is the whole. Thus, for example, what we may naively refer to as concrete immediacy is *already* mediated as a condition of its being grasped at all. This is even though our dialectical analysis through a *second* reflection may have progressed but a short way in the *recapitulation* of the pathway of knowledge and of actuality.

I sometimes refer to the analysis-synthesis of an actual occasion as a "second" reflection in order clearly to distinguish it from the *original* mediation (with its reflexive moment) by which concrete actuality and concrete knowing — the *living* occasion — are constituted, thereby leaving us something to work on.

the concept of which I have not considered here, is rendered superfluous, a reminder of precritical modes of thought.

(3) The need to discount the essential contribution of self-consciousness to the self-constitution of an actual occasion (with the increment of freedom this brings), which poses a hurdle to ethical theory, is done away with.

(4) A complete fact is not subject to error. This is to say, error, rather than being attributed to the concretely actaul, results exclusively from abstraction and hypotheses constituted by abstractions.

(5) The analysis-synthesis of a typical actual occasion in our cultural epoch with respect to its constituent contrasts — those aspects of propositions which are rendered concretely actual within the concrescence of an actual occasion — becomes the task of a critical process philosophy, which must be responsible to render a concretely specific account of concreteness. The methodological analysis-synthesis of contrasts, the respective members of which each function as accents within an identity inclusive of both by this approach, becomes a central methodological principle. An outcome is that the notion that precision in first philosophy is to be gained only at the expense of adequacy is, in principle, at least, laid to rest.

(6) Truth as a self-actualizing wholeness of discriminations (contrasts), climaxing in a coherent system, is secured against absurdity through inflation. It lends itself neither to inflation into an Absolute Spirit transcending all particular perspectives, into a concept of a universe such as could not even conceivably be concretized within any single particular occasion, nor into an analogously inflated concept of the self. Such inflated concepts can only be conceived as hypothetical notions. The necessary connection between self-evidence and perishing establishes especially epistemology, but also ethics, upon a fundamentally new basis.

(7) We are saved from the notion of theory-laden facts, which effectively eliminates the possibility of ever putting science upon a foundation of fact, by the process principle. In concrescence, a theory-laden fact may become a genuine (absolute) fact, a fact which in its season functions reliably as such, and which lends itself to intelligent and critical abstraction, its mortality being exposed to view. Abstraction is not of itself bad, and it can pose no terrors to critical thought when based upon concrete facts which have been subjected to a critical analysis-synthesis of the contrasts which are *the bedrock concrete language in which they speak for themselves.* It would seem not too much to anticipate that there is implicated in the system of contrasts constituting an actual occasion something at least ap-

proaching a perfect concrete language.[26]

(8) By virtue of the consideration that nonconscious occasions merely prehend and do not comprehend, they cannot be affirmed with certainty to be actual except insofar as they are comprehended within, and contribute with an appreciable grade of relevance to (that is, contribute determinable discriminations to),[27] a concretely actual occasion. Critical principles require on this account that they be relegated as a class to the status of being hypothetically actual. Hypothetically actual occasions await comprehension within a concretely actual occasion to be concretely actual, in the form of history actual within the present.

---

[26] It seems plausible to account for the disposition to construct ideally perfect languages in abstraction and after the fact as a kind of recapitulation through "rememberance" (see "*Er-innerung*" in the closing paragraphs of *Phän.*) of the structure inherent in concrete knowing and concrete actuality itself in every actual occasion.

[27] See SC, pp. 477-86.

III

CAN THE CONTRASTS CONSTITUTIVE OF AN 'ACTUAL OCCASION OF EXPERIENCE' BE SPECIFIED IN THEIR CONCRETE PARTICULARITY? ASPECTS OF A SOMEWHAT HEGELIAN CRITIQUE OF WHITEHEAD*

1. Introduction

For Whitehead the process of concrescence of an actual occasion was one within which polarities issue in contrasts. My intention in this essay is to consider what is entailed in proposing to provide a concretely specific account of the contrasts constitutive of some conscious occasion, such as Whitehead designated an 'actual occasion of experience'. Aside from being obviously, as I should suppose, inspired by Hegel, the question might otherwise appear to be quite innocent. As it turns out, however, the consideration of this possibility seems to force some not merely subtle changes in Whitehead's metaphysics, which are basically Hegelian but in some ways completely new, seeing that a critique of Hegel is also under way.

I must of necessity avoid becoming overly involved with some important issues pertaining to the interpretation of Whitehead and, even so, the treatment will be sketchy enough. In the first four §§ I shall principally be occupied with setting the stage. In §§5-7 I pre-

---

* Except for minor revisions and adaptations to the present context, particularly with reference to the notes, this essay was first published in, Herta Nagl-Docekal (Ed.), *Überlieferung und Aufgabe: Festschrift für Erich Heintel zum 70. Geburtstag* (Vienna: Braumüller, 1982). An earlier version was discussed by the membership of the Society for the Study of Process Philosophy, following advance circulation, on March 23, 1980, at Notre Dame University, South Bend, Indiana. I wish to express my thanks to George Allan and George L. Kline, who presented prepared commentaries, and to the other discussants. Most particularly, however, I owe my thanks to George Allan, Lewis Ford, and Paul Kuntz for their clarifying and stimulating correspondence following. I must nonetheless assume sole responsibility for the views herein expressed.

sent and summarize my account of what seems to follow upon the attempt concretely to specify the contrasts. In §8 I take note of some issues and limits pertaining to the execution of the proposed program.

At full concrescence, Whitehead's actual occasion is constituted a unity and wholeness of contrasts, the difference between the polarities characteristic of the early phases of the process of concrescence and the contrasts constitutive of the final phase consisting in that the paired aspects of a contrast are commensurate with one another. In the case of polarities this relation of commensurability, though implicit, has not yet been actualized and thus rendered internal to the respective contrasted aspects. Additionally to be noted is that, Categorial Obligation II and III in view (PR 26), it is clearly implicated, at least, in Whitehead's view, that each contrast is commensurable with the totality of other contrasts constitutive of the occasion within which it is concretized. Hegel proposed to delineate the contrasts constitutive of that species of occasions which attain to self-consciousness, with which I am herein to be principally concerned, namely, 'actual occasions of experience' (hereafter to be abbreviated 'occasions', 'actual occasions', etc.), in their concrete specificity. He did not explicitly employ this term: Where Whitehead refers to contrasts and contrasted aspects prehended and being prehended, Hegel refers to discriminations and discriminated aspects in process of being mediated, the dynamic of this process (the power of negation), ultimately being within the constitutive aspects of the actuality being mediated. The differences in terminology need not blind us to the basic parallelism of functions to be observed in the Hegelian concepts, though it will become evident that the concepts here in view in the case of the two thinkers serve somewhat different ends and different methodologies for the achievement of their respective ends.

Some would maintain that the intrinsic richness of Hegel's thought consists in the concrete specificity with which the dialectical stages of the development of thought and of actuality are delineated, discrimination by discrimination. Not a few persons who have rejected what they have understood as his "system", or his idea for a completed system (perhaps unrealized), have drawn heavily upon some one or more of his mediations on the way toward the realization of this grand design. The issue to which I am addressing myself might perhaps on this account alone be found of some interest; I hope, however, that it will be greeted by an interest more deeply involved with the system-idea of Hegel, because I think persons informed about Whitehead have a natural point of access to some Hegel-inspired notions that are rather common coin today and which have gone relatively unexplored within the of late relatively insular English language tradition of philosophy. I am of the opinion that there is a way, partly by selective reinterpretation and partly by revision, to reconceive Hegel's most daring and comprehensive aim and program so that it can be accomplished. In both the reinterpretation and the revision Whitehead can provide inspiration. I am thinking most especially here of Hegel's concept of presuppositionlessness, and its affirmative counterpart, his concept of the self-certainty of reason. The first term is as awkward as its German counterpart, and the second makes strange English; with the English reader in view, therefore, I prefer to substitute the term "self-evidence" for both, which term, interestingly enough, has no natural counterpart in German. Following this usage, the Hegelian counterpart to Whitehead's 'occasion' is self-evident by virtue of being a unity and wholeness of discriminations (*Unterscheidungen*) adequate to its explication. It contains all of the discriminations needful for its explication. Only if the discriminations constitutive of this Hegelian counterpart of an 'occasion' (hereafter 'occasion$_h$') can be specified in their concrete particularity can Hegel's concept of self-evidence be made to stand up. This program, as it stands, owing both to inaccessability (especially to English readers) and to some intrinsic problems and ambiguities, is in some degree less than completely successful.

2. Some Variations from Hegel's Program

Because the program in view is thus most basically Hegel's, it will be useful to note two points at which I shall be making departures from Hegel which are inspired by Whitehead have especially wide ranging ramifications.

1. Hegel would appear never to have doubted that all 'occasions' are constituted by precisely the same totality of contrasts (discriminations) being mediated. This belief on his part appears unwarranted and indeed to constitute a breach of his own critical principles, to which he generally adhered with some strictness.[1] Having rendered individuality the highest realization of Spirit in history, he thus nonetheless undercut the possibility of according status to the ***differences*** between individuals by reference to a difference in their constitutive discriminations.

In place of Hegel's unfounded dogma pertaining to the (abstract) universality of all contrasts throughout the plurality of 'actual occa-

---

[1] See CHSS, §1 or, for the most extensive treatment, SC, Book I.

sions', I propose a fourfold typology of contrasts construed with respect to their range of universality: Some contrasts are evidently universal to all 'occasions'. These constitute a kind of substantial set of conditions necessary to account for the possibility of experience and of actuality. In the case of others, we are in want of evidence that their range of universality extends beyond certain epochs or types of epochs of occasions, such as a cultural epoch or the epoch constituted by the life span of a human individual. Some contrasts, so far as can be determined, are unique to a particular occasion, and in this sense novel. Then there is the type of contrast which normally occurs once and only once within the particular type of epoch it helps to define, its effect being inherited throughout the series. Series of this type of contrasts, which constantly follow one another in a certain approximate order, define a species. Lordship and Bondage as construed within the epoch constituted by the life span of a human individual is an example of this type of contrast.

2. In not properly developing and accentuating the perishing of an 'occasion$_h$,'— a notion foreshadowed, in some degree, in his concept of the breaking asunder of the unity of the Begriff upon its attainment of concreteness, and in his concept of the Golgotha of Absolute Spirit — Hegel's truth that is the (concretely actual) whole becomes inflated and overbearing by seeming to survive its (lived) concreteness. This failure seems at points to be accompanied by a diminution of the centrality of the process principle intrinsic to his thought.[2]

The first of the above noted departures from Hegel is undeniably substantial in character. In the case of the second the issue appears so complexely involved with issues of interpretation as to be undecidable, but it involves at least a difference of emphasis with far-ranging consequences; pursued with consistency, moreover, it takes us somewhat outside of the Hegelian problematic.

3. Some Variations from Whitehead's Program

In presenting an 'occasion' reformed in accordance with post-Kantian critical pinciples (hereafter 'occasion$_r$'), I shall intend to overcome the pre-critical character of Whitehead's thought suggested by his remark that "in the main the philosophy of organism is a recurrence to pre-Kantian modes of thought" (PR xi). This character in Whitehead's metaphysic is most profoundly evidenced in his apparent

---

[2] The two criticisms of Hegel from which the foregoing departures move are developed in greater detail in Essay I.

failure to perceive the possibility of rendering a concretely specific account of the concretely actual, discrimination by discrimination, or (even more obviously in Hegel's language) of rendering an account of thought (which his system as a whole in view, ultimately turned out to be equally an account of concrete actuality) in its own native form. One of several errors which followed from this, resulting in a number of complications which contribute to the relative unaccessability of his thought, is his having excluded the understanding, interpreting subject from his 'actual occasion', which he nonetheless construed — mistakenly, I think — to be a complete fact (Essay II). An accompaniment of the non-inclusion of the understanding, interpreting subject within his 'occasion' is a failure to accord an essential role to this same subject in the constitution of knowledge and of actuality, to which this subject, except perhaps for vague perceptions of causal efficacy, remains externally related. His mistake was in not recognizing that reflection is a contrast: the discrimination of the understanding interpreting subject and the world present for this subject — along with, of course, the discriminated aspects, a concrete discrimination being unabstractable — being one of those essential to the self-explication of any 'occasion', and hence to the self-evidence with which every 'occasion' presents itself, as Hegel was well aware.

In view of this, his seeming at times to have forsaken the search for concreteness becomes understandable: "Philosophy is explanatory of abstractions, and not of concreteness" (PR 20), which sometimes appears to have been construed in a manner that rendered it, in itself, not knowable, and hence as not available to serve as a touchstone for those theories with the development and expansion of which into metaphysical generalizations he was so absorbed. A happy qualification is his concept of prehension, which can go some way toward presenting the *process* of concrescence as both concrete and in some sense known, a reading to which a Hegelian would be natively inclined.

4. Interpretational Presuppositions

In attempting to stipulate the alterations in Whitehead's metaphysics which seem to follow upon an attempt to specify the contrasts constitutive of an 'occasion', I shall presuppose the following notions in Whitehead, for each of which I think some considerable justification can be found, although this may not in every case be conclusive. The intent has been to state these positions so as to leave Whitehead's views minimally subject to criticism by, and maximally available for appropriation within, a (post-Kantian) critical construal of process philosophy.

Distinguishing marks of a critical process philosophy are: (1) to provide a concretely specific account of concreteness, or the pursuit of this ideal, (2) to displace speculation of a pre-critical sort within the province of first philosophy in preference for the analysis-synthesis of discriminations (contrasts) produced by our native faculties of reason in the constitution of the concretely actual, i.e., facts, (3) to conceive the concretely actual in a way that preserves the clear line of distinction between theory and concrete fact as a touchstone of theory which we all natively presuppose, (4) seeing that concretely actual facts and concretely actual facts alone function within their temporal context as absolute, to avert the absolutizing of anything else, i.e., particular discriminations, particular common languages, eternal objects, etc., which might tend in any manner to displace the authority of facts construed in a manner consistent with the function they actually perform for us.

I turn, then, to the presuppositions:

1. In general, Whitehead's characterization of an actual occasion may also be held to hold for his 'actual occasion', although the converse does not hold.

2. An 'actual occasion' at the stage of full concrescence climaxes as a unity and wholeness of contrasts, whereupon it perishes. What remains after perishing are its results. Regarded as abstract data separated off from the living process of their becoming, such results, except as they may be regarded as data for the subject of another occasion, are not actual, but potential.

This is not intended to take issue, e.g., with Jorge Luis Nobo, where he stresses that an occasion which is actual is actual both as subject and as superject, i.e., "whether its present existence is that of a subject enjoying the universe from which it arises or that of a superject functioning objectively in subsequent processes"[3] — although my emphasis is different. Indeed, I tend at several points in what follows, where I must presuppose an interpetation which cannot be justified here, to presuppose that of Nobo.

My interest, however, is not so much to deny the possibility of interpreting Whitehead in a different way as to lend such support as I can to the rescue of perishing, seeing that I am of the opinion that this notion, especially when Whitehead's 'Complete Fact' is rendered *in fact* complete, and with this self-evident, by the inclusion of the contrast between its comprehending subject and the world present

---

[3] *Process Studies,* Vol. 4, No. 4, p. 281.

for this subject, can save Whitehead, or, more properly, can save the best that lies at hand for successor 'occasions$_r$' to inherit from him. The view that results from the perishing of perishing seems to me to be unsoundly inflationary of knowledge — at least of what we ought here to mean by knowledge — and to be untrue to the human existence that should count as crucial in self-conscious 'occasions$_r$'. Following the present account, such are to be viewed as the only type of occasions which are concretely, and not merely hypothetically, actual.

3. It being assumed as unproblematical that on Whitehead's account of an 'actual occasion' prehensions are in principle all alike perceivable in the mode of causal efficacy, I wish to assume, which, so far as I know, may be problematical, that all such prehensions arise to consciousness in the form of contrasts, or ingredient aspects of contrasts, such as get expressed in propositions. So far as I have been able to determine, Whitehead does not address himself specifically to this issue, which figures crucially in what follows, although his concept of a complex contrast appears to be highly commensurate with this view.

> A multiple contrast is analysable into component dual contrasts. But a multiple contrast is not a mere aggregation of dual contrasts. It is one contrast, over and above its component contrasts. (PR 329)

A slight expansion seems here in order, leading into an addendum to the point in which I shall relate this consideration briefly to what I find to be Hegel's most central methdological principle. Contrasts, in the living context of the 'occasion' within which they are actualized, function for Whitehead as fully actual. The presupposition in the interpretation of Whitehead stated in the foregoing paragraph being allowed, they on this account turn out to function in a manner parallel to that of Hegel's philosophical (or speculative) proposition (or judgment),[4] which is thus dissimilar to Whitehead's proposition in that the latter is in part potential, a "hybrid", and insofar, I suppose we should be forced to conclude, essentially hypothetical.[5] It is owing to its character of being a hybrid that, following Whitehead's usual manner of reference, a proposition can function as a lure for feeling (PR 183ff).

The subject and predicate of Hegel's philosophical proposition are

---

[4] Hegel alternatively refers to *philosophischen* and to *spekulativen Sätzen*. "*Satz*" (the singular form) may be translated either "judgment" or "proposition", depending upon the context. See Essay I, §2, or SC, Book I, Chap. 1, pp. 75-123.

[5] The parallelism referred to is more readily understood when the focus is upon that function of Hegel's *philosophischen* or *spekulativen Satz* that is most properly translated "philosophical *judgment*" or "speculative *Judgement*" (rather than proposition), seeing that what is then in view is a *founding* judgment or a judgment *constitutive of* experience. This is a concept which Whitehead appears to have overlooked in Kant.

accents within an (discriminated) identity inclusive of both (*Phän.*, p. 51; or *Phen.* 120). This proposition is actual as a mediating process integral with the 'occasion$_h$,' as a unity and wholeness of contrasts in which it results. It follows from Categorial Obligations II and III (PR 26) that every part or aspect of an 'occasion' fulfills a necessary function throughout the occasion, apart from which it could not be the occasion that it is. In other words, to employ a Hegelian term, it is concretely universal throughout the occasion.

With respect to its actuality as process, Hegel's philosophical proposition is contrasted with the "habitual proposition" (or judgment), which is abstract, hypothetical, and after the fact. Following this account a proposition in ordinary language, which in some manner is a bearer of concreteness, has a philosophical proposition ingredient in it as a component aspect, and would in this sense also be hybrid. This being the case, the term "philosophical proposition" can be misleading, seeing that it is judgments which found ordinary experience and concrete language which are, in the final analysis, more prominently in view, these being the model for any distinctly philosophical utterances.

Therefore, if Whitehead's contrast as it pertains to 'occasions' is as precise a counterpart of Hegel's proposition as I take it to be, it would be natural to inquire as to whether it might make sense on the basis of Whitehead's account to propose that a contrast can function as a lure for feeling that in the final phase of concrescence is fully actual, being integral with its mediated result and without residual potency not concretized in this result, such as belongs to the "transcendent" aspect of a (hybrid) proposition. This is of course not Whitehead's manner of speaking. Even so, it seems not to do violence to his views. If I am correct in this, the ploy provides a test case for my contention respecting the closeness of the parallel between Hegel's proposition and Whitehead's contrast.[6] In view of the power which the former concept has exhibited within philosophically major language communities during recent decades, this is a matter deserving of the closest investigation.

4. As a number of writers have done, I wish to construe that an 'occation', given available data, is self-creating or self-constituting without qualification, even though Nobo may have rendered this view problematical to defend.[7] I have no interest in excluding Whitehead's

---

[6] See Essay II, §2 and SC, pp. 419-22.

[7] Jorge Luis Nobo, "Transition in Whitehead: A creative Process Distinct from Concrescence", *International Philosophical Quarterly*, Vol. XIX, No. 3 (Sept., 1979), pp. 265-83. See p. 278.

notion of transition, which figures crucially in Nobo's argument, but, in the model of 'occasion$_r$', transition must be relegated to an account offered from a hypothetical rather than from an actual perspective. Whitehead seems to undercut the possibility of this distinction by failing to observe the possibility of an actual perspective, except sometimes when he is discussing prehension or causal efficacy.

As will later become apparent, what I have in mind is not precisely creation out of nothing (which Nobo rejects), but merely out of nothing *actual*. A *self-creating* 'occasion$_r$' is most readily rendered compatible with its self-evidence.

5. I wish to assume that Whitehead's account of causal efficacy commits him, or should commit him, to the view that the mediation of the subjective and physical poles of contrasts within the concrescence of an 'occasion' may be felt, that such feeling may enter consciousness, and that, in the case in which they do, these feelings cannot with consistency be construed as purely or merely objective.[8]

5. Some Resulting Alterations

I shall now undertake to delineate some principal alterations which seem forced upon Whitehead's metaphysics by a serious attempt to specify in their concrete particularity the contrasts constitutive of an 'actual occasion'. This will provide additional background for an assessment of some accompanying problems in §7.

Whitehead certainly leaves us what may be regarded as some important clues as to some of the contrasts he would have listed as constitutive of every actual occasion had he attempted such a program as I have here in view. Space/time, subjective aim/physical data, mental feeling/physical feelings are among the most plausible candidates. If the universality requirement is dropped, it is possible to envision the list extended almost without limit to include the particular subject and the particular predicate of every proposition which at one or another time authentically affirms anything at all about actuality.

Seeing that Whitehead's contrast is non-abstractable [and insofar

---

[8] George Allan and Lewis Ford assisted me to see the complexity of the issues here touched upon, and to see that I had formerly understood perception in the mode of causal efficacy too much with reference to its purity and too subjectively. The net result is that Whitehead appears more nearly compatible with Hegel in respect to this point than I reflected in the previously circulated manuscript of this paper. It remains a matter of increased concern to learn that some Whitehead scholars wish to maintain that for Whitehead subjective feelings can only be known as objectified, a position that I think cannot be sustained. Suspecting that this interpretation may be placed in question, however, I have skirted the issue by allowing what I regard as a more generous one.

concrete (?)] — which I take to mean that it is identical with the relation between the contrasted aspects in their concrete particularity — and since we shall find it useful to talk of types of concrete contrasts, or generic contrasts, it is best to acknowledge the significant distinction between concrete and generic contrasts at the outset. Thus, when I refer to the space/time relations constitutive of the 'occasion' which arises when I turn left, this is a concrete reference. These relations constitute a different concrete set than is constitutive of another 'occasion' a moment later when I turn right. But space/time is the generic type of the two successively concretized schemata of contrasts.[9]

When one undertakes to specify the contrasts constitutive of an 'occasion' it becomes immediately apparent that I as a subject must in some manner and by some means comprehend (and not merely prehend) the occasion of which I am to provide an account, or at least I must comprehend 'occasions' of this general type. I must have a perspective and point of access to the knowledge of what I propose to talk about.

On Whitehead's account I as an understanding, interpreting subject stand in an "objective" relation to the data left upon the perishing of an 'occasion'. This is what I perceive clearly, i.e., in the mode of presentational immediacy and as abstract, and this perception is within the (earlier phases of the) successor 'occasion'. In addition to this I have access to perception in the mode of causal efficacy, by which I perceive the process of becoming of the data out of my causal past. The combining or mixing of these two "pure" modes presents us with symbolic reference (PR 121f, 167f). If we set aside the unfortunate impression left by Whitehead in these and some other contexts that each of the modes may enter into consciousness in its pure form, and then go on to construe that they are not so much modes as a contrast — an interpretation that appears to be allowed by some things he says, as, for example, when he refers to each mode as involving a direct and indirect knowledge of perception (the indirect one being for the other mode direct /PR 169) — a basis is provided for rendering this discrimination commensurate with the requirements of the present critique. A development of this basis would additionally require the stipulation that symbolic reference construed in this way cannot, as Whitehead alleges (PR 168) involve error, and this would point, in turn, to an abandonment of the term, seeing that it is

---

[9] For my contrast of concrete space-time with the more abstract here-now (*hier-jetzt*), the latter being more commensurate with the abstract usage within modern physics, see SC, pp. 211-17, 437f, and 482f.

concrete actuality and concrete language with which we end up, rather than with something symbolic of something else that of itself is not properly knowable. In other words, there being no knowledge which precedes symbolic reference, it is appropriately renamed; and symbolic knowledge, i.e., "knowledge of" (something objectively present) becomes an unconcretized construction of one or another sort formed from abstractions from an 'actual occasion$_r$,' which has perished.

The unfortunate impression sometimes left by Whitehead that the "pure" modes may each be perceived independently of the other can be moderated by noting the role of inheritance in perception in the mode of causal efficacy. Notwithstanding, the sense is left that in his less than systematic exposition of this discrimination he is laboring under a burden for not having admitted the subject into his 'occasion$_r$,' a step which results in a simplification that ought to recommend it for serious consideration, particularly since it can be made to seem self-evident to every person of common sense not corrupted by theories: that he finds himself situated in a relation of contrast to a world present *for* him, his self-concept and his world-concept sharing the same content. In other words, each self and each world presents itself as an accent within an identity inclusive of both. From this it is a short way to the view that all other contrasts are somehow comprehended by this complex contrast.

The contrast between the two 'modes' on this account become one such sub-contrast, except that what remains are no longer modes but abstractions from the becoming and the being of an actual occasion, respectively, perceived as integral, and as essential aspects, each of the other.

In no way does Whitehead's metaphysics more clearly bear the marks of its birth in the theory of science than by the exclusion of the comprehending, interpreting subject from his 'occasion' and by his apparent disposition that the consciousness of an actual occasion adds nothing to its metaphysical character (PR 53). To name the contrasts is of course to accord prominence to many which do not have any particular relevance to physical theory or to mathematics, such as that between the comprehending, interpreting subject and its world, and to settle the issue of reductionism in one fell swoop. This may be said to have been Hegel's way of giving the particular theoretical sciences their due without turning the work of philosophy over to them or modeling concrete facts upon their theories.

It is to be admitted, of course, that Whitehead's 'occasion' contains a ***prehending*** subject. The problem consists in that this does not permit an account of the contrast from an internal perspective because the content of such an account, the perception of which must of necessity be at least predominantly in the mode of persentational immediacy, by virtue of his not having perceived that reflection is a contrast, is on his theory external.

Whitehead portrayed felt contraries as "consciousness in germ", indicating that "when the contrasts and identities of such are felt, we have consciousness" which is the feeling of "the contrast of theory as mere theory with fact as mere fact" (PR 188). Had he specified the contrasts constitutive of an actual occasion, or of some one or more such, to have included the contrast of theory with fact — both sides being grasped in their mediation as accents within an identity inclusive of both, an inclusive and complete fact — this would have had the effect of including the understanding, interpreting subject *within* the occasion. It would additionally have resulted in according to consciousness as such an essential role in the constitution of experience and indeed — what Whitehead probably wished to avert but which cannot be averted — in the constitution of concrete actuality itself, thereby giving recognition to the increment of freedom we associate with the possibility of conscious decision making. All of these are things which Whitehead would have found himself in a cramped position to do (had he wanted to). These results could have been effected apart from sacrificing the theory-free character of facts — required if facts are to be construed in a way commensurate with their constituting an adequate basis for science. This is seeing that, as concretely actual, a fact stands free (if through assimilation) of any and all theories which may have conditioned its concrescence. *It is precisely in this way that the process principle rescues the theory-free status of facts.*

Once the notion is taken seriously that an 'actual occasion$_r$' ought to be self-constitutive in an unqualified sense as a necessary condition of our being able to account for its self-evidence (as a world and self climaxing in an episodic achievement of coherent unity of contrasts adequate to its explication), the externality of at least one of the modes of perception will not do. This is especially apparent when we note that an 'actual occasion' considered from an external perspective cannot possibly be more than hypothetically actual. Except for such relief from this result as Whitehead may have managed through his concept of perception in the mode of causal efficacy, by not admitting the understanding, interpreting subject into his 'occasion' he has recapitulated within his metaphysics what before the appearance of Gerold Prauss, *Kant und das Problem der Dinge an Sich* we used to follow Hegel and many others in supposing to be Kant's problem of an unknown thing-in-itself. If he unconsciously took on a vague reflection of this mythical error, this would be the nearest he came to entering upon the "critical" path of philosophy which had its inception in Kant. Quite naturally, then, he did not go on to seek the resolution of the problem within the further development of the same tradition.[10]

An aspect of the matter before us consists in that, if an 'occasion' is self-constituting, an 'occasion$_r$' must be self-evident as well, as a condition of being self-constituting. The character of being self-constituting on the part of an 'occasion' consists in its inclusiveness of all that from its perspective is actual, so that it is not rendered relative by external relations. This character would of course be compromised by the perceiving subject being external to it were it not for the fact that it is only upon perishing that the data of the 'occasion', as such, i.e., as its superject, is perceived. Perishing in an 'occasion', in addition to serving as a terminus to process, thus protects it (before perishing) from being relativized by being made a mere object of perception by the understanding, interpreting subject.

The understanding, interpreting subject is included within an 'occasion$_r$,' however, from which perspective all of the constitutive contrasts are in principle perceivable as a unity and wholeness of contrasts adequate to the explication of the 'occasion$_r$', thus accounting for the self-evidence with which it is perceived in its all-at-onceness. If any single contrast were not in principle perceivable to the subject (in some grade of relevance or other and commensurate emphasis) the inclusiveness of the 'occasion$_r$' of all action would be compromised, and with this, its self-constitutive character. An 'occasion$_r$' thus has no need of protection against being relativized by the understanding, interpreting subject. The perishing of an 'occasion$_r$' sets a hedge against the subject's immortalizing concreteness — the God-complex — by rendering derivative (hypothetically actual) actualities and concepts, such as the theory of electromagnetic events, absolute.

6. Some Further Resulting Alterations

In an 'occasion$_r$,' that comprehends as well as prehends, the comprehension displaces the superjective function, or in part. This is inevitable since knowing a 'concretely actual occasion$_r$' from *within*

---

[10] The problem of an unknown thing in itself continues to haunt philosophies that fail to accord a proper status to concreteness in its fullness and finality. The clearing up of its supposed association with Kant leaves us with Kant and Hegel being somewhat more proximate than has generally heretofore been suspected.

If Prauss' case is regarded as conclusive, Whitehead would appear to be innocent of having *in any obvious way* entered upon the critical path!

(from an *actual* perpsective) is to know it, on the one hand, as at once equally subjective and objective (Hegel's "true objectivity"), these contrasted aspects being accents within an identity inclusive of both, and, on the other, as the process of becoming and as the being of what has become, as yet integral.[11]

Seeing that account is being taken of self-evidence, i.e., of the fact that concreteness is known, it is inevitable that actuality will undergo a *fall* at the point of perishing, at which point Whitehead has it function as superject. Whitehead, for whom "philosophy is explanatory of abstractions and not of concreteness" (PR 20), by taking up his account of knowledge (at least of that in knowledge which is perceptually immediate) following this fall, finds it unnecessary to render an account of it.

To approach the issue in another way, I know concrete identities as discriminated results not yet separated off by abstraction from their process of becoming. I know these "same" identities, as no longer concrete but as generic, following abstraction, as generic because they are then functioning within another 'occasion$_r$'. They are not actual, however, as is Whitehead's superject (at least following Lobo), but hypothetical. This hypothetical status is especially from the standpoint of the first occasion, viewed as process and result not yet separated from one another. The difference thus indicated is more marked where the subjective aim of the successor occasion is significantly different in character from its predecessor. Viewed from the standpoint of the subjective aim of the successor occasion, inherited data are only hypothetical insofar as they are yet wanting in commensurability for forming contrasts constitutive of this 'occasion$_r$' in its final phase of concrescence.

It may be noted that I have not referred to the data abstracted

---

[11] In response to the judgment implicated in the foregoing paragraph and elsewhere in this paper that Whitehead describes actualities in general from the outside and hence hypothetically, Lewis Ford proposes in a letter, dated 1. IV. 1980, that what Whitehead rather undertakes is "a generic description of actuality from the inside, by imaginative generalization from his own particular experience, focusing on those features which might be appropriate for all actualities". I find this judgment plausible. Supposing Ford's representation, we are then led to envision an inner perspective that nourishes Whitehead's external perspective and that is effective behind the scenes, as it were, the imagination being accorded the task that might have been superfluous if the actual perspective, that on my account is native to self-consciousness in the first place, had been given center stage. Whitehead cannot accord it center stage, seeing that this would involve according to self-consciousness the status of being essential to an actual occasion, which would not serve his *wissenschaftstheoretische* interests. This all seems perverse, and I find the imagination to have principally, at least, a far more essential role than that of compensating for that perversion of the particular sciences that has up to now insinuated itself into much philosophy (or into much that passes under this name), namely that of making theory rather than *concrete* (and theory-free) fact the starting point from which inquiry moves.

upon the perishing of an occasion as objective. The foregoing account overlooks a complicating factor which is now to be introduced. Although this is not implicated directly with the specification of the contrasts constitutive of an 'actual occasion', it is required by the same critical principles which urge this specification. Critical principles disallow Whitehead's favoritism toward objective data, left upon the perishing of his 'occasion', to which he exclusively accords the immortality he denies to subjects, seeing that this favoritism is rendered possible only by virtue of his appeal to eternal objects to explain how new subjects come into existence. Where Whitehead's "complete fact" has been rendered *in fact* complete, no reason will be found for the introduction of such venturesome theoretical notions into first philosophy, which in its primary work — the analysis-synthesis of concreteness, discrimination by discrimination, at least once it familiarizes itself with the phenomenological basis of the facts with which it works — can very largely do without theory as such. Accordingly, the data left by an 'actual occasion$_r$,' upon its perishing are equally subjective and objective, although a different subjectivity is nonetheless at work in the process of concrescence of the successor occasion, on which account the character of being something hypothetical still clings to these data in the early phases of concrescence, before positive and negative prehension has effected priorities of emphases resulting in the commensurability of the mental and the physical poles.

There seems on the face of it no reason for pronouncing a subject dead when it has done its work. If the issue is to be approached from the theoretical standpoint, it seems more appropriate to say that the subjective and the objective aspects of the occasion continue in a passive state, and that in this passive state its parts and aspects fall asunder, or do so to some degree (depending upon their inherent stability and how they are appropriated by successor occasions), the point of clevange not, however, being necessarily between subjective and objective aspects. Insofar as the form of the concrescence which has preceded is preserved, subjectivity is in this passive state preserved. (Moreover, a hypothetical content completely without form is *unthinkable*.)

A further remark in regard to eternal objects. This concept was intended to serve to explain how internal relations can be known short of knowing everything (SMW 235). Where the contrasts constitutive of an occasion of experience in its end phase are specified, this function is rendered superfluous. An occasion being unambiguously and exclusively constituted by polarities being synthesized into contrasts and in its end phase by a wholeness and unity of contrasts, it is a complete fact, comprehending within itself all that from its perspective is actual, hence absolute, and there is no need to invoke a transcending principle to explain its being what it is. All of its constitutive contrasts are not equally emphasized, it is true; its concept is nonetheless in keeping with the self-evidence we experience every waking moment, and this suffices. Also, the need to appeal to a conceptuality brought "from elsewhere" is set aside, as, e.g., a traditional language, a dependence upon which would imply for the concrete the status of being *something merely hypothetical,* when, in fact, as absolute, it ***can speak for itself.***[12] Rather than upon eternal objects, the intelligibility of experience and the continuity of the universe, upon which the possibility of intelligibility rests, are founded upon such contrasts as are universal to all 'occasions$_r$,' or to sizeable epochs of them, which (along with all others) are in principle available to to analysis-synthesis. I refer to analysis-synthesis because the recapitulation in linear language for the understanding of the all-at-onceness of the contrasts constitutive of an 'actual Occasion$_r$,' cannot stop with analysis alone, it being the (recapitulated) synthesis of the aspects polarized by analysis which effects the overcoming of the disposition of the abstract understanding to construe them as being mere polarities. Thus synthesis is ever the complement of analysis. Also analysis/synthesis is a contrast, and one which appears to be constitutive of every 'occasion$_r$'. This has the force of proposing that every possible occasion is an internalization of external relations and in this sense a many becoming a one. That this is true in the practice of first philosophy in the explication of concreteness is ever a reflection of the character of the facts upon which it works, which are internalizations of external relations.[13]

Finally, and in view of the foregoing exposition, the concretely specific specification of concreteness signals the possibility of displacing the language of external relations, the language of theory, such as is characteristic of Whitehead's metaphysics, at least to a very large extent, by the language of internal relations. To state the matter more precisely, it signals the possibility of providing, from an internal (*actual*) perspective, an account of external relations being internalized.[13a] This has the effect of eliminating most of the fat of

---

[12] The philosophy of language here implicated has much in common with that of Erich Heintel, *Einführung in die Sprachphilosophie* (Darmstadt: Wissenschaftliche Buchgesellschaft, 1972) and with that of Renate Christensen, previously mentioned (p. 17, n. 27), a difference consisting, however, in that I, in common with Hegel (as I maintain) and Gadamer, accord ontological import to concrete language. See TCMM, §4.

[13] It is in this sense a many becoming a one. For a treatment of "that Natural Order is from Fact to Theory", see pp. 129-49 and Essay VI.

rumination from metaphysics, and moving it beyond the shadow land of theories modeled either upon some arbitrary "common sense" or other or upon modern physics.

Theory in metaphysics can serve no purpose at all if it does not guide us to the fact or facts the structure of which it is supposed to approximate, perceived from an internal (*actual*) perspective. It is at most a shadow. *Even a shadow, however, may serve to guide one toward the light, the self-evident fact, although the basis and natural point of beginning of an investigation is the latter.* The basic (theory-free) phenomena constitutive of facts are the feelings and results, as integrated aspects, of the process of discrimination, i.e., contrast formation.[13b] Thus, the process of concrescence might alternatively be

---

[13a] The foregoing statement is commensurate with a construal of second philosophy as performing its role within that of first philosophy, conceived as a Hegelian type phenomenology of concreteness. (Cf. Essay I, §6.) I later find it more consistent to say that an account of external relations being rendered internal can only be from a hypothetical (external) perspective, but that this must necessarily presuppose an account of concreteness from an actual (internal) perspective. Concrete actuality being grasped *a priori* as such, and thus as a system of internal relations, to speak of external relations priorly being rendered internal involves one in the absurdity of implying that something is prior to that which is *a priori*. This is possible only for hypothetical thought operating within the context of the hypothetico-deductive method, which is, of course, completely alien to Hegelian phenomenology. This correction, which I introduced into SC and other essays completed subsequent to the present one, seems not to qualify the force of the point I am making in the statement that immediately follows in the text, although I would now state it in such a way as to emphasize that an account of external relations being rendered internal is appropriately regarded as secondary to one of concrete actuality grasped *a priori* as such.

[13b] The foregoing statement has a background context in Hegel's dialectic of the natural soul, the feeling soul, and the actual soul (*Enzy.*, esp. §§388-412). What this dialectic has to show us for the present context is that even relatively undetermined feelings on Hegel's account, if they are grasped at all and sublated (*aufgehoben*) within his Begriff — i.e., concrete actuality grasped as such — are grasped as discriminated or as contrasts. This is an important aspect of Hegel's treatment of contents of consciousness that for most philosophers fall on the side of the non-cognitive, but which for Hegel is by sublation included within conceptual thought.

As pertaining to this theme, George L. Kline, in "Concept and Concrescence: An Essay in Hegelian-Whiteheadian Ontology" (in George R. Lucas, Jr. (Ed.), *Hegel and Whitehead: Contemporary Perspectives on Systematic Philosophy* [Albany: SUNY Press, 1986], proposes: "Whitehead goes further than Hegel in de-emphasizing the cognitive dimension of experience" (p. 139). If we proceed from the standpoint that for Hegel conceptual thought is understood so inclusively that nothing of which I can be aware is alien to its grasp, as I have indicated, then it would seem to follow that a de-emphasis of "the cognitive dimension of experience" could from Hegel's viewpoint only take the form of an emphasis upon the need for further negation. Also further negation, however, or the non-being thus encountered, will then be rendered determinate and *aufgehoben* within cognition, as well. Hence such a strategy can never finally succeed. If we view the matter from Hegel's point of view, perhaps there is no reason why it should. This is to say, there is no reason why we should wish to absolutize indeterminancy, which for Hegel might have come to much the same as the affirmation of a "false infinite".

I understand Kline to be maintaining that it is by "taking account of" prehensive relations so construed that cognition and consciousness are special cases that Whitehead effects

construed as the process of discrimination. This is so long as discrimination is construed primarily in terms of founding judgments constitutive of experience and of facticity, and only secondarily with reference to the results of analysis-synthesis, which, at least prior to *re*concrescence, are derivative recapitulations, i.e., *after the fact*. Theory, if it has served its Lord Facticity as a guide, is insofar rendered superfluous (in any given 'occasion$_r$'), its ultimate source and touchstone having been grasped as such.

a de-emphasis of the cognitive. With reference to this matter, the fact should not be concealed that the prehensions that we concretely know are mediated to constitute consciousness. These are such as one might alternatively view as concretely actual speculations. The more inclusive class of prehensions can be construed only by analogy with these conscious ones by hypothetical speculation. Since hypothetical speculation is posterior to actual speculation, we seem not to end up with very much of a basis for construing that a de-emphasis upon the cognitive might thus be effected. Perhaps we should not wish for this, given the inclusiveness of this category and the fact that what *is not* can only be construed with reference to what concretely *is*. (Kline, 147)

Before leaving this particular issue it seems appropriate to make reference to another contribution to the Lucas (Ed.) *Collection* that likewise implies in an especially conspicuous manner the mistaken understanding of Hegel as having centered his conceptual thought in hypothetical rather than in actual speculation. This is within the context in which Ernest Wolf-Gazo proposes, in "Negation and Contrast: The Origins of Self-consciousness in Hegel and Whitehead": "For Hegel, self-conscious thinking has inherited exclusively the function of negation, while for Whitehead, negation is already present in simple perception..." (p. 214). Thus Wolf-Gazo at once permits the part of perception and the dialectic of perception within Hegel's account to drop out of view, and alleges, in effect, that Hegel's self-conscious thinking is merely epiphenomenal to the concrete actuality that (I have noted) it determines. I know of no basis for such a claim in Hegel's writings — which it seems to me could give rise to little more than puzzlement were it to be found —, nor does its author point to any. Can this have any other basis than an excessive zeal to perceive Hegel as a kind of forerunner of Whitehead? The statement quoted is one of several on p. 214 of Wolf-Gazo's paper that seem to me to be about equally problematical.

I shall not here enter further upon the issue as it pertains to Whitehead, which I find to be somewhat more complex — both by involving the analogical character of such prehensions as are construed as not entering into consciousness and by his realistic theory of knowledge — and which is in any case marginal to the thrust of Kline's criticism.

There are other aspects of Kline's representation of the Hegel-Whitehead relation to which I might raise objections. Most of these seem to follow, at least in part, from a failure to accord adequate recognition to the very marked, and I believe irrefutable, difference that I find to obtain between what I have sometimes referred to as the type of actual speculation that is normative for Hegel and the type of hypothetical speculation that is normative for Whitehead. (See SC, notes on pp. 64, 92, 101, 209, and 436 and pp. 289ff below, n. 22*a*.) Consider the following passage:

[F]or Hegel the unifying, organizing activity of the Begriff (concept) is, in the end, cognitive and self-conscious, whereas for Whitehead the prehensive relation is a more general "taking account of", of which cognition and consciousness are quite special cases. As Düsing puts it: the "absolute identity", of the speculative Begriff is the "self-relatedness of a subjectivity which thinks itself". And again: through subject-object unity, "subjectivity not only knows itself in its object, but in this knowledge is also certain of the producing (*Hervorbringung*) of this object." Other recent commentators add that the Begriff is not only "a concrete system" but also "a conscious experience...an activity of [cognitive] self-differentiation [or self-specification]"; and

Even so, hypothetical thinking, which theories formalize, bridges between the peaks of climaxing, episodic, 'occasions$_r$,' thus contributing to the illusion that actuality is in a simple sense continuous. Hypothetical thinking in relation to fact is thus analogous to the fading visual image between the flicks of a motion picture, which, by filling in, yields the sense of motion to the perceiver. This is not to propose that there is no *actual* motion (process) underlying this, i.e., internal to the fact, which is being recapitulated (what we indeed perceive) but merely to call attention to the consideration that at the secondary level, process, rather than being self-evident, is merely inferred.

that it is a "reflexive or self-conscious grasp by subjectivity of itself as subject-object". I have no quarrel with these interpretations; they make vividly explicit the "intellectualist" or "theoretical" bias of Hegel's theory of the Begriff as compared to Whitehead's theory of the concrescence. (p. 147)

In overlooking the different status that Hegel accords to actual speculation, on the one hand — i.e., consciousness in its self-certainty including the world present for and determinative of it — and to hypothetical speculation, on the other, Kline in effect levels the former to the latter. This Whiteheadianism amounts to what I have elsewhere referred to as the arch-anti-Hegelian fallacy (SC, p. 64 and the two pages preceeding). This is despite the fact that he includes quotes from Düsing that might well have served to call his attention to this very discrimination. At the end of the quote Kline seems to imply that apart from entering upon this sort of adventure of hypothetical speculation, we will be in danger of falling prey, with Hegel, to an "intellectualist" or "theoretical" bias. At bottom this is surely a perverse contradiction in terms.

The passages quoted by Kline within the longer passage above quoted provide us with a faithful representation of much of the basis for Hegel's self-certainty of reason. This is a certainty that obviously cannot be carried over to mere hypothetical thinking. Without proposing here to enter upon the complex issue of what might constitute an "intellectualist" or a "theoretical" bias in Hegel, I propose merely that, if such biases are there to be overcome, it is not plausible to suppose that this might be by the strategy that Kline proposes, which amounts to a movement from what is grasped *a priori* as self-certain to hypothetical thinking of a sort that is not restricted by critical principles. Hegelian self-certainty cannot be mixed in willy-nilly with what passes as knowledge, or as a substitute for knowledge, within the framework of the hypothetico-deductive method, and yet retain status for us as such, and this goes also for what is demonstrated within an abstract system of one or another sort. Kline may not have considered this as being a loss, but from a critical standpoint it could hardly be regarded as other than a serious one.

That the force of the passages in the above that Kline quotes from Düsing and others has been passed over is also indicated in his brittle and, I maintain unjustified, defense of Whitehead where he asserts, "Hegel fails, or refuses, to make categorial distinction between subjects as *present* and objects as *past* (or *timeless*) which is integral to Whitehead's position" (p. 149). Conspicuously absent from his consideration is the fact that for Hegel *philosophy* — i.e., what I have referred to as the analysis-*re*synthesis of the Begriff — *is past*, after the fact, and with this, quite naturally, the priority of the Hegelian Begriff in its subjective and objective aspects (or poles) alike is affirmed, the reconstruction of which in secondary reflection follows after. All of this puts Kline in a different ballpark, and he has not provided his readers with any reason for joining him there.

Why should Hegel's self-certainty of reason have our respect? It should at the very least force the recognition that I know something like the self-certainty that is here in view every waking moment, this being a characteristic of consciousness. It seems to me entirely plausi-

The internal perspective, whether grasped in its all-at-onceness or delineated in linear (which may nonetheless be concrete) language, consists in contrasts that it is useful just here to construe as philosophical propositions or judgments, which as such are graspable. In such a judgment, constitutive at once of experience and of actuality, actuality is grasped concretely in its mediation. This is the immanent judgment constitutive of the fact. Its form is the same as that employed by hypothetical reasoning going about the business of preparing possibilities, theories, for concretion in future 'occasions$_r$', a function ever to be distinguished from analysis-synthesis after the fact. This latter is the primary role of first philosophy which, like the fact itself, stands prior to theory, as well as prior to the theory of science (*Wissenschaftstheorie*). The particular sciences and the theory of the particular sciences are done from an external (hypothetical) perspective (presupposing the character of the concrete facts with which they have to do),[14] *as though* one could somehow locate oneself outside of an 'occasion$_r$' inclusive of all that from its perspective

ble that a philosopher should proceed in such a way that he is not cut off from the possibility of relating responsibly to this kind of self-certainty as a point of access to what we may know, at least for the duration of a lived occasion.

Kline might have spared his readers confusion had he observed what H. K. Wells described as Whitehead's separation of qualities (and objects) from passage. By identifying qualities with particular (unchanging) eternal objects, Whitehead in effect eliminated the problem of dealing with them as processes, in which, e.g., "any concrete instance of a shade of red is at the same time becoming a *different* shade, and, indeed, in the long run becoming non-red." See H. K. Wells, *Process and Unreality*, esp. pp. 58f, or on pp. 58f, n. 4 above. Hegel's position here follows from his rejection of the laws of identity and of non-contradiction as first laws of thought and his **subordination of these principles within** lived process. This was a deliberate and well advertised move, made with full awareness of positions of the type of Whitehead's, which treat objects as knowable only in abstraction. If we are to speak of neglect within the present context, this would have to be on the part of Whitehead for reflecting no awareness of anything closely resembling Hegel's position with regard to the issue. A result is that Hegel's is the more thoroughgoing philosophy of process.

Bearing in mind these and other objections that I might raise, in the paper under discussion Kline has moved some way from one bearing the same title on which I was in Sept., 1977 invited to prepare a commentary, which I did and which appeared in SC, as n. 2 within the "Acknowledgements". I tend to assume that this was an ancestor of the present paper, even though I find the differences between the two versions to be more marked than their similarities, and I am pleased to observe that this is in such a way that my previous criticisms either no longer apply or apply with somewhat moderated force. Since he was the first with whom I shared the substance of this earlier critique, perhaps it has had a bearing upon the present revision, which I find to be more deserving of criticism. I can be relatively brief, since Hegel is somewhat less of a stranger to the English reader than he was a decade ago. I am also pleased to note that Kline here (p. 133) reverses the position that he had taken earlier in another paper, of which I was critical, in which he found Hegel to have left us with a vacuous actuality. (See my review of the earlier version of the paper under discussion.)

[14] For more extensive treatments of the relation of first philosophy and the theory of science, see Essay VII, §4; Essay II, §§4, 6; Essay VIII, §5; SC, pp. 434-39, 471-76.

is actual. It is on this account that critical principles obtaining in philosophy have little to contribute directly to these disciplines, which in their methodology must of necessity continue to have much in common with pre-critical rumination in philosophy. The perspective of an 'occasion$_r$' includes all that falls within its perceptual-conceptual-intentional horizon and history as actual within the present, particular features and aspects being accorded some grade of relevance and emphasis.

Whitehead's concept of an 'actual occasion' tends to be dominated by physical models, principally that of an electro-magnetic event. The point can be over-emphasized; after all, he does build biological and psychological aspects into this concept. Nonetheless, there can scarcely be any doubt but that it continues to bear the marks of its birth in physical theory. To the extent that this is so, there is at work within this concept, however subtly, a certain favoritism tantamount to a tendency toward physical reductionism. Where the contrasts are specified, this favoritism must inevitably be exposed to view, particularly if an account can be taken of the relative emphasis accorded to particular discriminations by having the order of explication reflect the relative inclusiveness of import of particular contrasts within an 'occasion$_r$'. A concretely specific explication of the contrasts constitutive of an 'occasion$_r$' typical of some epoch will reflect the 'biases' (considered with respect to massive averages) of the particular epoch of 'occasions' under consideration. An occasion within the epoch constituted by the life span of A. N. Whitehead, for example, will reflect one set of 'biases' (commensurate with those of an 'occasion'?). Another 'occasion$_r$' within the epoch constituted by the life span of Martin Luther King will doubtless reflect another set of 'biases'. In any case, however, the concrete specification of the contrasts issues in no 'biases' not actual within the 'occasion$_r$' subject to analysis-synthesis. It thus in an ***unbiased*** manner accords equal right to all constitutive contrasts. This is to be understood in a manner compatible with the consideration that some contrasts appear to be universal to all 'occasions$_r$'. Contrasts which figure importantly in physical theory, such as space/time, tend to be among these. But (abstract) universality (throughout the plurality of occasions) does ***not*** imply emphasis, or inclusiveness of import within the particular 'occasion$_r$'. From any actual perspective this will tend to fall to the contrast between the understanding, interpreting subject and the world present for this subject and to some of its principle sub-contrasts, generically considered.

7. Summary of Resulting Alterations

In summary of the two preceding §§, to undertake to specify the contrasts constitutive of an 'actual occasion' appears directly or indirectly to effect the following principal alterations upon Whitehead's metaphysics. (1) Whitehead's 'occasion', which he viewed as a "complete fact", is rendered *in fact* complete by the inclusion of the concrete discrimination between its understanding, interpreting subject and the world present for this subject. (2) The two modes of perception become a sub-contrast of becoming and being, accents within an identity inclusive of both, (self-)perceived in its unity and wholeness. Thus knowledge in the proper sense — that is, *concrete* knowledge — is equally subjective and objective, the highest subjectivity and the highest objectivity being each an accent within an identity inclusive of both. (3) An actual 'occasion$_r$', as complete, i.e., absolute, must be self-evident as a condition of its being self-constitutive. (4) The superjective function of an 'actual occasion', where the superject is construed as actual, is displaced by hypothetical data, a matter to be understood with a view to the manner and sense in which concreteness, following Hegel's account, is known. (5) The concept of objectively immortal data gives way to data which in their immortality are equally subjective and objective. (6) By rendering an 'actual occasion$_r$' a complete system of internal relations, the concept of eternal objects is rendered a superfluous reminder of precritical rumination. Continuity is explained by appeal to generic contrasts which are constantly reconcretized and in this sense are (abstractly) universal throughout all, or at least certain epochs of, 'occasions$_r$'. (7) In first philosophy, theory tends to be displaced by the analysis-synthesis of contrasts or discriminations. This is implicated with the subject's taking an inside (*actual*) perspective "upon" an 'occasion$_r$' which includes it. (8) In the construal of the causative aspects of an 'occasion$_r$' from the perspective of its stage of full concrescence, there is no bias for subjectivity or objectivity, every constituent aspect being equally causative of the unity of concrescence attained. (9) In shifting from theory — and most especially physical theory — as a point of beginning, to the contrasts constitutive of an 'occasion$_r$', a basis for possible bias that is present in Whitehead's method is overcome with respect to the aspects of actuality which are emphasized.

8. Some Limits

An 'occasion$_r$' that arises, completes itself, and perishes, by the time it can be subjected to an analysis-synthesis, contrast by contrast, will long since have perished. This is bound up with the consideration that an analysis-synthesis of contrasts requires abstraction after the fact, i.e.; after the perishing of the 'occasion'. The self-evidence with which the 'occasion$_r$' presented itself is, of course, prior to and (considered with respect to any particular case) completely independent of any analysis-synthesis, partial or exhaustive, which might follow. The self-knowledge of the occasion,[15] then, is not here at stake but the manner in which this self-knowledge is laid out for the understanding in linear language. These considerations in view, I take the following note of some built-in limitations upon the program that has been characterized in the foregoing.

1) The analysis-synthesis of the contrasts constitutive of an 'occasion$_r$' will inevitably pertain not so much to a particular 'occasion$_r$' as to one held to be typical of some relevant epoch. This might be a cultural epoch or the epoch constituted by the act of raising my arm to salute the flag. Undoubtedly some strictness is lost in the account when a *typical* 'occasion$_r$' is construed, especially in the case of a more inclusive epoch.

2) Seeing that analysis-synthesis necessarily involves abstraction, what results, as pertaining to the character of the self-evidence with which the occasion has undeniably presented itself, is a stipulation of the full set of conditions necessary to account for its possibility (as self-evident).[16] This is to say, the analysis-synthesis being *after the fact,* a necessary limitation is placed upon the results whereby these must be construed as transcendental conditions only. Critical principles of course require that we do not confuse transcendental conditions with facts.[17] Notwithstanding, in the case in which a contrast by contrast explication of an 'actual occasion$_r$' attains to an ideal completeness, and where there is no substantial break in the continuity of character of the members of a sequence of 'occasions$_r$' to which an account is to pertain, this distinction can have no practical importance. This is assuming that concrete discriminations are not

---

[15] Throughout this essay, where the term "occasion" occurs without quotes or a subscript, an ordinary non-technical usage is intended.

[16] I have thus dealt summarily with a very large topic, which I have treated more extensively, if also from a merely external perspective, in SC, pp. 93-107, 217-23, 471-77.

[17] Seeing that no 'occasion$_r$' contains accidental or non-essential aspects, the full set of conditions to account for its possibility (as opposed to the merely substantial set of conditions referred to earlier in this paper) includes, in addition to the contrasts (abstractly) universal to all 'occasions$_r$', all other constitutive contrasts as well.

displaced by generic ones. Insofar as the explication falls short of this ideal of completeness or there is "discontinuity" in the sequence of occasions, the distinction takes on significance. For most practical purposes, however, the differences here in view will be negligible. When the matter is strictly considered, nonetheless, and with specific cases in view, it constitutes yet another kind of limit with respect to how nearly the ideal of a concretely specific explication of concreteness can be achieved. A more adequate account of this matter would need to include reference to history as actual within an 'actual occasion$_r$,' which concept it seems preferable not to attempt to introduce here.[18]

In view of the variability of 'occasions$_r$', the transcendental conditions to which I have alluded will in some degree vary from one 'occasion$_r$' to another. The transcendental categories — the term "category" here being construed after the Hegelian model, i.e., as discriminations (contrasts) being mediated — are sublated in every occasion, a consideration which I must pass over here.

3) Allowance being made for the foregoing, if an ideally exhaustive analysis-synthesis of an 'actual occasion$_r$,' typical of some relevant epoch, whereby the self-evidence with which it presented itself may be laid out for the understanding in linear language and fully detailed, is in principle, at least, very nearly realizable in some cases, an additional, practical consideration may lie in the way of the execution of this ideal. It will assist me in rendering the point clear to note first that an 'actual occasion$_r$' at full concrescence, being completely determined, contains no accidents. This entails that, strictly speaking, an explication of its self-evidence requires an exhaustive explication of its constitutive discriminations (or contrasts), each of which plays a unique role in the satisfaction of the occasion at full concrescence. In the case of a given 'occasion$_r$', some discriminations may be novel or rare and their presence only implicitly perceived. Despite the fact that such figured crucially in the self-evidence of the occasion, from the standpoint of a causal analysis they may be lumped off with what is implicit merely because it is familiar and can in an every-day attitude safely be presupposed. A dialectical analysis-synthesis of contrasts cannot, of course, stop here.

---

[18] Especially outside of the critical tradition, this is a distinction, drawn out of decent modesty, which generally gets overlooked. To overlook it is an offense against the process principle, even though its force in the case of most 'occasions$_r$' will be relatively weak.

Also Kant scholars who write in English have frequently erred in respect to this matter in the interpretation of Kant. See, e.g., Klaus Hartmann, "Recent Anglo-American Literature on Kant", trans. by Terry Pinkard, *Contemporary German Philosophy*, Vol. 2.

Some Limits 69

If the dialectical explication of presuppositions does not of itself pose totally unfamiliar or unresolvable difficulties, the possibility and the possible frequency of novel or near novel contrasts (or discriminations) places a more notable limitation upon the achievement of the ideal of an exhaustive analysis-synthesis of contrasts. Art, religion, and philosophy each play a distinctive and crucial role in the rendering explicit of such novel and variant contrasts. Every occasion being a new creation, however, this is a continuing task which sets a challenge to the presently outlined program.

By way of summary it seems fair to conclude that in the case of some particular 'occasion$_r$', typical of some epoch, some limitations (both of principle and in practice) may lie in the way of an exhaustive account of the contrasts, the ideal can be closely enough approximated so that it can safely be said to remain a governing principle (which gets concretized and reconcretized) and, as such, an ideal for process oriented expositions of concreteness executed with due regard to critical principles.[19]

---

[19] Out of caution, and because I could not here enter upon some somewhat complex issues that pertain to what is involved in proposing to provide an account of the contrasts constitutive of an actual occasion sufficiently exhaustive to account for its self-evidence, I have doubtless made this undertaking seem more problematical than I in fact find it to be. An ameliorating factor consists in that it seems plausible to say that a complex contrast, such as subject ("I")–world, considered within a given 'occasion$_r$' contains precisely the same content regardless of the number of its sub-contrasts that are found to be explicit or that are made explicit in its anylsis-synthesis. This is to suppose that the increment of explicit sub-contrasts lends specific detail to the complex contrast apart from the addition of content. If we follow this direction, we are led to the view that simpler contrasts, e.g., (relatively) unconscious physical feelings, for example, detail more complex contrasts some of the more inclusive of which are prominent in consciousness, and that what we principally want to account for in the analysis-synthesis of an 'occasion$_r$' are discriminations that arise to explicit awareness. The richness of specific detail that lies potential to such an analysis-synthesis is then not strictly required to account for the self-evidence of the occasion. In short, to accomplish our aim, it suffices that we give an account of those discriminations that in fact present themselves (within the context of the occasion) as self-evident. See Essay VIII, n. 32, or, for a more extensive treatment of one aspect of the problematic, SC, pp. 93-108.

IV

WHITEHEAD'S "PREHENSION" AND HEGEL'S "MEDIATION": PARALLEL DYNAMICAL CONCEPTS AT THE SERVICE OF DIFFERENT METHODOLOGIES*

1.

Hegel and Whitehead are both prominently associated with speculative philosophy, Hegel with respect to his entire mature work, and Whitehead during the latter (American) phase of his career. An outstanding difference between the two versions of speculative philosophy will be seen to consist in the fact that Whitehead, moving from a position that all knowledge is hypothetical, busied himself with the construction of a forthrightly abstract system. Hegel, for whom, "Science can become an organic system only by the inherent life of the Begriff" (*Phän.* 44; *Phen.* 111), with certain minimally necessary qualifications, is attempting to arrive at the one system that *is* concrete actuality.[1] This system (as in the case of Whitehead's actual occasion) is conceived as an organism (*Phän.* 31; *Phen.* 95) that undergoes growth and development. Its conception must, nonetheless, in the end be graspable in abstraction as well, on which account it is the *universal* individual (*Phän.* 26; *Phen.* 89) and what *for* this individual is actual that Hegel intends to set forth. Indeed a principal value, if not *the* value, of such abstraction, however, consists in that the various stages of the growth of the system may thereby the more readily be retraversed and recapitulated by *particular* individuals assimilating (and perhaps reconstituting) their cultural heritage and

---

* This paper appeared in the *Review of Metaphysics,* Vol. XXXVIII, No. 2 (Dec., 1984), pp. 341-74, with varied pagination.

[1] Like the whole of Aristotle's philosophy, his logic really requires recasting, so that all his determinations should be brought into a necessary systematic whole — not a systematic whole which is correctly divided into its parts, and in which no part is forgotten, all being set forth in their proper order, but one in which there is one living organic whole, in which each part is held to be a part, and the whole alone as such is true. (G. W. F. Hegel, *Lectures on the History of Philosophy,* trans. by E. S. Haldane [London: 1963], p. 223).

thereby constituting themselves as individuals.[2]

2.

Commensurate with this difference, Whitehead provides us with brief and admirably clear statements of his method — at least as far as they reach, while for Hegel, any statement of his method must be provisional because, on his account, method is not finally separable from the content to which it pertains. Indeed, it is nothing other than the structure of the whole in its pure and essential form (*Phän.* 40; or *Phen.* 106). "This nature of scientific method, which consists partly in being inseparable from the content, and partly in determining the rhythm of its movement by its own agency, finds...its peculiar systematic expression in speculative philosophy" (*Phän.* 47f; *Phen.* 115). Before giving further consideration to this function of self-determination of "the rhythm of scientific method", I turn for contrast first to Whitehead's method for purposes of the philosophy of science, in order to show the point of approach he took to speculative philosophy, and then to his method for purposes of speculative philosophy. For the first I draw upon his *The Concept of Nature*:

> ...[A] science has...a certain unity which is the very reason why that body of knowledge has been instinctively recognized as forming a science. The philosophy of science is the endeavor to express explicitly those unifying characteristics that prevade that complex of thought and make it to be a science (CN 2).
>
> Nature is that which we observe in perception through the senses" (CN 3).

In sense perception nature is disclosed as a complex of entities whose mutual relations are expressible in thought. The fact of sense perception has a factor which is not thought, which Whitehead calls 'sense awareness' (CN 3). Sense awareness, following his account seems somehow to be complimented by "thinking homogeneously about nature".

> We are thinking 'homogeneously' about nature when we are thinking about it without thinking about thought or about sense-awareness, and we are thinking 'heterogeneously' about nature when we are thinking about it in conjunction with thinking either about thought or about sense-awareness or about both.
>
> I also take the homogeneity of thought about nature as excluding any reference to moral or aesthetic values whose apprehension is vivid in pro-

---

[2] Cf. *Phän.* p. 26; or *Phen.* p. 89. For Hegel the actualization of the spiritual individual is the highest achievement of the dialectic, in which his system culminates, as may be seen from his *Lectures in the Philosophy of Religion* or his *Lectures in the Philosophy of History*.

portion to self-conscious activity. The values of nature are perhaps the key to the metaphysical synthesis of existence. But such a synthesis is exactly what I am not attempting. I am concerned exclusively with the generalisations of widest scope which can be effected respecting that which is known to us as the direct deliverance of sense-awareness. (NT 5)

To be noted is that Whitehead's speculative philosophy as presented prominently in PR moves beyond thinking about nature to thinking comprehensively also about thought and sense-awareness in relation to nature, and this in such a way as to reflect concern for moral, aesthetic, and even religious values. I quote from chap. 1, the first page and a half. Echoes of this passage are found scattered throughout the work.

> Speculative Philosophy is the endeavor to frame a coherent, logical, necessary system of general ideas in terms of which every element of our experience can be interpreted. By this notion of 'interpretation' I mean that everything of which we are conscious, as enjoyed, perceived, willed, or thought, shall have the character of a particular instance of the general scheme. Thus the philosophical scheme should be coherent, logical, and, in respect to its interpretation, applicable and adequate. Here 'applicable' means that some item of experience are thus interpretable, and 'adequate' means that there are no items incapable of such interpretation.
>
> 'Coherence', as here employed, means that the fundamental ideas, in terms of which the scheme is developed, presuppose each other so that in isolation they are meaningless.... It is the ideal of speculative philosophy that its fundamental notions shall not seem capable of abstraction from each other. In other words, it is presupposed that no entity can be conceived in complete abstraction from the system of the universe, and that it is the business of speculative philosophy to exhibit this truth. This character is its coherence.
>
> The term 'logical' has its ordinary meaning, including 'logical' consistency, or the lack of contradiction, the definition of constructs in logical terms, the exemplification of general logical notions in specific instances, and the principles of inference. It will be observed that logical notions must themselves find their places in the scheme of philosophic notions. (PR. 3)

The methodology of speculative philosophy here set forth contains no reference to prehension, which along with Whitehead's closely related term "feeling" may safely be regarded as the central dynamical concept in rendering his account of the process of concrescence of an actual occasion, as I shall subsequently show. If some sort of phenomenology or quasi-phenomenology of prehension may be found in evidence in, or implied as lying behind, his speculative philosophy — an issue I shall be considering — such seems not to be accorded status within his various statements of method. In consideration of the history of philosophy during the past two centuries, certainly some readers may find this to constitute a curious deficiency. (We may thus be reminded of the extent to which Whitehead's intellectual roots lie within mathematics and theories [and *the* theory] of the natural sciences, disciplines within which less need has been found than in first philosophy to be apologetic about being openly speculative in the pre-critical sense that Whitehead seems to me principally to attach to this term.[3]) In my attempt to make a plausible comparison of his method with that of Hegel, I shall be considering whether this is indeed a "deficiency" that ought to be corrected.

3.

I return now to the determining of the rhythm of scientific method on Hegel's account. An important background thought here is that truth does not make its appearance by hypotheses, or, in his own words, by "the method of propounding a proposition, producing reasons for it and then refuting its opposite by reasons too" (*Phän.* 40; *Phen.* 106). Such propoundings and refutations rest ultimately upon the more or less systematic abstract language they presuppose, we can almost hear him saying. From the perspective of how (concrete) knowledge comes to be, it is of course possible to account for the arising of habitual distinctions such as are contained in common language and sometimes get set forth in dictionaries.

> ...[T]he important thing for the student of science (*Wissenschaft*) is to make himself undergo the strenuous toil of conceptual reflection, of thinking in the form of the Begriff. This demands concentrated attention to the Begriff as such, to simple and ultimate determinations such as being-in-itself, being-for-itself, self-identity, and so on; for these are elemental, pure, self-determined functions of a kind we might call souls, were it not that their conceptual nature denotes something higher than that term contains. The interruption by conceptual thought of the habit of always thinking in figurative ideas (*Vorstellungen*) is as annoying and troublesome to this way of thinking as to that process of formal intelligence which in its reasoning rambles about with no real thoughts to reason with. The former, the habit, may be called materialized thinking, a fortuitous mental state, one that is absorbed in what is material, and hence finds it very distasteful at once to lift its self clear of this matter and be with itself alone. The latter, the process of *raisonnement,* is, on the other hand, detachment from all content, and conceited superiority to it. What is wanted here is the effort and struggle to give up this kind of freedom, and instead of being a merely arbitrary principle directing the content anyhow, this freedom should sink into and pervade the content, should let it be directed

---

[3] "[I]n the main the philosophy of organism is a recurrence to pre-Kantian modes of thought" (PR, p. xi). I have indicated in Essay V, the second paragraph, the sense in which I conceive Hegel to be a philosopher working within the critical tradition.

and controlled by its own proper nature, i.e. by the self as its own self, and should observe this process taking place. We must abstain from interrupting the immanent rhythm of the movement of conceptual thought; we must refrain from arbitrarily interfering with it, and introducing ideas and reflections that have been obtained elsewhere. (*Phän.* 48; *Phen.* 116f)

The foregoing is one of the statements leading into the exposition of the basic unit of conceptual thought, Hegel's "philosophical" or "speculative" proposition. The subject and predicate of a philosophical or speculative proposition (*Satz,* which may be rendered either proposition or judgment within different contexts) are each accents within a mediated identity inclusive of both.[4]

In considering the distinction between such concretely particular meanings as those which philosophical propositions yield and ordinary abstract meanings, I can do not better than to cite the example of a philosophical proposition proposed by Josef Simon.

> It may not be amiss to introduce an example, not in Hegel's text, of a possible meaningful statement uttered in some situation or other and in some context, perhaps a descriptive one. In "this table is round", the subject-concept "table" does not mean something which, as a basis underlying the determination, could accept "accidents". What is meant is that this certain round table has not fortuitously *taken on* the property "round", but rather exists only in this shape. Further, the predicate does not signify a property which could "belong to" other objects as well. Only in a mathematical judgment could the "universal round" of a geometrical circle, constructed in pure intuition — that is, a concept that is to be constructed and not one *necessarily to be exemplified* — be intended, and only here could this constructed figure be the "basis" of the determination round, since in this case the free *action* of constructing is itself as "pure capacity" the "basis" of the various properties of figures. In this mathematical possibility, the categorial forms must synthesize an appropriate conceptual material, namely, concepts that have been constructed, with no reference made to an external, individual, real object. This possibility finally accounts for the form of the proposition, which "involves" the (fixed) "distinction between subject and predicate"[5] and thus refers to fixed meanings. In language, which is concerned with existent things,

---

[4] "Formell kann das Gesagte so ausgedrückt werden, daß die Natur das Urteils oder Satzes überhaupt, die den Unterschied des Subjekts und Prädikats in sich schließt, durch den spekulativen Satz zerstört wird, und der identische Satz, zu dem der erstere wird, den Gegenstoß zu jenem Verhältnisse enthält. — Dieser Konflikt der Form eines Satzes überhaupt und der sie zerstörenden Einheit des Begriffs ist dem ähnlich, der im Rhythmus zwischen dem Metrum und dem Akzente stattfindet. Der Rhythmus resultiert aus der schwebenden Mitte und Vereinigung beider. So soll auch im philosophisches Satze die Identität des Subjekts und Prädikats den Unterschied derselben, den die Form des Satzes ausdrückt, nicht vernichten, sondern ihre Einheit [soll] als eine Harmonie hervorgehen. Die Form des Satzes ist die Erscheinung des bestimmten Sinnes oder Akzent, der seine Erfüllung unterscheidet..." *Phän.,* p. 51; or *Phen.,* p. 120.

[5] *Phän.,* p. 51; or *Phen.,* p. 120f.

however, it is not the case that quiescent and passive "meanings" are linked together in a purely formal way. Rather, it happens that the subject with which a certain predicate is linked determines, on the basis of its meaning, that of the predicate, and the predicate determines the meaning of the subject.... According to Hegel, the "object"... "manifests itself as its development".[6]

With one additional quotation, a basis will be provided for the consideration of the philosophical proposition in what follows.

> The proposition ought to express what the truth is, in its essential nature subject. As such truth is the dialectical movement, the self-producing course of activity, advancing and returning into itself. (*Phän.* 53; or *Phen.* 123)

Such terms as "determines", "action", "development", and "movement" in the foregoing passages are indicative of the emphasis upon the mediation *process* as that which is actual in a philosophical proposition. The following additional points are to be especially noted as implicated in these passages: (1) The philosophical proposition functions in the determination of *original* and *concrete,* that is, *concretely particular,* meanings. (2) The subject and predicate of such a proposition (or judgment) at once come to be determined (and indeed in their concrete specificity *come to be*[7]), and *to be dis-*

---

[6] "Die Kategorien im 'gewöhnlichen' und im 'spekulativen' Satz", *Wiener Jahrbuch für Philosophie 1970,* pp. 9-37. See pp. 23f. The quoted passage is taken from the translation of this article by Gunther Heilbrunn in, *Contemporary German Philosophy,* Vol. 2 (University Park, Penn.: The Pennsylvania State University Press, 1983). So far as I have been able to determine, the passages quoted from this paper, so far as they reach, reflect in every detail the sense of Hegel's account in the Preface to his *Phän.*

For the final quotation within the citation, see *Phän.,* p. 49; or *Phen.,* p. 118. I have given attention to the developmental and cumulative import of dialectic, referred to here and following, in "Die Phänomenologische Methode Hegels und das Unbewußte", in, *Wiener Jahrbuch für Philosophie,* Vol. VI (1973), pp. 178-207, and more recently in Essay IX [which I was then completing]. See also "Hegel and a Philosophical Doctrine of God for Theism", *Indian Philosophical Quarterly,* Vol. V, No. 4 (1978), pp. 521-58.

[7] When Hegel's dialectic and the philosophical propositions that constitute dialectic are properly understood as not merely constitutive of thought but of actuality as well, the two — thought and actuality — being accents within an identity inclusive of both, it will be clear that the subject and predicate are actualized in their concrete specificity at the same time that they come to be discriminated. The immanent character of Hegel's dialectic, and for that matter of his proposition, within nature — a notion which has its parallel in Whitehead, who in effect made consciousness an unessential feature of (some) propositions — can be rendered clear from his statements of method.

Hegel's treatment of judgments in his *Enzyklopädie der philosophischen Wissenschaften 1830,* §§165-171, and Quentin Lauer's oveview of these §§ can be very helpful to understanding dialectic as immanent within actuality and knowledge. See Quentin Lauer, *Hegel's Concept of God* (Albany: SUNY Press, 1982), pp. 86-91.

Commensurate with the foregoing, equal weight is herein being accorded to the ideal and

criminated (*unterschieden*).[8] (3) These concretely discriminated aspects are neither abstractable from this concrete discrimination, nor is the discrimination abstractable from them. (This is the root of the ambiguity involved with talking about Hegel's method.) As concrete, this is to say, a particular discrimination and its mutually determined and mutually dependent discriminated aspects are integral. But one can go one step further.

Any particular discrimination is integral as well with other discriminations constitutive of any particular concrete identity. If this latter point is perhaps less than completely documented by the texts within the *Phän.* to which reference has been made, it will be suggested by "the object manifests itself in its development" if this assertion leads us to think of further determinations to be unfolded and more positively, perhaps, by the example of "roundness" which leaves one to consider that the table referred to, to be what it is, must surely possess other attributes as well.

Certainly Hegel's system, regarded in its entirety, can leave no doubt but that any particular identity is multiply discriminated or, otherwise said, that any particular identity is **constituted by** a multiplicity of discriminations.[9] The system of philosophical propositions, viewed in respect to the foregoing, indeed represents an attempt to explicate all of the discriminations constitutive of any particular identity, regarded in its completeness. "Philosophy.... is the process that creates its own moments in its course, and goes through them all; and the whole of this movement constitutes its positive content and its truth" (*Phän.* 39; or *Phen.* 105). Indeed such a system is complete by virtue of containing all of the discriminations needful for its explication.[10]

Although the term "mediation" is not used either in the above account of Hegel's philosophical or speculative proposition or judgment nor does it emerge prominently within the precise context of

---

the real aspects of actuality and of dialectic, and with this, the focus is upon the phenomenological basis of Hegel's enterprise, rather than upon the concept of a logical idea accorded some sort of status in itself.

[8] For Hegel's dialectical definition of *Unterschied*, of which *Unterscheidung*, which I am translating "discrimination", is a derivative, see Hegel's dialectic of identity and difference, *Logik*, II, pp. 26-40; or *Logic*, pp. 411-31.

[9] The following statement, understood in its context, will go some way toward documenting the point. "Philosophy.... is the process that creates its own moments in its course, and goes through them all; and the whole of this movement constitutes it positive content and its truth" *Phän.*, p. 39; or *Phen.*, p. 105.

[10] The preceeding three paragraphs are adapted from Essay I.

his explication of this methodological principle, it has been introduced prominently a few pages earlier (*Phän.* 21ff; *Phen.* 81ff), so that the process by which the subject and the predicate of a *spekulativen Satz* each in its radical particularity determines the other may be unmistakably identified as mediation. If the pages referred to are considered with care, it will be clear that "mediate" forms a contrast to "immediate", and that mediation consists in the dynamic self-movement that is the formal character of the development of the *Begriff*, an understanding reinforced by frequent subsequent usages throughout the major works which we have from Hegel's hand and, so far as I have been able to ascertain, nowhere contradicted.

The consideration of one additional example of a philosophical or speculative proposition will suffice for my present purposes of illustrating Hegelian mediation as a concept that is inextricably bound up with Hegel's method. This example has been chosen because it will subsequently assist me to develop the fundamental contrast that I see to obtain between the methods of Hegel and Whitehead. My example is Hegel's own, given as such near the close of the Introduction to his *Phän*. For the following to be seen to embody a philosophical proposition of the simplicity indicated in his account, the expression "consciousness of itself" may be read as the subject of the proposition and "consciousness of the object" may be read as its predicate.

> ...[C]onsciousness is, on the one hand, consciousness of the object, on the other, consciousness of itself; consciousness of what to it is true, and consciousness of its knowledge of that truth. Since both are the same consciousness, it is itself their comparison; it is the same consciousness that decides and knows whether its knowledge of the object corresponds with the object or not. (*Phän.* 72; *Phen.* 141)

In the paragraph following, we read,

> This dialectical process which consciousness executes on itself — on its knowledge as well as on its object — in the sense that out of it a new and true object arises, is prcisely what is termed experience (*Phän.* 73; *Phen.* 142).

From this concluding statement we may know that what Hegel here has explicitly in view by a *spekulativen Satz* is what we may most properly regard not as an abstract proposition but as a concrete judgment or proposition[11] ***constitutive of*** experience (and indeed of

---

[11] The allusion to a concrete proposition is intended to suggest the possibility that a discrimination immanent to the occasion of which it is constitutive may by virtue of being immanently uttered be accorded a status in addition to that of being an immanent judgment. For a working out of this idea, see, Essay IX.

actuality, as well). As a judgment, were it not that this might have an excessively Kantian ring (when, in fact, the position indeed goes *beyond* Kant), we might say that this **conditions** experience, as such, the principal point here being that there would be no self-consciousness and no world present *for* self-consciousness as actual apart from this judgment and its resultant discrimination or, to employ Whitehead's term, that I shall be showing to be somewhat parallel, its resultant "contrast" having conditioned such.

If the dialectic of knowledge and its object is internal to the constitution of experience, it will become progressively clear to the person who reflects on the matter that all of his dialectical categories are ultimately judgments **internal** to the constitution of experience, conditioning it prior to the fact of experience and prior to their being explicable as abstract.[12] This is even though, Hegel, in his concern to develop his dialectic *as a progression* often permits this consideration to fall out of focus (*Logik*, I, 30; or *Logic,* 49). Nonetheless, it represents the only position, so far as I am able to see, that is consistent with his concept of dialectic as a "deduction" (*Logik* I, 30; *Logic* 49) of what lies implicit within the Begriff from the standpoint from which he begins his dialectical exposition, and which needs only to be rendered explicit. This conclusion also finds support in the status of the dialectical mediation to which reference was made within the series that constitute Hegel's Begriff. These are themes that are played upon in various ways throughout his system.

I shall not undertake a full-scale justification of the point here, even though I think it needs systematic development as a corrective to a fairly common disposition current among some Hegel scholars to overlook the phenomenological aspect of his account or to level this down to some species of theory. I am at this point concerned to render clear that, should we be led to say that Hegel was formulating an inclusive theory constituted of generalizations of unrestricted scope, in the manner of Whitehead, this ought properly to form part of a *criticism* pointing to a failure in some degree on his part to accomplish what he set out to do and, as a result, ending up with a *mere theory*.

---

[12] See Essay II.

Quentin Lauer writes, "...what Hegel is looking for in his discussion of 'objectivity' is not a thought-process which 'from outside,' so to speak, *puts* the diverse moments of reality *together*, but rather a thought which *recaptures* reality's own process of *putting-itself-together* – is thought, to be sure. It is self-putting-together which makes sense only if the 'totalizing' (*Zusammen-schliessende*) concept is *not* merely the produce of subjective (finite) thinking." *Hegel's Concept of God,* p. 104.

I would hasten to add that I do not wish to take upon myself the burden of proof implicated with saying that he never theorized. It suffices for my present purpose to have pointed toward the phenomenological method that lies at the heart of his work, if we may trust his own account, the explication of the practice of which does not involve theorizing on the basis of a hypothetico-deductive model that within the present context we may properly associate with Whitehead's speculative philosophy and that we are today likely to associate with theory as such, and which uniformly is involved with predictions about the future, for which Hegel has no time.

On the basis of the foregoing, the following preliminary conclusion suggests itself. What Whitehead designated his speculative philosophy is a kind of "adventure of ideas". What Hegel sometimes desigated his speculative philosophy is a posterior analysis of concrete actuality after the fact of its concrescence — if I may use a Whiteheadian term — to which concrescence an adventure of ideas *may* have contributed. This concrete actuality is at once rendered concrete and *actually* known. The concern of the analysis — or it would be more appropriate to call it an analysis-resynthesis[13] — is to grasp (*begreifen*) its discrete phases as a unity and thus to comprehend the speculative function native to reason as immanent within actuality.[14]

---

[13] My use of the term "analysis-synthesis" is intended to reflect a taking account of the consideration that in philosophical usage, the function of neither half can ultimately stand alone. Each is an accent within an identity of meaning inclusive of both, as every Hegelian, apart from awaiting Quine's deliberations in the matter, which led him to a similar conclusion, should know. Neither can analysis ultimately yield any truth, in the Hegelian sense of that term, apart from a complimentary synthesis. The analysis of a term with a view to discovering the generic discrimination it contains must be followed by an experimental synthesis of its constituents. This may lead to the discovery of its similiarity to a discrimination in concretion, or even contribute to such a concretion.

[14] The suggestion that something in some way analogous to a process of concrescence is to be found in Hegel opens a complex issue that might be the theme of another paper. What is principally in view within the present context is that (not the grasping but) the analysis-*re*synthesis of Hegel's Begriff progresses from abstract to concrete, and that the concreteness — as a wholeness and unity of discriminations — in which it culminates on this account bears a certain similarity to the unity and wholeness of contrasts attained within the phase of full concrescence of Whitehead's 'actual occasion of experience'. Certainly there are marked differences in the methods by which, and the perspectives from which, the two philosophers go about reconstituting the occasion after the fact. In view of these differences, one might be tempted to suppose that Whitehead, in deliberately proceeding by the use of hypothetical reason, might be providing us with an account at least some part of which — perhaps the early or even middle phases of concrescence — are to be referred to a process *yet prior to* Hegel's *a priori* concrete actuality grasped as such, that in principle might not present themselves as phenomena and thus be accessible to a phenomenological account.

To be noted here is that such a proposal would almost certainly be presupposing, in opposition to Hegel, that not all of the discriminations required for the explication of an

4.

Were this all that is to be said, it would be difficult to imagine two more methodologically variant enterprises than Hegel's and Whitehead's versions of speculative philosophy. Is it possible despite this vast apparent difference to bring them into some kind of proximity, so that some overlapping functions might come into view? In raising this question, my cue comes from John B. Bennett, among others, who in "Husserl's Crisis and Whitehead's Process Philosophy"[15] in essence proposes that in opposing scientific materialism, Whitehead's approach is threefold: (1) through the exploration for compatibility of developments within physical science itself, (2) through a confrontation among and an ultimate harmonizing of, different perspectives upon reality, of which science is but one, (3) through an appeal to immediate experience.... "a more concrete analysis, which shall stand nearer to the complete concreteness of our intuitive experience" (SWM 66f).

My comments to follow, centering upon Whitehead's concept of prehension, principally pertain to the third of these aspects. Under this head, Bennett notes that "my experience *as I live through it at the present moment* is Whitehead's *paradigm case* of an actual entity." In a similar vein William A. Christian, noted two years earlier:

> In *Symbolism,* Whitehead is in the process of explaining what "the most concrete actual entity" is (S 27). He says that when we talk about any actual individual, such as a human being, "we must mean *that man in one occasion* of his experience" (S 27; italics mine). He goes on to claim that a proper name, such as "Julius Caesar", may have different meanings, but "the *most concrete* of all meanings [is] 'Caesar in *some one occasion* of his existence'" (S 27f; italics mine). He goes on to explain that Caesar the society is more abstract than Caesar the single actual entity.
>
> But perhaps Whitehead has changed his mind in *Process and Reality*....
>
> For example, Whitehead is discussing the traditional mind-body problem in PR pt. II, ch. 3. There he is trying to *explain* the *unifying control* exhibited by animals, "by reason of which we not only have unified behavior, which can be observed by others, but also *consciousness of a unified experience*" (PR 165; italics mine). He goes on to account for this

---

actual occasion are contained within it, thus relinquishing the notion that concrete actuality as *a priori* self-evident (if perhaps through assimilation) stands theory-free.

What I am unable to attribute to Hegel by way of rendering his Begriff **understandable within the context of a system of theoretical ideas** is in a way the very thing I am elsewhere proposing, but in such a way that its completeness and self-evidence is not thereby compromised. See my SC, pp. 224-26.

[15] John B. Bennett, "Husserl's *Crisis* and Whitehead's Process Philosophy", *The Personalist*, Vol. 56, No. 3 (Summer, 1975), pp. 289-300, see p. 291.

phenomenon in terms of his theory of "the presiding occasion of human experience" (AI 299).[16]

In the characterization of Whitehead's concept of prehension as this figures in the method he actually appears to be practicing in speculative philosophy, I shall from time to time note a parallel to Hegel's method as I have sketched it in, paying particular attention to his concept of mediation. In the course of the discussion and following, I shall take note of some differences pertaining to Whitehead's prehension and Hegel's mediation that seem not to be explained away, by calling attention to those aspects of Whitehead's "more concrete analysis, which shall stand nearer to the...concreteness of our intuitive experience."

For Whitehead, "The ultimate facts of immediate actual experience are actual entities, prehensions, and nexūs. All else is, for our experience, derivative abstractions." (PR 20) Further along he writes,

> The sole concrete facts, in terms of which actualities can be analyzed, are prehensions, and every prehension has its public side and its private side, Its public side is constituted by the complex datum prehended; and its private side is constituted by the subjective form through which a private quality is imposed on the public datum. (PR 290)

Parallel 1: Hegel's mediation and Whitehead's prehension are both alike immanent to the self-constitution of concrete actuality.

"For Berkeley's *mind*", he writes, "I substitute a process of prehensive unification" (SMW 102). This and several passages in what follows may at first seem to leave us with an unambiguous sense that prehensions in some manner make their presence felt in conscious awareness. But then Whitehead sometimes explains to us that he uses the term prehension for uncognitive apprehension, by which he means that apprehension may or may not be cognitive. (SMW 101)

> The cognitive perception of a sense-object is the awareness of the prehensive unification...of various modes of various sense-objects... (PR 103) ...[P]erception is cognition of prehension. The actual world is a manifold of prehensions; and a 'prehension' is a 'prehensive occasion': and a prehensive occasion is the most concrete finite entity, conceived as what it is in itself and for itself... (SMW 104f)

Following Whitehead's account "an actual occasion may or may not be conscious of some part of its experience." "Its experience is its complete formal constitution including its consciousness, if any" (PR 53). On this account the difficulty we face in evaluating the status of prehensions in knowledge arises from the fact that they

---

[16] William A. Christian, "John Lango, *Whitehead's Ontology*", *Process Studies*, Vol. 3, No. 1 (Spring, 1973, pp. 44-64, see p. 51).

may not be cognitive, hence may not be perceived.

> In Cartesian language, the essence of an actual entity consists solely in the fact that it is a prehending thing.... A 'feeling' belongs to the positive species of 'prehensions'. There are two species of prehensions, the 'positive species' and the 'Negative species'. An actual entity has a perfectly definite bond with each item in the universe. This determinate bond is its prehension of that item. (PR 41)

Indeed, positive prehensions are sometimes simply termed feelings by Whitehead (PR 220).

If the phrase, "I prehend therefore I am" is construed to pertain necessarily to noncognitive prehensions, and to cognitively perceived prehensions as well, in case in a given instance there are such — in other words also to consciousness, if any — it certainly lacks the quality of being indubitable that we associate almost automatically to the Cartesian *cogito*. This is because the status of prehensions in knowledge on Whitehead's account is curiously affected by the fact that noncognitive prehensions alone are accorded the status of being essential to the constitution of an actual occasion, *even though they are obviously ever being imaged to us by analogy to their cognitive counterpart that have only the status of being accidental.* This points rather decisively in the direction of the conclusion that Whitehead's method, as pertaining to the explication of the concept of prehension, is more accurately described as an imaginative reconstruction based upon analogies to first person *conscious* experience than as a phenomenological analysis of conscious experience and the world present for consciousness. This seems to rule out the possibility that we should expect to find more than a quasi-phenomenological aspect present in his method.

> **Parallel 2:** Hegel's mediations in a parallel manner may be explicitly or merely implicitly constitutive of the Begriff.

> [E]very prehension consists of three factors: (a) the 'subject' which is prehending, namely, the actual entity in which that prehension is a concrete element; (b) the 'datum' which is prehended; (c) the 'subjective form' which is *how* the subject prehends that datum.

> **Parallel 3:** "Subject" and (prehended) "datum" in the above may be read as parallel to "subject" and "predicate" being mediated to become accents within an identity inclusive of both within Hegel's philosophical or speculative proposition (or judgment).

In another context Whitehead portrays prehensions as analysable into five factors, rather than three. The effect may be to render the parallelism above suggested less apparent, but it seems not to detract from it, once perceived.

A feeling — i.e., a positive prehension — is essentially a transition effecting a concrescence. Its complex constitution is analysable into five factors which express what that transition consists of, and effects. These factors are (i) the 'subject' which feels, (ii) the 'initial data' which are to be felt, (iii) the 'elimination' in virtue of negative prehensions, (iv) the 'objective datum' which is felt, (v) the 'subjective form' which is *how* that subject feels that objective datum.

> Parallel 4: Something like a Hegelian synthesis might be made out of iv and v combined, in the above, which would reflect the fact that for Hegel knowledge is equally and at once both subjective and objective, these aspects being accents within an identity inclusive of both; to abstract either of these accents from the other would thus be equivalent to rendering both alike abstractions.

If for the present purpose we overlook the ontological character of Whitehead's concept of prehension previously mentioned, it is possible to make out something of the same notion in his speculative philosophy that I have just noted in Hegel's. A bit of reflection on the longer quotation near the beginning of §6 below (from PR 235) will render this apparent. Here one finds a reflection of Whitehead's view that the subjective and the objective poles of an actual occasion are mutually constitutive each of the other throughout the process of concrescence. What in Whitehead's case detracts from this imaging of the situation, however, is his notion that the ideal for knowledge is to be purely objective and that "objectification is abstraction" (PR 101) following upon the perishing of the occasion from which it is derivative. That objectivity on Whitehead's account is not achieveable within the living occasion as an accent within an identity of subject and the world as objective, as on Hegel's account, amounts to an anti-Hegelianism that I believe cannot ultimately be sustained.

What Whitehead says about intuitive judgments within the context of his treatment of propositions may be considered to provide some sort of additional support for what I should like to see strengthened or justified in his account with respect to this matter.

> Having regard to the fact that judgment concerns the subjective form of an impure feeling arising from the integration of simpler feelings, we note that judgments are divisible into two sorts, There are (i) intuitive judgments and (ii) derivative judgments. In an intuitive judgments the integration of the physical datum with the proposition elicits into feeling the full complex detail of the proposition in its comparison of identity, or diversity, in regard to the complex detail of the physical datum. The intuitive judgment is the consciousness of this complex detailed comparison involving identity and diversity. Such a judgment is in its nature correct. For it is the consciousness of *what is*....
>
> In an intuitive judgment the subjective form of assent or dissent has been restrained, so as to derive its character solely from the contrasts of the datum. Even in this case, the emotional force of the judgment, as it passes

into purpose, is derived from the whole judging subject. (PR 192)

The intuitive judgment is thus a consciousness of *what is*. Can such a judgment on Whitehead's account rise to consciousness apart from the objectification associated with abstraction and the perishing of the occasion? If so, and if knowledge requires equally a subjective and an objective dimension — as I think we must surely conclude to be the case on Whitehead's as well as on Hegel's account — then its physical data would be objectified also within the living occasion and not merely upon its perishing. Whitehead to my knowledge never refers to objectification as taking place within an actual occasion prior to its perishing. On the contrary, as I previously noted, for him "Objectification is abstraction." This seems to place the issue, which is too complex to be considered in detail here, and which so far as I have thus far been able to make out may well be undecidable, at least in doubt. If so, I suspect that in any case we will be forced at least to conclude that subjective forms in general and intuitive judgments in particular on Whitehead's account provide a necessary substratum *within the living occasion* for consciousness (as well as for knowledge) *subsequent to its perishing*. If so, then what must here be recalled as a qualifying factor is that following his account it is not judgments but propositions that are possible candidates for knowledge, which on his account is public, and "A proposition emerges in the analysis of a judgment; it is the datum of the judgment in abstraction from the judging subject and from the subjective forms" (PR 193).

That Whitehead affirms the possibility of intuitive judgments within the living occasion that are "correct" but that such correct judgments nonetheless cannot rank as knowledge (which designation he reserved for abstractions!), may be taken to indicate how radical a shift of emphases and indeed of substantive doctrine — ultimately, as I intend to show, traceable to a marked difference in method — would be required to render his position compatible with that of Hegel with respect to this central issue.

5.

Jerome Ashmore has observed concerning the concreteness of a prehension,

> Actual entities may be analyzed in an indefinite number of ways, but most analysis will lead to abstractions, for example, awareness, private sensations, emotion, purpose, appearance, or causation. Whitehead calls such abstractions "Ghosts of the old 'faculties', banished from psychology, but still haunting metaphysics" (PR 27). But abstraction may be avoided by

an analysis of an actual entity into prehensions. Prehensions maintain concreteness and yet have a subjective form and aim, and may involve emotion, purpose, valuation, and causation (PR 28). Intrinsically prehensions are not atomic and can be divided into other prehensions and combined into other prehensions, yet "a prehension, considered genetically, can never free itself from the incurable atomicity of the actual entity to which it belongs."[17]

As though to emphasize the latter point, Whitehead writes, "A feeling cannot be abstracted from an actual entity entertaining it..." (PR 221).

> **Parallel 5:** In like manner, the mediation of a philosophical proposition, following Hegel's account, is concrete, its meaning being, of course, contextual, its context being the Begriff, i.e., all that is concretely actual.
> Also to be noted, the subject and predicate of Hegel's philosophical proposition have been seen to be radically particular, on which account the discrimination that is formed in their being mediated is non-abstractable. In a similar manner, as we may conclude from the foregoing, also a particular prehension within Whitehead's account is not abstractable from the context of the occasion within which it is prehended.
> Hegel and Whitehead attach different meanings to "concretely actual", seeing that for Hegel concrete actuality must contain not only a prehending but a self-conscious (*com*prehending) subject.

It was noted in the above that prehension may involve emotion, purpose, valuation, and causation. Supposing that all of these types of relations may be constitutive of a single 'occasion of experience', how then are they organized?

> In a process of concrescence there is a succession of phases in which new prehensions arise by integration of prehensions in antecedent phases. In these integrations 'feelings' contribute their 'subjective forms' and their 'data' to the formation of novel integral prehensions, but 'negative prehensions' contribute only their 'subjective forms.' The process continues till all prehensions are components in the one determinate integral satisfaction". (PR 26)

It seems most natural to consider the manner of organization of progressive inclusion within more inclusive prehensions by reference to Whitehead's concept of a contrast. "What are ordinarily termed 'relations' are abstractions from contrasts. A relation can be found in many contrasts; and when it is found, it is said to relate the things contrasted." (PR 228f)

> '[C]ontrast' — as the opposite of incompatibility depends upon a certain simplicity of circumstance; but the higher contrasts depend upon the assemblage of a multiplicity of lower contrasts, this assemblage again exhibiting higher types of simplicity. (PR 95).

---

[17] Jerome Ashmore, "Diverse Currents in Whitehead's View of Time," *Process Studies*, Vol. 2, No. 3 (Fall, 1972), pp. 193-200, see pp. 197f.

Although I have not found a text that seems quite certainly to import this, I think we may very nearly conclude from the two passages last cited that in the case of even the simplest prehension, a contrast exists between the datum (as a feeling) and the subject (or subjective feeling) prehending that datum.[18]

> Parallel 6: Insofar as this conclusion is justified, a parallelism exists between Hegelian discriminations (philosophical propositions) and Whiteheadian contrasts throughout the various levels and orders of actuality to which each of the two concepts respectively pertains. Each is concretely actual within the context of the whole of actuality, the one as mediated (or as being mediated [?]) and the other as being prehended. This is of course not to imply an identity of Hegel's discrimination and Whitehead's contrast, although it does seem plausible to say that in the case of every Hegelian discrimination, a Whiteheadian contrast obtains between the discriminated aspects and that in the case of every Whiteheadian contrast, contrasting aspects have been or are being discriminated. This seems to require qualification by what I shall have to say about Whitehead's theory of knowledge as "purely objective", set over against Hegel's phenomenology of knowledge as ever equally subjective and objective.
>
> To be noted just here is that the parallelism noted extends to Whitehead's proposition only insofar as it embodies a realized (prehended) multiple contrast. Insofar as Whitehead's proposition is "a hybrid", being in part only potential and in this sense transcending actuality, it is radically dissimilar to Hegel's philosophical proposition.

The following citation from Whitehead will complete my observation concerning how the relations constitutive of an 'occasion of experience' are organized.

> The term 'multiple contrast' will be used when there are or may be more than two elements jointly contrasted, and it is desired to draw attention to that fact. A multiple contrast is analysable into component dual contrasts. It is one contrast, over and above its component contrasts. (PR 229)
>
> Parallel 7: The manner of organization by successive inclusion within a multiple contrast finds its rather precise parallel within the progressive inclusion in series of dialectically determined discriminations constitutive of Hegel's Begriff.

6.

The following passage, although perhaps one of the densest in PR, seems to me especially important for showing us how Whitehead works back from the "public" side of prehension in abstract and objective knowledge to the reconstitution of their "private" side, also by reference to their subjective form, which, as I shall further be

---

[18] I understood Charles Hartshorne, in a personal conversation in late Aug., 1983, in Montréal, to indicate agreement with me with respect to this point.

noting, we may presume, in the case of a given 'actual occasion of experience', that is, an occasion that is conscious, in some manner and degree to be a datum of conscious awareness.[19] Here again an awareness of subjective form *in general* is assumed to be a datum of consciousness in terms of which he can proceed to show us what he means by prehension. Especially the second paragraph is of crucial importance here, although this is to be considered within the context of what follows.

> The prehensions in disjunction are abstractions; each of them is its subject viewed in that abstract objectification. The actuality is the totality of prehensions with subjective unity in process of concrescence into concrete unity.
>
> There are an indefinite number of prehensions, overlapping, subdividing, and supplementary to each other. The principle, according to which a prehension can be discovered, is to take any component in the objective datum of the satisfaction; in the complex pattern of the subjective form of the satisfaction there will be a component with direct relevance to this element in the datum. Then in the satisfaction, there is a prehension of this component of the objective datum with that component of the total subjective form as its subjective form.
>
> The genetic growth of this prehension can then be traced by considering the transmission of the various elements of the datum from the actual world, and — in the case of eternal objects — their origination in the conceptual prehensions. There is then a growth of prehensions, with integrations, eliminations, and determination of subjective forms. But the determination of successive phases of subjective forms, whereby the integrations have the characters that they do have, depends on the unity of the subject imposing a mutual sensitivity upon the prehensions. Thus a prehension, considered genetically, can never free itself from the incurable atomicity of the actual entity to which it belongs. The selection of a subordinate prehension from the satisfaction — as described above — involves a hypothetical, propositional point of view. (PR 235)

Parallel 8: With reference to the final sentence in the above quotation, I can have no doubt but that it can be shown that the selection of a particular mediation within Hegel's Begriff for explication in abstraction involves a hypothetical point of view. This I would judge to be the reason that he resorts to ordinary as well as to philosophical propositions — especially in prefaces, introductions, illustrations, and addenda — to render his dialectical expositions more readily understood.[20]

---

[19] The pains taken by Whitehead in informing us how it is possible to reconstruct the process of concrescence of an 'actual occasion of experience' from objectified remains suggests that, his assertion about the intuitive grasping of *"what is"* in the passage cited from PR, p. 192, notwithstanding, he does not find himself in a position to affirm that such a judgment arises to consciousness within an 'actual occasion of experience' while it is yet living and prior to the objectification of the occasion *that for him seems to come only after the fact*.

With reference to the above quotation, I have already called attention to the status of (purely) objective knowledge, which, following Whitehead's account is a product of abstraction following upon the perishing of the occasion. Especially in consideration of the fact that we must allow that the subjective form of an actual occasion may lie completely below the threshhold of consciousness or that the occasion may stand free of any association with consciousness (it being nonetheless construed by analogy to conscious prehensions, as was previously considered), this must on the present account figure very large. (1) Following Hegel's account, the mediation of a discrimination, whether explicit or merely implicit, and its grasping (*Begreifen*) *all take place within, and constitute features native to,* the Begriff in its radical completeness.[21] (2) It is thus that Hegel's absolute knowledge, as this grasping, can be equally subjective and objective, as on his account true objectivity must be.

The contrast can be carried even further. Whitehead maintained that "you cannot think without abstractions" (SMW 85), even going so far on one occasion as to assert that "Philosophy is explanatory of abstractions and not of concreteness" (PR 20). Whatever one is to make of this assertion,[22] a couple of years previously he would seem to have made it clear that he was not denying that philosophy has as one of its tasks to give an account of concreteness.

> I hold that philosophy is the critic of abstractions. Its function is the double one, first of harmonising them by assigning to them their right relative status as abstractions, and secondly of completing them by direct comparison with more concrete intuitions of the universe, and thereby promoting the formation of more complete schemes of thought. It is in respect to this comparison that the testimony of great poets is of such importance. Their survival is evidence that they express deep intuitions of mankind penetrating into what is universal in concrete fact. Philosophy is not one among the sciences with its own little scheme of abstractions which it works away at perfecting and improving. It is the survey of sciences, with the special objects of their harmony, and of their completion. It brings to this task, not only the evidence of the separate sci-

---

[20] My reasoning that here pertains will be found reflected especially in Essay IX and HdS. esp. chap. 2, "Der Bereich des Hypothetischen und Potentiellen: Erfassen, (Begreifen), Erbschaft, Gesellschaften, und Vorgänge". Regrettably, I have not as yet found an opportunity to consider closely how much of this can be documented as present in Hegel's works.

[21] See pp. 33-37.

[22] Charles Hartshorne has noted, "Whitehead had rhetorical gifts, indeed he has passages of great prose poetry; but not all his uses of this gift were adequately subordinated to his main purpose, which was to be as definite and clear as possible". *Insights and Oversights of Great Thinkers* (Albany: SUNY Press, 1983), p. 319.
See pp. 33-37.

ences, but also its own appeal to concrete experience. It confronts the sciences with concrete fact. (SMW 126f)

This seems to say, among other things, that philosophy confronts the sciences with concrete fact, i.e., the deep intuitions of mankind penetrating into what is universal in concrete fact, and that we are especially indebted to the great poets for bringing these deep intuitions to our attention. If I correctly understand Whitehead in regard to this matter (a proper treatment of which would require another paper), like Heidegger, he points us toward the great poets of mankind for the last word, to the taking account of whose deepest intuitions the philosopher can only aspire. If this is a fair reading, then in point of emphasis at least, he is quite far from following Hegel's example of according to philosophy the status of transcending and containing the meaning of art. This is to say, to the extent that the latter is grasped at all, following Hegel's account, this is in mediated concepts. To state the matter more precisely with respect to the present context, Hegelian mediation — also when considered merely as a "philosophical concept" in an external sense and apart from having regard to its being the dynamic principle immanent within creation (and hence also as the dynamic principle of the poet's *coming to his deeper insights*) — is at work also in our grasping the insights of the poet, which grasping is an indispensable aspect of the grasping of "the truth that is the whole", and as such conceptual, following from Hegel's inclusive use of this term to signify all that is mediated. Obviously, for several reasons intrinsic to the foregoing exposition, a function that is at all closely parallel cannot be attributed to Whitehead's prehension.

In all of this it is to be noted that while for Whitehead the term "thought" is applicable to our activity in the use of abstractions, for Hegel also the *grasping* (*das Begreifen*) of concrete actuality is an activity of thought — perhaps one that is not ultimately completely separable from thought as such — and this does *not* depend upon an appeal to abstractions.[23]

---

[23] Were this not to be the case, this would be tantamount to making the Hegelian Begriff out to be less than inclusve of all that is concretely actual; and this would rob us of a standpoint from which the arising of consciousness can be accounted for in a situation in which there is no possibility of theory even seeming to play a role.

The proposal that concreteness is grasped apart from abstractions is not of course intended to suggest that its analysis-resynthesis after the (concrete) fact proceeds apart from abstraction.

In a letter dated Aug. 25, 1983, John Cobb notes of Hegel and Whitehead: "One uses thought to include all the activities of experience, the other, only certain high grade ones." Granting Cobb's principal point, this of course leaves us to decide whose criteria for judging which thoughts are "high grade" are to be counted the most appropriate.

Following from Whitehead's disposition in these matters, our knowledge as such is found to be radically pluralistic, and needs to counter the loss of concreteness by philosophy conceived as the critique of abstractions. As william S. Sullivan has noted, in characterizing this position,

> Philosophical thinking attempts to reunite in our awareness the elements of perception separated in the process of becoming conscious. This is the sense in which philosophy is the "critic of abstraction". It shows the apparently discrete atoms of our experience to be aspects of an emerging environment whose members are constituted by mutual interaction, much as in the example of an ecosystem. Concrete experience at its most primitive is the strong felt sense of togetherness in the drive toward satisfaction. Abstract awareness at the point of "disinterestedness," as in the classical "theoretical" attitude, is in danger of losing the sense of the relevance of the parts in their aim at synthesis. At this stage the task of philosophy is to renew the sense of connection. Whitehead called this rationalization, "the partial fulfillment of the ideal to recover concrete reality within the disjunction of abstraction". (MT 170f)[24]

Hegel as well proposes that philosophy has the critique of abstractions as a central task. Far from supposing that the elements of our awareness are separated in the process of coming to consciousness, however, he found consciousness to be precisely an aspect of concrete actuality as a realized whole that, indeed, cannot present itself in discrete isolated aspects but only in its integral unity, i.e., as "the truth which is the whole". Thus consciousness as an accent within an identity of subject and world-present-for the subject is inherently a unity that knowingly sets derivative abstractions from this whole in their place, calling them what they are.

The difference just noted may serve to illustrate that Hegel and Whitehead are indeed methodologically poles apart. We may begin to perceive just how far apart when it is observed that Hegel's system is in essence a system of internally related philosophical (or speculative) propositions, internal to the actuality they collectively constitute.[25] Whitehead's system of speculative philosophy, in being insistently hypothetical, is a system of exclusively external relations.

---

[24] William S. Sullivan, "Two Options in Social Theory: Habermas and Whitehead", pp. 87f.

[25] I have elsewhere proposed that both of these languages can be brought relevantly to the explication of an actual occasion conceived as external relations being rendered internal. In dual complimentary roles, I conceive it to be the task of the language of internal relations to explicate concrete actuality from an actual perspective internal to some actual occasion regarded as typal of a commensurable society of such occasions, and the task of the language of external relations to prepare possibilities for concrescence from a hypothetical perspective, which trades upon relations between actual occasions and aspects of actual occasions conceived as externally related. See SC, Book II, Part III.

Even when it ventures analogically to talk *about* concreteness (which Whitehead, despite protestations to the contrary, does indeed *seem* to undertake to do), we should not be led to suppose that his language is supposed to reflect the concreteness attributed to his subject matter. He is thus very far from undertaking to explicate reason, i.e., the concretely actual, "in its own native form", as Hegel undertakes.

The foregoing judgment as it pertains to Whitehead seems to me to stand even when the force of the following trenchent interpretative remark by F. Bradford Wallack is taken into account, although it does suggest a limit to its applicability:

> The relations among occasions, being made within them, are an integral part of their internal nature. That is to say, relationships are inevitably internal: "...the concept of internal relations requires the concept of substance as the activity synthesizing the relationships into its emergent character" (SMW 180).[26]

That all *actual* relations on Whitehead's account are ultimately — i.e., after negative prehension has done its work and an actual occasion achieves full concrescence — internal, however, cannot consistently be construed to render his *talk about them* internal. After all, no mere theory could on the basis of his account be a part of an actual occasion at full concrescence. As a matter of fact, propositions as Whitehead conceives them, being in part merely potential (and insofar hypothetical), are never fully internal to an occasion at full concrescence. Rather, they transcend it. This is what distinguishes them *fundamentally* from Hegel's philosophical propositions.

Having said this, I must hastily add two disclaimers: I do not wish to imply that Hegel had no need to employ also ordinary propositions to guide his readers into the meaning of philosophical propositions. Indeed he makes such frequent use of such that uninitiated readers are sometimes mistakenly led to suppose that these constitute the substance of his doctrine, because they are readily grasped apart from having the slightest understanding of the subtilities of his method. Neither do I wish to imply that Hegel was fully successful in the execution and employment of his method. To treat this sort of question as pertaining either to Hegel or Whitehead would take us far beyond the manageable scope of the present essay.[27]

---

[26] F. Bradford Wallack, *The Epochal Nature of Process in Whitehead's Metaphysics* (Albany: State University of New York Press, 1980), p. 49.

[27] See my RAtP and TCMM.

7.

The parallels I have drawn between Hegel's mediation and Whitehead's prehension seem to me collectively to constitute a parallelism of functions of these two concepts, and, considered in context, to show each to be the central dynamical principle of the system to which it belongs. My attempt to seek out Whitehead's appeal to a "more concrete analysis, which shall stand nearer to the complete concreteness of our intuitive experience" has served this effort, even though what results seems not to provide a basis for affirming that the method he in fact practiced justifies a phenomenological adjunct to his declared method.

To pursue the point in a thoroughgoing way would require the development of a set of criteria as to what minimally constitutes a phenominology, which in view of current variations in usage might not be easy. The following four points — the first two being a restatement of points already made — are intended to indicate that there would appear to be insufficient reason for pursuing the issue this far. (1) Although the case is somewhat ambiguous, strictly speaking it seems necessary to consider Whitehead's characterization of the role of prehension as analogical (to conscious apprehension) rather than phenomenological. (The two do seem to be mutually exclusive.) (2) His theory of knowledge as purely objective, following abstraction, seems to place an additional difficulty in the way of assigning status to the prehending subject of an actual occasion — the "I", and not merely the me — commensurate with the self-certainty that may be suggested by the phrase "I prehend therefore I am" regarded as a parody on the Cartesian *cogito,* and that is a datum of consciousness. This is a point that the Personalists were raising already in the early decades of the century. Without wishing thereby to make a case for a narrowly conceived philosophical idealism, it is nonetheless difficult to see how a phenomenology can proceed on the basis of less than such a self-certain "I". (3) If elements of a kind of account of consciousness may be found, e.g., in his detailed portrayal of the stages of concrescence — which I have not taken up — these strike me as far more of the order of theoretical interpretation of phenomena of consciousness than an account of them as present to consciousness. Otherwise, he seems frequently to be trading upon analogies to what in a very general way is familiar to consciousness. (4) Whitehead cannot be said to provide us with a phenomenology in a proper sense because, as pertaining to method, he moves from the hypothetical to the actual, and this not merely in search of a point of beginning that lies beyond theory. A defense of this point would commit one to showing that (i) also when portraying the process of concrescence as a complex of interrelated prehensions, his language is purely theoretical, with the effect that methodologically he does not move from a portrayal of narrow types, much less of particular,[28] felt prehensions in rendering an account of how this transition takes place, (ii) this order, understood in the manner indicated, is alien to phenomenology as such, and (iii) it is possible today to reverse this order. This latter is especially in consideration of the fact that I am skeptical as to the prospect of justifying a claim that Hegel brought this off, although he would seem to have apraoched success nearly enough to render the prospect attractive.

These points contribute to the conclusion that Hegel and Whitehead are doing quite different and indeed ***very nearly mutually exclusive*** things. Hegel is doing a phenomenology of concrete actuality — of subjective mind and what is present *for* the subject — and Whitehead is doing an adventure of ideas that at once presupposes self-consciousness and the world present for self-consciousness, the very thing Hegel is working out. In his airoplane flight of speculation Whitehead doubles back to cover some of the same terrane from a quite high altitude, from which the concrete particularity of a phenomenological account of the type of Hegel's is not what is of interest This is, rather, part of an adventure of speculative ideas that have not yet settled down to become the concrete actuality that Hegel wants to reconstruct after the fact by running through its constitutive discriminations as they are concretely mediated. Hence Whitehead is only correct in informing us ever and again that what he is doing is merely forming a hypothesis. Hegel on the other hand, purports to reconstitute the given. Both claims have to be taken with complete seriousness, it seems to me, to make much sense of what the claimant is undertaking; I find no reason for considering one to be either more or less innocent or suspect than the other. Especially important as one considers enterprises so different in character is not to conflate them, or to level either down to the other. Seeing that

---

[28] See Essay III.
Whitehead's method in combination with his concept of prehension leaves open a place for accounting for the creativity of particular individuals and cultures. Hegel's method, as embodying his concept of mediation, when certain correctives are introduced, affords us the opportunity to fill this open place with particular concrete contents, seeing that anything that we might call creativity on the basis of his account would have to be personal and cultural in character. Moreover, the open place for accounting for the creativity of particular individuals and cultures left by Whitehead's account, when this is filled in, is filled in by historical consciousness. The pre-history of philosophy can no more be rushed than can its history, of course; the open place left by Whitehead's account nonetheless awaits filling. This is one of the senses in which Whitehead's theory awaits concrete actualization.

we seem to have no good reason to believe that the language of one is even translatable into that of the other, an effort at rendering the two enterprises compatible seems potentially more productive than comparison with the idea of establishing a translation manual. There are parallels aplenty to be found, of which I have noted a few, but identities are scarce or non-existent.[29] I find the area of compatibility and complementarity between the results of these quite different undertakings manifold and impressive, however, and *not less because they are fundamentally different.*

---

[29] I am in agreement with Hartshorne when he portrays Hegel and Whitehead as providing us with a contrast, as when he says, "It is hard to imagine Whitehead having much communication with Hegel. He is not a Hegelian, even a radically revised one, but rather a radically revised Leibnizian...". Charles Hartshorne, *Insights and Oversights*..., p. 313. This is although, considering how different our receptions of Hegel are, this agreement may be merely a coincidence. Also, I think he makes the contrast out to be somewhat stronger than it actually is, perhaps by virtue of a failure to take into account the fact that also Hegel was importantly infuenced by Leibniz. See, e.g., Joachim Christian Horn, *Monade und Begriff: Der Weg von Leibniz zu Hegel* (Vienna and Munich: Verlag R. Oldenbourg, 1965). This may be an important part of the reason that Hartshorne construes Hegel's method, so far as I have been able to determine, with complete disregard to the dynamic dimensions of negation and mediation (which I regard as the affirmative counterpart to negation), and is on this account left with a dialectical logic as static as mathematical logic but wanting in the precision that in this type of logic could stem only from the *dynamic* (eventlike) relations obtaining within and between its constitutive categories. On this account it cannot seem strange that such parallels as I have mentioned between Hegel's mediation and Whitehead's prehension should have escaped his notice, and that he should suppose Whitehead's concept of prehension to have been as original a contribution to the history of philosophy as he believes it to be when he writes, "in principal prehension is the whole story of causality and freedom. I know of nothing like this extraordinary generalization in the entire history of philosophy previous to Whitehead", Charles Hartshorne, "Whitehead's Revolutionary Concept of Prehension", *International Philosophical Quarterly*, Vol. XIX, No. 3 (Sept., 1979), p. 256.

To trace out the list of confusions that follow from this error of oversight as Hartshorne undertakes to record the insights and oversights of Hegel would require a paper, which, considering the respect with which I regard the achievements of this remarkable scholar, who in my estimation as a metaphysician has considerably outstripped his mentor, Whitehead, would not be easy for me to write, especially in consideration of the fact that commenting on Hegel is certainly one of his more trivial philosophical avocations, carried over from a time when, if one wrote in English, taking pot shots at Hegel, like praising motherhood and democracy, was one of the safest indoor sports in which a philosopher could indulge himself. (In this regard, I find Hartshorne's performance less stupifying than that of Karl Popper and a dozen other prominent contemporaries whom I might name.) I will therefore limit myself to commenting on only two of Hartshorne's objections to Hegel that are traceable to this oversight and that I find unjustified or at least very stilted.

1) Hartshorne writes, "What is missed both by Hegel and common sense is the vast 'ocean of feelings' that Whitehead discerned as the message of Wordsworth's poetry" (*Insights and Oversights*..., p. 199). Had he understood Hegelian mediation in its dynamic dimension, he might have perceived that all of the types of feelings mediated within Hegel's account of subjective spirit are dynamically connected, also, e.g., with the aesthetic, religious, and philosophical concepts the mediation of which is set forth within the dialectic of absolute spirit. I have written a number of papers that in one way or another touch upon this theme, including, "Hegel's Phenomenological Analysis of Mental Disease and Freud's

Having prepared a number of essays that play upon aspects of this theme, I shall restrict myself to suggesting only one area of complimentarity here. Hegel I think has gone a good way toward showing

Psychoanalysis", *International Philosophical Quarterly*, Vol. VIII, No. 3 (1968); "The Theory of Mental Derangement and the Role and Function of Subjectivity in Hegel", *The Personalist*, Vol. 49, No. 4 (Autumn, 1968); and "Die phänomenologische Methode Hegels und das Unbewußte", *Wiener Jahrbuch für Philosophie 1973*, Band VI.

When Hartshorne finds that "what Hegel seems to miss entirely is the wealth of microstructures that are quite blurred in our sensing" (*Insights and Oversights...*, p. 198), he seems to me to indicate a want of clarity with regard to how Hegel's dialectical method proposes to proceed from concretely particular to concretely particular types of mediation, leaving theorizing about mass groupings to side comments or (more largely) to other types of accounts (of which he gives only a dialectical account). In addition he seems in effect to be criticizing Hegel for not theorizing about what lies beyond anything that could possibly fall under descriptive phenomenology and which we can only approach in theories of the expansive sort that typify Hartshorne's own work and that of Whitehead, both of whom apparently believed do not need to be made answerable to methodological restrictions of this sort.

2) Hartshorne objects that "Because Hegel does not see the true relations of universal and particular, he cannot properly relate philosophy and religion, or philosophy and art" (*Insights and Oversights...*, p. 209). Although there are aspects of Hegel's conception of the relations of art, religion, and philosophy that I should not wish to defend, and others that I can accept only with qualifications, the fact that Hartshorne has failed to perceive the dynamic meaning of Hegelian mediation seems to me to have blinded him to the character of the mediation of particularity and individuality, on the one hand, with (concrete) universality, on the other — one of the most central mediations within the Hegelian system, as I trust I have rendered sufficiently clear in the foregoing — with the fulfillment of which the system climaxes, as it were, in spiritual individuality. The priority of concrete universality, and of the concrete universality of the particular, might, I suppose, trouble Hartshorne even if he had a grip on the dynamic dimension of Hegelian mediation, but in this case, at least, he could not be led to associate Hegel with a vague, unresolved, or somehow static relation between particularity and abstract universality.

Hartshorne writes, "Those who learn much from Hegel tend never to become really clear or rigorous thinkers" (*Insights and Oversights...*, p. 205). This kind of remark has always both worried and challenged me. Dialectical logic is a logic proximate to organic, and indeed to lived, processes. Aspiring to be the forms of such processes, it stands proximate to something Hartshorne might hopefully be tempted to call the logic of prehension. Interestingly enough, it embodies a kind of *logic of perfection* in that also an occasion conceived along Hegelian lines achieves completeness. Where conceived as the logic of a concretely lived actuality, I can see no way of avoiding the conclusion that it is more or less radically particular in orientation — even though precisely this radical particularity can only be explicated contextually and in terms, as well, of its concrete universality. So conceived, it is precise and rigorous insofar as it conforms to the particular it is supposed in a certain way to image. There would seem to be no reason for believing that, pursued disinterestedly, it need be less precise and rigorous than mathematical logic at its best. Even so, apart from a dialectical exposition of concreteness being understood from very nearly the same perspective from which it was made, it may seem not only vague but fanciful and, viewed, through the eyes of a mathematician, perhaps even annoyingly so. The logic of such an exposition does not, however, exclude mathematical logic from doing its work, once the occasion has been reconstituted after the fact that can serve as a suitable field — I would prefer to say, as a language sufficiently proximate to "concrete language" (See Essay IX) — worthy of its application. Even though it thus presents us in some way and degree with something like an ego-centric or community-centric predicament — also when we acknowledge the social character of our self-consciousness and world present for self-consciousness —, it seems not too much to say that it *is* the logic of concreteness, *par excellance*. This is the case, at least,

us how a philosophy of concreteness must proceed. Whitehead has perhaps gone as far toward showing us how possibilities are prepared for (possible) concrescence. The first undertaking requires a perspective internal to some one actual occasion inclusive of all that is actual, in other words, an actual perspective. The other requires a hypothetical perspective, from between or above a plurality of such occasions, which is of course not actually (but only hypothetically) possible. Both undertakings consider essential functions of human reason, and each proceeds with language uniquely suitable to its task. To make Whitehead's effort over into an attempt at a philosophy of concreteness against his will would be a mistake. To cast Hegel's brand of speculation as an adventure of hypothetical ideas seeking to approximate concrete actuality would be only slightly less wrong-headed.[30]

---

if we are to think historically and operate in terms of a doctrine of continuous creation. Mathematical logicians attempting to settle issues of philosophcial method have all too often escaped into their own particular kind of precision in some artificial language, and to have only a vague notion as to what this might *concretely* come to, i.e., how this might match up with the language of a particular occasion or a more or less homogeneous — but nonetheless far from uniform — historical epoch. The capacity to manipulate abstractions with precision is a powerful gift, when one knows *and comprehends philosophically* the concreteness from which they are abstracted. Dialectical logic — aspiring to be the logic of creation — can assist us to achieve a somewhat comparable precision in knowing the latter. Even when it is granted that either type of logic can be conceived in some sense to "include" the other — if, as I suspect, each (contextually considered) has indeed proven to be an accent being mediated within an identity inclusive of both — observing the distinction remains essential to clarity and rigor of thought, especially with respect to the kind of conversation that Hartshorne has here enjoined. If Hartshorne reflected any degree of clarity about this distinction at all, he would be in a better position to judge whether or not people who have learned much from Hegel do or do not tend to become clear and rigorous thinkers. As things stand, I find his polemic in this vein to be shockingly unworthy of so able a mind.

In a world that may be about equally divided between philosophers predominantly oriented, with respect to method, toward dialectical logic and philosophers predominantly oriented toward mathematical logic, the issue that lies here can hardly be a trivial one. The kind of extreme polarization that one commonly finds today with respect to this distinction, especially in the West, that is here exemplified by Hartshorne, may indeed be *the most significant single negative contribution that philosophers presently make to the cause of understanding and of peace in the world.*

[30] This essay was prepared in response to Charles Hartshorne, "Whitehead's Revolutionary Concept of Prehension", *International Philosophical Quarterly*, Vol. XIX, No. 3 (Sept., 1979). It contains the elaboration of remarks that I made in the discussion that followed an oral presentation by Hartshorne under a similar title at Louvain, Belgium, Nov. 10-12, 1978.

Postscript

In making his shift from the philosophy of science — which term in his usage I would prefer to render "theory of science" (*Wissenschaftstheorie*) — to metaphysics and cosmology, Whitehead, if the matter is considered with care, virtually overlooked two hundred years of methodological development in first philosophy. That he could have been so presumptuous testifies to the excitement that centered around theories attached to the natural sciences in the early decades of this century, upon which his essentially precritical ruminations are to a significant degree based. The idea of one day being in possession of a completed science of physics, complimented by the reductionist ideology, has been an intoxicating one, that even today is sometimes experienced as heady wine. Even though Whitehead was known to have disavowed the first of these notions and no more than a qualified form of the second is to be found reflected in his work, he wrote in such a way as to be open to their force and they formed prominent features of the context of thought within which he worked, that counted importantly in his reception. In addition to having learned to be more skeptical about affirmations of the supposed finality of comprehensive theories in the particular sciences that we have in the past somehow accustomed ourselves to think of as "hard", we have in recent decades become somewhat more aware that the critical movement in philosophy that had its inception in Kant was very much more than the temporary accommodation to the incommensurabilities of Euclidean geometry and Newtonian physics with developments of science and knowledge in the modern period that Whitehead (along with many others) would appear to have supposed it to be, to be rendered dispensable as soon as our conceptuality has been put more nearly in systematic order.

It seems not to be too late to observe that the limits of reason pertain also to the status we may properly assign to theories in the particular sciences and not merely to forthrightly metaphysical assertions. This is not to suggest that these limits can longer be supposed to be such that we ought never to exceed them, but that we ought to be aware of them when we do so and to know that we have in a certain way distanced outselves from the concrete actuality that we actually and concretely know. My suggestion is that it is these limits, in the final analysis, that render it inevitable that Whitehead's type of speculation presupposes as its basis and foundation a phenomenology of mind and world that it should be the enduring, inexhaustible, and principal task of first philosophy to render explicit. The parallelisms I have noted provide a background for the suggestion that this foundation can most naturally be provided by a phenomenology that in its most basic character is Hegelian. In my opinion an essentially precritical system of the type of Whitehead's must today finally owe what credibility it can claim to its degree of commensurability with such a phenomenology, which by all possible means to the greatest extent possible ought to be not merely intuitively felt or willingly presupposed but rendered philosophically explicit — and thus *made public* — as well. This is to express the view that to whatever extent the impulse to pursue the goal of a scientific first philosophy is to be correctly guided, it will issue in philosophical presuppositions *being rendered explicit* (not merely as theories but) *as phenomena.*

V

A HEGELIAN CRITIQUE OF PEIRCE*

1.

Had I been permitted time to justify the position I shall be pressing as entirely implicated, at least, in the philosophy of Hegel, this paper might have been entitled, "Hegel's Critique of Peirce". This should have served to symbolize that the philosophy of Hegel is very much living today, for anyone who might have some residual doubt. Even in this case, however, it might have been safest to leave it "A Hegelian Critique of Peirce", seeing that, in point of emphasis, at least, the standpoint from which I shall level my critique at Peirce will be somewhat removed from Hegel, if in a direction which it seems plausible to believe that he might have taken, had he been confronted with the climate of opinion in American philosophy of the present time, to which Peirce contributed.

I view Hegel as a critical philosopher working within the tradition of critical philosophy which had its inception in Kant. To be a critical philosopher in Hegel's sense implies, in my understanding, a commitment to three principles.[1] (1) First and foremost it means that one must provide a sound basis for drawing a clear line of distinction between what one considers to be concretely actual and what is to be counted as merely hypothetical or conjectural. The very possibility of scientific inquiry requires this. Commensurate with this requirement, the first task of philosophy is the exposition of the concretely actual, which must serve as a touchstone for judging what is merely hypothetical or conjectural. (2) It requires, in addition, that no aspect of the concretely actual be regarded as in

---

* This paper was initially published in *The Owl of Minerva*, Vol. 13, No. 1 (Sept., 1981), following its having been presented to the Charles Sanders Peirce Society, Oct. 5-7, 1978, at Bloomington, Indiana.

[1] The summation of critical principles to follow is a close paraphrase of my treatment of this theme in CHSS.

itself absolute. Thus, no single discrimination may of itself legitimately be regarded as absolute. Conversely, every discrimination, even when dialectically exhibited and defined, is relative to what it concretely discriminates and to other discriminations. (3) Only concreteness as fully discriminated, all of its aspects in unity, can lay legitimate claim to being absolute. To be critical, then, requires as well that one reflect in one's philosophy a capacity to take account of all aspects of the concretely actual as they present themselves in their integral unity. In respect to this point, to be uncritical is to fail to be discriminating.

Central to the critical dimension of Hegel's thought is his conviction, which he maintained to be native to reason as such, that the concretely actual is self-evident. Along with this it is self-constitutive, completely determinate, absolute, and free. These are interrelated concepts, the definition of any one of which must involve an appeal to some, at least, of the others. What is self-evident is absolute, and this by virtue of containing within itself all that determines it. This self-determination amounts to being free. But it is the characteristic of being self-evident, which must here be emphasized.

There is no literal counterpart in German to the English term, "self-evidence". I have chosen this term as a translation for Hegel's "die Selbstgewißheit der Vernunft" (for which there is no native counterpart in English). Self-evidence as I shall employ the term will reflect not only the self-certainty of reason, however, but Hegel's concept of presuppositionlessness as a property of concrete actuality as well. Presuppositionlessness I understand to express negatively what is expressed affirmatively as the self-certainty of reason. This is to say, reason, following Hegel's account, achieves certainty of its own autonomy precisely when, and to the degree in which, in its comprehension of the concrete it is freed from a dependence upon presuppositions. The concrete being discriminated (*unterschieden*)[2] and being in fact constituted a unity and wholeness of discriminations, is grasped with self-certainty precisely when, and insofar as, it is comprehended in terms of discriminations (*Unterscheidungen*) internal to itself. The concepts implicated with these discriminations do not need to be brought from some external source to the exposition of the concretely actual because the discriminations which constitute it also constitute reason. This is to say, reason is identical with its object, even while discriminated from it, the discrimination being one of those constitutive of both.

Two additional remarks will suffice to establish the background

---

[2] ***Conceptual*** presuppositionlessness is here in view.

for the critique to follow. (1) I shall presuppose the pluralistic interpretation of Hegel, who made individuality the highest achievement of his dialectic, rather than the interpretation of him as an all-too-simple-minded monist, in the generally dominant mood of the Anglo-American tradition, the Personalists excepted.[3] What Hegel in the final pages of each of several of his principal works, including the *Phen.* and the *Logic*, refers to as the falling asunder of the unified Begriff into its constituent dialectical moments,[4] I shall refer to as the perishing of an actual occasion. Although he certainly might have been more fully explicit in regard to what is here implicated than he was, it seems to me that at least some appreciable justification for this venture of interpretation can be made out. I shall be introducing some additional Whiteheadian terms, as well. Allowance being made for the possible exception of the reference to perishing, however, my intent will be to restrict these to an entirely Hegelian import. Thus, for Hegel's Begriff as fully determined, i.e., as rendered fully concrete, I shall substitute the term "fact", by which I shall mean a complete or absolute fact. (What Whitehead called a complete fact was not complete, by reason of not including a conscious understanding subject along with the discrimination of subject and world, and by virtue of the circumstance that it could contain error.[5]) This terminological switch will side-track some old caricatures and assist me in other ways.

My critique of Peirce consists in three points, which I shall first list in shorthand form, and then consider at greater length, each in turn.

1) The theory-futuristic oreintation of pragmaticism, epitomized in the pragmaticist maxim, represents an abandonment of critical principles.

2) Within Peirce's semiotics, concreteness should be (re)presented by Thirdness rather than by Firstness.

3) A concept of concrete universality — which is amenable to be-

---

[3] Following Hegel's account, nothing can be universal apart from at the same time being particular (or individual), and vice versa, these concepts being accents within an identity inclusive of both.

[4] For my analysis of these "anti-climactic passages" see "Hegel's Altar to the Known God", *Hegel-Studien*, Beiheft 11 (Bonn: Bouvier, 1974), pp. 219-30; and "Hegel's Justification of Christianity: Serious or Sophistry?", in *The Southern Journal of Philosophy*, Vol. XIV, No. 4 (winter, 1976-77), pp. 413-30. The latter first appeared in a French translation in *Archives de Philosophie*, Chantilly, 1976.

[5] On Hegel's account, a concretely actual occasion can contain no error, which has to do exclusively with abstractions.

ing rendered self-evident — should be substituted for abduction and related notions in Peirce, which fill a necessary function within his 'system' but which are speculative in a pre-critical sense.

2.

With respect to the first criticism, it will be well to have the pragmaticist maxim before us: "Consider what effects that might conceivably have practical bearing you conceive the object of your conception to have. Then your conception of those effects is the WHOLE of your conception of the object". (*Collected Papers*, 5.422)

Whitehead once wrote, in a moment of rare insight which, so far as I have been able to discover, he did not follow to its logical conclusion in his own philosophy:

> ...[I]t is hardly an exaggeration to say that the very meaning of truth is pragmatic. But though this statement is *hardly* an exaggeration, still it is an exaggeration, for the pragmatic test can never work, unless on some occasion — in the future, or in the present — there is a definite determination of what is true on that occasion. Otherwise the poor pragmatist remains an intellectual Hamlet, perpetually adjourning decision of judgment to some later date. (PR 181)

Peirce's pragmaticism in effect projects Kant's transcendental unity of reason onto a future in which, if we take the optimistic view, it is gradually to be realized in the form of theories which are with increasing probability justified.[6] For the pragmatist following his maxim, facts, rather than being accorded a certain reliable status, are reduced to future expectations. More than that, this is a receding future at which we seem never to arrive. Should one attempt to follow this exclusively theory-oriented aspect of Peirce's philosophy, taken by itself, one would be in want of a *presently* viable concretized concept of fact adequate to render the concept of theory meaningful by virtue of being discriminated from fact. But it is the self-evidence of precisely those facts which we all experience as facts within the horizon of our present experience, and as compelling apart from what may occur in the future and apart from any philosophical argument or discipline, of which a philosophical account needs to be given, in order to provide a meaning-yielding contrast to, and a foundation for, theory.

---

[6] The work of K.-O. Apel would appear in some measure to share this characteristic of Peirce's pragmaticism. See, e.g., *Die Erklären: Verstehen, Kontroverse im transzendental pragmatischer Sicht* (Frankfurg a/M: Suhrkamp, 1979).

Science can have no other basis than facts, which function as absolute. There can be no compromising this principle. If we wish to provide a philosophical basis for science, we must therefore explicate the character of an absolute fact. The myth that there are no theory-free facts is *just a myth,* seeing that facts are precisely concrete actualities, insofar as the latter are theory-free.[7]

In a non-trivial sense of grasp, we in fact grasp a here and how concretely actual occasion which, by virtue of including within itself all of the discriminations needful for its explication, is self-constituting. One of these discriminations, and one which happens to be universal to all occasions, is that between the subject and his (or her) world. A practical outcome of the fact that this particular discrimination (with others) is constitutive of any actual occasion is that the understanding and interpreting subject of an occasion is interior to it. Were the understanding and interpreting subject outside of the occasion (as for Whitehead) we should never be able to explicate the self-evident character which facts self-evidently possess. Rather, we should find them merely somehow to be there *for* the subject, fundamentally alienated from them, and even finding, as Whitehead does, that they can contain unresolved error, *as though they were merely theories.*

This is not intended to deny that theories may contribute to the concretion of new fact. What is important is that a fact, once concretized and before its being sundered into its constituent aspects, is grasped in its purity as theory-free.

A concretized fact is a system achieved as the climax of a concrescence. This system is "the truth which is the whole". This is a discriminated, or better, a *being-discriminated,* whole; and it is on this account that as a mediating process, it can be grasped. The world of objectivities (as well as the subject itself) are first grasped as integral aspects of the mediation process within which they are actualized, before they are abstracted. This system is most conveniently conceived as a unity and wholeness of discriminations, including, of course, subject-world.

The particular discriminations constitutive of an actual occasion are explicable through an analysis-synthesis of the occasion in *spekulativen Sätzen* (speculative propositions or judgments, hereafter *spek. Sätzen,* or in the singular, *spek. Satz*). The subject and the predicate of a *spek. Satz* are each accents within an identity inclusive of both. In the concrescence of an actual occasion this identity of

---

[7] The philosopher's concept of concrete fact is to be rendered sufficiently rich deductively to account for its functioning as such. See p. 67, n. 19.

discriminated aspects presented in *spek. Sätzen*, which, as well as constituting concrete language, are immanent in nature, is actualized, or better, is **being actualized**. An actual occasion — or an absolute fact, together with its sub-identities (or sub-facts) — is a system of discriminated aspects, at the climax of the concrescence of an occasion. This realized system — or, better, this system *being realized* — is the truth which is the whole, rescued from an absurd old age in which freedom has spent itself into actuality, by perishing.

The subject and world within an actual occasion are accents within an identity inclusive of both. Both are aspects of the reflexive act, within the occasion and prior to its perishing, when they are rendered abstract results, detached from the lived process of their becoming. (The allusion again is to the falling asunder of the unity of the Begriff.)

Peirce is rescued from some of the force of this criticism by the fact that there are other dimensions of his thought than pragmaticism. If his pragmaticism had been rendered compatible with these other dimensions he might perhaps have been more nearly rescued. In affirming that we perceive relations (5.55), for example, he seems at least sometimes to have assumed that the truth of these relations as perceived does not await a future verification. This suggests that something, however attenuated, is here and now self-evident. More importantly, perhaps, following his "scholastic realism", Peirce maintained that "general principles are operative in nature" (5.101). "... [T]he uniformity with which stones have fallen has been due to some active general principle..." (5.100). Peirce, in arguing that, when I drop a stone, I directly know this principle, would seem at times to have been referring to a here and now knowledge and not merely to a future expectation. Furthermore, when a man reasons, following Peirce's account, he thinks he is drawing a conclusion which would be justified in every analogous case (5.108). One might wish to interpret this as meaning that here and now knowledge of a law of nature *also* affects my expectation of what will obtain in the future, rather than giving it the pragmaticistic interpretation, following which I must await the future before certifying my knowledge in the present instant. All of these indicated suggestions of a direction which I should like to have found justified in Peirce seem withdrawn as possible interpretations when he declares that all abductive inferences, presumably including the direct perception of relations, are after all no more than suggestions as to what may in the long term future prove to be true.[8] Before returning to this finally more dominant side of his thought, which from a Hegelian perspective bears all of the earmarks of a cop out, permit me to pursue the earlier line of thought with regard to abduction. In his third cotary proposition under "Pragmatism and Abduction," Peirce writes:

> On its side, the perceptive judgment is the result of a process, although of a process not sufficiently conscious to be controlled, or, to state it more truly, not controllable and therefore not fully conscious. If we were to subject this subconscious process to logical analysis, we should find that it terminated in what the analysis would represent as an abductive inference, resting on the result of a similar process which a similar logical analysis would represent to be terminated by a similar abductive inference, and so on *ad infinitum*. (5.181, 3rd. cotary)

Had Peirce consistently pursued this line of thinking, and not made remarks elsewhere calling the veracity of sense certainty into question, he might well have arrived at a concept of self-evidence adequate to form a meaning-bestowing contrast with theory, which might have saved his pragmaticism from the fate of Hamlet. In what immediately follows the above citation, however, he develops further another direction which is in this regard unhelpful:

> This analysis would be precisely analogous to that which the sophism of Achilles and the Tortoise applies to the chase of the Tortoise by Achilles, and it would fail to represent the real process for the same reason. Namely, just as Achilles does not have to make the series of distinct endeavors which he is represented as making, so this process of forming the perceptual judgment, because it is subconscious and so not amenable to logical criticism, does not have to make separate acts of inference, but performs its act in one continuous process. (5.181, 3rd cotary)

I am of the opinion that the separateness of occasions of perception is intrinsic to their character as self-evident and not merely a character of their logical analysis, as Peirce proposes. In this respect Whitehead had the correct view, along with Hegel, if I have not translated his account of the breaking asunder of the unity and wholeness of the Begriff (together with certain other suggestions which point in this direction) too freely in calling it the perishing of an occasion. This is although, as I noted, Whitehead failed to percieve an actual occasion to be the complete fact that it must be to be self-evident.

3.

I come now to the second criticism of Peirce. Within his semiotics, concreteness should be (re)presented as Thirdness, rather than as Firstness. By way of fleshing out this criticism, I would add that

---

[8] A consideration of these notions in their earlier development and apart from being made completely subservient to Peirce's pragmaticism might have resulted in a different emphasis. See the essay immediately following.

concreteness, being constituted by not merely one but, minimally, by a plurality of discriminations, must involve the unity of a plurality of Thirdnesses.

Peirce does not make frequent reference to concreteness. Where he does make reference to it, so far as I have been able to discover, it is considered to be Firstness. Thus he remarks that the *first* and simplest character to be noted is something present to the mind in its *presentness*.

> The present is just what it is regardless of the absent...utterly ignoring anything else. Consequently, it cannot be abstracted (which is what Hegel means by the abstract) for the abstracted is what the concrete, which gives it whatever being it has, makes it to be.... The first category, then, is Quality of Feeling, or whatever is such as it is positively and regardless of ought else.[9] (5.44)

The issue which lies here is rendered fussy due to a certain ambivalence respecting the possibility of directly perceiving firstness, as such, and apart from a contrasting feeling. His nominal position, however, would seem to have become that there is no perception of Firstness or Secondness apart from their being mediated to Thirdness (5.90).

> Not only does Thirdness suppose and involve the ideas of Secondness and Firstness, but never will it be possible to find any Secondness or Firstness in the phenomenon that is not accompanied by Thirdness (5.90).

This position is most readily rendered systematically integral with other concepts of his mature thought, including the notion that perception is always the perception of a relation. This being the case, it would seem that, even when the matter is considered within his own frame of reference, within which relations are, after all, counted as real, Peirce might well have accorded to concreteness the status of a unity and wholeness of thirdnesses. We should then have been presented with the possibility of conceiving truth as a wholeness of internal relations after the model of a complex Thirdness as an inclusivity of Firstness and Secondness, which, although they contain a past rendered actual in the present and an anticipated future, are presented in the here and now as self-evident.

From a Hegelian perspective this would have eliminated concreteness as Firstness in Peirce, which it is possible to view as a ghost of *"the thing in itself"* that has frequently been attributed to Kant, despite his avowals that he has laid that ghost to rest. The primary con-

---

[9] Peirce ultimately comes to adopt the same position as Hegel, when he acknowledges, or in effect, that Firstness as such is only to be arrived at by abstraction from a mediating process.

sideration is that Firstness is known only in its being mediated. If it is found to be actual only as a pole of a mediation process, then this process is what should count as concretely actual, and the positing of a fixity behind this is a multiplying of entities beyond necessity.

4.

The third criticism pits the concept of concrete universality against abduction, on the grounds that the former is required by critical principles while the latter remains, at most, something merely intuited — if this term, with deference to Duns Scotus, from whom Peirce drew inspiration, may here be invoked — or necessary to be presupposed as intuited to account for facticity, and, at least, as a way of regarding theories.

This presupposes of course that the two concepts function in some degree analogously within the respective conceptualities to which they belong. They appear to function analogously in three principal respects. (1) Each of these concepts stand for a speculative function maintained to be native to reasoning activity and indeed to consciousness as such. In this regard it is to be observed that Hegel's concrete universal is constituted by *spekulativen* Sätzen, his principle by which meaning (and ultimately, if the matter is properly persued, being, as well) is generated. And for Peirce, "Abduction is the process of forming an explanatory hypothesis. It is the only logical operation which introduces any new idea..." (5.171). (2) In addition, the concepts share a commonality of function with regard to the central role each plays in the becoming or achieving of facticity. The concrete universal is 'a' concrete fact, and one ultimately implicating a complex of equally concrete sub-facts. Although Peirce denies the absoluteness of all here and now facts, at least in so far as we have in mind something more than a Firstness, as such — in principle unaccessible — what most nearly approaches reliable here and now facticity is derived by abduction. If account is taken of his understanding of perceptual judgments as relational in character (relations being real) and as "the extreme case of abductive inference", the parallelism of functions which I am indicating is rendered especially clear. (3) A third commonality of function consists in that, following Peirce's second cotary proposition, he writes, "...perceptual judgments contain general elements, so that universal propositions are deducible from them...". Acknowledging that the term "general" in this usage is synonymous with "abstractly universal" — precisely what one would anticipate, seeing that Peirce had no concept of universality suitable to an account of internal relations

— the function here alluded to finds its parallel in Hegel's concrete universal, from which abstractly universal propositions are derived, following the breaking asunder of the occasion into its (abstract) component stages of development.

As was noted, Peirce regarded perceptual judgments as the extreme case of abductive inference. This is even though, unlike other types of abductive inference, they stand beyond criticism. Their standing beyond criticism is not, I think, to be understood to mean that they may not be in error. At least if one is to make systematic sense of Peirce, one must conclude that in the final analysis he intended to exempt nothing from the need to be rendered certain in the future as a condition of its being regarded as true. "The abductive suggestion comes to us like a flash. It is an act of insight, although of extremely fallible insight" (5.171). "Abduction merely suggests that something *may be*" (5.171). It may be safely ventured that it is precisely the extension of this fallibility principle even to immediate sense perception which renders the concept of abduction commensurable with the maxim of pragmatism:

> If you carefully consider the question of pragmatism you will see that it is nothing else than the question of the logic of abduction. This is, pragmatism proposes a certain maxim which, if sound, must render needless any further rule as to the admissibility of hypotheses to rank as hypotheses, that is to say, as explanations of phenomena held as hopeful suggestions ...(5.195)

Viewed in this way, Peirce's theory of abduction does nothing to rescue his philosophy from the fate of Hamlet and of pragmatism.

He writes, "Abduction consists in studying facts and devising a theory to explain them. Its only justification is that, if we are ever to understand things at all, it must be in this way" (5.145). If we can overlook Peirce's seeming obsession to assimilate all knowledge to theory, as though concreteness can never make itself known except in theories *about* it,[10] we must agree with this statement as far as it reaches. This is not, however, very far. Far from being the explication of the self-evidence of a thing — which, pursuing a generous interpretation, Hegel in his concept of presuppositionlessness at least goes very far toward achieving — his concept of abduction is little more than a name of a mystery. Peirce should nonetheless be credited with according this mystery *the dignity of a name,* and this at a time when the critical impact of Hegel's concept of a concrete fact had hardly really begun to be assimilated to philosophy, least of all

---

[10] The skepticism thus engendered is countered by according the status of actual to the mediating *process,* a standpoint commensurate with a semiotic in which Firstness and Secondness are mediated to Thirdness.

within the Anglo-American tradition. *To accord a name to a mystery, however, is very far from according to it a systematic explication, following a specified methodological principle.*

I understand the concrete universal to be a system of internal relations such that every aspect and element has the status of being something essential to, and present throughout, the system. To call attention to the pluralistic dimension in Hegel, I have been calling this an actual occasion.

Not only is the whole more than a simple sum of its parts; in addition, the whole of the system is implicated by the character of every part. Every part and aspect is thus concretely universal throughout the system. This means that every part and aspect might appropriately be construed as determining every other part (and the whole) in its progressive determination, i.e., in its process of concrescence. Otherwise stated, freedom being equally in nature (the world as objectively presented for the subject) and on the side of the subject, either might be said to have determined the occasion, as well as to have been determined by it.

It is most convenient and most in keeping with critical principles to conceive the constituents of an actual occasion as discriminations. For one reason, we may readily accord ontological as well as epistemological status to discriminations. With each discrimination are implicated the discriminated aspects. The actuality of both — a discrimination and the discriminated — however, consists less in a realized result of discrimination than in the mediating process by which discrimination is *being* achieved. It is the process which is grasped as concretely actual, before the occasion perishes. Of course certain discriminations are apparently ever being concretized anew,[11] in every new occasion.

Concrete living language (as opposed to a traditional language), as an accent within an identity of language and being, expresses the actuality of this process. Concrete language, as consisting of *spekulative Sätze*, being an accent within an identity of language and being, is **presentational**. Traditional or ordinary language is constituted of abstractions derived from living occasions which have perished, and is thus *representational*.

An upshot of this for a semiotic is that within every Thirdness as concretized within a here and now concretely actual occasion, is contained a Firstness and a Secondness, and that this concretization is not subject to error. When upon the perishing of the occasion these

---

[11] Hegel's dialectical circle consists in a return to abstract immediacy, its point of beginning, with which is implicated the necessity for a recurrence to the entire circle of dialectical determinations.

moments come to be abstracted from one another and hypothetically combined in new ways — whether spontaneously or in the interests of deliberately performing an experiment — these combinations may or may not prove capable of contributing to new concrescences. If this remark is considered with care, it will be seen that a basis has now been provided for asserting that authentic perception — by which is meant perception which is concrete[12] and which is not in part constituted of abstractions — like the actual occasion which constitutes it, is in principle self-evident. In a language which more nearly approximates that of Peirce, the abduction which constitutes authentic perception is rendered no longer subject to proof or correction in some remote future (as though some derived standard could suffice for this), even while abduction as a recombination of abstractions derived from past occasions continues to retain the status of being a mere suggestion. Such a suggestion becomes the more interesting, of course, the more proximately it stands related to what is *actually* concretized. Should it be concretized, and following this, successively *reconcretized*, it may pass into the commonplace and be no longer of any great interest, except to persons learning a language and philosophers interested in unearthing the in principle presuppositionless character of the concretely actual and that history that *actually* determines us and our world in living occasions.[13]

What is perceived within one occasion will of course not be what is perceived within another, even when considered in respect to constitutive explicit discriminations.[14] And the truth which is the whole of one occasion will of course not correspond entirely with the truth which is the whole of another, subsequent occasion. Facts — even as abstractly conceived by taking massive averages — have in this situation no certain tenure. And concrete facts are of the instant. Even so, there is an acknowledged standard against which to hold theory which can account for our designating it such. And there is fact in terms of which to judge error, which on this account — even on the philosophical account of it — may not be said to have been derived merely by pre-critical rumination. The sole source of error,

---

[12] By "perception which is concrete", I refer, of course, to "the Truth which is the whole," the subjective side of which might be abbreviated, "perceptual-conceptual-intentional comprehension".

[13] Abduction might thus be accommodated within a critical perspective.

[14] Constitutive discriminations are viewed, not generically, but with reference to their concrete particularity, commensurate with a concretely specific account of concreteness. They are thus subject to what I call this "the settlement effect". See SC, pp. 237f.

following critical principles, consists in what we do with abstractions, and most particularly in substituting them for concreteness.

Abstract universality is *derived*. It pertains to the *plurality* of actual occasions. It presupposes concrete universality within a single occasion or series of such. Furthermore, the affirmation of the abstract universality of a concept is necessarily in certain respects hypothetical and can never in a particular case be affirmed with certainty. It involves *a predication about the future — a liberty which Hegel on critical principles never permitted himself.* I have elsewhere argued that abstract universality must be a hypothetically entertained notion, also because *no one could at any time have gotten outside of that some one occasion which constitutes him and his world at a given instant, seeing that an actual occasion includes within itself all that from its perspective is actual.*[14a]

5.

The intended force of the foregoing critique notwithstanding, Peirce develops a number of themes within his philosophy, in ways which render them available for appropriation within a critical philosophy of concreteness apart from being rendered subordinate to pragmaticist principles, *which cannot pass through this narrow gate.* His approach to such themes as "general principles operative in nature", "whenever a man reasons he thinks he is drawing a conclusion such as would be justified in every analogous case", and "in perception two objects really do...react upon one another", are cases in point. And there is much else in the conception and practice of the semiotic enterprise, based upon its three categories — recognized also by Peirce as having a fundamental kinship with the Hegelian triad — which lends itself to being so considered.

[14a] By the insertion of this reference to history as actual within the present for the second printing of this article, I wish to suggest a reconception of *Wirkungsgeschichte* which stands more proximate to Hegel than does that of Gadamer, from whose usage the term is adapted, and which is commensurable with my reconception working from Hegel. See Hans-Georg Gadamer, *Wahrheit und Methode* (Tübingen: J. C. B. Mohr, 1965), pp. 283ff.

VI

WAS HEGEL 'ACCORDING TO PEIRCE' "THE GREAT VINDICATOR" OF PRAGMATICISM?*

If Hegel was not actually guilty of the principal error that Peirce found him to have committed, we should be compelled to view him, if we take Peirce at his word, as "the great vindicator" of pragmaticism. My intention is to show that Hegel is not guilty of this error, and, following, to show that from Hegel's point of view to be regarded as a vindicator of pragmaticism could only have been an unwanted "honor". In addition, I propose to show that, certain restrictions being observed that take account of what it seems plausible to believe would have been Hegel's principal objections to pragmaticism, the possibility of what a Hegelian could recognize as a scientifically pursued semiotic based upon Peirce's doctrine of the categories is not on this account rendered unthinkable.

I

At the close of "What Pragmaticism is," an article published by Peirce in *The Monist* in 1905, he wrote,

> The truth is that pragmaticism is closely allied to the Hegelian absolute idealism, from which, however, it is sundered by its vigorous denial that the third category (which Hegel degrades to a mere stage of thinking) suffices to make the world, or is even so much as self-sufficient. Had Hegel, instead of regarding the first two stages with his smile of contempt, held on to them as independent or distinct elements of the triune Reality, pragmaticists might have looked up to him as the great vindicator of their truth. (CP, 5.436)

In another context Peirce remarks that

> ...the doctrine of Hegel is to be commended who regards Category the Third as the only true one. For in the Hegelian system the other two are only introduced in order to be *aufgehoben*. All the categories of Hegel's

---

* Translated and revised for the present context from "War Hegel nach Peirce 'der Begründer des Pragmatizismus'?"

> list, from Pure Being up, appear to me very manifestly to involve Thirdness, although he does not appear to recognize it, so immersed is he in this category. (CP. 5.80)

I propose to show that Peirce, by virtue of a false understanding of Hegel's concept of *Aufhebung*, erred in his interpretation of "Thirdness" in Hegel and that Hegel's position with respect to what Perice called Firstness, Secondnesss, and Thirdness in various ways stands very much closer to Peirce's own position than he would seem to have perceived. More specifically, Thirdness according to Hegel as much as according to Peirce *includes* Firstness and Secondness. It was then equally true for Hegel and for Peirce that every actuality is ever also a case of thirdness, with which are implicated Firstness and Secondness, which are necessarily constitutive of Thirdness. This is because also according to Hegel's concept of *Aufhebung*, Firstness and Secondness, as they pass over into Thirdness, retain their integrity as discriminated Aspects. What Peirce apparently failed to understand was that Hegel's concept of identity is one which contains discriminations within itself, or better, that it is **constituted** of discriminations and discriminated aspects. Before I give a more adequate account of these matters, I wish to introduce another aspect of Peirce's relation to Hegel as a further specification of his position with respect to this theme.

> 90. I have thus far been intent on repelling attacks upon the categories which should consist in maintaining that the idea of Reaction can be reduced to that of Quality of Feeling, and the idea of Representation to those of Reaction and Quality of feeling taken together. But meantime may not the enemy have stolen upon my rear, and shall I not suddenly find myself exposed to an attack which shall run as follows:
> We fully admit that you have proved, until we begin to doubt it, that Secondness is not involved in Firstness nor Thirdness in Secondness and Firstness. But you have entirely failed to prove that Firstness, Secondness, and Thirdness are independent ideas for the obvious reason that it is as plain as the nose on your face that the idea of a triplet involves the idea of pairs, and the idea of a pair the idea of units. Consequently, Thirdness is the one and sole category. This is substantially the idea of Hegel; and unquestionably it contains a truth.
> Not only does Thirdness suppose and involve the ideas of Secondness and Firstness, but never will it be possible to find any Secondness or Firstness in the phenomenon that is not accompanied by Thirdness.
> 91. If the Hegelians confined themselves to that position they would find a hearty friend in my doctrine.
> But they do not. Hegel is possessed with the idea that the Absolute is One. Three absolutes he would regard as a ludicruous contradiction *in adjecto*. Consequently, he wishes to make out that the three categories have not their several independent and irrefutable standings in thought. **Firstness** and **Secondness** must somehow be *aufgehoben*. But it is not true.

They are in no way refuted nor refutable. Thirdness it is true involves Secondness and Firstness, in a sense. That is to say, if you have the idea of Thirdness you must have had the ideas of Secondness and Firstness to build upon. But what is required for the idea of a genuine Thirdness is an independent solid Secondness and not a Secondness that is a mere corollary of an unfounded and inconceivable Thirdness; and a similar remark may be made in reference to Firstness.

In Hegel's language the concluding sentence immediately above affirms that the first and second moments of the Begriff constitute necessary conditions of its synthesis. One might add that the principal objection to Hegel in the passage above quoted might be summarized under two points. (1) According to Hegel, the *Aufhebung* (sublation) of Firstness and Secondness into Thirdness is equivalent to their being done away with. Peirce maintains that Firstness and Secondness shall be retained as distinct elements of the threefold character of reality. This is bound up with the insight that it will never be possible to find a Secondness or Firstness in a phenomenon that is unaccompanied by Thirdness. (2) All of Hegel's categories according to Peirce should involve Thirdness, and he believed that for Hegel this was not the case. This corresponds to Peirce's conviction that representation (as Thirdness) as such requires the influence of Firstness and Secondness. In other words, Firstness and Secondness correspond to relations internal to every representation. This understanding quite naturally did not for Peirce exclude the possibility that a representation, as a case of Thirdness, could stand in a relation to another representation either in a relation of Firstness, Secondness, or Thirdness. Were the possibility that a representation might stand in an external relation to another representation — relations that we consider as secondary with reference to those of Firstness and Secondness contained by each representation — to be disallowed, it would be impossible to frame any new hypotheses, i.e., hypotheses that had not previously been concretized. Neither would it be possible to introduce new meaning into a term.

Talk of internal and external relations will doubtless seem strange to some readers of Peirce, seeing that that thinker, in his attempt to view concreteness as Firstness,[1] of which little more could be said than that it is a feeling of being present, found no need for this discrimination. One might doubtless interpret the future truth and

---

[1] "The present [Firstness] is just what it is regardless of the absent.... utterly ignoring anything else. Consequently, it cannot be **abstracted** (which is what Hegel means by the abstract) for the abstracted is what the concrete, which gives it whatever being it has, makes it to be.... The first category, then, is quality of Feeling, or whatever is such as it is positively and regardless of ought else." (CP, 5.44)

actuality that Peirce anticipated in his pragmaticistic maxim as a system of internal relations — Thirdness and a unity of Thirdnesses — that are to be arrived at in a remote future. This concept is, however, very far removed from a present concreteness as Thirdness and as an (absolute) system of Thirdnesses that at once condition and constitute actuality and consciousness of actuality. It is concreteness in this latter sense that Hegel undertook to explicate as a basis for theory (that, however, is itself not a theory).

This is not to be understood to suggest — also not for Hegel — that concrete actuality contains no anticipation of the future, but that it does not await the future in order to be and to be certain of itself, i.e., self-evident.

With an eye to Whitehead, whose teaching concerning concreteness — especially in his concept of a concretely actual occasion — is interpretable in part as a further development of Peircean beginnings, in preference to concreteness, I prefer to refer to the ***process of concrescence*** as that which is actual. This process, moreover, for its brief temporal duration, will be considered to be absolute, and this by virtue of achieving a coherent system of internal relations (inclusive of all that is actual) and because, by the perishing of the occasion the way is left open for varying successor occasions that are, each in turn, in like manner absolute.

The principal point that is here to be kept in mind, however, is that for Peirce anything thinkable is a representation and therefore an instance of Thirdness. Hegel as well as Peirce saw this. This is, for example, indicated by the fact that each of the relatively abstract concepts that lay on Hegel's dialectical route in the explication of Absolute Spirit contains Firstness and Secondness. Peirce apparently failed to recognize or understand this dimension of Hegel.

The principal error in Peirce's understanding of Hegel consisted in his failure to take note of Hegel's technical usage of his term *Aufheben*. This is although this usage by Hegel is consistently made clear and explicit from the appearance of his first principal work in 1807 until his death in 1831. It will suffice to quote from Hegel's *Remark* concerning his use of this term at the close of the first chapter of his *Logic*:

> ***To sublate***, and the ***sublated*** (that which exists ideally as a moment), constitute one of the most important notions in philosophy. It is a fundamental determination which repeatedly occurs throughout the whole of philosophy, the meaning of which is to be clearly grasped and especially distinguished from ***nothing***. What is sublated is not thereby reduced to nothing. Nothing is ***immediate;*** what is sublated, on the other hand, is the result of ***mediation;*** it is a non-being but as a ***result*** which had its origin in a being.

'*To sublate*' has a twofold meaning in the language: on the one hand it means to preserve, to maintain, and equally it also means to cause to cease, to put an end to. Even 'to preserve' includes a negative element, namely, that something is removed from its immediacy and so from an existence which is open to external influences, in order to preserve it. Thus what is sublated is at the same time preserved; it has only lost its immediacy but is not on that account annihilated.... Something is sublated only in so far as it has entered into unity with its opposite; in this more particular signification as something reflected, it may fittingly be called a *moment*.[2]

II

Peirce wrote that if, according to Hegel Firstness and Secondness were not done away with in Thirdness — the allegation that I have considered in the foregoing — pragmaticists might look to him as the great vindicator of their truth. Since it will be fairly clear from the foregoing quotation that Hegel did not err in this manner, it may now be inquired whether Hegel might have regarded it as an honor to be considered the great vindicator of pragmaticism. The answer must be a decisive, *in no way.* No utterance of Peirce shows with more clearity how little he understood Hegel than this association of his name with pragmaticism. In order to see clearly the great gulf that separates Hegel and pragmaticism, it is only necessary to call to mind that his entire system consists in an exposition of concrete actuality. Truth and actuality do not await a remote future to be established for what they are, as in the case of a theory — even such a philosophical theory as pragmaticism, (also) on Peirce's account. Following Hegel's teaching, the phenomenology of concreteness must take priority over every other scientific undertaking, i.e., undertakings of the particular sciences. It may with confidence be said that for Hegel concrete actuality is the concretely factual with reference to which *only* a theory can have any meaning at all, and that apart from this reference it would not even be identifiable as such. Concrete actuality is presupposed by the sciences other than first philosophy; for philosophy, however, it is no mere presupposition. Philosophy has as its first task the explication of the fact that concreteness is *in and for itself,* i.e., thus self-constitutive, and that it contains all of the discriminations needful for its explication. Consider Peirce's pragmaticist maxim with reference to this thought.

> Consider what effects, that might conceivably have practical bearings, we conceive the object of our conception to have. Then, our conception of these effects is the whole of our conception of the object (CP, 5.402).

---

[2] *Logik,* I, pp. 93f; or *Logic,* pp. 106f.

Principally because of its futuristic orientation it would have been impossible for Hegel to have reconciled pragmaticism with his concept of concrete actuality. He understood full well that *in actuality* — i.e., from a perspective internal to some one actual occasion inclusive of all that is actual — we do not await a future before we know something as true (which "something" will in any case turn out to be "the truth that is the whole"). He was so far removed from the spirit of the pragmaticist's maxim that, on methodological grounds, he could permit himself to make no prediction concerning the future at all in the name of philosophy, e.g., in considering the probability of a philosophical theory being true. To have made such a prediction would have been to go beyond the limits permitted by his critical method.

For Hegel concreteness consisted in a unity and wholeness of discriminations. The truth is the whole, and this whole, precisely considered, is a wholeness of discriminations and discriminated aspects. Each aspect and particle is a necessary aspect of this whole, on which account the whole is implicated in every part. This is the defining characteristic of concrete universality.

I have elsewhere attempted to show (Chap. III and SC, Book I) that Hegel's concept of concreteness is interpretable as a "complete fact", a term that I have adapted from Whitehead. If we formulate the defining characteristic of concrete universality in this terminology, we might say that each aspect and each particle of an identity or of each of its sub-identities — each fact or sub-fact — is universal, and that each is equally the cause of the whole.

If we consider Hegel's discriminations with reference to the Peircean semiotic, we ought to consider that each discrimination of a concrete identity or sub-identity presents us with a speculative (judgment or) proposition. The subject and predicate of a speculative proposition are each accents within an identity inclusive of both (*Phän.* 51; or *Phen.* 120). This is a discriminated identity, and what is discriminated within this identity is Firstness and Secondness. The identity viewed as inclusive of both is thus Thirdness.

If we work out this translation of the Peircian categories further and in a consistent manner, it will be found that concreteness for Hegel consists in a unity and wholeness of Thirdnesses and that every concrete identity lends itself to being considered as a wholeness of constituting Thirdnesses. Seeing that these consist of all of the discriminations that are needful for the explication of the occasion, it is presuppositionless and in this sense absolute. As absolute it can for Hegel serve as a measure for all hypothetical thought, constituted by mere abstractions. When the matter is seen in this light, one cannot even recognize a theory as such until one has set it in relation to what is in this sense self-evidently actual.

III

With certain reservations, it may be said that Hegel's principal objections to pragmaticism raise no particular problem for a scientifically executed semiotic based upon Peirce's categories. This is seeing that pragmaticism, although it forms an aspect of the semiotic, must not necessarily be considered to be its most essential aspect. The doctrine of the categories, by way of contrast, stands at the very center. Thus, the doctrine of pragmaticism is separable from the semiotic, while the doctrine of the categories is not. One should also consider that the pragmaticist's principle is irreconcilable with Hegel's concept of concreteness only insofar as it is considered as a form of first philosophy or as a substitute for first philosophy. Within the framework of a theory of the sciences (*Wissenschaftstheorie*) it may retain a certain status, provided that it is founded upon a proximate concept of concreteness and can be subject to criticism with reference to such a standard. In other words, a form of semiotic that is divorced from pragmaticism posing as a first philosophy, or as a substitute for first philosophy, does not close out the possibility that aspects of the pragmaticist doctrine might be applicable with reference to external relations, once an ontological (being-becoming) basis for such is constituted through a system of internally related Thirdnesses (of which each includes Firstness and Secondness). Such a basis is a concept of concrete actuality as at once an identity and a system of identities that includes all of the discriminations needful for its explication. The explication of concreteness is thus describable through a semiotic analysis-synthesis. In a parallel manner can the analysis of theories (and ordinary synthetic propositions) and their criticism with reference to their measure, concrete actuality, be carried forward through semiotic analysis.

I close with one additional remark. The fact, also recognized by Peirce, that Firstness, Secondness, and Thirdness stand at once at the center both of his semiotic and of Hegelian dialectic, forms a bridge between semiotic in the Peircean tradition on the one hand, and the Hegel inspired dialectical-hermeneutical tradition, on the other hand, that has up to now gone almost unused. With reference to this matter, it remains the task of philosophy in the Hegelian tradition to bring us back to concreteness — a principal aspect of the Hegelian teaching that to Peirce as to so many others has remained totally unknown, and apart from which — even with the most absurdly heroic effort — little that Hegel says can ultimately be made to yield very good sense. Above all it remains to be seen what light semiotic may shed upon the (internal) constitution of concreteness in our own temporal era — which must inevitably become a principal interest of philosophy in the Hegelian tradition.

VII

A HEGELIAN CRITIQUE OF
POPPER'S THEORY OF OBJECTIVE KNOWLEDGE*

1. Introduction

The consideration that Hegel made the explication of concrete actuality the highest aim of his dialectical philosophy has often, and perhaps characteristically, been deemphasized by commentators, passed over in embarrassed silence, or made a matter of apology. I have taken the opposite tack of rendering this aspect prominent, and of inquiring why this enterprise, which I find no reason for regarding at the outset, at least, as having been wrong-headed, could not by a certain reconception (and a cutting short of potentially endless interpretative discussion) be made to succeed. Following this tack, the determination of the relevance of Hegel today would seem to hinge largely upon locating him as a philosopher who went beyond theory to the explication of concrete actuality and concrete fact.

If I am correct in this, and if the effort to rethink his conceptuality, and in particular his concept of presuppositionlessness, to render it more consistent with this basic aim, seems in any way justifiable, one way of putting the enterprise to the test might be by making it the basis for a critique of Karl R. Popper, according to whose theory of objective knowledge all knowledge is assimilated to theory, or in effect. This is what is here undertaken.

Popper has provided us, in his theory of objective knowledge, with an in many ways original *evolutionary* and *biological* approach. Both of these accents are in principle highly compatible with the present

---

* For the views of Karl R. Popper I have drawn for the most part upon two of his comparatively recent works, *Objective Knowledge: An Evolutionary Approach* (Oxford: Clarendon Press, 1972), and *The Self and its Brain: An Argument for Interactionism,* coauthored with John C. Eccles (Munich: Springer International, 1977), Part I (authored by Popper).

perspective. What he has in view is within the Hegelian perspective called understanding (*Verstand*), however, and on a Hegelian account, understanding must ever be completed and given context within reason, which is more inclusive. To be kept in view, in this connection, is that if the understanding is sublated (*aufgehoben*) in Hegelian dialectic, its products and its function are ever preserved within the context of reason in its dynamic fullness and actuality — inclusive also of the living aims of the subject for whom objects of the understanding are present. This being the case there need be no basic conflict with objective knowledge, also on Popper's account, for which the autonomy of absolute truth is not claimed. This is although Popper appears to be in error in seeming not quite to acknowledge that objective knowledge is a product of abstraction. That he acknowledges some sort of role for the subject in knowledge and that he claims at most only some relative grade of truth for objective knowledge nonetheless contributes to the area of potential complementarity. What to my thinking is most conspicuously missing from Popper's perspective, which he appears at points expressly to disallow and which can be provided by the perspective of my critique, is the world as settled fact — more adequately, the world as *actual* and as a *becoming* of some settled fact and its sub-facts. I have in mind such an actuality as includes its understanding-interpreting — and hence knowing — subject. If the knowing of such a subject is a thing of the living instant — and hense as settled only *in a very special sense* — it is nonetheless, by virtue of being a self-evident knowing, adequate to serve as a touchstone for theory. The self-evidence to which I refer is *a throb of creation,* complete in itself and hence at once self-conscious knowing as well as the world present as known, an episode climaxing in the correspondence of the two within a truth which is the coherent whole of this and other constitutive discriminated aspects.

The treatment to follow turns out, in the final analysis, to be less a critique of particular points of doctrine than a reflection upon where Popper's theory of science (which he presents as philosophy) leaves off and what I call first philosophy begins, and how the former should not be used as an immunization against the latter, which can provide the needed foundation in (concrete) fact. If one sets aside statements by Popper that tend to restrict philosophy to concerns of the theory of science, with its more or less exlusive orientation towards objective knowledge, most aspects of his theory can be seen to be at least not in conflict with the somewhat Hegelian perspective I have been developing. As I hope to show, often they can lend themselves to being made complementary.

Introduction

Richard McKeon once remarked that "Metaphysics is abandoned when criteria and methods of establishing objective knowledge are sought as a basis for determining what is".[1] If for "metaphysics" the term "first philosophy" is substituted, this statement is in the present context rendered applicable to Popper's theory. The perspective that I am proposing as first philosophy in its primary exposition and intention is not so much metaphysics as phenomenology, and it assumes the character of the former only to the extent that the ideal of a complete, discrimination by discrimination, explication of concreteness for practical reasons goes unfulfilled. This is the ideal of a completed philosophy, an ideal that lies potential for fulfillment with respect to every actual occasion, which is a new creation. With respect to the totality of occasions, hypothetically viewed, however, this ideal can never be fulfilled, except perhaps in God.

My critique of Popper consists principally in three points, which I shall first list in shorthand form, and then consider at greater length, each in turn.

1) A disposition to assimilate all knowledge to theory, which will not do.

2) A reversal of the natural order of knowledge, which is from fact to theory.

3) His theory needs first philosophy as a companion piece.

2. The Assimilation of all Knowledge to Theory

As integral with his evolutionary approach to objective knowledge, Popper proposes the following as "some cosmic evolutionary stages":

World 3 (the products of the human mind)	(6) Works of Art and of Science (including Technology)
	(5) Human Language. Theories of Self and Death
World 2 (the world of subjective experiences)	(4) Consciousness of Self and of Death
	(3) Sentience (Animal Consciousness)
World 1 (the world of physical objects)	(2) Living Organisms
	(1) The Heavier Elements; Liquids and Crystals
	(0) Hydrogen and Helium (SB 16)

---

[1] "Ontology, Methodology, and Culture", Raymond Klibansky (Ed.), *Contemporary German Philosophy* (Firenze: La Nuova Italia Editrice, 1969), p. 97.

What for my present purposes is deserving of emphasis is World 3, regarded as *products* of the human mind. While acknowledging that World 3 is conditioned by World 2 as well as World 1, and hence that our subjectivity is involved in its creation, Popper wishes to focus our attention upon these products, *as such,* insisting that whatever we understand about their production must be primarily with reference to them as result.

His disposition in this regard parallels somewhat Whitehead's disposition to restrict knowledge to what is purely objective — more specifically, to knowledge of the abstract data residual upon the perishing of actual occasions, a disposition on account of which I have characterized the latter's metaphysics as a more or less inflated theory of science.[2] An effect of the resultant tendency to conflate all knowledge to theory is that an account cannot be given of the self-evidence with which I seem to know things whenever I observe. This is to say, what is sometimes (if naively) referred to as "immediate knowing", that which at least in the lived moment seems to possess an indubitable character, must be regarded as a species of theory and as dubitable. From the present perspective anything that I might regard as thus immediately known is already mediated, or better, *being mediated,* so that it presents itself either as the truth which is the whole — the entirety of the occasion as which it is actualized — or at least as some aspect of this whole in context. There is no appropriating of disperate and isolated aspects each by itself, whether one has in view percepts (or sense data), concepts, intentions, or any other aspect that might be construed as the most basic building block of knowledge, truth and actuality being all-or-nothing inclusive occurrences. This understanding, if found acceptable, will seem to render the conflation mentioned less than probable. The process will be carried a step further if an actual occasion is viewed as constituted by a unity and wholeness of discriminations adequate to its explication. Such an occasion, by virtue of needing nothing outside of itself to be what it is, seems to take unto itself a birthright to actuality such as can hardly be attributed to a theory, which, after all, is a dependent creature, at least prior to its being somehow demonstrated as exhibiting the shape of actuality, and probably thereafter, as well.

If our conceptuality were as impoverished of discriminations as it must be supposed to be when all knowledge is thought to be restricted to the knowledge of (more or less fallible) theory, we should have no touchstone for theory by virtue of which to know it as such and as distinguished from such meaning-entities as actuality, fact, truth.

---

[2] For comments lying in this direction, see pp. 49-53.

Apart from the possibility of such a meaning bestowing contrast, there seems good reason to believe that we cannot be making good sense. If Popper often vaguely appeals to "realism" i.e., "we conjecture the entities of the physical world to be real" (O.K. 36), etc., at least with reference to a particular concrete case it is made to seem that this appeal must always be suspect, i.e., to involve no more than a provisional assignment of the status of real to what is not certainly warranted to be so. He is concerned (with Tarski) with the rehabilitation of the correspondence theory of truth, according to which "... truth is simply correspondence with the facts" (O.K 308). But what for him are the facts? We seek in vain what from the present perspective can serve as satisfying answers to such questions, seeing that what may provisionally be regarded as facts do not stand up as such, but rather prove finally to be no more than provisionally warranted theories or their functions.

While maintaining that all theories are hypotheses and may be overthrown, he wishes nonetheless to maintain that "... *we do justify our preferences by an appeal to the idea of truth:* truth plays the role of a regulative idea. We test for truth, by eliminating falsehood" (O.K. 29f). He later elaborates:

> Like the descriptive use of language, the argumentative use has led to the evolution of ideal standards of control, or of 'regulative ideas' (using a Kantian term): the main regulative idea of the descriptive use of language is *truth* (as distinct from *falsity*); and that of the argumentative use of language... is *validity* (as distinct from *invalidity*) (O.K. 237).

From whence arises this regulative idea of truth? Popper writes, "There is no doubt that corresponce to the facts is what we usually call truth, rather than coherence or pragmatic usefulness" (O.K. 316). He wishes to maintain that the correspondence theory permits us to speak of a reality different from theory. "The realist wants to have both a theory and a reality or the facts... which are different from his theory about these facts, and which we can somehow or other compare with the facts" (O.K. 317). Here we find Popper in search of a meaning bestowing contrast between theory and fact, i.e., what the theory *is about.* This search leads to his concern, with Tarski, to rehabilitate the notion of correspondence (O. K. 318), which he thinks is to be accomplished through the discovery that "in order to speak about correspondence between statements S and a *fact* F we need a language (a meta-language) in which we can speak *about* the statement S and *state* the fact F" (O.K. 316). If space permitted, I think I could show a direct and close parallel between this move to a meta-language as essential to speaking of correspondence on Popper's account and some particular phases of Hegelian negation and mediation, notions of which Popper seems to me to have displayed little understanding. It must here suffice to note that he has left me fully persuaded, if this was needed, that this move to a meta-language is indeed an important aspect of the manner in which we do speak and indeed have spoken even since long before the discovery. The issue, however, becomes one of what it is in the nature of actuality — what constitutes the hardness of its facticity — that leads us to require this character trait in our language. Popper proposes that by the constant elimination of falsehood what is left over may be regarded as provisionally true, i.e., the best that we have to go on. This seems hardly sufficient. For one thing, it leaves the matter of a criterion wrapped in deep mystery. If it should be the case that we in fact *are* in possession of "being-mediated" knowledge that presents itself self-evidently, we ought not accept such an answer to our problem until we have at least looked into the character of this self-evidence to see whether it is actually as pernicious as Popper finds all claims to absolute knowledge to be, and indeed as they are so long as what we are thinking of is theory. I am persuaded that Popper falls short of providing a satisfactory reply to this ***fundamentally philosophical*** question, required if a foundation is to be provided to his contributions to evolutionary theory as pertaining to objective knowledge.

I must be content just here to no more than suggest how I propose the criticism is to be met. Popper seems mistaken in his assertion that all knowledge is theory-impregnated (and on this account can remain no more than conjectural) in that, once concretized, the concrete fact and its sub-facts stand theory-free, regardless of how much or many theories may have contributed to the process of concrescence. This is a process within which potentialities are actualized. His mistake follows from having taken up a perspective before, rather than during and after, the concrete fact and from having failed ***intellectually*** to acknowledge both its received presence and its transient character.

I will build upon the principal themes I have mentioned in what follows. To be borne in mind is that *no demonstration is intended.* Indeed such an attempt would be presumptuous and absurd, seeing that the intended outcome of the position is that it lends itself to being found self-evident and that anything at all that is subject to being self-evident lies beyond the reach of demonstration. (That this is the case ought to assure us that truth is not merely of our making.) In this regard the position advocated, by comparison with that of Popper, is disadvantaged, a disadvantage owing to the fact, however, that it attempts more — more, that is, at least from a ***philosophical*** standpoint. This ***more*** consists in the effort to go beyond theory and the theory of science (*Wissenschaftstheorie,* the area within which Popper's expertness seems most at home) to concrete fact that can serve as a touchstone for both, a consideration that in any case is reserved to first philosophy, because it is an undertaking that proceeds by a quite different method.

This way of stating the matter is admittedly apologetic, intended for persons who, by virtue of living in a theory oriented century and culture, share Popper's theory-oriented dispositions, perhaps even in their private affairs. This is perhaps the currently most pervasive form of alienation from both self and world. *Actually* the natural beginning point in knowledge is not theory, as Popper supposes, but actuality, which, with a bow to Whitehead, but taking some liberty with his concept, I wish to refer to as *concrete* fact.

3. The Natural Order is from Fact to Theory

Popper maintains that theory — interpreted biologically and in the broadest conceivable way to include expectations and preconscious and unconscious dispositions as well — is prior to what most nearly approximates a knowledge of concrete actuality.

> I believe that theory — at least some rudimentary theory or expectation — always comes first; that it always precedes observation; and that the fundamental role of observations and experimental tests is to show that some of our theories are false, and so to stimulate us to produce better ones (O.K. 258).

This knowledge as well turns out to be theory, following his account, although this is not what I wish now to emphasize. Here to be noted is that the fundamental movement on his account is from theory to what most nearly approaches knowledge of actuality, i.e., what from the present Hegelian perspective I have referred to as *concrete fact.* I wish to maintain that the fundamental movement is *from fact to theory,* this being the case not only in the order of being (ontologically) but in the order of knowing (epistemologically), as well. It is the fact of concrescence that makes this doctrine true, and I wish to maintain that it lends itself to being rendered self-evident. I shall now enlarge upon this theme.

A central feature of Popper's view is that an organism is at a given temporal instant possessed of given dispositions to act, "an inner state". Physically identical stimuli may at different times produce different reactions, and physically different stimuli may result in identical reactions. (O.K. 343)

> I assert that every animal is born with expectations or anticipations, which could be framed as hypotheses; a kind of hypothetical knowledge. And I

assert that we have, in this sense, some degree of inborn knowledge from which we may begin, even though it may be quite unreliable. This inborn knowledge, these inborn expectaitons, will, if disappointed, **create our first problems;** and the ensuing growth of our knowledge may therefore be described as consisting throughout of corrections and modifications of previous knowledge. (O.K. 258f)

We often become aware of dispositions to act when prevented from doing so. For example, an unexpected step in one's path may serve to make one aware than an even surface was anticipated. Such disappointments force the correction of expectations, which is learning. (O.K. 343f)

Seeing that an observation always presupposes the existence of some system of expectations (which may take the form of queries) in need of being confirmed or corrected, an at least implicit hypothesis on Popper's account precedes every observation and, indeed, every perception.

> At every instant of our pre-scientific or scientific development we are living in the centre of what I usually call a 'horizon of expectations', By this I mean the sum total of our expectations, whether these are subconscious or conscious, or perhaps even explicitly stated in some language. Animals and babies have also their various and different horizons of expectations though no doubt on a lower level of consciousness than, say, a scientist whose horizon of expectations consists to a considerable extent of linguistically formulated theories or hypotheses.
>
> The various horizons of expectations differ, of course, not only in their being more or less conscious, but also in their content. Yet in all these cases the horizon of expectations plays the part of a frame of reference: only their setting in this frame confers meaning or significance on our expectations, actions, and observations.
>
> Observations, more especially, have a very peculiar function within this frame. They can, under certain circumstances, destroy even the frame itself, if they clash with certain of the expectations. In such a case they can have an effect upon our horizon of expectations like a bombshell. This bombshell may force us to reconstruct, or rebuild, our whole horizon of expectations; that is to say, we may have to correct our expectations and fit them together again into something like a consistent whole. We can say that in this way our horizon of expectations is raised to and reconstructed on a higher level, and that we reach in this way a new stage in the evolution of our experience; a stage in which those expectations which have not been hit by the bomb are somehow incorporated into the horizon, while those parts of the horizon which have suffered damage are repaired and rebuilt. This has to be done in such a way that the damaging observations are no longer felt as disruptive, but are integrated with the rest of our expectations. If we succeed in this rebuilding, then we shall have created what is usually known as an **explanation** of those observed events [which created the disruption, the problem]. (O.K. 345)

Thus neither man in the natural attitude nor man as scientist begins from scratch (or from a *tabula rasa*) as a mere receptacle free of dispositions and assumptions. He is always possessed of a horizon of expectations with which his perceptions interact. How deeply dispositions are on Popper's account imbedded in our experience and actuality is suggested by the following passage.

> The continuity producing memory... has to be understood in its biological function, interpreted theoretically in the light of a theory of our position in the environment, represented by a 'feeling' of our body and its place in a kind of model or map. This theory too is unconsciously and dispositionally held. (S.B. 131)

Popper's structure of expectations is compatible with the perspective of this critique, a stipulation being permitted to assist us to account for the ingredient of unity and compatibility that gets worked into experience and actuality as we know it. Our expectations and dispositions must again and again be brought into the unity of focus that issues in action. Sometimes we are aware of the tug of contending dispositions and feelings just prior to acting. This unification I wish to designate the stage of full concrescence of an actual occasion, without denying that this stage may rise and pass repeatedly, and with rapidity, apart from our being aware of these passages. Just here the principal idea I wish to introduce is that of unification, in alternating instants, that maintains the horizon of expectations — which between instants is renewed by data inherited from the causal past — the organized structure that we ever experience it *as becoming*.

From the somewhat Hegelian perspective of this critique we should at this point be talking about the natural selection of concrete facts more than about the natural selection of theories, not because theories (in the broad sense intended) do not go into the making of concrete facts, but because self-consciousness arises as an aspect of a concrete fact *as something being achieved. What presents itself self-evidently is actual and not the potentiality that went into its making.* Every actual occasion presents a subject and a world present for that subject (with its component of sub-contrasts) *being* constituted or settled. In other words the process of concrescence yields definiteness by transforming potentiality into actuality. Thus a part of the function of Popper's 'horizon of expectations' is displaced; i.e., some of what he considered to be dispositions and theories are now settled "facts", at least for the duration of particular given occasions, or for short or lengthy epochs of occasions. The matter may at least at first be viewed in this way.

A settled fact within an epoch of occasions is settled in the sense that it is reconcretized within each occasion. Seeing that every actual occasion is unique, a new creation, a "settled disposition" that is reconcretized within each occasion within an epoch will be constitutive of that occasion as the distinctive *concrete* fact that it is. In other words, the context of each particular occasion is determinative of what a particular "settled disposition" really comes to within that particular occasion, and this disposition will in turn be concretely universal throughout the universe comprehended by the occasion; this is to say, it will have exactly one necessary function within that occasion. Let this phenomenon be called "the settlement effect". The upshot is that what is referred to within the language of theory as "settled dispositions" is from a hypothetical perspective that transcends any particular occasion — the transcendence of the occasion that is being lived and that includes within itself all that is actual being possible *only for the imagination and not actually* — not finally so very settled after all. This statement goes very far toward showing how the settled concrete fact and its sub-facts — settled, that is, within the context of particular actual occasions, each regarded in turn from an internal perspective — can be compatible with what from a hypothetical perspective such as Popper's must appear as unsettledness. Continuity and the possibility of hypothetically anticipating the future require the former, despite the manifestly shifting character of theories and the only relatively more stable character of our structures of expectations, the latter each regarded as a whole. The biological dimension of his theory of knowledge in view, Popper cannot consistently restrict knowledge to the objective sphere, as he sometimes attempted to do.[3] His later and more mature position in the matter is perhaps fairly well represented by the following:

> Now I wish to distinguish between two kinds of 'knowledge': subjective knowledge (which should better be called organismic knowledge, since it consists of the dispositions of organisms); and objective knowledge, or knowledge in the objective sense, which consists of the logical content of our theories, conjectures, guesses (and, if we like, of the logical content of our genetic code).
>
> Examples of objective knowledge are theories published in journals and books and stored in libraries; discussions of such theories; difficulties or problems pointed out in connection with such theories; and so on.
>
> We can call... the world of the logical *contents* of books, libraries, computer memories, and such like 'world 3'. (O.K. 73f)

Notwithstanding his bow toward subjectivity under the term "organismic knowledge", where it is theories that can sustain critical scrutiny that are in view, the principal, if not exclusive, appeal is to the objectivity of knowledge.

Admittedly, the activities or processes covered by the umbrella term 'un-

---

[3] See O.K., Chapters 5 and 6.

derstanding' are subjective or personal or psychological activities. They must be distinguished from the (more or less successful) *outcome* [[emphasis added]] of these activities, from their results: The 'final state' (for the time being) of understanding, the *interpretation*. Although this *may* be a subjective state of understanding, it may also be a third-world object, especially a theory; and the latter case is, in my opinion, the more important one. Regarded as a third-world object, the interpretation will always be a theory;... (O.K. 162f)

The appeal to objective knowledge is carried out by interpreting the subjective act of understanding in a strictly objective way, through the following three theses, the emphases being added.

(1) That every subjective act of understanding is *largely* anchored in the third world;
(2) That *almost all* important remarks that are made about such an act consist in pointing out its relations to third-world objects; and
(3) that such an act consists *in the main* of operations with third world objects: we operate with these objects almost as if they were physical objects.

This, I suggest can be generalized, and holds for every subjective act of 'knowledge': all the important things we can say about an act of knowledge consists in pointing out the third-world objects of the act – a theory or proposition – and its relation to other third-world objects, such as the arguments bearing on the problem as well as the objects known. (O.K. 163)

Continuing, Popper is critical of the view that "we cannot do without such procedures as sympathetic understanding or empathy, or there-enactment of other people's actions (Collingwood) or the attempt to put ourselves into another person's situation by making his aims and problems our own" (O.K. 163f). His proposal is that a subjective state of understanding as well as the processes which lead to it "must be analysed in terms of third world objects in which they are anchored....[[and]] can be analysed *only* in these terms" (O.K. 164). Thus he is led by a very loose kind of argument to conclude that "an activity of understanding consists, essentially, in operating with third world objects". Statements of this sort leave the impression that even while acknowledging a subjective dimension to knowledge, in the particular propositions and terms he is less interested to pay systematic attention to this dimension than were either Hegel or Peirce, for whom Firstness, Secondness, and Thirdness were logical categories modeled somewhat upon the Hegelian triad.[4]

In this appeal to objectivity Popper is sharply critical of the quest for certainty, which, so far as I have been able to ascertain, he uni-

---

[4] For Peirce every thirdness includes firstness and secondness. *Peirce Papers*, 5.90. Also see Essay V.

formly construes as a (correctly or incorrectly drawn) result of demonstration, a construal that follows consistently his assimilation of all knowledge to theory. To explain his position in this regard he formulates two statements that he finds to be characteristic of the common sense theory of knowledge.

(a) Knowledge is a special kind of belief or of opinion; it is a special state of mind.

(b) In order that a kind of belief, or a state of mind, should amount to more than 'mere' belief, and should be capable of sustaining the claim that it amounts to an item of knowledge, we require that the believer should be in possession of *sufficient* reasons for establishing that the item of knowledge is *true with certainty*.

Of these two formulations, (a) can easily be so reformulated that it becomes part — a small part — of an acceptable biological theory of knowledge; for we can say:

(a') Subjective knowledge is a kind of disposition of which the organism sometimes may become conscious in the form of a belief or an opinion or a state of mind.

This is a perfectly acceptable statement, and it may be claimed that it merely says more exactly what (a) was intended to say. Moreover, (a') is perfectly compatible with a theory of knowledge that gives full weight to objective knowledge; that is, to knowledge as part of world 3.

The position of (b) is totally different. As soon as we take objective knowledge into account, we must say that at best only a very small part of it can be given anything like sufficient reasons for certain truth: it is that small part (if any) which can be described as ***demonstrable*** knowledge and which comprises (if anything) the propositions of formal logic and of (finite) arithmetic.

Rather than demonstrable knowledge, what we for the most part achieve is verisimilitude: theories that are better than others and have not as yet been refuted. Popper maintains in fact that "A scientific result cannot be justified. It can only be criticized and tested" (O.K. 265).

I have...merely sketched a programme of combining Tarski's theory of truth with his calculus of systems so as to obtain a concept of *verisimilitude* which allows us to speak, without fear of nonsense, of *theories which are better or worse approximations to truth* (O.K. 335).

From the present perspective it would seem that the possibility ought with certainty to be left open that a firmly established scientific result *may* become an aspect of the concretely actual, at least within the present cultural epoch. (We seem to have no right to assume that the future will always resemble our past — and prediction of the future is in any case no proper business of first philosophy.) What more frequently results is doubtless less than a firmly established result, i.e., something that must still be classified as a theory. In practice it is difficult to determine the precise point at which a well-accepted and problem-free theory may pass into fact, but the occurrence, if a decision in this regard may occasionally be subject to being reversed, is inconspicuous. A rule of thumb is that so long as a scientific theory remains of interest *as such*, it has *not* passed into fact but remains in some degree problematical. As such it is constituted by one or more propositions that serve as "lures for feeling"[5] at the level of (self-conscious) comprehension (and not merely at the level of prehension), which propositions, however, are eliminated by negative prehension from the final phase of concrescence, or at least for the most part, to be displaced by (unconscious) prehensions.

The unconscious dispositions or judgments represented by the latter are contributary to the wholeness and unity of discriminations that constitute the truth of an actual occasion by being sub-moments within propositions that can both accommodate them and be compossible with other propositions the mediations of the subject and predicate of which contribute discriminations constitutive of the occasion in its phase of full concrescence.

The gain when a theory passes into concrete fact, i.e., when it can be entirely expressed within a body of propositions consistent with one another and with other propositions constitutive of the occasion within which it is "settled", is an increment of discriminations for the occasion, consistent with the power for fine-grained explication. Seeing that the subjective form of an occasion is reflected in the organization of the static data left upon its perishing (on which account even explicitly "objective data" is, strictly speaking, never *merely* objective), an increment of discriminations tends to be inherited, especially through a relatively stable epoch. In the case of a theory that achieves a relatively secure status, short of passing into fact, the ideal I have described may be nearly approximated.

The difference between propositions and judgments consists in that the process by which judgments are mediated — by which, this is to say, the subject and predicate in a particular case each become an accent within an identity inclusive of both — may not be fully explicit to self-consciousness as actual and as felt. Where there is reference to judgments in the foregoing, it is judgments *constitutive of* experience and of actuality that are in view. Judgments may not be explicitly identifiable as such apart from being deduced from actual

---

[5] The term is Whitehead's. See PR, pp. 148-89. Whitehead's "contrast" appears more nearly to duplicate the function of the Hegelian *spekulativen Satz* than does his concept of a proposition, in that it does not transcend the occasion but completely spends its potentiality (its power to lure) in it. See pp. 28-33.

occasions as conditions necessary to account for their possibility or recapitulated on the basis of data, in the form of abstract result, residual upon the perishing of occasions of which they are constitutive.

Theories that have passed into fact are reconcretized in successive actual occasions as propositions that are explicit or implicit to the conscious subject of every occasion. Unlike Whitehead's propositions, such propositions are concretized *without residual* in every occasion, their potentiality — their "lure" — being spent into actuality *without residual.*[6] (Only thus can the occasion be complete, and hence self-evident in the senses in which we experience it as being complete and self-evident.) Where such propositions are implicit to consciousness only, they are nonetheless felt, and in principle available to being rendered explicit in some subsequent occasion through attention.

If concrete actuality is episodic and climactic in character as I propose, and if truth is to be construed commensurably, i.e., in terms of systems (each an actual occasion) that successively achieve coherence, each in turn, as a unity and wholeness of discriminations adequate to its (self-)explication and hence self-evident, and perishes, Popper's concept of verisimilitude will be seen to pertain less to the realm of truth than to that of the abstract and the possible, i.e., to the horizon of expectations, which from the present perspective is derived by reconstruction on the basis of abstract data residual from occasions that have perished. I say "less...than" rather than "not at all" in the above statement to make allowance for "the settlement effect".[7]

A theory will thus be said to be the best available when it accords

---

[6] A reminder of some ground that has been covered may here be in order. From the present perspective, it is found necessary to maintain, in opposition to Whitehead, that the subject of an actual occasion *comprehends* as well as *prehends*. This is owing to the consideration that, were the occasion not to include its own understanding, interpreting subject, it could be known only as relative to a subject outside of itself, and could on this account not with certainty to said to be actual. (Thus we would be haunted by a form of "the problem of the thing in itself".) Seeing that to be complete an occasion must include all of the discriminations needful for its explication, however, the inclusion of the discrimination between its subject and the world present for that subject is also implicated. Only on this condition can we account (at least in principle) for its self-evidence, the fact to be explicated. In addition, the standpoint taken is post-Hegelian and post-Buberian in that the subject, being self-conscious and therefore able to know its own occasion to be actual (from an inside and hence actual perspective) before its perishing, seeing that its life for its brief duration is his or her own, can directly intuit its character as discriminated and hence can directly know the more emphasized constitutive discriminations that condition its self-evidence, these being expressed or expressible in concrete spoken language, in propositions (*spekulativen Sätzen*) the subject and predicate of which are in the act of communication *being mediated.*

[7] See pp. 147f.

best with the structure of our expectations regarded in its entirety, this, however, having nothing directly to do with truth as self-evidence. The structure of expectations, otherwise called "nature as a 'permanent' possibility of experience", is on this account largely constituted of theories which, although they contribute to the concrescence of actual occasions by serving as lures for feeling, may never as such be concretized as aspects of truth, i.e., may never as such or as a whole pass into concrete fact.

The gap between theory and truth is on this account wider than Popper leaves it. This is most fundamentally, perhaps, because what is self-evidently true can never be arrived at by demonstration alone. It must be concretized (and this anew or originally) and not merely shown to have been actual or to be deserving of this status within an abstract system of concepts or a conventional or habitual language.

It should be acknowledged that Popper appears to have been careful never to close out the possibility that we might have some very modest amount of certain truth. This is although he makes no effort to affirm this to be necessarily the case or explicitly to indicate how such a minimal content of certain truth might serve a necessary role as a touchstone for theory, much less to develop the concept concretely, i.e., discrimination by discrimination, and with the logical rigor to which a concrete fact as a complete system of internal relations should lend itself. This criticism would have no cogency were he proposing to be doing the theory of science rather than philosophy, and *following Hegel,* at that. As the case stands, it must prove very serious indeed, ultimately not less because it is shared (along with a general disinterest in, or distaste for, philosophy) by many of his contemporaries.

This criticism necessarily moves from the presupposition that we all know some things self-evidently in every waking temporal instant, a presupposition, however, that might hopefully be rendered superfluous by the discrimination by discrimination explication of the self-evidence of an actual occasion. One discrimination that I trust every reader can find to be self-evident at the very instant that he is reading this line is that of himself as subject (as "I", not some "me" worked up from abstractions after the lived moment) and the world present for him or her.[8] This is not to propose to demonstrate either the concrete authenticity of this one discrimination or that of a system of such, the members of which can be serially subsumed within this one, or self-evident as such. It is rather to say that the explica-

---

[8] For a sense of the variety of types of some of the sub-discriminations within this one, I must here commend Hegel's system, beginning with the *Phen.,* construed critically and otherwise in a manner commensurate with the present perspective.

tion may reach a point at which the hearer or reader might recognize in him- or herself this identifiable characteristic of lived experience and actuality.

For the theoretician I am talking about the most basic and fundamental all-or-nothing phenomenon, which I take to be the genus of all other types. To know this as it is in (and for) itself, however, is quite a different matter than to understand, or agree to, a theory about it. It seems to me that there is nothing at all mysterious about this, whatever may be found wanting in my account in pointing out its obviousness.

To my way of thinking the entire strategy of attempting to demonstrate knowledge to be true, for which Popper attempts to provide a foundation by the appeal to objective knowledge as the equivalent of the propositions of logic and arithmetic, is mistaken. True knowledge cannot be demonstrated because it is concrete and not abstract. If it could be abstract and yet true — absolutely and not merely relatively true — this might be within an abstract system, such as demonstration necessarily presupposes. Where the reference is to concrete truth, to speak of logical demonstration is a contradiction in terms which it is perhaps not too soon to designate a hybris of the logical mind, one, I would say, of which I think Hegel may sometimes have been guilty, although there is much more to be said on this issue. What is concretely true is self-evidently so and what is not cannot be made so by human ingenuity alone. To demonstrate truth in this sense would be the equivalent of artificially creating a living occasion and then performing logical operations within it while it was yet actual. The first may well be impossible and the second certainly is. This way of putting the matter will nonetheless suggest that the attempt to construct a perfect language should be with reference to a self-evident concretely actual occasion as its most proximate model.

4. The Two Perspectives

I have already intimated that Popper's theory of objective knowledge belongs most properly not to philosophy but to the theory of science (*Wissenschaftstheorie*), more particularly, to the theory of knowledge, which within the present context, as frequently, it is misleading to translate "philosophy of science" (as though it were some kind of philosophy). From the perspective of the present critique the basis is provided for a fairly definite distinction between these two kinds of disciplines, pursued by the employment of quite different methodologies.[9] The remarks to follow are intended to "locate" Popper's work with reference to this distinction and thus establish the basis for a potential complementarity with the Hegelian/Whiteheadian concept of self-evident actual occasions that I have proposed. My initial account of this distinction will emphasize that internal relations characterize actuality, while contingent relations — which may be a mixture of internal and external relations, but which consist at least in part in the latter — characterize possibility. This is only provisionally adequate. Following I refer rather to two perspectives, each with its characteristic language and roles.

Philosophy has as its task the explication of the concretely actual — i.e., one occasion regarded as typical, from each relevant (cultural?) epoch — discrimination by discrimination, from an internal, hence *actual,* perspective. The perspective affords us access to the occasion as a system of internal relations. No one has ever *actually* stepped outside of that some one occasion that at a given instant is constitutive of him and his world and that includes within itself all that from its perspective is actual. Hypothetically, however, we do quite commonly take up outside perspectives, which are characterized in the language of relations *between* occasions. The fact that human individuals can undertake this feat of seeming has the most profound consequences, for thereby the range of possibilities that, viewed from a hypothetical perspective, can be prepared for new concrescences is augmented. The theorizing which is characteristic of the particular sciences and upon which the theory of science patterns itself is an extension of this disposition, by which we individually constitute nature as a permanent possibility of experience.

The foregoing account is provisional in the following two ways:

(1) Every actual occasion, viewed from a hypothetical perspective, is *a process wherein external relations are rendered internal.* Only in its end phase, the phase of full concrescence, is it quite adequately portrayed as a system of internal relations. On this account the statement is now to be revised to shift the emphasis to the differences of perspective upon the process. The perspective from *the end*

---

[9] A question may arise as to the methodology being employed in this essay. It will be obvious that I am not here doing an analysis-synthesis of an actual occasion, which aims to be descriptive. Rather, this is to be classified as at once a metaphysical and methodological theory. It is on this account that I am employing for the most part Whitehead's language (pertaining to external relations) rather than Hegel's *spekulative Sätze* (the language of internal relations) and this despite the fact that I am appealing to the latter as the mode in which philosophy should, to the greatest extent possible, go about its principal task. The present essays, considered with respect to the reconception they introduce, can serve as no more than a kind of explanatory preface.

phase of concrescence, from which the occasion presents itself in its self-evidence, characterizes self-consciousness as such. This is a perspective which can only be portrayed in the language of internal relations, the language of *spekulativen Sätzen* (speculative propositions and judgments) the subject and predicate of each of which are **being mediated** to constitute a discriminated identity, the totality of discriminations being adequate to the self-explication of the occasion i.e., the concrete fact and its sub-facts.

The various particular sciences and the theory of science are all characterized as taking up a perspective amid or above the plurality of occasions, *as though this were possible.* They are engaged in viewing the many becoming a one from the perspective of the not-yet-unified-many and by the employment of the language of external relations, the language of the understanding. We might designate this the pluralistic perspective, were it not for the fact that the unified occasion viewed from the perspective of full concrescence, although a *unified* plurality, *is not on this account any less pluralistic.* This is through being constituted by discriminations and by virtue of the fact that the one and the many, each as accents within a discriminated identity inclusive of both (the way plurality can exist, and indeed the very principle of plurality), is one of the contrasts constitutive of every actual occasion. As an alternative, however, the hypothetical perspective might safely be designated contingent, seeing that from the perspective of full concrescence an actual occasion is fully determined and no contingency remains, thus forming a contrast. A concrete fact is what it is because everything determinative of it is definitely set. This is just prior to its perishing.

2) An actual occasion contains a record of its causal past within it — serialized data from perished occasions. As data taken up by the subject of the occasion now actual, it is (if for the most part not consciously) part and parcel of this occasion and hence actual in the present (*Wirkungsgeschichte*).[10] It is history as actual within the present that provides us with a model for hypothetical thinking, i.e., thinking that *posits* inherited data as yet identified with serially ordered occasions which have perished in a past, proximate or remote, from which it has inherited, and which also *projects* future possibilities commensurate with this past. Important to note is that the past as prior to the occasion that is actual is a hypothesis. This is an inevitable outcome of the consideration that knowledge arises **within** the

---

[10] H. G. Gadamer, *Wahrheit und Methode* (Tübingen: J. C. B. Mohr, 1965), pp. 283ff. My usage of the term is **reminiscent** of that of Gadamer.

occasion, a standpoint earlier defended, the abandonment of which from the perspective of this critique would be tantamount to the abandonment of all critical principles.[11] The positing of inherited data as yet identified with occasions that have perished is a hypothesizing on the part of natural reason, and the prototype for the hypothetical perspective among or above the plurality of occasions, *as though this situation were possible.*

Popper's hypothetical perspective thus follows the line of a natural function of reason in the preparation of possibilities for concrescence. It reflects the skepticism appropriate to this perspective, pursued without regard to the self-evidence yielded by an actual perspective. Especially when pursued with cognizance of the concretely actual — the concretized from the standpoint of full concrescence, the *actual* standpoint — it fulfills a necessary role, though one that can never replace creation, i.e., fully determine it in advance of the fact.

It may be thought strange that I should have insisted at the outset that no one has ever taken up a position outside of that some one actual occasion constitutive of him and his world when that occasion, as it turns out, bears the traces of its causal past as history actual within the present. Would it not be as plausible to begin by emphasizing the stage at which movement from many to one is *a not yet unified plurality,* and with reference to its historical heritage? From this alternative standpoint it might be supposed that I may actually be as much at home amid *the not yet unified many.*

So long as we have grounds for insisting that the self-conscious subject is within the occasion (which is required to account for its self-evidence), the mere reference to "I" in the above undercuts this possibility, seeing that such a reference is then possible only within the unified occasion, i.e., *from the actual perspective.* This is to say, the subjective aim unifies the occasion and in so doing emerges as fully determined (which within the present context, as opposed to Whitehead, means as conscious),[12] one side of a contrast of self and world-for-self, each being an accent within a discriminated identity inclusive of both. The individuality of an occasion as an achieved fact is a principal characteristic of it, and the perspective from which its self-evidence is exhibited is the only one which can exhibit this individuality with due regard to all of its determinative constituents. From the present perspective these constituents are not purely objective, as an apologist for Popper, wishing to make out a maxi-

---

[11] See my statement of critical principles in Hegel's sense in Essay V, 2nd par. (pp. 101f).

[12] See Essay II.

mum of complementarity of perspectives, might propose. They are rather mediating processes, within which an objective pole is actual *as, and only as, an aspect* of the *process*. This pole, regarded as *something in itself*, should be seen as an aspect of an account of objectivities as abstract result. As such, it is only hypothetical, as are they.

The foregoing paragraph should not be understood as compromising the claim that concrete fact (constituted at once [to be all too brief] of onsciousness and the world present for consciousness as a contrast being mediated) is natively prior to theory. It is theory that is self-consciously maintained to be such that is here in view. This is even though, where theory-conditioned occasions in this more restricted sense of theory are in view, we experience the felt contrast-in-mediation of fact and theory as a constitutive aspect of concrete actuality. Whitehead went too far in making this contrast essential to the self-consciousness of an actual occasion, in the case of such as he found to be self-conscious: "Consciousness.... is the feeling of the contrast of theory, as *mere* theory, with fact as *mere* fact" (PR 188). Consciousness takes its rise apart from *explicit* theory playing any role whatever. It is to be noted, however, that fact as something that stands in contrast to theory is actual only as becoming fully concrete, i.e., it is a sub-fact within the comprehending context of the complete (concrete) fact. Every sub-fact requires for its status as actual the context of the complete (concrete) self-evident fact. This amounts to the stipulation that every part has the whole implicated within it. Regarded as an abstraction, i.e., as merely something in itself, however, a sub-fact can only hypothetically be held to be actual. It is thus in fact no more than a theory. *Exaggerating the status of a theory must evoke from a serious Hegelian a feeling of uncertainty, bewilderment, perhaps even disgust, comparable, perhaps, to what the naive empiricist feels when a theory is not directly anchored in the illusion he calls sense immediacy. This is because he perceives that the basis for anchoring everything in hard (concrete) facts has been undercut.*

I have in effect said that *it is only from the actual perspective that the subject of the occasion is adequate to the apprehension of the plurality of phenomena.* There is an additional reason for saying this. In the final analysis neither truth nor theory are recognizable apart from their relation to one another. Like husband and wife, each names a relation, from one perspective. It would seem sensible to conclude that whenever we are concretely aware of a theory, that each — truth and theory — is within the then actual occasion being mediated as an accent within a discriminated identity inclusive of both. If we understand theory in the inclusive biological way that Popper proposes, i.e., to include expectations and unconscious as well as conscious dispositions, for the preceding statement a simpler one might be substituted: In every actual occasion each — truth and theory — is *being mediated* as an accent within a discriminated identity inclusive of both. This would cover the case of an actual occasion in which consciousness is coming to birth in an infant or foetus that had no prior conceptuality and hence no opportunity for self-conscious theory-making. But if every occasion has its dispositional and unconscious dimensions, especially seeing that it is in any case a new creation, I do not in the final analysis see the infant coming to consciousness as a special case. It is only special, this is to say, in that it may assist us to see more clearly what is entailed in the problematic of an actual occasion conceived as a concrete fact that *can speak for itself*.[13]

An authentically philosophical account of objective knowledge that is pluralistic in tone and made from the hypothetical perspective may recognize objective knowledge as result, as does Popper, but this must be in such a way that actuality, i.e., the mediating process of which it is the result, is not dismissed from view in preference for some vague common sense realism somehow critically assessed without having either a criterion or touchstone of truth, other than a theory that may (someday) lend itself to being demonstrated to be true within some abstract system. By actuality I here mean a completed process, in which process and result are yet integral, prior to the abstraction of the result. Popper's reference to truth as a regulative idea seems not to suffice to save him from the force of this criticism, apart from our being shown more about the unknown source of this notion.

In the preceding paragraph I have specified one plausible role for the philosophy of the particular sciences. Such an account as that to which I made reference would be *second philosophy*, a quite proper undertaking insofar as it recognizes the role of first philosophy in pursuing the idea of rendering presuppositionless its foundation in concrete fact. The *initial* fact to be explained in philosophical investigation is self-evidence. We dare not overlook it, or — following an initial distortion — dis- or as-similate it to theory. Moreover, *even as theories have truth as their touchstone and ought to be subordinate to truth, so their characterization ought to be subordinate to, and in conformity with, the characterization demanded by truth.* In the present approach, this statement has the status of a methodological

---

[13] See HFSI and SC, Book II, the final Chap, pp. 457-86.

axiom.

The first task of philosophy being unavoidably the explication of the concretely actual, Popper (to be doing philosophy) would seem to have begun from the wrong perspective. Even so, there are doubtless many persons who are so thoroughly theory-oriented that it has been somehow necessary, and perhaps sometimes even possible, to discover philosophy by this route. *The natural movement is nonetheless from concrete fact to theory — from light to shadow — rather than the reverse.* We grasp fact as such and as that with which we have to deal; perhaps better, it presents itself irresistably, *grasping us* like an impulse, a kind of spasm, before we can be aware of how or why it occurred or the dispositional propensities that went into its making or *being grasped.* As a settled world, it has no doubt at some point been disposed, as Popper might readily remind us, but is no longer. *Whatever disposition or theory has gone into its making, now concretized, is no longer disposition or theory but fact.* This all-or-nothing episodic and climactic phenomenon of concrescence is what determines irrevocably the natural directionality of our knowing,[13a] which is from fact to theory, and it is the insight that finally most decisively separates the present position from that of Popper. There is nothing mysterious or behind-the-scenes about this phenomenon: every concrete proposition and every concrete judgment exhibits it in the mediation of subject and predicate to the status of accents within an identity inclusive of both. All of this is inextricably bound up with a certain *theory,* however, and the problematic thus involved must now be taken up, insofar as this is plausible within the present context.

It is to be noted that the perishing of an actual occasion is inaccessible from an inside (actual) perspective, nor could it be, seeing that, where this to be knowable, this could only be from the perspective of a successor occasion. After all, death is simply *ceasing to be,* i.e., ceasing to be *actual.* The acknowledgement of this as an occurrence — the funeral celebration, as it were — must be in a successor occasion, if indeed it can be known at all. As pertaining to relations *between* two occasions, then, it would necessarily be hypothetical. *Death is a theory.* The reference here is to my own death. What I concretely know is merely *change.* Death thus turns out in fact to be *incurably* theory. But I must explain what I here have in view.

There is no *change* within an actual occasion, as Whitehead saw. It merely *becomes.* How then do I concretely know change? In the

---

[13a] This same directionality ultimately determines, as well, that a cause must be prior to — hence must occur 'before' — its effect.

above I referred to a hypothesis of the serially ordered (from the proximate to the remote) causal past made by natural reason on the basis of direct knowledge of history as actual within the present. A hypothesis is a possibility for concrescence in a subsequent occasion. A concretized hypothesis as to the serially ordered causal past may contribute to history as actual within the present. This being the case, it is correct to say that *an actual occasion that becomes but does not change can contain a serially ordered record of change as a part of what is becoming.* It is in this way that we know change in continuity, namely in the continuity of becoming.[14]

This explains why as I look out of my window upon the Fortress Hohensalzburg, situated in the center of the old medieval City ca. two kilomenters distant, and see smoke rising slowly from a chimney in the foreground, I know with certainty the smoke (within the context of the then actual occasion) at each minute stage, in turn, of its rising. Moreover, I know with equal certainty that these events occur in the succession that I actually perceive, conceptualize, and 'intend' them (in the broadest conceivable sense of "intend", including expectations and preconscious and unconscious dispositions, as well). This is the case even though, as each in turn (within the context of its constituting occasion)[15] is displaced by the next in the series, the previous one is no longer self-evident (nor would it be even if the smoke were not rising, but hovering instead), and hence if I am honest and forthright, I must not affirm it to be more, in any case, than hypothetically actual. Its compelling power has passed, so to

---

[14] "...in every act of becoming there is the becoming of something with temporal extension; but that the act itself is not extensive, in the sense that it is divisible into earlier and later acts of becoming which correspond to the extensive divisibility of what has become" (PR, p. 69).

I tender the above account as an example of a use of language in theory construction that reflects the concrete correlativity of the terms yielded by a concretized (mediated) contrast that I shall briefly commend: Change and continuity form a contrast that, generically considered, may apparently be found to be reconcretized in every actual occasion. This is to say, there would appear to be little room for doubt but that the analysis-synthesis of any actual occasion at all, or, what would come to the same, the reconstruction of a concrete language constitutive of an actual occasion, cannot be rendered complete apart from the inclusion of an account of this contrast.

"The continuity of becoming" referred to in the above text is *actual* time — and not temporality, which is hypothetical (pertaining, as it does, to relations between occasions), e.g., measured (clock) time. Each occasion creates its own space and its own time, or, in language that more nearly reflects the concrete situation, its "space-time". See p. 54 (n. 9) and X; and SC, pp. 100, 216f, 213, 477-86.

[15] As I employ the term, an "event" is concretely actual (and not merely hypothetically actual) only when it is present "for" a subject, both event and subject being comprehended within some actual occasion. Otherwise it may of course be hypothetically held to be actual, i.e., be affirmed to be hypothetically actual.

speak.

I cannot point to the exact points of death, as though they were somehow calibrated on the smoke rising from the chimney. It is rather that there is presented a continual 'flow' or passage away of what was (self-evidently) actual. That this flow is discontinuous — that it consists of a myriad of instances — may well escape me, it is true, and this even though, if I consider the matter philosophically, I might be led to anticipate that the individual occasions sequentially constitutive of this epoch each in turn climax in actuality and truth and that the actuality/truth-crests, being bridged by theory, yield the effect of the steady rise of the smoke that I apprehend. As I said, death is a theory. It assists me to explain *how* a series[16] of actual occasions, each a coherent and fully determined unity of discriminations can, by virtue of being complete in itself, be self-evident.

It might at first be supposed that the fact that the death of an actual occasion is not given self-evidently, but as an inference from change, might compromise the possibility of explicating the self-evidence of a particular occasion, or of approaching this ideal. If we are satisfied that this possibility resides solely and completely in the adequacy of its constitutive discriminations to its explication, which is the position that I wish to maintain, however, it will at once be clear that this is not the case. This is seeing that the perishing of an actual occasion, although it seems, within the framework of a hypothetical perspective, to follow as a necessary inference from its character as self-evident, neither conditions this self-evidence nor is it intrinsic to its character.

Theory proves to have a necessary role in the scheme of things within the process-actuality of which an account is being rendered when we proceed to take up a hypothetical perspective transcending the self-evidence of the here and now actual occasion, and in the task of explicating this self-evidence at both ends, as it were, of the process of concrescence. In the movement toward full concrescence, it takes the form of possibilities for actualization. At the terminus of concrescence, it provides us with the necessary notion of perishing. Accordingly, what appears most wrong-headed in Popper's concept of objective knowledge is not that he appeals to theory or presents us with theories to which, though acknowledging their fallibility, he accords (as a class) all but exclusive right, but that, for a person who proposes to be speaking for philosophy, he takes up an unjustifiable,

---

[16] The position that I wish to maintain is that this theory is not required to explain the self-evidence of any *one* actual occasion, that one being in its instant of actuality inclusive of all that is actual and in need of no conceptuality from without to speak for it.

regrettably exclusivistic (at least in development and emphasis), and I believe uncritical and *simply wrong*, perspective upon theory.

Even so, there is a high degree of complementarity to be observed in the two approaches when they are conceived as describing the same process from different perspectives — namely from the internal (actual) and the external (hypothetical) perspectives. If the translation of the language of external relations into that of internal relations, and vice versa, presents problems — perhaps insurmountable ones — the two kinds of accounts, within which the one or the other type of language counts as most essential, and indeed as normative, can nonetheless shed light upon one another, at least in a general way, not less because they form a distinct *contrast*. To be maximally complementary, however, they need to be made each with a certain cognizance of the other. Hypothetical thinking should be done, or at least begun, in a language loosely approximating the discriminations concretized in actual and proximate occasions, considering alternatives with a view to what has lent itself to being rendered actual in the past. And the analysis-synthesis of discriminations constitutive of actual occasions representative of selected relevant epochs — the task of first philosophy — should typically proceed with a cognizance of clues provided by ordinarly language as well as by the sciences and the theory of science as to what discriminations are being presupposed, as measured against what commonly gets reported as self-evident in the sense herein indicated.

To my earlier remarks with reference to "the settlement effect" the following may now be added. This effect, understood from a hypothetical perspective — the perspective of the theory of science — is such that, strictly speaking, a particular law of nature is by virtue of variations in contextual determination shaped somewhat differently within different occasions. It nonetheless retains its identity (as a generic type) by virtue of the fact that, in the case of occasions likely to be significant for selective comparison, such variations are likely to be of negligible import. This effect in view, a law of nature may be provisionally regarded as an emulation of a kind of massive averaging of its particular concretions. The true story, however, is rather that within any personal society[17] of actual occasions, e.g., the

---

[17] For Whitehead, "...a society of the 'personal' type....[is] a linear succession of actual occasions forming a historic route in which some defining characteristic is inherited ....A society of this sort is an 'enduring object'." (PR, p. 198) Seeing that I restrict the term "actual occasions" to conscious human occasions, Whitehead's usage [excepting its reference also to human occasions as a type of enduring objects (PR, pp. 89f)], is made to pertain to what I call "actual events" (see note 15).

society constituted by the life span of a given human person, it is inherited and reconcretized in successive occasions, ever in slightly variant form and with variations that may come to have cumulative import. There is thus a potential directionality and tendentiousness even in its mere "continuance", apart from, but sometimes paving the way for, the more decisive breaks implicated with mutation.

Aware of the Whiteheadian background of the concept of an actual occasion herein proposed, some readers will almost certainly have inquired at various points as to whether my reference is to a microcosmic occasion or to a macrocosmic one, and whether this distinction might not parallel the two perspectives. To the latter query the answer is a qualified "yes". The qualification consists in that the distinction seems at least initially problematical from other than a hypothetical perspective. We may initially be reminded that, there is no *actual* perspective from which two actual occasions might be compared, one microcosmic and one or more being macrocosmic. Is the case different when we consider a single occasion from two points of view? If the parallel holds, we would in effect be asked to accommodate two perspectives within the same occasion. I find myself unable to accomplish such a feat as to entertain two perspectives (*as such*) within a single occasion while it is yet actual.

From a hypothetical perspective the distinction has its usefulness in assisting us to envision many actual occasions each of which includes all that is actual within it, centered in such ways as to constitute (concretize) a plurality of definite and compatible spacial relations, i.e., the perceptual horizons of the respective occasions. This in view, the following two statements by Whitehead (the latter with bracketed amendations to take account of the fact that, within what I previously described as a critical process philosophy, in referring to what is real or actual one can properly have in view only what is self-evidently so) approximately reflect the perspective of this critique.

> The initial fact is macrocosmic, in the sense of having equal relevance to all occasions; the final fact is microcosmic, in the sense of being peculiar to that occasion.... The initial fact is the primordial appetition, and the final fact is the decision of emphasis, finally creative of the 'satisfaction'. (PR 47f)

> There are two species of process, the macroscopic process, and microscopic process. The macroscopic process is the transition from attained actuality [[in prior concrescences]] to actuality in attainment; while the microscopic process is the conversion of conditions which are merely real [[I should say hypothetical]] into determinate actuality. The former process effects the transition from the 'actual' to the 'merely real' [[I should say hypothetical]]; and the latter process effects the growth from the real [[I should say hypothetical]] to the actual. (PR 214)

5. Some Related Themes

There are three themes taken up by Popper that are relevant here that I have not mentioned up to now because they are not focal for my criticisms. As occasioning remarks indicative of some degree of compatibility, if not complementarity, however, they are equally deserving of notice.

1) *On Induction:*

Induction is a muddle, Popper concludes, and, because the problem of indication can be solved in a negative and straightforward manner, it turns out to play no integral part in epistemology or in the method of science and in the growth of science. (O.K. 85)

Within broad limits, this judgment can from the perspective of this critique be accepted, as can Popper's statement that "we proceed by a method of selecting anticipations and expectations or theories, which is often taken for indication because it simulates induction" (O.K. 272)

Popper's alternative is bold speculation.

> ... [W]e should dare to put forward bold hypotheses that open up, if possible, new domains of observation, rather than those careful generalizations from 'given' observations which have remained [ever since Bacon] the idols of all naive empiricists (O.K. 355).

This alternative, however, especially if it is insisted that bold speculation be done in the name of philosophy, does not appear to be the simulation of induction that we seek, both because it seems to be altogether too suggestive of speculation in a "pre-Kantian" sense, as though philosophy were still at such a stage that it can be content merely to practice the kind of speculation that is associated with the hypothetico-deductive method of the particular sciences, and also because we need to be taking account of the proximate character of concrescence and of what this has to do with the *constitution* of experience and of actuality. I propose that one ought to permit creation, – new, felt, and discoverable in its original act in every occasion – the basic structure of which is rendered explicit and specified as the elegantly simple dialectical-logical structure of the process of discrimination, to displace a part, at least, of the urgency of this counsel to somehow be inventive.

2) *On Mind-Body Interactionism:*

Popper believes that mind-body interactionism dominates the entire philosophical tradition from Plato and Aristotle down to the present day (O.K. 157-71, 178f) and he wishes to regard the notion as in some sense normative. That it has been peculiarly associated with Descartes and that it has on this account borne the brunt of heavy criticism is held to be owing to the fact that Descartes' concept of physical causation is incommensurable with it (O.K. 181f, 186).

The Hegelian/Whiteheadian perspective herein developed places the emphasis upon the process of interaction, as yet integral with its result, and not yet separated off by abstraction. Mind and body each become accents within a discriminated identity inclusive of both, the mediation and the discrimination being one of those that, as abstractly universal to all occasions, is reconcretized within each. Indeed, neither body nor mind are on the present account actual except as integral aspects or components of their mediation. As discriminated results, after the occasion has spent itself, they are mere potentials (for further mediation in new occasions). It tends to leave interaction as a theory, i.e., as 'true' from a hypothetical perspective, intact. "'True'" here means that it is congruent with the abstract character of the perspective and with theory of science usage.

3) *On Reductionism:*

Popper argues, in opposition to Paul Oppenheim and Hilary Putnam, that reductionism, although important as a research program, is not one that finally succeeds (O.K. 17-30). The reductionist idea is that the events or things on each level of such biological systems as the following, and their parts, should be explained in terms of the lower levels.

(12) Level of ecosystems
(11) Level of populations of metazoa [[sic.?]] and plants
(10) Level of metazoa and multicellular plants
(9) Level of tissues and organs (and of sponges?)
(8) Level of populations of unicellular organisms
(7) Level of cells and of unicellular organisms
(6) Level of organelles (and perhaps of viruses)
(5) Liquids and solids (crystals)
(4) Molecules
(3) Atoms
(2) Elementary particles
(1) Sub-elementary particles
(0) Unknown: sub-sub-elementary particles? (S.B. 17)

As a "rationalist", he hopes for a reduction of biology to physics. At the same time he writes, "... I think it quite likely that there may be no reduction possible: it is conceivable that life is an emergent property of physical bodies" (O.K. 292).

Indeed it is his concept of emergence that renders Popper cautious with respect to how far reductions can be carried.

> I do not believe that anybody who has ever seriously gone into any chapter of the history of ideas will think that a reduction of these ideas could ever be successful. But I take it as my task here...to argue...for the need to recognize and describe...emergent *entia* before one can seriously think about their possible elimination by way of reduction. (O.K. 297)

Setting aside Popper's hopes for a reduction of biology to physics, this line of reasoning, so far as it reaches, is highly compatible with the present perspective, which, however, provides the basis for a more decisive position in keeping with emergent evolution. I shall outline this position under three points.

a) An actual occasion is itself a reduction — a reduction to compossibles — though not one prejudiced against the "higher", or for that matter the "lower", evolutionary levels; also it is not one which can lend itself to further reduction, the truth being *its* whole.

b) An actual occasion cannot be affirmed to be actual from an external perspective. This is to say, to attempt to do so would be merely to register a belief or theory *about* actuality. Actuality now means self-evidently known actuality. The present standpoint can permit no compromising this point, the counterpart of the empiricist's insistence upon an appeal to sense perception, protocol sentences, or first person experience, apart from which all intellectual discipline goes by the board and anything is permitted.

c) Reductions of the higher to the lower levels of actuality do not work because actuality and truth are given only in wholes, i.e., particular concrescences, any aspect of which can only contextually be, and be known, for what it is. Moreover, seeing that the function of any aspect is concretely universal throughout the whole, any attempt at reduction will be confronted by the fact that equal claim can be made for any particular component aspect being that to which all others are reducible. Any discrimination constitutive of a particular occasion is equally essential to its being that occasion, whether belonging to its mental or physical pole, even if unique to it. Thus of the discriminations constitutive of an actual occasion, those unique to the human sciences are as essential as the space-time of physics. This stand against reductionism is of course not intended to discourage theorizing from abstractions appropriate to the area of investigation. It rather urges that such theorizing be done with a cognizance of *particular* concreteness — which only as *particular* can be (concretely) *universal* — conceived in something like the manner proposed. The concept of concrete universality must somehow be rehabilitated.[18]

---

[18] Having proceeded in this article in complete disregard of Popper's various statements in these and other works [most importantly, *Conjectures and Refutations* (London: Routledge and Kegan Paul, 1963), Chap. 15, "What is Dialectic", pp. 312-36] with reference to Hegel, I should perhaps enter a comment in this regard.

While I do not find his reception of Hegel uninteresting, three considerations have prevented me from treating it systematically. (1) The theme is one that would require a more extensive treatment, and one principally centered on Hegel. (2) Popper appropriates the notion of dialectic at such an entirely different level and in such a partial way that it seems to have little to do with the Hegel from whom I make selective appropriations for my Hegelian/Whiteheadian perspective. For him Hegelian dialectic is something purely external and pertaining exclusively to arguments in a language ready made (apart from dialectic having anything essential to do with this making) about a reality somehow (if vaguely) presupposed as ready made (also apart from dialectic). From the present perspective, Hegel understood in this way could only be considered to have been a very, very bad theoretician of science. Hence it is not surprising that Popper finds him to be a very, very bad philosopher. (3) Some considerable portion of what he says with regard to Hegel in the final analysis centers upon objections which it seems to me have often enough been replied to by Hegel scholars in the past, so that, at least so long as we stand in want of evidence of significant direct influence, these should no longer need to be of concern. Even so, I shall briefly mention three such objections.

1) Popper proposes that Hegel somehow denied the law of (non-)contradiction (O.K., pp. 126, 297). It is interesting to note that despite this objection, he somehow finds it possible to say, "My various schemata such as P_1 - - - TT - - - EE - - - P_2 may indeed be looked upon as improvements and rationalizations of the Hegelian dialectical schema: they are rationalizations because they operate entirely within the classical logical organon of rational criticism, which is based upon the so-called law of contradiction... contradictions, whenever we discover them, must be eliminated". (O.K., p. 297)

Even with the assistance of Popper, I have never been able to find a basis in Hegel for this allegation, popularized by Bertrand Russell, which has received far more attention in print than it ever deserved. I am convinced that it is only by systematic *misinterpretation* that it has gained plausibility in certain quarters. The situation is rather that Popper and Hegel do not in the least differ with respect to the propriety of the law of (non-)contradiction *within the province of abstract logic.* Hegel's principle of negation, linked with the *Aufhebung* of that which is negated — the fundamental characteristics of his *spekulativen Satz* — are a quite different matter, as even my selective interpretations should have gone some way toward rendering evident. Popper's error in this regard consists in not having located Hegel's undertaking and *method,* which is not really possible so long as one considers all conceptual comprehension to take the form of theory, *or in effect.*

For a fresh approach to the issues here involved, see Friedrich Kaulbach, "Subject Logic and Predicate Logic", trans. by Louis Agnosta, *Contemporary German Philosophy*, Vol. 1. The German original was published in, Manfred Riedel and Jürgen Mittelstrass (Editors), *Vernünftiges Denken* (Berlin/New York: de Gruyter, 1978). Also see, Josef Simon, "The Categories in the 'Habitual', and in the 'Speculative' Proposition: Observations on Hegel's Concept of Science", *Contemporary German Philosophy*, Vol. 2. The German original appeared in *Wiener Jahrbuch für Philosophie,* Band III; or H. K. Wells, *Process and Unreality,* or my remarks on pp. 25f, n. 4.

2) Popper objects that what he calls "the autonomy of the third world, and its feedback effect, becomes with Hegel omnipotent..." (O.K., p. 125). In so judging he would appear to have assumed that Hegel was a theoretician something like himself, operating adventurously within the hypothetico-deductive method. He displays no understanding of the senses in which phenomenological method is intended to be descriptive of mental and historical phenomena (including speculation), and finally, at least by implication, of nature and of actuality, as well. Far from having rendered Popper's third world omnipotent, Hegel had no place for predictions about the future, and hence with theorizing of the sort that pertains to

the prediction of the future. I think it is genuinely doubtful that he could have admitted such a body of concepts freefloating above a world of merely possible perceptual objects. After all, the discriminations constitutive of sense perception on his account are *aufgehoben* in the understanding and reason, each in turn, which means, among other things, that they are *preserved* within each, in turn. Reason thus never cuts itself free of perceptual objects on Hegel's account. Popper's problem would seem to be that he has identified Hegel as a speculative philosopher and attached his own free-wheeling meaning to the term "speculation".

3) Popper objects that for Hegel spirit is not only conscious but a self, in opposition to which he maintains that his third world ideas are totally different than consciousness (O.K., p. 126). This difference, I contend, is a weakness and not a strength in his position, unless one is prepared simply to dismiss from consideration all forms of thought that might be classified as idealistic.

VIII

HENRY NELSON WIEMAN AND THE CRITICAL TRADITION*

By "the critical tradition" I shall have in view that tradition in philosophy that had its inception in Kant. I understand the history of philosophy from Kant through Hegel as a phase by phase development of this tradition that continues down to the present day. A distinctive mark of this tradition is the recognition of a limit, or limits, of reason that renders impossible a return to metaphysics or ontology pursued in a pre-critical manner.[1]

If creative interchange came, in the latter phase of Wieman's career, to be one of his central categories, some of his previous references to the critical tradition are, in spite of their vagueness, so grossly inaccurate in what they assert or imply as hardly to invite any sort of interchange at all. Of the sources upon which this essay is based,[2] it is in SHG that he most exposes himself in this regard.

> We cannot know anything, and nothing can make the slightest difference in our lives unless it be an event or some possibility carried by an event. Transcendental realities literally have nothing to do after we have dis-

---

* Presented to the 1984 Wieman Centennial Conference on "Philosophy of Creativity as Creative Interchange: A Critical Analysis", August 16-19, at the Southern Illinois University at Carbondale, Illinois.

[1] "Pre-Critical" in this usage is not to be understood as applying equally to all philosophy previous to Kant. An authentically "phenomenological" dimension is to be readily made out in both Plato and Aristotle, e.g., by virtue of which much that these philosophers say does not fall under this ban. By the same token, although much that Wieman says is "pre-critical" in spirit, passages are to be found in which his reflections are less given to rumination and stand more proximate to the dynamic of occurrences as they are concretely grasped.

I have sometimes applied the term "Post-Kantian Critical" to Hegel, principally to remind the reader of English of the Critical tradition, which Hegel addressed and within the framework of which he to a significant extent is to be understood. See, e.g., CHSS.

[2] See the items listed with abbreviations following the text.

covered that all value, all meaning, and all causal efficacy are to be found in the world of events and their possibilities. Therefore, the transcendental must be ignored, except as an imaginative construction of the human mind. Since we never shall know everything, the transcendental might be retained as a mythical way of representing what is yet to be discovered. But that device has proved so confusing and misleading that we think it is better dropped. (SHG 8f).

Kant, as well, might have uttered the first two sentences of the above, had it ever occurred to him to affirm such things as transcendental *realities*. Wieman's misleading insinuation in this matter would seem to be of a piece with his conflation of the meanings of "transcendental" and of "transcendent". This is with the result that Kant's refusal to attribute ontological import to his transcendental forms of intuition, categories of the understanding, and principles of reason, which he conceived to condition the possibility of experience, is overlooked, a conflation that I suppose no proponent of the critical tradition would find acceptable. Wieman thus sets the stage for perversely construing both notions narrowly as products of otherworldly speculation. This is out of place. In this same vein, he conveniently overlooks Kant's renunciation of traditional metaphysics as exceeding the limits of reason, an oversight that becomes all the more striking when it is noted that the kind of speculation in which he himself engages must surely fall under the Kantian ban.

Since the foregoing criticisms pertain to features of Kant's thought that are so familiar that they may be found reflected in virtually any handbook in the history of philosophy, I allude to them only in passing. Later in SHG he proposes a task for philosophy that, with some shifts in terminology and a deletion, within this context, of his reference to matter, can readily be found commensurate with a Kantian perspective, as far as it reaches.

> The dispute between several philosophies.... support[[s]] the claim that the method of philosophy is the kind of reflective analysis which seeks knowledge of those ingredients found in all perceptual events because they are indispensable preconditions of everything else that man can experience. The human mind is such a necessary precondition. So also is matter, so also is form or structure, so also are events and quality. Since every one of these is a necessary precondition of all experience, the dispute about which of these is "ultimate" seems to be more pragmatic than metaphysical.... All these may be called "ultimate", not in the sense that they are outside and underlying experience but only in the sense that they are ingredients always present because no experience is possible without them. (SHG 206f)

On the page immediately following the foregoing, Wieman again takes up his running polemic against that vast army of straw men —

Chap. VIII, Wieman and the Critical Tradition

including somewhere among them proponents of one or another phase of what I am referring to as the critical tradition — that are always vaguely present as the backdrop against which he works, or at least waiting in the wings, and with whom he is ever and again fighting some sort of battle to the finish, and this with an implied originality that he gives the appearance of being unable to doubt.

> There is another kind of metaphysics which claims to know about a reality inferred or intuited from the world of events but not itself a part of this world. This kind of philosophy does not stop with the necessary preconditions of all experience, which are themselves events or the form or the mind or the quality in experience, but claims that these and everything else in experience can be rendered intelligible only if we postulate or infer or intuitively acknowledge something that is beyond all these. This something beyond may be God, variously interpreted; or the "Absolute", also variously interpreted; or the "Unconditioned", which cannot be interpreted at all; or some flux of energy or dance of atoms, inferred but never experienced. This Something which is not events or ingredient in events may be called "Reality", while events are "Appearance" only....
>
> The transcendental kind of philosophy just mentioned we shall not discuss here. The controversial issues concerning it are too recondite and complex. Its defenders have always been exposed to attack and have developed great subtlety and elaboration of defense until the devious routes of the dispute lead on endlessly and there is no conclusion. Therefore, we shall pronounce upon this transcendental philosophy the words *Pax vobiscum*. This we can do because the kind of philosophy we are considering, kept within the bounds of events, deals with elements inescapable to every one. Even the transcendentalist must examine and analyze events, if to no other end than to declare them to be illusion. On the other hand, the transcendental realm does not force itself upon those who refuse to take the further step leading beyond events. So we humbly keep within these bounds where all philosophers must walk, even though the giants are able to step beyond into Superhistory, the Unconditioned, the Absolute, the Hidden Deity, the Noumenon, or whatever they may call the nature of the Great Beyond. (SHG 208f)[3]

In writings subsequent to SHG that I have considered, I have found no inaccuracies with regard to the critical tradition of a comparable grossness, nor an instance in which he displays himself as so puffed up with humility at the implied expense of this tradition. This is although MUC contains the following simplistic interpretation of Kant's moral philosophy.

> Kant sought his ultimate moral standard by this dialectic of reason and reached the conclusion that rigorous, universal rational consistency was

---

[3] For further references by Wieman to "transcendental philosophy", see esp. SHG, pp. 33-37, 268, and ETW, pp. 372f. For comments in secondary sources relating to transcendentality, see esp. ETW, pp. 85, 310, and CI, p. 204.

sufficient in itself to make valid moral judgments. The limitation of this method appears when we note that the human mind undergoes creative transformation from infancy to old age, from one period of history and culture to others, and from one group of associates to another. (MUC 117f)

I know of no instance in which Kant proposes that a possible maxim of moral action might be adopted apart from regard to the situation, as Wieman here implies. Even so, Wieman seems here to be pointing, if bluntly, to a problem that has long been associated with Kant where the formalistic side of his ethical theory is accorded emphasis. Here and elsewhere, what I find to be a principal weakness in Wieman's critique is that he seems to be interpreting Kant in terms of a concept of reason restricted to its functions in the manipulation of abstractions, characteristic of his own usage. For Kant reason is dynamic and actual and not merely a faculty pertaining to what is theoretical. It consists in a theoretical *and a practical* faculty, and is the unity of these two that is realized in action. By the time we get to Hegel, the emphasis is placed upon the function of reason as a unity in the grasping (*begreifen*) of actuality in its *a priori* truth prior to abstraction. This primary function is also present in Kant, especially in the *Third Critique* and following, although in a less developed form and less uniformly emphasized.

If such barriers to creative interchange between Wieman's thought and the critical tradition as I have indicated were to be removed, what might result from such an interchange? Commensurate with the theme of this conference, I shall limit myself to some indications as to the direction in which I think it might lead as pertaining to Wieman's philosophy of creativity as creative interchange. With the consideration in view that Wieman's ethical views have already been subjected to a fairly thorough "critical" scrutiny,[4] I shall further restrict my focus to ontological and epistemological aspects of the concept of creative interchange.

Gary Kessler observed that a central problem with Wieman's philosophy consists in his not having satisfactorily bridged the dichotomy between the empiricist and the mystical aspects of his thought.

> It appears incongruous, if not contradictory, that an empirical theology and philosophy which insists that scientific reason is the only path to knowledge should have at its heart a profound mystical vision. Yet such is the character of Henry Nelson Wieman's philosophy.
> Much of the reaction to and discussion of Wieman's thought centers on

---

[4] See Clark A. Kucheman, "Creative Interchange and Moral Obligation", CI, 196-207.

Chap. VIII, Wieman and the Critical Tradition

> the empirical and scientific aspect...at the expense of its mystical aspect. Perhaps the incongruity between mysticism and empiricism leads to this oversight. Yet in many respects mysticism is more central to his thought than empiricism. (CI 122)

A few pages later Kessler drops the following suggestion, which, as he moves on to reflect what I judge to be a Husserlian type transcendental phenomenology, he leaves virtually undeveloped:

> If the incongruity between mysticism and science is to be removed as well as the dichotomy between the "two sides of living", there must be a genuine overcoming in the Hegelian sense. Some third synthesizing notion is required. I submit that this third notion is creative interchange. (CI, 128)

I propose in the remainder of this essay to follow up this suggestion as a point of access to some Hegelian themes that I think might have assisted Wieman to a more consistent and adequate development of his concept of creative interchange, had he been more open to them, reinforcing certain of his "second thoughts" that I shall mention, and that he himself failed to follow up. First I must set the problem in context with the resolution of which I am to be concerned.

For Wieman, "All knowledge must depend ultimately upon science, for science is nothing else than the refined process of knowing. Scientific method is simply the method of knowing". (RESM 23) With this many of us might agree, at least until we come to entertain doubts that science as he conceived it is of itself adequate to yield knowledge. Wieman's concept of science draws heavily upon Ralph Barton Perry, whom he quotes as follows.

> "Scientific description, then, is governed by two motives, on the one hand, unity, parsimony, or simplicity, the reduction of variety and change to as few terms as possible; and on the other hand, exact formulation. When a scientific description, satisfying these conditions is experimentally verified, it is said to be a law...". (RESM 160f)

He takes note of Perry's appeal to Galileo's formulation of the law of the acceleration of falling bodies, calling particular attention to his having ignored everything about the body save only certain very specific properties of time and space, namely "d", the constant variation in distance from the starting point, and "t", the constant variation in time. That the body passes me as it falls, that it reflects the light of the sun, or that it may crush a flower as it hits the ground are irrelevant to the kind of concept he was formulating. Moreover, he was seeking an elementary conception of uniform acceleration, a description of motion, which, however, neither seeks to account for nor justify what it describes. It is an analytic description, in that it expresses motion as a relation of the terms, such as *d*, *t*, etc., into which it can be analyzed. It is exact, mathematically formulated. And it simplifies through the discovery of an identity underlying difference. (RESM 163) The generalization arrived at that pertains to the scientifically defined and controlled data permits prediction (RESM 148). Scientific method thus proceeds by ignoring much. Wieman quotes W. F. Cooley as follows.

> The fallacy of simplification consists in assuming that, when a natural mechanism has been traced out and described the phenomena characteristic of it have been *fully* set forth and accounted for. As a matter of fact, however true and valuable the mechanical description may be, it is after all an account of part of the facts, not of the whole of them. (RESM 165)

The foregoing will suffice to suggest the simple model for science that Wieman seeks to find uniformly applicable to all areas of inquiry. Even while conceding that physics became a science long before psychology, "because its data were much more simple", the expectation is that sociology will follow in its path. Conceding that the datum of religious experience is yet more complex, so that "no method has yet been devised which is to treat it scientifically", he nonetheless optimistically notes, "we are working in that direction. (RESM 23f)

Wieman seeks to bridge the gap between scientific method, construed in the manner indicated, which of itself is supposed in some way to yield knowledge, and the kind of awareness of the "total fact" which yields religious experience, for which he draws upon the mystical tradition. He thus finds scientific method and religious experience to be "two sides of life" (RESM 119-159), the most extreme expressions of a duality and an opposition that runs all the way from the lowest biological level of the human being up through the social level, both constituting demands that life makes. "The contrast may be called roughly that of efficiency versus appreciation; or that of adaptation versus creativity" (RESM 119).

Of the members of this contrast he can then say,

> Scientific technique....vastly magnifies our efficiency in procuring anything we want and have the capacity to enjoy; but it greatly diminishes our capacity to enjoy. It gives us wonderful instruments for achievement, but narrows and distorts our vision of what is to be achieved. (RESM 186)

Human creativity consists in bringing together these two sides of discovery, open awareness and theorizing, with its analysis, discrimination, definition, and experimentation. "When these two are unified and rightly balanced, human life leaps forward like an open spillway or a hound unleashed" (RESM 197).

The object is thus found to be very much more than what it is described to be by scientific theory. Even a correct scientific theory falls short of the totality of the object as it is given in contemplation (RESM 73). In another context he notes that to reduce the depth and richness of experience to abstractions would "deprive human living of almost everything that makes for good" (MUC 141).

> The swing of the pendulum of interest from mysticism back to scientific method and from scientific method to mysticism, is of value only if it serves in each swing to build up a little more the wealth and fullness of that which we contemplate" (RESM 84).

It seems to me that Wieman renders his position respecting what constitutes knowledge problematical if not untenable by utterances such as the foregoing, that leave the distinct impression that we do not, after all, properly know anything until we grasp it within a holistic context, within which what we were previously led to suppose that we know scientifically is no more than a necessary aspect. Notwithstanding, he maintains explicitly in SHG, in consistency with his plaudits for what he maintained to be the one and only scientific method (and apparently never disavowed), that "truth is *never* the whole of any concrete embodiment of value but always one abstract feature *ingredient in concrete value* as experienced by human beings" (SHG 168, emphases added). In the course of clarifying this standpoint, he proposes, "The totality of all structure includes far more than can ever be specified" (SHG 169). Behind this statement seems to lurk the assumption of a sharp line of demarcation between cognitive and non-cognitive belief, shared with many positivists of his time.

> In each case a proposition is cognitive only when its acceptance is determined by evidence, evidence being correspondence between a specified structure and observed events. When a belief is otherwise determined it is not knowledge....The tests of truth are three — observation, agreement between observers, and coherence. All three apply to every proposition alleged to be true". (SHG 211)

Wieman, if he was serious about bridging the gap *philosophically* between "science" and the "total fact", ought to have introduced systematically the concept of dialectical mediation (*Vermittlung*), with particular cognizance of Hegel's development of this concept.[5]

---

[5] For an introduction to Hegel's concept of mediation, see the Preface to his *Phänomenologie des Geistes*, Hoffmeister Ed. (Hamburg: Meiner, 1952), pp. 21ff; or *Phenomenology of Mind*, trans. by J. B. Baillie (New York: Macmillan, 1955), pp. 82ff.

Students of Wieman may find certain parallels I have drawn between Hegel's mediation and Whitehead's prehension in Essay IV useful as a point of access to Hegelian mediation.

Had he been in a position to accord this concept status within a science of knowledge (*Wissenschaft*) more inclusive in scope than the science he defended, this concept might then have served in place of such colorful metaphors as the swing of a pendulum, an open spillway, and a hound unleashed.

Mediation is the dynamic relation between the first and second moments of Hegelian dialectic whereby they issue in a synthesis. As such it may perhaps best be understood as the affirmative counterpart of negation, an import of which is that any ideal or real entity is what it **concretely** is by virtue of being determined by what it is "up against", i.e., by what it is *not*, even as what is not is equally determined by this same limit or boundary. A philosophical proposition, as such, is indeed on Hegel's account a process of mediation whereby the meanings of a radically particular (or concrete) subject and a radically particular (concrete) predicate each mutually and exclusively determines the other, to become an accent within an identity inclusive of both.[6] I have argued that any given mediation may alternatively be viewed as a discrimination, which, being non-abstractable is neither more nor less than the mediated relation between its discriminated aspects.[7] Thus conceived a dialectical account becomes an account of the discriminations constitutive of concrete actuality and of our knowledge of concrete actuality, these being commensurate with Hegel's mediation of subject and substance within each actual occasion, if I may adapt a term from Whitehead,[8] and accents within a mediated identity inclusive of both. Each of these accents is conceived as containing sub-discriminations within it.

The relation between scientific method and religious experience, which Wieman understood in terms of mysticism, is essentially one of mediation. Had he understood it as such, proceeding from *the lived fact* that we do indeed concretely mediate these polarities in every actual occasion, he would have taken upon himself the task of

---

[6] *Phän.*, p. 51; or *Phen.*, pp. 120. The term "Vermittlung" (mediation), is not used in the relevant passage, although it is implied, having been introduced by Hegel previously. (See n. 5.)

[7] See, Josef Simon, "Die Kategorien im 'gewöhnlichen' und im 'spekulativen' Satz", *Wiener Jahrbuch für Philosophie*, Band III (Vienna/Stuttgart: Braumüller, 1970); or, in English trans. by Gunther Heilbrunn, in *Contemporary German Philosophy*, Vol. 2.

[8] The use of the term "actual occasion" for Hegel's *Begriff* is for present purposes intended to suggest an interpretation of Hegel as a pluralist, commensurate with the tradition of interpretation of pluralistic personalism. For a further development of this usage, see CHSS, RAtP, and TCMM.

For my critique of Whitehead, some aspects of which pertain to Wieman as well, see esp. Essays I and II.

describing this mediation in its concrete actuality of becoming. In this case, he would not have subordinated its status as such to science viewed exclusively as a method of dealing with abstractions. Also, he would have introduced not merely one, but many types of discrimination-generating mediations, commensurate with the inherent complexity of the problem that he was attacking.⁹ To perceive that Wieman struggled with the duality of scientifically quantified aspects of knowledge to bring these even vaguely into some kind of relation to more inclusive ordinary consciousness — apart from which, as even he would seem to have half perceived, these aspects could not even be found intelligible — it is indeed regrettable that he should have

---

⁹ By way of illustration, and to occasion some further observations, I shall now indicate how I propose that the concept of mediation, accorded the status of a methodological principle, might be made to strengthen the philosophical foundations of Wieman's concept of creative interchange at two specific points, releasing it from dominance by a science too narrowly conceived.

A number of authors have accused Wieman, directly or indirectly, of illicitly moving from "is", to which his scientific method may pertain, to "ought", to which it cannot pertain (Edward John Carnell, ETW, pp. 309f). If careful account is taken of the statement by Wieman previously cited, that "truth is never the whole of any concrete embodiment of value but always one abstract feature *ingredient in concrete value* as experienced by human beings", this criticism is not, I think, fully justified. It is clear, nonetheless, that he has legitimized the concern of his critics by passing over this matter much too lightly. Wieman might have strengthened his position, insofar as he was seeking to give expression to a philosophy of creativity, and been more forthright, had he been in a position to trace out the lineaments of a dialectic of fact and value, and the process by which these aspects are mediated to become accents within a concrete identity inclusive of both, this being one of the central discriminations at once constitutive of actuality and of knowledge alike. It is possible that he vaguely presupposed such a dialectical phenomenon. If so, this should not suffice. I put the matter thus because I believe that the tracing out of such mediations points unavoidably toward the concept of a unified reason, an important heritage of the critical tradition that can be put to the service of a philosophy of creativity and creative interchange. Wieman's objection that "the totality of all structures includes far more than can be specified", previously noted, has, after all, no force whatever if by totality we mean, with Hegel, what actually is *explicitly* grasped (*begriffen*), including feelings, discursive concepts, and intentions all at various levels of determinateness and of explicitness. To this it may be added that Hegel provided for *implicit discriminations*, which might even be necessary to the grasping of an actual occasion; but the fact that such in a given historical epoch might not be explicit, would seem, following this account, not to have resulted in a self-consciousness and a world present for self-consciousness being less than certainly known, but merely in a want in the philosophical comprehension of this dimension of the self-certainty of reason.

In addition, Wieman especially needs an explicit dialectic of quality and quantity. He certainly struggled valiantly to accord status to qualities as well as to quantities in experience, seeing that also qualities were found to lend themselves to mathematization and thus yield unity amenable to what he regards as scientific method. If I am correct in this, he is presupposing something very much like the outcome of Hegel's dialectic of quality and quantity (that yields measure). If this is so, would it not have been more forthright were this matter to be set forth in a manner that reflects the dynamic process of reason undertaking (and ultimately, at the primary level, *undergoing*) this process of mediation, rather than being merely vaguely adumbrated, perhaps as *a theory about* polar aspects of actuality and of our apprehension of actuality?

proceeded without awareness of Hegel's extensive efforts, drawing upon the entire historical tradition up to his time, to resolve this very problem. What we may learn from Wieman's want of success in mediating scientific method and mysticism is that this cannot be resolved within the purview of scientific method as he conceived it, nor at the level of abstract thought alone or initially, no matter how precise an artificial language might be invoked. Of course Wieman was "primarily a theologian and philosopher, and not a historian", as he noted,[10] but this acknowledgement only raises the issue as to whether theology and philosophy are not *inherently* historical disciplines. It is only fair to note, however, that Wieman records some second thoughts which lend themselves to being construed as moving in a direction compatible with my critique. Thus in SHG we read,

> If the structure of qualitied events and the possibilities relevant to them, as determined by noncognitive reaction of the organism, must undergo change in the very process of achieving knowledge of them, the objector might say that they are never known. Only that modified form of them is known which can reach knowledge. But if this modification is precisely what must always occur when one knows anything at all, it is useless quibble to say that this modification renders knowledge of them impossible when, in fact, it is precisely what must occur when any knowledge is ever achieved. So we conclude that it is quite proper to say that we come to know the structure of events determined by noncognitive feeling-reactions, even though this structure is modified by the inquiry issuing in knowledge.
>
> While we believe that truth can in this way be identified with the total value-structure of events relative to the non-cognitive feelings of associated organisms, we shall not adopt this alternative. The complexity of existing reality so far exceeds any competence of language to designate it that we must simplify whenever we can. It is much more simple, and hence less staggering to our limited abilities, if we identify truth with that possible structure which is actualized in events to the degree that correct knowledge is achieved but does not characterize events completely and perfectly until complete and perfect knowledge of them is attained. (SHG 167f)

Shortly following he is led to the conclusion that "truth is never the whole", a proposition that directly contradicts Hegel's well-

---

[10] John Broyer, "A Final Visit with Wieman" (CI, p. 91). It is interesting to note that even though Wieman is engaged in speculative thought, in proceeding with relatively little regard to the history of his discipline he followed the lead of logical positivists of his time who disavowed the right of speculative enterprises.

A more plausible objection to Wieman's having taken over uncritically the simplistic concept of science and knowledge built upon the undoubted power of abstraction, mathematization, and inductive generalization might be that as a theologian his principal business was not to settle issues in the philosophy of science so much as to meet the crisis of faith as reflected in the religious fellowships of his time to which he addressed himself.

known utterance, "The Truth is the whole".

The "complete and perfect knowledge" referred to in the above is no doubt the knowledge of abstractions, set within some sort of context of value, that Wieman wishes to attribute to science. The criteria here in view, even though the introduction of a context of value certainly seems to introduce a strain into the concept of science to which he proposes to adhere, are I think inadequate to the concept of a science that of itself could yield holistic contextual knowledge. I have here in view the kind of self-certain (presuppositionless) knowledge of which Hegel intended to provide a dialectical account for his own time. This account includes within it not merely the results of a single science of abstractions of the sort Wieman takes up, but of a veritable encyclopedia of scientific methods all sublated (*aufgehoben*, transcendended and contained) within the inclusive structure of (organic) actuality, with its constitutive discriminations, as it is known (as method, ie., the Logical Idea) as such.[11] This would have involved the sublation of the methods of empiricism within every actual occasion, however, and rendering these subordinate to a more comprehensive principle, namely the principle of reason as self-determining and as (at once) self- (and world-) determination. Given his point of beginning in a certain conception of exact science, this would have been a difficult step for Wieman to have taken. The following passage will nonetheless suggest that he entertained the idea of a move in this direction.

> If reason should be identified with creativity as creativity has been interpreted in this writing, it would be very different from reason identified with the tests distinguishing true from false statements. It is confusing to use the same word to refer to matters which have almost nothing in common. Therefore we shall be thinking of reason not as the creation of insights but as the methods and operations by which true statements are tested and distinguished from false statements, from dreams, aesthetic and artistic creations, fanciful imaginings, and much else of like sort. (MUC 137)
>
> Reason, as the word is here used, can be most simply defined as the method of analysis, observation, inference, prediction, experiment, and logical coherence....
> As said before, reason cannot itself produce the insight, the theory, the innovating idea, the hunch, the clue, or the suggestion to be tested.... Without this method of reason for distinguishing true from false, fact from fiction....we cannot know what a new idea really is....But the new idea, the insight, the suggestion cannot be produced by reason. The new idea is the grist for the mill of reason but reason cannot create its own grist.

---

[11] G. W. F. Hegel, *Enzyklopädie der philosophischen Wissenschaften 1830*, edited by Friedhelm Nicolin and Otto Pöggeler (Hamburg: Meiner, 1959).

Creativity produces that. (MUC 138f)

On Hegel's account reason — sometimes God — creates its own grist, and whatever creativity there is is the creativity of reason. I have proposed that a Hegelianized actual occasion that perishes provides for the possibility of a new birth of freedom and of creativity in each occasion.[12] An upshot of reason creating its own grist is that it becomes possible to acknowledge that the self-conscious individual knows his world and self *a priori* in a particular occasion for the actuality that it is, i.e., prior to abstraction and to the sharing of such aspects of this occasion with other persons as may lend themselves to being shared,[12a] and also prior to any possible unpacking and reconstitution of the occasion in secondary reflection. This is impossible on Wieman's view, who thereby relegates the "total fact" to an uncertain status, because he thinks that scientific method intrudes before we can know anything. On the basis of Wieman's account, which in this regard flies in the face of what seems to me to be one of the most reliable dispositions of common sense, knowledge is incurably public.[13] On this account he cuts himself off from the possibility of providing an adequate account of what may well in the final analysis be the most certain, if not indeed the *only* knowledge each of us ultimately has, leaving us in the shadow land of theory.

My view, following Hegel in the main, is that such "knowledge" as Wieman attributes to science, being the knowledge of abstractions,

---

[12] This is with the acknowledgement that since the idea of ("my own") death can in principle never have more than the status of a theory (because my own death cannot present itself as a phenomenon for me), what I experience is *change* in continuity.

[12a] The foregoing statement reflects the view that the lived occasion might privately be grasped as such and that all language might be public. In the preparation of this paper, I was attempting to avert the issue as to whether there might be such a thing as private language. As I subsequently came to reflect systematically upon the issue from the perspective herein being developed, I came to see with increasing clarity not only that conventional language but what I have come to call concrete language, as well (in which creation speaks for itself), must be as inherently social as is self-consciousness for Hegel.

The social status of concrete language may for present purposes be summed up under the following three principal considerations. (1) It is *only* within an organism that all aspects and relations are concretely universal, including authentically concrete utterances, and a being-lived occasion is an organism (and this not merely in a metaphorical sense). (2) In an I-Thou relation a given occasion, by virtue of including at least one person other than its subject, is intersubjective in character. (3) Utterances of authentically concrete language, which occur *within* the occasion as yet actual and are presentational (and not merely re-presentational) in character, as expressive of this intersubjective character, are inherently 'intended' for all who share the occasion. See Essay IX, Part I; Essays X and XII; and in SC, consult the index under "language, concrete".

[13] SHG, p. 211. That knowledge is *a priori* should not be interpreted as implying that language is not social in character. See Essay IX.

can have only the status of something derived, its derivation being at once both from concrete knowing and the concrete actuality known, each an accent within a mediated identity inclusive of both. Such scientific "knowledge" may contribute possibilities to the concrescence of a new occasion, thus contributing to knowledge in a proper (actual) sense, but the story of science coming to the knowledge of abstractions, is not, as such, a creation story, but something after the ("total") fact.

How do Wieman's creative event and creative interchange bear upon the problem of mediating between scientific method and the experience of the "total fact" and with non-cognitive meanings that he associates so largely with religious experience? In SGH we read,

> The ultimate determinant of truth and knowledge is the creative event generating the rational principles of the mind and the structure of matter in mutual determination of one another. Also this progressive creation rears a culture which shapes the reactions of the human body, the directions of attentive consciousness, and the technology, so that empirical findings will yield reliable knowledge inductively established within this framework of order shared in common by the mind and its appreciable world. (SHG 201)

If Wieman's concept of creative interchange, which of the sources I have consulted surfaces especially in MUC, may be regarded as an outgrowth of his concept of the creative event, then I think he comes very close to saying, if not quite directly, what Kessler thought he should have been saying, namely, that creative interchange plays the crucial role in bridging the gap between scientific method and religious experience.

> Creative interchange is that kind of interchange which creates in those who engage in it an appreciative understanding of the original experience of one another. One gets the view point of the other under such conditions that this original view derived from the other integrates with one's own personal resources. This integration modifies the view derived from the other in such a way that it becomes a part of one's own personal resources. This integration modifies the view derived from the other in such a way that it becomes a part of one's own original experience....
> Creative interchange has two aspects which are two sides of the same thing. One aspect is the understanding in some measure of the *original* experience [[emphasis added]] of the other person. The other aspect is the integration of what one gets from others in such a way as to create progressively the original experience which is oneself. This creative interchange creates the unique individuality of each person while at the same time enabling each to understand the individuality of others....[A]ll this is partial, incomplete, infected with error and distortion. Nevertheless it can be more or less complete, comprehensive, and correct. (MUC 22f)

If we understand the reference to "original experience" in the above as referring primarily to what we can maximally grasp of the integral wholeness of the occasion that another person lives,[14] so as to be able in some degree to understand that person empathetically, then it seems to me that Wieman's creative interchange in the ideal case might be said to mediate between the knowledge of abstractions associated with scientific method and the non-cognitive meanings associated with the "total fact" that is open to a broadened religious awareness. Thus interchanges that may begin with ordinary shared meanings, including the weather, the time of day, and the knowledge of science, may move to the level of a sharing of whole persons. If I am correct in this, what most conspicuously distinguishes creative interchange from Hegelian mediation is that in Hegel's account *mediation is a (if not the) central feature of his concept of scientific method,* both with reference to the particular sciences and with reference to knowledge. In Wieman's thought it appears (as creative interchange) as a kind of adjunct to his more narrowly conceived scientific method, apart from being assigned a definite methodological status. Additional distinctions consist in the certainty of absolute knowledge on Hegel's account and its *a priori* character, by virtue of which it stands free of any possible manipulation or doubt. Certainly these differences are not trivial. I have the impression that Wieman has an *a priori grasp* of creativity and creative interchange, but that, with regard to method, he is not well situated to give an account of this grasp.

In my opinion a phenomenology of mediations ought to provide the foundation of a philosophically developed concept of creative interchange. In this case creative interchange could become the name of a certain group of mediations that operate at the level of personal relations.

It seems to me that if the concept of creative interchange is deserving of the status Wieman in his later work accords to it, it would be only consistent with this evaluation to integrate this function into the very concept of reason. (So readily is the principle of mediation illustrated!) But if creative interchange is a species of mediation, then it is more proper to follow Hegel in construing mediation as constitutive of reason and as reason's procedure for its self-constitution. The development of the concept of creative interchange as a species of Hegelian mediations inclusive of such mediations as obtain in personal relations could strengthen Wieman's

---

[14] "A serious danger threatens our society as mechanized communication prevails and the speech of creative interchange declines" (SENA, p. 184).

enterprise at what may well be its weakest point, which I think Kessler correctly spotted, by assisting us to explain the mediation of scientific methods obtaining in the particular (abstract) sciences and religious experience, on the one hand, and assist students of Hegel to see the personal and social outworkings and implications of a reason adequate to the mediation of nature and spirit, on the other.

It may be maintained that I have overlooked a phenomenology that is somehow at work in Wieman's thought. If this is so, I find such a phenomenology only vaguely present and in such a way that it becomes confused with "empirical method", with which it has almost nothing in common, and therefore not as such clearly recognizable, certainly not for a reader who is naturally led to associate empiricism with that historical development the fundamental tenet of which is

> that all knowledge of matters of fact always derives ultimately from sense-observation in some form, which is what it is, independent of conceptual, theoretical or logical connections; and any statement or proposition expressing the brute facts so observed is logically independent of every other such statement.[15]

A phenomenology of mediations and an empirical investigation carried out in consistency with philosophical empiricism thus conceived are quite different enterprises, seeing that for the phenomenological account, precisely those isolated derivatives from sense observation in some form are perceived (in the primary sense) *only in the process of their being mediated.* From the standpoint of a phenomenology of mediations the empiricist's account of isolated derivations from sense observation can only be arrived at by abstraction from a concretely actual (lived) occasion after the fact. What results is a representation not so much of actuality as of possibility, epitomized by J. S. Mill's concept of nature as a permanent possibility of experience. Wieman's central methodological mistake was in beginning with empirical method, most fundamentally pertaining to possibilities of experience worked up from abstract ideas. When he came to explicate his concepts of creativity and creative interchange he appealed to concretely lived experience, and perhaps, if vaguely, to what we should learn to call concrete mediations. Because his starting point was wrong, however, he was led perversely to make these pertain primarily to the abstractions with which he began. The order needs to be reversed. The phenomenology of mediations is the creation story, with which, to be methodologically circumspect, he

---

[15] Errol E. Harris, *The Foundations of Metaphysics in Science* (New York: Humanities, 1965), p. 26.

should have begun, and empirical generalizations built up out of abstractions after the fact pertain to the search for hypotheses for the preparation of possibilities for *future* creations.

ABBREVIATIONS

ETW   Robert W. Bretall (Ed.), *The Empirical Theology of Henry Nelson Wieman* (Carbondale, Ill.: Southern Illinois University Press, 1963).

CI   John A. Broyer and Wm. S. Minor (Eds.), *Creative Interchange* (Carbondale, Ill.: Southern Illinois University Press, 1982).

CW   William Sherman Minor, *Creativity in Henry Nelson Wieman*, ATLA Monograph Series, No. 11 (Metuchen, N. J.: The Scarecrow Press, Inc., 1977).

RESM   Henry Nelson Wieman, *Religious Experience and Scientific Method* (Carbondale, Ill.: Southern Illinois University Press, 1971, the vol. having originally appeared from Macmillan, 1926).

SHG   _____, *The Source of Human Good* (Carbondale, Ill.: Southern Illinois University Press, 1946).

MUC   _____, *Man's Ultimate Commitment* (Carbondale, Ill.: Southern Illinois University Press, 1958).

SFNA   _____, *Seeking a Faith for a New Age: Essays on the Interdependence of Religion, Science and Philosophy*, edited by Cedric L. Hepler (Metuchen, N. J.: The Scarecrow Press, Inc., 1975).

IX

THE SOCIAL CHARACTER OF CONCRETE LANGUAGE*

I

§1 If it should be found that belief in some one idea could even conceivably have the effect of resolving or leaving readily resolvable all or most of the basic problems that are the business of first philosophy, we should feel compelled to give this idea most careful scrutiny and to see its implications spelled out in every relevant context. This would be the case, moreover, even if this notion were initially to be found to be counter-intuitive, at least to most inquirers. Truth proving stranger than fiction is a familiar enough phenomenon in the twentieth century.

§2 More than ten years ago, quite by accident, I happened upon an idea that seemed to have an importance of this dimension, namely the idea of a necessary connection between the self-evidence and the perishing of a concretely actual occasion of experience. (I thus state the matter in language proximate to that which I have come to find most appropriate for the resultant conceptuality.) By "self-evidence" I mean something like Hegel's self-certainty of a presuppositionless reason. By "perishing", I mean something like what Whitehead meant by this term. Whitehead developed the concept of perishing as a way of building into his concept of an actual occasion[1] the character of an electro-magnetic event in physical theory. He

---

* A shorter form of this paper was originally prepared for the First International Social Philosophy Conference, held in Montréal, August 19-23, 1983, and for the film edition of *The Journal of Social Philosophy* dedicated to the proceedings of the meeting. In Part I, I outline the concept of concrete language, with an eye to its social character, that I find implicated with what I have previously proposed as a necessary connection between the self-evidence and the perishing of a concretely actual occasion. In Part II, I outline my case for maintaining that such a concretely actual occasion can be *re*constituted after the fact through secondary reflection.

[1] The term "actual occasion" is adapted from Whitehead's usage. Where it occurs in the singular, i.e., to designate concrete actuality inclusive of all that is actual, I have been rather free in my Hegelianizing of it. Where it occurs in the plural, its reference being to hypothetical entities, it retains much more of its original sense in Whitehead's usage. Seeing that an actual occasion may be thought of in a Whiteheadian way, as a process within which

apparently did not consider setting this within the context of anything like a self-evident occasion, however, and indeed, this would have been out of keeping with what I prefer to call the *wissenschaftstheoretischen* standpoint that dominates his conceptuality, even when doing his metaphysics.² It is within this new context that the notion of perishing seems to take on a decidedly new significance, and this apart from the loss of its function within Whitehead's conceptuality.³ If absolute freedom consists in everything being determined and *in my knowing what determines me,* as Hegel proposed, then the perishing of the occasion within which this occurs could clear the way for a new birth of freedom within a successor occasion, with different determinants. The effect would be something like Hegel's absolute knowing within the context of the whole that is the truth, and this would be reconcilable with a world in which things *change* from one occasion to another. Absolute knowing would then be the end-phase of a process of mediation that climaxes in concreteness fully discriminated by an *immanent* dialectic (implicated with the identity as discriminated of subject and substance) and thus fully actualized. This end phase would be inclusive of the entirety of its process of mediation, i.e., the *becoming* of its being and the *being* of its becoming. *Change* would thus be rendered reconcilable with *absolute knowing* within respective successive occasions. The process of mediation being one within which a plurality of data are mediated to unity, moreover, the perishing of the occasion would leave open the way to a renewal of this process. The effect would be to render the hard phenomenological core of Hegel's system available for appropriation *as a method* for the analysis-synthesis of actual occasions in our own epoch by contributing the principal ingredient of a complementary theory to serve as a supplement, to enable us to understand aspects of our experience — such as change — that lend themselves less readily, at least, to a phenomenological analysis that follows the Hegelian model. The hard determinism within any single

---

a plurality of data, derived from many occasions (that were), are mediated to unity — a process that may be described either from an actual perspective (from within an occasion that includes all that is actual) or from a hypothetical perspective (*as though it were possible* to take up a perspective upon a plurality of such occasions) — this adaptation of the term finds its justification. Moreover, this later perspective is the one from which we prepare possibilities for possible concrescence.

² See pp. 53-57, esp. pp. 55f, and Essay IV.

³ To show that I retain also the principle of this concept that is exhibited within Whitehead's conceptuality, it would be necessary to make reference to my concept of an "event". As in the case of Whitehead's actual occasion, an event can be an object *for* a subject existing outside of it. Within my proposal, it needs only to be included within a concretely actual occasion to be itself concretely actual.

concretely actual occasion that would find justification if this idea were to prove itself would warm the heart of every thoughtful cyberneticist, at the same time suggesting a standpoint from which to explain human error while exempting his or her ideal robot from it.

§3 That the outworking of the idea of a necessary connection between self-evidence — Hegel's self-certainty of a presuppositionless reason — and the perishing of an actual occasion should have laid claim to so much of my time — and the task to this point appears to me to be no more than well under way — is due to the fact that, although the phenomenology of self-evident occasions seems to lend itself to being made self-evident, *the idea of perishing can in principle never rise above the status of being a theory.* For this to be clear it is only necessary to note that a concretely actual occasion, to be complete in Hegel's sense, must contain all of the discriminations required for its explication, including that between its understanding, interpreting subject and the world present for this subject (RAtP). On this account the reference must here be to the death of the only subject fully privileged to the occasion, i.e., to "my own death", which, whether as the conclusion of one actual occasion or of that epoch of occasions constitutive of my life span from birth to death, can of course never be a part of a phenomenological account, either of mind — myself as subject — or of the world-present-for me. This is the case, moreover, even if death may *seem* as certain as taxes, since we here have to do not with worlds of mere *seeming*, but with what is concretely *known*, i.e., known as settled (if only for its brief season) concrete fact.[4] If the notion of my own death can thus never be accorded status as being more than a theory, the concept of self-evidence as pertaining to the occasion that is actual seems to lend itself no less on this account to being found to be self-evident.

§4 The notion of perishing will at first seem counter-intuitive. As a critic of Whitehead remarked, "What I experience is not a world jerkily coming into and out of existence, but continuity and a flow of consciousness". Can this experience be explained if it is maintained that occasions that are complete in the Hegelian sense perish? I believe so, and the fact that my own death can never present itself as a phenomenon seems, at least at *second glance,* to serve this explanation rather than stand in its way: Since I cannot experience the

---

[4] My "concrete fact" is an alternative way of designating a concretely actual occasion, a usage that was suggested by Whitehead's application of the term "complete fact" to his actual occasion, which, however, I have shown not in fact to be complete, and this by virtue of its non-inclusion of its understanding, interpreting subject, which Whitehead locates in a successor occasion (Essay II).

death that I hypothesize to account for how each member, in turn, of a series of actual occasions can climax in a coherent whole that is the truth, what I experience is (merely!) *change* between successive occasions that are, *each in turn,* self-evident.[5]

§5   If it is inquired what is self-evident, my reply, if presented with some new accents, can now, on the whole, be quite Hegelian. What is self-evident is the entirety of the occasion as fully concrete, i.e., fully discriminated, inclusive of its causal past as this *in some manner and form* has been rendered actual in the present. If we consider this whole, one aspect at a time *in context,* what is self-evident is a concrete proposition. My concrete proposition, like Hegel's philosophical (or speculative) proposition, is constituted by a subject and a predicate *being mediated* to constitute accents within an identity inclusive of both (*Phän.* 51; or *Phen.* 120). This definition should prove adequate if two qualifications are borne in mind. (1) This is a discriminated identity, and its discriminations do not dissolve into the Absolute, do not pass away, at least not prior to the perishing of the occasion. Rather, the absolute (occasion) *is constituted by these very discriminations,* which, as concrete, are not abstractable from the elements or aspects discriminated. (2) The reference here is not to abstract universals,[6] but to a subject and predicate each in its

---

[5] This line of argumentation must be carried forward within the context of a treatment of history as actual within the present. See SC, pp. 477-86.

If the idea of my own death must in principle ever remain an unconcretizable theory, assuming that the only way in which I could actually know the death of another would be by analogy to my own — precisely parallel to the manner in which I derive the idea of power in another being by analogy to my own feeling of decision-connected muscular power —, then it would appear that I must conclude that death as such can have no more secure status. In any case, I have come to put little stock in this particular theory, seeing that to accept its consequences would render me unable to understand, much less to account for, what I maintain to be my own most rational decisions and actions, a consideration that I suppose I should have had little difficulty in explaining to Kant, were he present to hear me. Having come to believe that, Hegel having "stood the world on its head", it has since for some of us in any case been right side up, I see no reason for not acknowledging, at least as a faith affirmation, that within the context of many occasions I seem to have made decisions without regard to personal consequences (that were sometimes in fact quite adverse). Such a notion will be spurned by no one who has experienced the power of an endless life. This is indeed a faith that I find to be irresistable, that lends to life the dignity required for it to be lived worthily, and one in the way in which no good reason stands.

Even though the theory of death is, to say the least, questionable, I nonetheless maintain that, for the order and clarity it can bring to philosophical issues viewed from a temporal perspective, it can nonetheless serve as a very useful fiction.

[6] Concrete universality is prior to abstract universality, even as concrete fact is prior to theory, the latter in both cases being derived, residual of the living occasion upon its perishing.

radical particularity as exclusively determinative of the other within the context of other discriminations also being mediated within the occasion.

§6 If the first of these qualifications is borne in mind, it may not seem unduly strange that a concrete proposition is alternatively conceivable as an act of discrimination (*Unterscheidung*). What are discriminated are the subject and predicate of a proposition, which are actual, however, only as related each to the other, i.e., as being discriminated. Because a concrete discrimination is non-abstractable from the elements or aspects discriminated, it is in fact these elements or aspects viewed as particulars with respect to their boundary relation to one another.

§7 A concretely actual occasion as it climaxes at full concrescence is constituted by a unity and wholeness of such discriminations. This unity and wholeness of discriminations might alternatively be viewed as a perfect language, each of its propositions and terms having a concretely specific role within the totality, apart from which the occasion would not be the occasion that it is, and being in its working out concretely universal throughout. This is a totality that, certain qualifications in view (Essay III, §8), it is in principle possible to reconstitute after the fact through "secondary reflection".[7] It does not (of course) gain its self-evidence through being reconstituted in abstraction after the fact.[7a]

---

[7] An actual occasion is absolute *prior* to the abstractions that follow upon its perishing, which are derived. The priority of the whole that is the truth here referred to is more readily perceived for purposes of the present context if we permit the term "secondary reflection" to refer to the analysis and *re*constitution (or secondary synthesis), of the discriminations constitutive of an actual occasion *after the fact*. This will be to adopt a clearer line of distinction than does Hegel, or at least to be more constantly reminded of it, between the primary reflection (mediation) that is constitutive of concrete actuality and the recapitulations of the mediations constitutive of concrete actuality after the fact. It is small wonder that this distinction sometimes gets blurred in Hegel's works, seeing that we have here to do with a matter that can be consistently spelled out only after one has fully faced up to the necessity of the perishing of an actual occasion as a theoretically necessary companion piece to its absoluteness, *the latter being understood within a consistently pluralistic and temporal perspective.*

If one achieves clarity in this matter, the qualitative difference in which the possession of philosophical self-consciousness in *something like* Hegel's sense must manifest itself will turn up in occasions that succeed the one that is undergoing secondary reflection rather than in an occasion being *re*constituted.

[7a] That the distinction between primary and secondary reflection under discussion is clearly implicated in Hegel's account will be immediately obvious to anyone who notes that the *Phän.* climaxes with the Begriff entering into consciousness (*Phän.*, p. 563; or *Phen.*, p. 806). This marks the completion of the account of how consciousness comes to be, which has taken up the entire *Work* preceding. Of course it was an already conscious individual

§8 A concretely actual occasion is self-evident (or certain of itself) by virtue of including within itself all of the discriminations needful for its explication. A language does not need to be brought from elsewhere, i.e., from some other occasion to this task — *as though this were possible*, the occasion being inclusive of all that is actual, in some grade of relevance and commensurate emphasis.[8]

§9 An utterance of concrete language is *concrete actuality speaking for itself*. This is regardless of what discrimination constitutive of an occasion — dialectical (and in this sense rational) to its very bottom — is being uttered. It is not a mere story *about* creation, but *creation affirming itself*. Its truth is self-evident, at least to the subject of the occasion, the speaker, and in this sense is absolute knowing, lying beyond the range of possible doubt. One way of portraying the situation is to say that the subjective idea of an objective situation and the objective situation itself are each accents within an identity inclusive of both, this being a discrimination that is mediated within and constitutive of the occasion. A correspondence test between these two accents being mediated having been "passed",[9] as it were, as an immanent aspect of the self-constitution of the actual occasion, the result (so long as it is not yet abstracted from the living process of its being mediated) stands clear of the possibility of being called into question.[10]

---

who was rendering the account all the while. At this point, however (to state the matter in terms of an explicitly pluralized Hegelian perspective), this individual finds the account adequate to the living occasion within which he finds himself. The internal (actual) perspective upon which he has been drawing all the while has now been made explicit without qualification. What possible alternative procedure could have served the explication of the Begriff — concrete actuality grasped *a priori* as such?

[8] See Essay II. It would of course be as superfluous as it would be absurd to propose to demonstrate self-evidence. The foregoing statement is merely an explanation to assist the **Understanding**. Insofar as *this* understanding can be concretized within an actual occasion constitutive at once of the reader and the world present for him or her (each — self and world — being an accent within an identity inclusive of both), it will be rendered self-evident.

[9] See my "Das Problem der Verifizierbarkeit historischer Dialektik", *Philosophisches Jahrbuch der Görres-Gesellschaft*, 84. Jahrgang (1977), pp. 126-34.

[10] The case is somewhat similar to that of an empiricist who holds forth for a sense immediacy that stands free of doubt. The difference is that what we are here considering is not some fictional entity which we have no reason to believe can, as such, have any status in actuality, but the entire body of concretely specific discriminations constitutive of an occasion being mediated as something like Hegel's truth which is the whole. The barest consciousness presents this truth, however few of its aspects may be explicit and however few (if indeed any) of its aspects have been subjected to an analysis and resynthesis after the (concrete) fact.

§10 Such an utterance may, however, be thought of provisionally as having a dual role to perform, in that, in addition to speaking an occasion forth, it has the "silent" (implicit) role of being a mediation between inheritances from occasions that were priorly actual. That these roles are not only reconcilable but ultimately one is owing to the character of an actual occasion as *a mediation of a plurality of data and occasions (that were) to the unity of a single occasion:* The mediation *process* between (personal) occasions, *viewed from the perspective of full concrescence,* i.e., the truth that is the whole speaking for itself, is a concretely actual (and concretely universal) part or aspect of the occasion.

§11 Error consists in the vocal or written utterance of an abstraction as though it were concrete. Illusion consists in the belief that it is concrete. A deliberately inauthentic utterance may for present purposes be thought of as one form of error. An abstraction the utterance of which constitutes an error belongs to some phase prior to the final phase of the concrescence — the phase of full concrescence — of the occasion out of which it is uttered. The truth of error — that and how it is such — comes from seeing it within the total context of the occasion *out of which* it is uttered.

§12 An authentically concrete linguistic utterance is ever an invitation by the speaker to the hearer to mutual recognition and understanding. This is whether or not the invitation finds fulfillment in an equally open response. It may draw an impersonal, or an even more flagrantly dissimulating response. In its function as an invitation to mutual recognition and understanding a concrete linguistic utterance is, as such, an enactment of social relation, regardless of the specific content or what shared understandings may result. For this reason, as well as because specific social relations "inherited" from one occasion to another in some grade of emphasis, normally beginning with the sibling-mother relation, form an important part of the contents of an actual occasion constitutive of a person and his or her world at any given temporal instant (the effects of which, being concretely universal, permeate the occasion), concrete language is inherently social in character.

§13 Following the present understanding, the cry of a new-born baby is an authentic linguistic utterance, even though instinct-domi--nated, insofar as the invitation to mutual recognition and understanding that constitutes it as such makes no intentional use of mutually recognized common symbols of meaning. The first cry of an infant is typically understood by the mother and others, nonetheless, as an enacted symbol of helplessness and the need of nurture. Where more intentionally shared symbols are used in concrete language, they are made *the servants of the occasion,* and are contextually determined. Language at its birth is concrete, but old symbols may be reborn, and thus be given new form and new life within an occasion that is actual.

§14 Insofar as what is rendered actual within the present is explicitly constitutive of self-consciousness, it may properly be said to constitute history as actual within the present (*Wirkungsgeschichte*). By virtue of its being inevitably under the sway of desire, thus taking the form of intentionality seeking and carrying forward the pursuit of new or modified ends, history as actual within the present brings with it the barest beginnings of distinctly human freedom, and it is by virtue of this freedom that it is living and actual. History as actual within the present, insofar as this is my causal past rendered explicit to consciousness, renders possible the positing of a future commensurate with the past, selectively appropriated with respect to what receives emphasis, that is potential for concrescence.

Historical consciousness arises through the expansion of history as actual within the present to encompass relations, especially social relations, which, *viewed in a merely external way,* might be supposed to have only an *indirect* bearing upon the subject's own person. It nonetheless renders the past of a culture and people the internal dynamic of its own being, with which the subject is self-consciously identified, even while remaining an individual discriminated within this identity as an accent.[11]

§15 One might feel tempted to portray the ideal communication situation as one in which a hearer, by virtue of sharing the same occasion as the speaker of an authentically concrete linguistic utterance, participates equally in its self-evidence with the speaker. This "ideal" would then be most nearly approximated in shared ecstatic

---

[11] In the foregoing discussion of enacted social relations, I am presupposing what I think must prove to be the most basic ingredient in Hegel's solution to what has somehow fastened itself upon modern philosophy as "the problem of psychologism": Precisely the same discriminations, *generically viewed,* may be constitutive of psychology as one of the particular sciences (as well as its subject matter, construed from the vantage point appropriate to this science) on the one hand, and (so far as they reach) of first philosophy, on the other. The difference consists in that these discriminations, viewed in abstraction, as external, and hence, at best, as authentic features of a likely hypothetical construct, are psychological. Within the context of a concretely actual occasion, which it is the business of first philosophy to explicate in its wholeness and unity, they are, by virtue of being contextually determined *actual.* If the explication is worthy, its concrescence will be approximated within subsequent occasions belonging to the same homogeneous socio-cultural epoch, and insofar rendered evident.

moments, such as sexual orgasm (also a kind of utterance) or in meditation. Most communication phenomena can on the whole be better explained, however, apart from a virtual loss of distinctive identity of two proximate occasions and their respective subjects, with proximate presuppositions standing in for what is wanting on the part of a hearer to share in the self-evidence of the occasion as known by the speaker. This is the case especially if there is a basic assurance in memory that, if he or she places himself in the proper situations, concrete discriminations will be at hand upon demand to displace, and in turn approximately to certify, particular presuppositions.

§16 Two factors ultimately render this "ideal" of "perfect communication" just referred to unattainable. One is that the two occasions that are constitutive, respectively, of each of two persons at a given temporal instant are bearers of different life histories inherited from occasion to occasion within the particular society that constitutes the life span of each. The other is that discriminations, being concrete and hence indistinguishable from their discriminated aspects or elements, do not pass away, at least not previous to the perishing of the occasion that they constitute; the discrimination between two individuals mutually participating in one another's occasions can be no exception.

§17 These two factors in view, it turns out to be less problematical to conceive most linguistic communication, at least, not so much as a direct sharing on the part of a hearer in the self-evidence of an authentically concrete linguistic utterance on the part of the speaker as a sufficient sharing in one another's occasions, in part on the basis of shared (abstract) understandings and in part on the basis of perceived presuppositions on the part of the hearer that admit of proximate "translation" into what he or she has known self-evidently in the past and that can be summoned into relevance and rendered actual within a present occasion. In this way the hearer may be led to believe the speaker's concrete linguistic utterance and in an ideal case to discover a proximate utterance (drawn out of his own causal past that can be rendered actual within the present) to be self-evident within the actual occasion presently constitutive of him (or her) and his (or her) world. I use the term "proximate" in the foregoing sentence because the entirety of an actual occasion being present in an utterance that is by this route discovered to be self-evident for the hearer will not be precisely the same as that which was self-evident for the speaker. This difference as it pertains to the only relative precision and adequacy of "laws of nature", I have elsewhere referred to as "the settlement effect' (*"die Einbettungswirkung"*). The natural (and in a certain sense necessary) ambiguity of shared language would appear to have its source in this peculiar relation between shared occasions whereby, although the respective subjects of each may share similar utterances as self-evident, each is in principle precisely determined but not precisely identical with the other.

§18 Participants in an enacted social relation may, however, know it each from the perspective of an accent formed by his or her participation, being at the same time necessarily cognizant of the other accent as a condition of the self-certainty each of his or her own. Thus in an *I-Thou* relation each of the participants are at once self-certain and certain of the other as a participant in this self-certainty — this mutual knowing of each both as him- or herself and in the other. The relation is thus certain (and, indeed, so far as we are able to judge, it may be identical) for both, even though it is highly unlikely that either may know with a like certainty the entirety of the context of discriminations within which this relation is for the other embedded. The invitation to mutual recognition and reciprocity that is concrete language achieves its ideal fulfillment in the *I-Thou* relation, falling short of which other levels of recognition are to be made out, such as the recognition of another abstract thing, meaning, or individual merely as having use *for* me.

§19 It is with such a discrimination that self-consciousness (and with it self-certainty and self-evidence) enters into the epoch constituted by the life span of a human individual.[12] In this case, as well, each participant in the relation brings to it a causal past — whether, or to whatever extent, this may be recollected or not — made actual in the present that plays a role. Unlike the case in which a hearer must first "translate" a linguistic utterance into a proximate discrimination within his own causal past in order to know it as self-evident, however, the past in this case plays a subordinate (background) role in the encounter, which is the identifying characteristic of the occasion. Thus self-consciousness can come originally to birth in a relation of encounter in which there is priorly no explictly recollected past that is present for it as actual within the present.[13]

---

[12] In "The Ontological Priority of Recognition in Human Existence", presented to the International Society for Metaphysics held in London in 1980 (if perhaps under a different title), Oliva Blanchette has treated the theme from a broadly Hegelian perspective in a manner that seems to complement what I have here in view.

§20 I noted in the above that what is self-evident includes the causal past as this is in some manner and form made actual in the present. Our knowledge of the past as actual in the present is known as self-evidently (within its context) as any other aspect of a self-evident concretely actual occasion. The doctrine of inheritance, which I adapt from Whitehead to account for how this has occurred, pertaining as it does to relations *between* concretely actual occasions, *as though one could step outside of one such occasion inclusive of all that is actual and perceive others,* can, however, at best be no more than a likely story, the sort of guesswork and conjecture that Whitehead apparently supposed *exclusively* to constitute first philosophy, because he was unaware that the phenomenological method had already effected a revolution in this discipline which was (and, so far as I am able to see, remains) irreversible. This story, adapted from Whitehead to the present account, goes as follows.

§21 Upon climaxing at full concrescence, the data left upon the perishing and falling asunder of the occasion, although it may hypothetically be maintained to be actual (and in this sense to be hypothetically actual), is in reality merely potential. As I have already noted, even the perishing of the occasion is excluded from the self-evident "truth which is the whole" of the occasion, and from any possible phenomenological investigation — the obvious reason, as I judge, why Hegel, in his attempt to be a consistent phenomenologist, regardless of the historical occasion he was depicting, busied himself ever with the reporting of his *one Begriff* inclusive of all that is actual. Hence only an in principle unconcretizable theory can tell us how the past may have come to be actual within the present. Thus, although what is, insofar as it exists proximately, i.e., within the perceptual-conceptual-intentional horizon (§32) of the presently actual occasion, is self-evident and thus amenable to being expressed in concrete language, change is unalterably contingent. A particular change is a possibility; insofar as this possibility is concretized, it is no longer possibility, but concrete fact. Concrete language, which is self-evident (to the speaker), does not report change. *This is unless the term is made to pertain to the becoming of an actual occasion, that, as such, includes its development out of its causal past,* insofar

---

[13] Relevant thereto, Henry Sussman proposes, "Lordship and Bondage" and "The Unhappy Consciousness" which immediately follows it in Hegel's *Phän.* "*translate* the dynamics of the physical world into intersubjective relations and the history initiated by them...". "The Metaphor in Hegel's *Phenomenology of Mind*", CLIO, 11. 4 (1982), p. 380.
  I find this apropo, although on the present account history, as actual time, is also in nature, insofar as we are concerned to view it as a dynamic — and in some sense an evolutionary — process and as actual.

as this past has, by whatever means we may hypothesize, been rendered actual (in some grade of emphasis and relevance) within the present. This is an important exception, although I myself prefer to reserve the term for usage with respect to what is contingent.

> *Remark:* The attribution of change exclusively to the hypothetical perspective has given rise to a problem in the minds of certain of my hearers and readers. To some I will seem thereby to have in some way cheated process of actual status. I shall undertake to reply to this here, and to show that the issue is at least principally verbal. As I indicated in a letter to Giacomo Rinaldi of August 13, 1987, it is my view that "[e]xcepting theories that never get concretized, the two [[actual and hypothetical]] perspectives have, or may (in the case of a particular occasion and its derivative abstractions) have, the same contents and sorts of contents..." Some readers will find this to be in conflict, or at least in tension, with certain statements in §21 preceding until I now explain my usage of the terms "change" and "becoming".
>
> Consider, e.g., the statement in the above, "change is unalterably contingent". This was made with a bow toward the conventional usage of the term "change" and with the intent of admitting the explication of particular and contingent change to be principally a task of the particular sciences and of *Wissenschaftstheorie*. Seeing that "change" in this usage is construed as belonging exclusively to the hypothetical perspective, its counterpart within concrete actuality is "becoming". But, at least when the thus stipulated relation between the two terms is considered **philosophically**, the term "counterpart" does not quite carry the sense we need. A particular living occasion being **prior** to the hypothetical perspective that is derivitive from it, the becoming of that occasion, considered both in its entirety and with respect to its component aspects in context, is of course equally prior to the relations of contingent change that are associated with its after-image in derivitive abstractions.
>
> One might perhaps prefer to use the term "change" in a perspective-neutral way. In this case one might make reference, e.g., to actual change and either to its representation, or to **possible** change, in hypothetical thinking. In a technologically oriented civilization disposed to assume that a change reported by "science" must somehow be implied to be actual and one reported by philosophers need in no case be so considered, however, this option might more readily lead to confusion than the one that I have adopted.
>
> It may be worth calling attention to the fact that the conceptuality within which I am working contains some terms, such as "change", which are governed more immediately by language conventions than by a perceived relation of proximity to an available dialectical exposition and justification. In this connection, attention is called to terms accorded a special role in the formulation of the *theory* of alternating perspectives, which are in this way **relatively** removed from their dialectical birthplaces. Since this *is* a theory (and, indeed, incurably a theory), seeing that it can never become an aspect of the phenomenology of concreteness, the case could not be otherwise. For certain purposes I regard this distancing, in which philosophy exceeds the stricter limits of natural reason, as legitimate, so long as the fact that such terms must ultimately prove to be commensurable with terms that have their birthplaces in concreteness is not permitted to slip out of view.

§22 What is concretely actual — and what, as such, bodies forth in *and as* concrete language that is self-evident to the speaker and often fairly convincing to selected other persons to whom it is intended authentically to communicate — is the *process* of mediation of concrescence, within which a causal past and a future of expectations converge, as it were, to form a living now, together with its result, the latter not yet being abstracted from its process of becoming through the perishing of the occasion. This process of mediation may be otherwise designated time. *More concretely* considered, it is space-time. *Most concretely* considered, it is space (concretized as nature)-time (concretized as history), a concept relatively remote from the needs of the theoretical physicist but indispensable for the purposes of a philosophy of concreteness. This latter is but another name for the occasion as a whole that is actual.

II

§23 Leibniz' "complete concept" — one of the more notable antecedents of the concept of an actual occasion that I have described — is the concept of an individual substance or a complete being, which he described as "a conception so complete that the concept suffices for the understanding of it and for the deduction of all of the predicates of which the substance is or may become the subject".[14] With Jürgen Mittelstraß, I am forced to the conclusion that such a concept, by virtue of its inclusion of the infinite, *if we follow Leibniz' account,* is not in fact analyzable.[15] I have maintained, following Hegel, not only that the concept of the basic unity of concrete actuality, but concrete actuality itself, certain qualifications in view, *is* analyzable, and I hope to make a somewhat better case for this than did Hegel, also without sharing what may have been his view that precisely the same totality of discriminations, whether explicit or merely implicit, is constitutive of actuality in all occasions, for which evidence is wanting. What results will not, of course, be quite the same. The foregoing characterization of concrete language, if it is to be counted for more than mere conjecture, must, indeed, find support in a convincing claim that the *re*constitution of an actual occasion after the fact can be carried out in secondary reflection. In

---

[14] *Discours de Métaphysique* §8, *Philosophische Schriften,* vol. 4, p. 433 (trans. from: Leibniz, *Selections* [ed. Ph. P. Wiener (New York: Charles Scribner's Sons, 1951)], p. 300).

[15] See Jürgen Mittelstraß, *Substance and Concept in Leibniz,* in *Studia Leibnizians, Truth, Knowledge, and Reality; Inquiries into the Foundations of Seventeenth Century Rationalism* (Sonderheft 9), p. 153.

the remaining §§ I shall state my case, insofar as I can do so apart from giving a fuller exposition of the concept of seriality in dialectic[16] than is possible here.

§24   A discrimination that contains other discriminations within it is a complex discrimination.[17]

§25   That each discrimination constitutive of an actual occasion is implicated within every other discrimination within the same occasion follows from its concrete universality. This is the reason that, strictly speaking, there can be no rank order of discriminations *in actuality*, but only in discriminations that were actual within a living occasion and are now, as "after the [[concrete]] fact", abstract.

§26   The character of concrete universality, *that* (upon the perishing of the occasion) *was*, registers itself more strongly upon some discriminations than upon others. Where it registers itself less strongly, concrete language gives way more readily to lumped-off common meanings, sometimes no more than vaguely similar to what was given in the living occasion. Such complex discriminations as are such by reason of having been accorded emphasis within the living occasion, tend, upon abstraction, to preserve more of their pristine integrity — i.e., their sharpness, like rocks broken out of a formation on the side of a mountain, before they are worn round in the stream below[18] — at least so long as they are yet proximate to their source.

§27   Emphasis registers itself within living occasions. The rank order of inclusiveness of import of simple discriminations within complex discriminations refers to the "natural" order of their analysis-synthesis in second reflection, moving from the simple toward the complex. This latter frequently appeals to (more or less) common language use for its justification. In other words emphases manifest themselves *in actuality* and these tend to have inclusiveness of import of the resultant abstract discriminations as their counterpart in the hypothetical world, following upon the perishing of the occasion.

---

[16] I have made a beginning in this in SC, pp. 93-107 and 217-24, esp. the latter.

[17] A "complex discrimination" is analogous to Whitehead's 'multiple contrast': "A multiple contrast is analysable into component dual contrasts. But a multiple contrast is not a mere aggregation of dual contrasts. It is one contrast over and above its component contrasts". (PR, p. 229)

[18] Cf. Eugen Fink, "Ontological Problems of Community", trans. by Michael R. Heim, in *Contemporary German Philosophy*, Vol. 2, pp. 1-18.

§28 This is to say, the order of discriminations within discriminations in abstract (hypothetical) thinking is *in part* determined by emphasis, in the sense that in a series of concrete utterances, each made within a different member of a series of occasions that inherit from one another and together constitute an enduring society, each will give primary emphasis to a single discrimination that, upon analysis-synthesis, will be perceived as containing within it as sub-discriminations a plurality of other discriminations constitutive of the occasion (that was) *within which* it was uttered. The upshot is that the order of emphasis and commensurate rank of discriminations approximately inherited throughout a series of occasions tends to change with each utterance in the series.

§29 Where I shall find it expedient in what follows to refer to an order of inclusiveness of discriminations within an actual occasion, what I shall have in mind, consistent with the foregoing, is emphases that will tend to be abstracted as an order of meanings belonging to a serial order of discriminations ordered by reference to their inclusivity.

§30 That the order of emphasis and commensurate rank of discriminations approximately inherited throughout a series of occasions tends to change with each utterance in the series is not to propose that the discrimination mediated in a linguistic utterance is the *most inclusive* discrimination constitutive of the occasion. It seems that we must generally reserve this status for the discrimination between the subject of the occasion, the "I", and the world present for this subject, and this even in the case in which this status for the discrimination goes virtually unacknowledged and remains largely implicit. There are a fair number of other discriminations that in a similar manner, generically construed, are constitutive of all actual occasions and must be accorded a high rank in the order of inclusiveness of import, whether explicit or merely implicit, and which may by virtue of emphasis take the highest rank. Space-time is one of the more obvious and inclusive, which with its concrete and particular filling of discriminations, is for most purposes more appropriately referred to as nature-history. Within many occasions, however, it is not emphasized, and we may judge this to reflect a bias for "pure objectivity" (as though objectivity were achievable other than as an accent within an identity of object and subject!) in our cultural epoch whereby space and time are more prominently associated with the objective/physical pole of actuality and knowledge than with the subjective/conceptual pole.

§31 The discriminations constitutive of an actual occasion may most appropriately be understood as contained within one complex discrimination, in series. Thus, for example, the total content of the occasion now constitutive of me (as subject, "I") and the world present for me is given in this single discrimination. A subdiscrimination has content, as well, but this is held in common with the complex discriminations, respectively, that contain it in series. Although it would not be possible to reconstruct an occasion after the fact upon the basis of the single discrimination named, seeing that a minimal language for the reconstruction of even a relatively simple occasion is constituted by a sizable plurality of discriminations, *an analysis and resynthesis gains no new content by the explicit detailing of sub-discriminations.*

§32 These considerations in view, an analysis-synthesis of an actual occasion, to be complete, need be only sufficiently detailed to account for those discriminations that are explicit to its subject. In other words, it must analyse those very discriminations that are to be accounted for as constitutive of the occasion. The understanding of self-evidence as consisting in an actual occasion's including all of the discriminations needful for its explication thus turns out to be tautological.

§33 Discriminations that are explicit to consciousness are determined by what receives emphasis by virtue of its relevance, i.e., by what lies within and proximate to the perceptual-conceptual-intentional horizon of the occasion. The term "perceptual-conceptual-intentional horizon" is intended to suggest the plurality of dimensions and aspects of fully discriminated, and in this sense concrete, actuality. What is given self-evidently is "perception bound" to a given spatio-temporal region. In an analogous manner it is conceptually and intentionally "bound" to the spatio-temporal "region" that is at once perceptually, conceptually, and intentionally determined and grasped (*begriffen*) as the truth that is the whole of its constitutive discriminations. Sub-discriminations that do not arise to consciousness, such, e.g., as arise beyond the horizon of the occasion, *normally* contribute dynamically, i.e., they selectively contribute emphases *to* (or, as the case may be, *through*) discriminations that do, thus contributing qualitatively and quantitatively to their specific characters.[19] In this way many of the differences between generic and

---

[19] Where sub-discriminations contribute *abnormally*, they express themselves "autonomously" and "spuriously" in activities and ideas not channeled through the order or orders of discriminations that have nominally contained them, we are confronted with an ontological source both of creative novelty and of a plurality of classifiable types of somatic and psychic pathology. See my "Hegel's Phenomenologcial Analysis and Freud's Psychoanalysis", *International Philosophical Quarterly*, Vol. VIII, No. 3 (Sept., 1968), pp. 356-78.

concrete discriminations are to be explained, as well as phenomena connected with "the settlement effect" to which I made reference in Part I.

§34 An indispensable condition of our being able to reconstruct an actual occasion after the fact is the persistence of the identity of an explicit particular discrimination, first as actual, and then, upon the perishing of the occasion, as abstract and merely potential. This is indeed the slender, *but very strong*, thread upon which it appears the possibility of a scientifically pursued first philosophy in the critical tradition must ultimately hang.

§35 Seeing that those discriminations that are explicit to the subject of an occasion may each in turn be accorded priority in a series of concrete linguistic utterances, each representative of an actual occasion within a relatively "stable" linear society, it is possible in principle to *re*constitute a single occasion approximately representative of a normally homogeneous epoch of such, e.g., the life span of a human individual or of a culture.[20]

---

[20] It will have been noted that I consider concrete propositions (*being mediated*) to be exclusively constitutive of actuality. An alternative formulation would involve the affirmation that, in the case of every occasion that explicitly speaks for itself, concrete language and concrete actuality form accents within an identity inclusive of both. This might seem to commit us to a more moderate and perhaps a "less objectionable" form of idealism, and it would be compatible with the principal thrust of the present formulation, based upon giving absolute priority to concrete actuality over what is merely possible and hypothetical. This is provided that we went on to affirm, in the case of a particular occasion, that the form of the concrete proposition likewise characterizes actuality in its concrescence, herein construed as constituted by sub-discriminations not as such explicit to consciousness.

The question thus posed cannot be answered upon the basis of a phenomenological analysis-synthesis of an actual occasion except as this pertains to the discriminations we are wont to employ in talking about nature, here understood as closely analogous to what discloses itself in the phenomenology of self-consciousness (and world *for* self-consciousness) and as contributing sub-discriminations to occasions that are explicitly conscious. Within the present context, I prefer to retain the term "concrete proposition or judgment" as the generic name for that which is constitutive of actuality throughout its various levels, seeing that this can assist us to grasp the structure of becoming (and thus of actuality) in its elegant simplicity and uniformity and as one with the structure of our language and knowing. Being aware of the alternative I have mentioned, whereby concrete propositions and concrete actuality are each in any authentically concrete linguistic utterance *being mediated* as accents within an identity inclusive of both, can, however, serve as a safeguard against any disposition to hypostatize such a generic name by making it out in an overly simple sense to signify something concrete.

X

HOW IS IT THAT A (CONCRETE) FACT CAN SPEAK FOR ITSELF? PROCESS PHENOMENOLOGY AS AN ALTERNATIVE TO PHILOSOPHICAL EMPIRICISM*

Preliminary Remarks:

1) The concept of process phenomenology that I shall be developing builds upon a Hegelian-Whiteheadian Synthesis pertaining to method in first philosophy that I set forth within a series of essays, concluded in 1983.[1] I shall be alluding to these proximate ancestors of notions that I shall be developing, but I do not conceive it to be a part of my present undertaking to relate to them in a detailed way.

2) I conceive the task I am undertaking to be broadly Hegelian, principally by virtue of reflecting a working out of the *a priori* status of knowledge and of actuality. The notion that concrete actuality and knowledge are *a priori*, i.e., prior to possibilities and derivative abstractions, is often permitted to drop out of view even in Hegel interpretations today, particularly in English, except perhaps in the Marxist form of Hegelianism, in the pale form of the doctrine of an inevitable class revolution.[2] This is although the notion is seldom

---

* An earlier version of this essay was presented at the University of Iceland, Sept. 16, 1984, and subsequently distributed to the membership of the Philosophical Society through their Newsletter.

[1] The list of "Other Essays Belonging to the Same Systematic Unit" appeared with "Can Hegel's Concept of Self-Evidence be Salvaged?", *Idealistic Studies*, May, 1984.

[2] Even if this doctrine could be warranted, its futuristic character would serve to render it no more than a weak form of what can qualify as *a priori* knowledge. Hegel's concept of speculation, herein reflected, provides no place for ruminations, at least not of the type that might be directly implicated with predictions pertaining to the future, all of which would for him have fallen within the scope of the particular sciences and *Wissenschaftstheorie*, a quite different discipline than *Fundamentalphilosophie*.

neglected by critics of Hegel, who have generally proposed it to be absurd.

I have taken a different tack: if *the truth is the whole,* as Hegel proposed, it seems reasonable to propose that *the truth of Hegel* is the whole *of Hegel.* If so, the *a priori* character of knowledge seems too central a concept not to take into account. Accordingly, I have adapted the strategy of providing this notion, by a certain reconception, with a context within which it can be at home.

3) My undertaking reflects Whitehead by the adaptation of his concept of the perishing of an actual occasion, which he developed by analogy to the concept of an electro-magmetic event in physical theory, and in other ways. I want to show this notion in particular to be useful to the conception of an actual occasion rendered inclusive of a human subject, to which subject occasions conceived in something like this way are rendered accessible. I shall be reflecting some other Whiteheadian dispositions as well that pertain to my concern to take account of particular differences between actual occasions and their constituents.

4) Toward the close of my remarks I shall be broaching the topic of metaphor, concerning which I am not very well informed,[3] but which has of late forced itself upon my thinking. What I shall be stating is the position with regard to metaphor that seems required by the reconstruction under way.

5) Following a few introductory remarks, I have numbered the §§ (or short paragraphs) principally comprising my paper from 1 through 31, which I will indicate for convenience of reference.

* * * * * * * * * *

For the sake of simplicity, the account of a concrete fact to follow will take a dogmatic form. This will serve to suggest that it should be considered at first for its systematic character, not that it is not subject to question and possibly to revision.

It reflects and builds upon an effort, moving principally from Hegel and Whitehead, to salvage a type of rationality that is distinctively Hegelian by a certain recasting along lines that were initially suggested by Whitehead's metaphysics and cosmology. I have long been convinced that every conscious human individual knows some things in the living and lively present that serve as touchstones for

---

[3] At the time this paper was written I had only begun systematically to involve myself with the extensive literature treating metaphor.

hypothetical thinking. i.e., for "theories about" this and that, and that apart from such touchstones hypothetical thinking would not even be identifiable as such because there would be nothing to which it would stand in a relation of contrast. A theory needs something which *it is not* to set it off. Even a supposedly thorough-going skeptic has to know something that forms a contrast with that of which he is skeptical, even if he chooses not to talk about this something.

In a way it is the sorts of things that every skeptic knows, if he is forthright, to which I shall be calling attention. Within the empiricist tradition this something that even a skeptic knows has often been referred to as **the immediately given.** This concept has always been problematical, however, at the very least because percepts without concepts are blind. This suggests the more encompassing problem that no mere fragments of what presents itself to awareness can be, and be known as, something in itself apart from its accompanying context. Thus, to choose examples of types of such fragments, neither a percept, a concept, nor an intention can be grasped by itself apart from its context. This is what prompted Hegel's well-known utterance, "The truth is the whole". The context in question is grasped as an organic whole and *only* as an organic whole. This must be qualified: it is self-grasped from a perspective within itself as an organic whole (Essays VIII and XIV). There can be no standpoint outside of such a whole to grasp it as merely objective, for then it would not include its comprehending subject, and on this account it would not include all that is actual within itself (Essay III). Thus it is a subject grasping an objective realm, and a reflection of itself in this act of grasping. Its basic nature is thus that of a complex contrast (Essay IX, §24), a theme I shall be further developing.

I call such a whole an actual occasion, adapting the term from Whitehead's usage, in part as a way of calling attention to the tradition that interprets Hegel as a pluralistic personalist. I wish now to propose a hypothesis as to the generic make-up of an actual occasion. I hope in time to evoke in my hearers an awareness of occasions that they have concretely lived that are similar by virtue of a commonality of generic contrasts.

§1 An actual occasion *includes all that from its perspective is actual.* This is to say, it includes all that from its perspective is actual *in some grade of relevance and emphasis.* This "all" includes both what lies proximate within its perceptual, conceptual, intentional horizon and what is more remote.

§2 An actual occasion is a *process* within which a plurality of abstract data are brought into a unity of concrescence and thus rendered actual by virtue of a common subjective aim.

§3 Such an occasion, once its potentiality is fully actualized in and as a coherent unity of concrescence, *perishes*, leaving abstract data for successor occasions to inherit.

§4 An actual occasion is a process of concrescence within which *polarities are mediated to constitute contrasts and discriminations*. A contrast is not a discrimination or vice versa, but where a contrast is present, the contrasting elements or aspects are discriminated, and where a discrimination is present, the discriminated elements or aspects are contrasted. Thus, e.g., space-time may alternatively or at once be construed as a contrast and as a discrimination. For the dialectician this imports that they are polar opposites that in concrescence mutually determine one another, to become contrasts.

Were the account to stop here, this process might seem as abstract as on Whitehead's account. What I shall subsequently add to it will effect a further Hegelianization that will render it more concrete in character and suggest parallels to consciously lived occasions.[4]

§5 One of the contrasts and discriminations found to be constitutive of every such occasion is that between its subject and the world present for that subject, *subject and world each mutually determining the other*. A Cartesian thinking "substance" and an extended world ("substance") are mere moments within such a mutual determination, actual only in their dynamic relation of mutual determination, i.e., in their *being mediated*.

Anyone inclined to doubt this should attempt to explain who he or she is apart from a reference to his or her world, or what *"the world"* is apart from reference to the self as the subject for whom *a* world is present. The result will be a mere idea or ideal, at most, and nothing concretely actual. By "concretely actual" I refer to something in a determining relation, otherwise known as a mediation (*Vermittlung*) of one or another sort.

§6 It will serve my present purposes to universalize the concept of mediation by noting that it is otherwise construable as the relation of mutual determination obtaining between the subject and the predicate of a concrete proposition. *Thus the subject and predicate of*

---

[4] If the subject that is one of my hearers or readers is not to find him- or herself to be within some actual occasion, recognizable as such on the basis of the account here adumbrated, he shall not have been led to a discernment of the concreteness that I have intended to build into my account, rendering it suitably proximate to what I describe as concrete language in what follows.

Chap. X, How is it that a Fact Can Speak for Itself? 193

a concrete proposition are each accents within a (being-)mediated identity inclusive of both.[5]

§7 Seeing that every such proposition constitutes at once a contrast and a discrimination, an actual occasion, which I noted to consist in a unity and wholeness of contrasts and discriminations, may alternatively be thought of as a unity and wholeness of propositions.

§8 Such a unity and wholeness of propositions, being constitutive as it is of a coherent system, may be thought of as *a perfect language.*

§9 An authentic concrete proposition that is explicitly uttered within an occasion is *true within the context of the occasion prior to its perishing.*

§10 The truth of such an utterance is certain and self-evident to the subject of the occasion and to other persons, insofar as, and to the degree in which, these other persons may properly be said to be "comprehended within the occasion."

§11 If a stranger or mere acquaintance should be present where there is an utterance in concrete language, he would very likely hear nothing more than a mere conventional statement or form of words in a conventional language, such as that which results from abstraction following the perishing of the occasion.

§12 Far from comprehending this form of words within the context within which it was uttered, he or she would interpret it within a context of presuppositions more or less foreign to it. Even if it should come to be considered as probably true within such a context, "true" could here mean no more than hypothetically probable, something very different than being concretely self-evident and thus certain.[6]

---

[5] The subject and predicate of a speculative or philosophical proposition on Hegel's account are each accents within a mediated identity inclusive of both. In this connection, the following statement needs to be considered within its context:

> Die Form des Satzes ist die Erscheinung des bestimmten Sinnes oder der Akzent, der seine Erfüllung unterscheidet: daß aber das Prädikat die Substanz ausdrückt und das Subjekt selbst ins Allgemeine fällt, ist die **Einheit**, worin jeder Akzent verklingt (*Phän.*, p. 51).

In my appropriation of this insight, I accord emphasis to the *process* of mediation, and in such a manner that the discrimination between the subject and the predicate is preserved within their identity rather than being done away with or vanishing.

[6] To address an issue here that has been with us since antiquity, knowledge ($\dot{\epsilon}\pi\iota\sigma\tau\acute{\eta}\mu\eta$) is more than warranted belief ($\delta\acute{o}\xi\alpha$). This "more" is creative process, i.e., concrescence, in essence mediation. A logical demonstration of a "necessary" connection between abstract

§13 To be comprehended within an occasion of which one is not the subject is to be present within it in such a way as approximately to comprehend the body of discriminations explicitly constitutive of it and, in addition, to share with the subject of the occasion significant discriminations that are merely implicitly constitutive of it, at least as presuppositions.

§14 Such a presence in an occasion constitutive of another subject and his world will ordinarily not be possible apart from a situation in which two or more persons contribute to the constitution of the occasion. To describe how this can occur, I now introduce two concepts: the concept of a personal society of occasions and the concept of inheritance. Consider inheritance first.

§15 The inheritance of the abstract data left by one occasion for another, either in part or entire, is by the assimilation of its data to the subjective aim of a successor occasion.

In this transport phenomenon,[7] the subjective aim of the occasion that has perished being now spent, it nonetheless persists in the form of objective data that is available for assimilation to a new subjective aim. This is a consideration that is crucial to my understanding of intersubjectivity.

§16 A personal society of occasions is a linear series constitutive of the life cycle from birth to death of a human individual.[8] Each

---

ideas does not render them concrete, i.e., does not stand in for creation. (To decide otherwise would be arbitrarily to fall victim to an objectionable form of idealism.) This is although in a given instance a necessary connection of abstract ideas may anticipate, and possibly even contribute to the constitution of, their concretization. This is a possibility that renders the particular sciences, which are theory-constituted and theory dominated in a way that first philosophy, which is obliged to make its utterances proximate to concreteness and to provide a critique of abstractions, dares not be, exciting and engaging for us, and this even though, strictly speaking, they cannot provide us with truth.

The self-evident truth, of which it is the principal business of first philosophy to provide an account, stands theory-free, if this is by virtue of the fact that such theory as may have gone into its making, because it has been assimilated and concretized within the creative process is no longer theory but concrete fact, grasped as such. It is thus that the attribution of actuality to *process* effects the rescue of the theory-free status of facts (See Essay II, esp. p. 150, summary point no. 7 and HCP, p. 2, col. 2, which appears absolutely essential if science is to be permitted to know what it is talking about insofar as it reaches into concreteness.

[7] The term "transport phenomenon", from cell-biology, must appeal to a non-technical sense of the term "phenomenon". This is in consideration of the fact that such a transport as can obtain between actual occasions, each of which includes within itself all that is actual, as in the case of the concept of inheritance, is incurably hypothetical and hence cannot present itself as a phenomenon. History as actual within the present, i.e., *Wirkungsgeschichte*, presents itself as a phenomenon.

[8] This usage is not to be confused with Whitehead's term, "personal society".

member of such a series, which might also be called an epoch, inherits in turn from its predecessors a commonality of subjective aim, and with this a developmental pattern that unfolds to become progressively explicit throughout the series.

§17 An occasion within a personal society, in addition to inheriting from the series of occasions constitutive of its own distinctive epoch, may inherit from other epochs as well. Self-consciousness being inherently social in character (Essay IX), inheritances of this sort are indeed essential to providing an account of how a personal society arises and especially for providing an account of how it actualizes its potential for *personhood,* where this occurs.

§18 Intersubjectivity — more concretely designated intersubject-objectivity, seeing that subject and world present for the subject (i.e., extended substance) are actual *only as being mediated* — occurs when the subject of one occasion inherits from the subjective aim of another occasion belonging to a different personal society. It follows from §15 above that the inheritance of a subjective aim is the inheritance of a *form* of objective data that lends itself to being assimilated to the aim of the comprehending occasion intact, apart from distortion.

§19 My friend Mike, with whom I have an authentic I-Thou relation, hears my concrete utterance for what it is and is persuaded of its truth by virtue of standing within the occasion of which I am the subject and by virtue of inheriting its mediated subjective(-objective) form relatively intact. His standing within the occasion of which I am the subject is supposed by our sharing certain presuppositions both explicitly and implicitly, due to our having "inherited" from one another's occasions over an extended temporal period and due to a certain openness and transparency to one another. Indeed, the fact that we have over an extended period of time stood within one another's occasion — thus, e.g., within an occasion constitutive of the other as subject and of the world present for him, as being mediated — accounts for an interpenetration of comprehensions such that each in a typical occasion participates in the self-certainty and self-evidence of the concrete utterance of the other. In the case in which Mike does not share the self-certainty and self-evidence of my authentically concrete utterance, he is in any case very likely to be understanding of my disposition in making it.

§20 The power of an utterance in concrete language is a function of its concrete universality throughout the occasion within which it is uttered, i.e., throughout the perfect language constitutive of it at full concrescence. By concrete universality I mean that every such proposition serves a single role throughout the extension and intention of the occasion. If any concrete proposition constitutive of the occasion, whether expressed or implicit, were different, the entire occasion would be a different occasion than it is.

§21 From the concrete universality of a concrete proposition throughout the occasion within which it is uttered, and from the fact that no two actual occasions are identical,[9] it follows that any abstract proposition taken up into a new concrescence becomes subject to being shaped within the wholeness of discriminations that constitutes the particular occasion. In other words, where abstract language is put to the service of an actual occasion speaking for itself, it becomes "the servant of the occasion".

§22 Either of two results may follow from this, or in combination: (1) The proposition may be reduced to a sub-context of negligible emphasis within the new occasion and thus for most purposes practically eliminated. (2) It may be reconcretized with an appreciable emphasis, perhaps in a variant form, within the new occasion, thus being rendered *explicitly* constitutive of it.

§23 By virtue of its concrete universality, a concrete proposition is expressive of the entirety of the occasion in its uniqueness within which it is uttered.

§24 Lying behind the preceding statement is the assumption that at full concrescence an actual occasion conceived in the manner proposed, being completely determined, consists in a unity and wholeness of exclusively internal relations. In hypothetical thinking we then have a system of external or contingently mixed internal and external relations, which from a hypothetical perspective we are inclined — as a likely story — to regard as derived from a system of internal relations.[10] The story is likely only up to a point, and it has a deceptive potential, as I suggest also in note 12 to follow.

§25 What in a conventional language might be regarded as a metaphor, as an utterance in concrete language becomes the literal truth of the entirety of the occasion. The status of a metaphor being perspectival, if the perspective is actual, i.e., internal to the occasion,

---

[9] As Whitehead viewed the matter, each occasion is different at least by virtue of inheriting from one more than did its predecessor.

[10] This is a matter to which I have accorded further attention in SC (consult the index under "relations, internal") as well as on pp. 246f.

what is properly called a metaphor will be such in relation to something literally true within that occasion. What from a concretely actual perspective appears as a metaphor thus has a dependent status.[11]

§26 Having thus acknowledged that the truth that is the whole of an actual occasion may contain metaphor, what is to be emphasized is that concrete language as such tends to bear the status of being the literal truth and abstract language as such, being the language of hypothetical thinking, carries with it the air of the analogical and the metaphorical.

§27 *Creation speaking for itself does not speak in metaphors* but in normatively literal language from which all types of conventional lan-

---

[11] In "Davidson's Rejection of Metaphorical Meaning" (*Philosophy and Rhetoric*, Vol. 16, No. 2, 1983), Thomas Leddy takes account of Donald Davidson's argument that

> Metaphors...cannot work their wonders unless every term in the metaphorical statement retains its literal meaning. The power of metaphor rests not in its special meaning content but in the way that it uses ordinary meanings to tease the reader into creative perception of the world. (65)

Davidson's felt need to appeal to literal meanings in his account of how a metaphor functions is basically compatible with the standpoint herein reflected. Insofar as he bases his concept of what constitutes literal meaning upon lexical definitions (see pp. 63ff of the Leddy article), however, he appears mistaken. The position I wish to maintain is that it is necessary to discriminate concrete meanings from ordinarily accepted meanings, including lexical meanings, and to accord *absolute* priority to what is concrete.

Carl R. Hausman writes,

> Speech is the mode of human expression that is active, unrepetitive, and not wholly dependent on a fixed lexicon, for it is that human activity which produces language. It is the ground breaking activity that presents rather than represents.... What is present for the first time cannot be something represented. ("Philosophical Creativity and Metaphorical Philosophy", *Philosophical Topics*, Vol. 12, No. 3 [Winter, 1981], p. 197)

It is this presentational aspect that I have in view when I refer to concrete language. What distinguishes my position most markedly from that of Hausman is that where he refers to metaphor, he appears to mean very nearly what I mean by the literal truth of the occasion that is actual. This is due to a difference of perspective. He addresses the issue from a standpoint that regards conventional language as normative in a sense that appears to be out of keeping with the representative (and derivative) status that he appropriately attributes to it. Appealing to the living occasion and to concrete language uttered within the living occasion as normative, I find no need to accord *the same sort* of normative status to conventional language. This is because Hegel's having stood the world on its head seems to me to have resulted in its being at long last right-side-up. I would prefer not to see it flipped again, and indeed, for those who are not duped by thought categories of a dehumanizing, technology dominated, culture, I have serious doubts that it can be.

The priority that I attribute to facts that speak for themselves yields the effect of making derivative conventional languages subject to constant modification and particularization (from a theoretical point of view) through reconcrescence. Short of such reconcrescence, however, a conventional language is only potential. For it to be actual, creation

guages and metaphors are derivative and secondary.¹²

§28 A process phenomenology reconstitutes an actual occasion typical of some relevant epoch after the fact. *This is possible owing to the continuity of the identity of any given discrimination at first as actual within the living occasion and subsequently as hypothetical following its perishing.* The reconstitution of an actual occasion in secondary reflection after the fact proceeds by an analysis-*re*synthesis of its constitutive discriminations.

§29 How one is to conceive the relation of the process phenomenology that I have adumbrated to philosophical empiricism will of course depend somewhat upon how one conceives empiricism. I wish briefly to reflect upon one conception, which seems to me fairly to represent the classical form of empiricism, to which any variant form will be almost bound to be related.

> ...that all knowledge of matters of fact always derives ultimately from sense-observation in some form, which is what it is, independent of conceptual, theoretical or logical connections; and any statement or proposition expressing the brute facts so observed is logically independent of every other such statement.¹³

---

must intervene. Hausman seems sufficiently impressed by the status of what he calls metaphor so that I may hope that this idea may not seem very alien to him. If so, I may further hope that he will be tempted to accord to it the rank of literal truth, commensurate with the authority it actually has for us in lived occasions.

¹² Ascribing the status of the literal truth of the occasion to what from a hypothetical perspective might have been regarded as metaphor is to grant to the latter a status commensurate with the authority it carries.

The following observation made in KWdT (between notes 11 and 12 under point 5) will here be in place: A hypothetical perspective does not present itself as such to an actual perspective. What is rather presented is recollection (*Er-innerung*, or *anamnesis*) including the recollection of what might have been but is not. This that is not, its merely negative worth notwithstanding, has a kind of status within history as actual within the present (*Wirkungsgeschichte*), this latter being strictly distinguished from the past as past, i.e., from the succession of happenings construed in a linear fashion that constitute what is merely temporal history and that can never have more than a hypothetical status.

From a hypothetical perspective that erroneously is considered to be actual, every actual perspective is considered to be contingent. This error, which consists in a form of the "arch-anti-Hegelian fallacy" – i.e., the substitution of hypothetical for actual speculation (SC, pp. 62ff) is rendered understandable by the fact that every actual perspective may be said upon its perishing to become hypothetical. This way of regarding things carried a temptation to conflate the perspectives and to lose concrete actuality with its status of being grasped *a priori* in a veritable see of seeming. To avoid this we should ultimately prefer to say in this context not that such a transformation is undergone, but that the two perspectives continuingly alternate with one another. Where this situation is not thus construed in a way that is in keeping with critical principles, a temptation to wholesale deception presents itself as built into the process of reflection by virtue of which we are human.

Chap. X, How is it that a Fact Can Speak for Itself?

§30 Process Phenomenology stands most markedly in contrast to empiricism thus conceived by denying status in anything deserving to be called knowledge to abstract entities conceived as static and as not *being mediated,* and by its insistent appeal to the truth as a wholeness of discriminations being mediated.

§31 Stating the matter in this way invites the question as to whether some position which it might make good historical sense to designate empirical might be reconcilable with process phenomenology as I have conceived it. I confess that I know of no such, and, seeing no point in destroying the usefulness of the term by broadening it to include all manners of allegiance to facticity no matter how conceived, I am disinclined to add yet another to the numerous varieties of philosophy to which the empiricist label has been attached. It is on this account that I have proposed process phenomenology to be an *alternative* to philosophical empiricism.[14]

---

[13] Errol E. Harris, *The Foundations of Metaphysics in Science* (New York: Humanities Press, 1965), p. 26. Behind this statement lies Harris' in depth critique of empiricism in *Nature, Mind, and Modern Science* (London: George Allen & Unwin Ltd., 1954), esp. part 3.

[14] My quarrel, I would hasten to add, is not with empiricism as a method and program in some way and degree practiced by the particular sciences, but with *philosophical* empiricism, and especially with such philosophical empiricism as proposes to set itself up as, or as a substitute for, a first philosophy.

XI

RECOLLECTION, IMAGE, AND METAPHOR IN HEGEL'S *PHENOMENOLOGY OF SPIRIT*

Having learned to appreciate the pedagogical value of contrast, I shall in this paper develop my perspective on the stated theme by interaction with Donald Phillip Verene's *Hegel's Recollection: A Study of Images in the Phenomenology of Spirit* (Albany: SUNY Press, 1985), This *Work* is admirably suited to my needs, because I find myself in disagreement with its author with regard to most issues of Hegel interpretation. It is therefore only fair to call attention at the outset to several features of it, beginning with the following statement by the author in the Preface, which tend importantly to qualify the force of some of the criticisms to follow:

> I do not regard the views I express to be exactly what Hegel himself meant. Nor do I intend what I say here to be simply my own philosophical view imposed upon Hegel's work. My approach falls between these two. In each chapter I have sought to uncover ideas that are within the text, but which, once uncovered, do not always point to what we have come to expect the text to mean. They are ideas that often lead out in their own directions. Uncovering these ideas allows us to look at Hegel differently and can allow us to raise in a new way the question: what is living and what is dead in Hegel? (xi)

Following this Verene notes, "Hegel invites the reader to participate in his work, not just to think about what it says but to think with it, to extend it and bring it to life" (xi). Not only has Verene thought "beyond" Hegel at points through the *Work,* drawing richly upon such thinkers as Ernst Cassirer, John Findlay, and Ernesto Grassi: some of the most basic aspects of the position he develops owe so much to the work of others and to his own ingenuity that this *Book* may best be regarded as a constructive synthesis of aspects of Hegel's *Phän.* with some other streams of thought, with some of which, however, I find it to be less compatible than does he. If at points he does seem to impose his own views upon Hegel, some readers may find the resulting synthesis not less interesting on this account. This not quite fully acknowledged mediating character of the work does not prevent him from shedding some important light upon Hegel's enterprise at points along the way, especially upon its literary character and upon background influences within German literature that are at work in it. Indeed it seems to me that it is precisely in the attention that Verene accords to these themes that his most important contribution may lie. This is important to note because my focus is to be upon issues pertaining to Verene's appropriations from Hegel as a systematic philosopher. It is also important to note that I intend to be doing Hegel interpretation, even though, strictly speaking, Verene does not. This is except where I leave qualifying cues of one or another sort to indicate that I am or might be going beyond Hegel.

As pertaining to his appropriations of Hegel, I wish here, right at the start, to call attention to some problems I find with his basic approach, as these are germane to the status he attributes to image and metaphor in Hegel's *Phän*. On page 3, in reply to the question as to what it means to claim that the key to Hegel's *Phän*. is *Erinnerung* (recollection), Verene replies, "Simply put, it claims that speculative knowing, *spekulatives Wissen*, presupposes recollection". The concept of recollection is certainly central to Hegel's enterprise, especially in his *Phän.*, and a service is rendered in thematizing it. It is also to be acknowledged that there is an undeniable identity to be affirmed between Hegel's Begriff and speculation, on the one hand, and these sundered categories that are recollected, and to the recollection of which Hegel's *Phän*. has led us, on the other. For Hegel the Begriff and its history — its path of becoming that gets payed out as a series of disparate images — are ultimately maintained to be one and the same. The issue I wish to raise pertains only to how this identity is to be conceived. What needs here to be observed, it seems to me, is that absolute knowledge, being *a priori* — the Owl of Minerva flies only at dusk — no more awaits recollection than my present certainty of myself and the world present for me within this present occasion awaits an explicit and detailed laying out of the various strata of phenomena that may subsequently be seen to have constituted it. Verene's statement that specific knowing presupposes recollection is very likely to mislead the reader into concluding otherwise. Anyone inclined to question the importance of this point may be reminded that Hegel's absolute knowledge can be the closed system of internal relations that it is only because, precisely by being past, it is no longer subject to change.[1]

These considerations seem to me to point toward a position that regards recollection as the means whereby what explicitly constituted my self-certainty is reclaimed for the abstract understanding. This is although, so far as I have been able to ascertain, Hegel does not leave clues that are adequate to maintain this unproblematically, perhaps because he could not properly do so within the strictures of his method. In part because his position is less than explicit at this point, I do not wish to emphasize it here, although it seems worthy of note that this way of regarding the matter fits in nicely with Verene's correctly understanding (so far as his account reaches), that images are to be associated with functions that Hegel assigns to representations (*Vorstellungen*). In this connection, it is proper to be reminded that representations are for Hegel always representations **of the understanding,** with a commensurate status as abstract and, where the naive consciousness stands in for knowledge proper, they prove on this account to be no more than provisional and hypothetical. If we are clear that recollection presupposes knowledge rather than knowledge presupposing recollection, as Verene proposes, it will be equally clear that the understanding is derivative from, and an abstraction from, the Begriff and not the Begriff from the understanding.

A reader disposed to regard this shift as less fundamental than I propose it to be might maintain that for consciousness in the natural attitude — say the level of sense immediacy — because the Begriff is at this level only very partially explicit, it is as proper to regard what of this sense certainty is explicit as derived from a form of mythopoetic consciousness as from an undetermined Begriff. This is a strategy that seems to be ruled out by Hegel's *Phän.* itself, however, which is surely intended to render explicit what previously was only implicit in the Begriff, also at the level of the natural attitude.

Another move to minimize this shift might consist in the proposal that the relation of representations and Begriff would in any case be circular, i.e., from one occasion to another, with the result that it cannot be too important with which one begins. What this argument overlooks is that to explain the understanding as the source of the Begriff requires a perspective that is hypothetical in a way that an actual perspective is not. On Hegel's principles, and it seems to me in fact, an actual perspective can only begin where concretely actual consciousness begins, namely as full blown (even if only very

---

[1] I am presupposing here that for Hegel the knowledge presented within any historical occasion is as unalterably complete as the Begriff itself, even though aspects may be only implicit, these being subject to being rendered explicit in the course of the further unfolding of history.

partially understanding itself), and with no theories presupposed as to the wherefore or whence of its origination. To regard the starting point as arbitrary would be tantamount to exchanging phenomenology for pure theory as theory is employed in hypothetico-deductive thinking from the outset. This seems not to be a move that a serious student of Hegel's *Phän.* can undertake with indifference, seeing that it implies either ignorance of, or the abandonment of, the very character of what Hegel is undertaking.[2]

Some additional considerations may now be brought into the issue. For one thing, we should be careful to note what the author points out in his Preface, that he is not claiming that Hegel's fundamental interest is the image and not the Begriff. Hegel, he proposes,

> is fundamentally concerned to create a concrete version of the concept, the *Begriff*. To do this he must free it from the image, the *Bild*. The *Phän.* is a grand project to accomplish this separation of the concept from the image" (xii).

A further qualification of Verene's position is to be noted. He acknowledges that Hegel does not employ *Bild* in the *Phän.* as a "special term," and that he himself has introduced the contrast of *Bild* and Begriff to refer to the general, systematic problem posed by the separation between image and Begriff that he finds in the *Work*, noting, "Hegel's own contrast is between *Vorstellung* and *Begriff*" (xii). It is to be noted that *Vorstellungen* (representations) within Hegel's account are assigned to the level of the abstract understanding. Continuing in this vein, Verene writes.

> *Vorstellung* in its general usage need not refer to thought involving an image but only to a mental process that is not as such conceptual. I mean *Bild* to refer to all modes of *bildhaftes Denken* — all forms of imaginative thought, religious, aesthetic, and mythical, that is, forms of thought that depend upon the metaphorical power of language. My use of the term *Bild* is most directly suggested by Hegel's description of his work as a *Galerie von Bildern,* a picture gallery, at the end of the *Phän.* (xii)

Already here we may be able to discern the influence of Cassirer's polemical construal of Hegel. Rather than being presented with a Begriff that Hegel presents to us as concrete actuality grasped *a priori*[3] as such — that is, a Begriff that enters the consciousness it

---

[2] The sort of theory that I here have in view ventures beyond the truth that is the whole of concrete actuality to posit something outside of and prior to this whole which is thought of as conditioning it. This is something that can, of course, only be done from a hypothetical perspective, which in principle cannot be actualized.

[3] In SC, Book I, I enter upon an exposition of Hegel's philosophy as it pertains to his conception of concreteness that concerns itself to take note of some of the many ways in which he witnesses to the consideration that his Begriff presents itself *a priori*. Although it is

constitutes as the truth that is the whole full blown, thus constituting the climax of his *Phän*.[4] — we are presented with something that from the author's point of view counts as more primordial, namely the *Bild*! Thus the for Hegel crucial difference between a phenomenological analysis of what has **already constituted** science and knowledge, on the one hand, and the sort of adventure of hypothetical reason that proposes what we might theoretically construe to be the antecedents for this to have been, on the other, tends to be blurred if not erased from the outset of Verene's account.

Concerning Cassirer Verene writes,

> In the second volume of *The Philosophy of Symbolic Forms*, which contains his theory of mythical thought, Cassirer refers to Hegel's passage on the ladder in the *Phän*. This is the passage in the preface in which Hegel says that science should provide the individual with a ladder to show him the way to the Begriff. (Hoffmeister, p. 25). Cassirer says: "If then, in accordance with Hegel's demand, science is to provide the natural consciousness with a ladder leading to itself, it must first set this ladder a step lower."

By a step lower Cassirer means that Hegel begins his account of consciousness with epistemologically neutral heres, nows, and I's. In the stage of sense-certainty the object is simply being sensed as a neutral content, neutral as to its primordial feeling qualities. As Cassirer shows in his theory of mythical *Dasein*, the object is first sensed not as a content but as a force. The object is felt in primitive consciousness as a friendly or

---

not practical to list the pages that pertain to an issue this thoroughly embedded throughout a systematic treatment, notes on the following pages of the *Work* will assist the reader to perceive the magnitude of the issue that I judge to be here at stake: 8f, 61-64, 85f, 92f, 111f, 117f, 133, and 145f. See also p. 499, where I conclude: "There is perhaps no fallacy that has so dogged the tradition of Hegel scholarship — in English more, to be sure, than in German — than the failure of interpreters to accept and consistently to appropriate the *a priori* status that Hegel accords to his Begriff. I am convinced that apart from understanding this matter correctly, we can never even find the right ballpark, much less play Hegel's kind of game sufficiently well to perceive his philosophy to offer the methodological basis, at least, of a live option."

[4] *Phän.*, p. 563; or *Phen.*, p. 806. This "transition (*Übergang*) of the Begriff into consciousness" is not to be understood as though there was consciousness all along and now this consciousness is somehow to be enriched. Rather, it signals that Hegel has now reached the terminus of his account of how consciousness **comes to be**. This coming to be I understand to be an all at once truth that is the whole (replete with the world determinative of it and present for it) that does not come to be in the bits and pieces of its analysis-resynthesis in linear language. In other words, the consciousness, and indeed the self-consciousness, that, insofar as the account is as yet incomplete, has all along been merely presupposed at this point gives way to the self-consciousness of which an account has now been given. The self-consciousness of which an account has been given as of something external to the self-consciousness being presupposed, however, at this point becomes that very self-consciousness. This is not, however, as merely presupposed but as known from an internal (actual) perspective. This internal actual perspective was, of course, necessary to the account all along, but it is first here that it becomes fully explicit as what it is. This, then, is absolute knowledge — the absolute knowledge that consciousness, as such, proves itself inherently to be.

foreboding presence. Usener, in his classic study of *Götternamen*, a work that was important for Cassirer, sees the first use of language by which consciousness frees itself from the immediacy of the moment of pure being as involving "momentary gods"....Immediacy is first formed not as a this but as a god, a god of the moment. (31)[5]

I shall enter four remarks pertaining to the foregoing quotation. (1) The Hegelian Begriff entering consciousness I take to be an all at once, all-or-nothing occurrence, quite apart from the degree to which this consciousness, except for a certain minimal awareness of certain discriminations, is explicit in a given occasion. Each level and aspect of the history that consciousness, together with the world present for consciousness, immanently contains I understand to be concretely universal[6] throughout the Begriff, and this in the case of any particular occasion, so that from the standpoint of an account of the type of Hegel's no one is more fundamental or more primordial than another. In other words, *within concrete actuality*, in an account of this type, dialectic is not determined by a serial order; serial order is introduced only where an applied dialectical method must necessarily issue in an exposition of this actuality in linear language.

To be noted parenthetically here is that I am assuming something that Verene seems at times to deny (e.g., 11), namely that there is in Hegel's conceptuality something we may plausibly call dialectical method.[7] I have previously proposed that a dialectical account

---

[5] Cassirer very probably derived inspiration for the last statement in the foregoing from Hegel. As Errol E. Harris reminds us, "for Hegel every category of the Logic ⟦within which indeterminate being is made the starting point⟧ is a provisional definition of the Absolute...". "The Contemporary Significance of Hegel and Whitehead", in George R. Lucas, Jr. (Ed.), *Hegel and Whitehead*, p. 22.

[6] For discussions of concrete universality, see SC, pp. 226, 243f, and 444-48.

[7] Hegel identifies his method with his *Logik*, excluding "die Elementarlehre" (*Logik*, 36f; or *Logic*, 54f). Again, "The method is nothing else than the structure of the whole in its pure and essential form" (*Phän.*, 40; or *Phen.*, 106). I use the term with reference to his logical idea insofar as it lends itself to being regarded as a procedure that may be applied. The term "dialectical method" permits me to distinguish Hegel's method from such methods of theoretical speculation as involve themselves with predictions of the future.
For my justification for referring to dialectic as immanent within determinate actuality, see SC, pp. 83f, n. 12.
Verene writes,

> The dialectic is not a method. Hegel is clear on this — that it is no method in any known or ordinary sense. The dialectic is not a method but a name for ingenuity, ingenious activity itself, which takes a continually varying shape depending on the content before it. (11)

The reader must judge from passages such as the following — and they are not difficult to find — taken from Hegel's *Logik*, whether Verene's statement is not misleading:

construed to be representative of the individuals within, e.g., a given community, could lend itself, at least within limits, to variation in the serial order of its representation. This usage and approach I find useful, especially where the ghosts of empiricism are still being invoked. It assists us to avoid confusion with all forms of the hypothetico-deductive method, which we associate prominently with futuristic hypothetical thinking such as pertains to how we prepare possibilities for actualization. It is not essential to the point about concrete universality that I have just made, however, which seems as though it might represent a departure of the Cassirer/Verene program from that of Hegel in addition to the reversal of the order of derivation of Begriff and image (as a species of understanding) previously noted. We shall forestall a decision, however, until some other considerations are brought in.

(2) I suspect that the "weakened form" of the claim for the serial ordering of Hegel's dialectic that I have thus in the preceding paragraph construed with some degree of freedom from Hegel may to some extent be made out in his position. Even were it to be found attributable to him, however, although I suspect this might weaken the force of Cassirer's critique, from which I have quoted, insofar as this is directed toward what I refer to as the serial ordering of his dialectic, I could not on this basis alone totally exempt Hegel from its force. This is even if it is presupposed that this issue is to be kept separate from, and made secondary to, the fact that Hegel's Begriff, being grasped *a priori*, stands prior to its constitutive recollections. In other words, consciousness (which is always at least implicitly the bearer of absolute knowledge) stands *a priori* and prior to the explicit recollection, as such, that is for the most part, at least, only retrospectively perceived to have constituted it.

The supposed necessity of the serial order of Hegel's dialectic, and with this the order of the implicated recollections, has always been subject to one sort of attack or another, and I believe with good

---

Hitherto philosophy had not found its method; it regarded with envy the systematic structure of mathematics and, as we have said, borrowed it or had recourse to the method of sciences which are only amalgams of given material, empirical propositions and thoughts — or even resorted to a crude rejection of all method [[is this what Verene does, even suggesting that this might be in the name of Hegel?]]. However, the exposition of what alone can be the true method of philosophical science falls within the treatment of logic itself; for the method is the consciousness of the form of the inner self-movement of the content of logic. In the *Phän.* I have expounded an example of this method in application to a more concrete object, namely to consciousness. (*Logik*, I, p. 35; or *Logic* [adapted from the Miller trans.] pp. 53f)

The passage that I have just quoted is followed by an instructive reference to "des logischen Satzes", the force of which, at least for present purposes, is moderated in the Miller translation by the rendition, "the logical principle", the reference clearly being to the philosophical proposition (and judgment) regarded in its function as a logical principle.

reason. This order appears to be principally determined by the principle of progression from categories we are predisposed from the outset to regard as simpler and hence, following his architectonic, more abstract, toward categories we are predisposed from the outset to regard as more complex, and hence, following his architectonic, as more concrete. Hegel proposes to find these categories, regarded collectively, to present us with a kind of skeleton of historical development *per se*, from which we may derive the order in knowing consciousness. He may at times be moving in the opposite direction, of course, from the order in the knowing consciousness to historical order. In either case, things have seldom appeared to his critics to work out as neatly as his proposed identity of the two orders requires, perhaps in part because they had different histories or different concrete knowledge, or because, as I have elsewhere proposed, emphases and implicated dialectical orders of discriminations may shift even from one occasion to another even throughout a series the members of which are successively constitutive of the same subject.[8]

(3) The preceding two points in view, I return now to a point I made earlier. What seems to me to be most fundamentally alien in the Cassirer/Verene position when set within the context of a Hegelian problematic is the proposal that images are prior to what is imaged, representations prior to what is being represented. Having thus restated this issue (if in a slightly different way), I must acknowledge that Verene appears sometimes, especially later in the *Work,* to be moving beyond the position I have thus been led to attribute to him. This is in contexts within which he leaves the impression that perhaps metaphors and images are not, after all, grasped merely as such (i.e., as abstract understandings), but only within the particular contexts of individuals and temporal moments within which they yield particular conceptual meanings. Although I am less than certain how these passages are to be reconciled systematically with some others of the sort I have noted, the insight they reflect seems to me to render it important to take them prominently into account. In this vein, consider, e.g., the following passage:

> The view of metaphor that I am applying to Hegel's procedure in the *Phän.* derives from Grassi's view that the real always appears to us through metaphorical speech and the original meaning the metaphor bears is never cancelled or surpassed in the logical development of the word (65).

This might seem to suggest that the effect of a metaphor might be concretely universal throughout the occasion of which it constitutes

---

[8] See Essay IX, § 28 (p. 185) or SC, esp. 444-46, also 93-108, 217-24.

an aspect. Viewed as within a Hegelian perspective, it seems at least to be saying that conceptual truth (and I should suppose that literal truth is here in view) to the grasping of which a metaphor is retrospectively seen to have led — self-consciousness aware of itself and the world present for it — is not something that can be separated off and regarded merely in abstraction apart from the loss of its actuality.

It is by a similar kind of reasoning that I have been saying that with any utterance in what I (without appealing directly to Hegel) call concrete language is implicated the entire occasion — something resembling Hegel's "truth which is the whole" — within which the utterance occurs.[9] With the passage above quoted, then, the difference between the Verene/Grassi account, which seems just at this point quite fittingly read into Hegel, and my account seems to me to pertain less to an issue of the truthfulness of the interpretation than to one of emphasis. Pursuant of Hegel's emphasis upon absolute knowing and his deemphasis of understanding (to which metaphor, as Verene has indirectly perceived, at least some of the time, belongs) I propose a very special type of language — namely concrete language — as the expression of absolute knowledge. An alternative formulation that would serve equally well to meet the present issue is that where a metaphor is grasped as such, its concrete meaning — and I would be inclined also to say its literal meaning for the time and situation of the perceiving consciousness — is grasped with it, so that it is not merely a blank check, so to speak.

The passage above cited seems to allow, at least, of this interpretation. Again, when he writes, "When we grasp the meaning of the image we take it up as the concept" (112), it seems that Verene might be heading in the direction that I am urging and that he does better justice to Hegel's enterprise than in those passages I have called attention to as marked abberations from Hegel (that he seems not to have recognized as such). In this same vein, I could also say with Verene that with absolute knowledge "we learn to distinguish between... that which presents meaning through another medium and that which presents meaning through its own medium. For the philosopher the image, the *Vorstellung* or the *Bild*, must always have a meaning other than itself" (112), properly attributing the sense of this utterance to Hegel.

The three passages that I have quoted from Verene in the imme-

---

[9] For my development of this concept, see Essay IX, (pp. 175-78), HFSI, esp. §§23-26, and in SC, consult the Index of Terms under "language, concrete (facts that speak for themselves, creation speaking for itself)".

diate foregoing all seem to imply, or at least to adumbrate, what with an eye to Hegel I would refer to as the concrete universality of both aspects, metaphor (or image) on the one hand and the particular conceptual meaning that the metaphor (or image) in a particular situation and (for purposes of simplification, shall we say) for a particular individual within the same occurrance or event, on the other. They might thus be regarded as accents within an identity inclusive of both parties to a mediation. This relation is actual in a speculative proposition or judgment, concerning which I shall shortly say more. What is to be appreciated just here is that one may with plausibility describe such an inclusive identity from the standpoint of either of its accents, because neither is complete, nor indeed even actual, except as an accent within the whole. Verene's taking over this important Hegelian idea is qualified, however, if attention is called to his proposal that speculative knowing presupposes recollection, since this seems to render speculative knowledge external to recollection. This is in addition to posing a contradiction in terms, since for Hegel a speculative proposition or judgment quite clearly sets forth no other relation than one that is internal to the subject and predicate it mediates. A concept of knowledge is thus presupposed that is narrower than Hegel's wholistic concept. In other words it is an abstraction. We must conclude, I believe, that knowledge construed narrowly enough to be derived from imagery must belong to a quite different program than Hegel's, and one linked more intimately with, or at least confused with, hypothetical thinking placed at the service of the hypothetical-deductive method than with a Hegelian type phenomenology.

(4) With reference to the issue as to whether Hegel needs to set his ladder a step lower, it seems to me entirely plausible that the first human knowledge may have been primitive in the sense that it was not far from the sense immediacy of other animals. The productions of minds that human beings typically associate with dreaming and mytho-poetic thinking belong, I suspect, to a strata of accomplishments, being "higher" on the ladder, that presuppose such sense immediacy in its imaging and representation, and one that we have not recovered from the need to nurture, as though it were there in primitive roots to which we only needed to return. Having said this, I for my part would not entirely disallow the possibility that a quite different serial order of dialectic might with plausibility be made to obtain, with a commensurately differing lower rung of the ladder, for some culture or situation.

Consider again Verene's statement that I quoted from page 112: "When we grasp the meaning of the image we take it up as the concept." Does the concept as which we take up the meaning of the image include the image? Hegel's reply to the question is of course a resounding "yes". Verene's position appears ambiguous. So long as we hold him to his statement that the Begriff presupposes images, since we are quite naturally led to interpret this and related utterances as implying an abstract knowledge external to the image or images it presupposes, his posture seems unHegelian and indeed antiHegelian. The Begriff is certainly, to use Verene's phrase, "that which presents itself through its own medium", however, and if we emphasize this point, his position comes out very much more Hegelian.

Again, Verene's accent upon image and metaphor, especially insofar as he implicitly acknowledges them to belong to what for Hegel is the mere understanding, seems unHegelian. It is as though for him the image includes its meaning, the concept, rather than, as Hegel would more typically express the relation, the concept includes the image. We should move quite cautiously on this point, however, because, if we consider every aspect of Hegel's Begriff to be concretely universal throughout its compass, i.e., throughout concrete actuality, grasped as such, we must, I believe, ultimately discover this to imply that the whole is implicated in every part.[10] In this case the comprehension of the truth that is the whole primarily from the standpoint of this one accent cannot be false. This presupposes the propriety of setting images and representations (*Vorstellungen*) on virtually the same footing within Hegel's conceptuality. Given that all merely representative thinking for Hegel falls short of concrete actuality and of the knowledge that it images or represents, the differences here involved can be only relative, as Verene seems to perceive.

---

[10] The notion that the whole is implicated in every part might in the following way be found to assist us to see the positions of Verene/Cassirer, on the one hand, and what I have presented as that of Hegel, on the other, as broadly compatible even though they issue from quite different methods.

In connection with the proposal that Hegel's ladder needs to be set one step lower, Verene proposes myth itself to be "the original artisan of the thought of the whole" (p. 32). This is an aspect of his proposal to construe Cassirer's mytho-poetic consciousness as the ground of Hegel's Begriff. This position may at first seem to reflect a quite radical departure from Hegel in that the unity and wholeness of the Begriff that the *Phän.* has as its task to render explicit is now in some way maintained to be explicitly present in its ground. Given this arrangement, commensurably less remains to be accomplished by the dialectic to follow. Certainly it is to be acknowledged that some extensive changes would be required to render Hegel's account commensurate with such a newly introduced point of beginning. If we construe that the unity and wholeness that is being attributed to the point of beginning is what is actually being rendered explicit throughout the course of the exposition, this whole being properly construed to be implicated in every part, however, it begins to seem as though the required adjustment could be made out to consist less fundamentally in a shift in the attribution of ultimate priorities than in a thoroughgoing reordering of the account.

I have proposed (point 3, pp. 208f above) that for Hegel images are not prior to what is imaged nor are representations prior to what is represented. It may now be added that, strictly speaking, this that is prior is for Hegel no mere part or aspect of knowledge but the truth which is the whole. Whatever representative thought there is — all of which is more or less image, simile, or metaphor — is an abstraction from this whole. It can on this account prove misleading to refer to what can be represented — as though it might be some supposed thing in itself, which, perhaps even as actual, could be set over against the representation — when in fact it includes, but is more comprehensive than, the representation. To state the situation that I believe to hold for Hegel more adequately (although I might be hard put to justify this with certainty), representation and that which is represented being actual only as poles of a mediation, as totally abstract elements they can have no greater status than that of possibilities. This is to say, they image possibilities for actualization, but are not themselves actual. To properly appreciate what is here involved is to perceive the speculative proposition (together with the speculative judgment), to which I shall shortly turn, as the dynamic and process principle by which potentiality is in mediation actual.[11]

It is my view that in applying the dialectical method to represent immanent concrete actuality, we **merely represent** this actuality. This representation, as in the case of any and all representative thinking, can present only a shadow of that which is represented. What are represented are the speculative judgments the unity and wholeness of which are concrete actuality grasped as such. What distinguishes this case of representation is that what is being represented was just previously known or grasped within the lived occasion, and the identity of what was known persists in its vivid remembrance. The upshot of my analysis is that speculative propositions should be considered to be ultimately representative of speculative judgments, the latter being internal to, and exclusively constitutive of, concrete actuality grasped as such. They are certainly known, but when we pay out what is known in linear language in the systematic analysis-*re*synthesis of the lived occasion upon its perishing, we do this in speculative **propositions.** This way of formulating the problematic permits us to accord to the discrete terms that issue from speculative propositions citizenship in a conventional language. This citizenship is by adoption or naturalization after first presenting themselves as natural born citizens of concrete language, which, being *a priori*, is certainly prior.

---

[11] This reading is the only one that I can find to be consistent with Hegel's affirmation of creation as *ex nihilo*, on which issue he distinguishes his position from that of Spinoza.

This way of construing things - which has of course taken me somewhat beyond Hegel — assists us to deal with a problem to which Hegel did not devote sufficient attention. His concern having been with "the ascent to the Absolute" (for which purpose the speculative proposition and speculative judgment function brilliantly), he did not render explicit enough how one might descend from the dialectical ladder into the everyday world of ordinary things construed as externally related and of representations of these ordinary things in ordinary language. Indeed not even in his method did he make proper provision for this descent, which cannot be accomplished, much less accounted for, by concretely speculative propositions or judgments, i.e., internal constituents of a Begriff that is grasped *a priori* subjected to analysis-*re*synthesis after the fact. Rather, it requires hypothetical speculation and futuristic thinking within the framework of the hypothetico-deductive method. Here we are descending into a morass where the empiricist convinces himself that he can be at home, but for which Hegel had little time. It seems to me that some attention needs to be accorded to this descent even properly to locate and appreciate what Hegel was doing. In addition, it can assist us to speak to the role of image and metaphor in the preparation of possibilities for possible actualization within some future occasion.

In our concern as to whether concrete actuality, grasped as such, is prior to hypothetical thinking or the reverse, we should not forget that the consideration at hand also has a circular and cumulative aspect. This is not, however, to propose that we here have to do with an issue of no more moment than which is first, the chicken or the egg, which may be unanswerable and ultimately trivial. In the present case, if knowledge does not come first, we never achieve it, and this appears to be deeply untrue and to introduce us to a game that is not to be won and that is pointless to play and dehumanizing. It is cause for wonder that anyone could ever have thought that this might be the way to a scientific first philosophy.

To this suggestion I hasten to add that what I have in view is not an accommodation to the Cassirer/Verene view that proposes to make the mytho-poetic consciousness the primoridal source of our conceptuality. This is because I can foresee no problem in reconciling this position, at least substantially, with what I am representing as Hegel's view, provided only that the latter is construed as adaptable to variations in the serial order that may obtain in historical accounts. I perceive no problem here because the two belong to entirely different types of accounts, which will finally be found to be generally compatible if we can only avoid rendering either vague through confusing it with the other. The potential confusion to which I refer is illustrated by reference to what I perceive to be an ambiguity in Verene's disposition with respect to the status to be assigned to images within Hegel's *Phän.*, in that he is disposed, on the one hand, to perceive them to be a species of representations, which in effect assigns them to the understanding, and, on the other, he wishes to make them out to be the founding source for Hegel's creation of a version of concreteness (cf. page xi)! I suspect that the latter disposition may be the more fundamental one for Verene. Aside from the issue as to whether it can stand as Hegel interpretation, if both of these dispositions were to be given a context within the same type of account we would need to know that they can be reconciled.

One of Verene's defenses of the status that he wishes to accord to images as prior to and as conditioning Hegel's Begriff consists in the proposal that they are not conceptual, and also not so in the sense of Hegel's *spekulativem Satz*.

> The *spekulative Satz,* the speculative proposition...in which the substance of the judgment passes from subject to predicate, requires powers of mind that are not in themselves logical, nor can they assume logical form. These powers are...the constant companions of speculative knowing, but, by their very nature, cannot take the form of the speculative propositions.... to recollect is not to form a proposition, but to form an image. An image is not a proposition nor is it implicitly a proposition. But an image can give access to the proposition. (3)

I find no evidence to support the view that recollection, which on Verene's account proceeds through metaphors, ingenuities, and images, does not present itself in speculative propositions in Hegel's sense, but in images. Here again, the passage reflects more influence by Cassirer than by Hegel. It seems especially out of keeping with Verene's above mentioned proposal that images pertain to what Hegel classifies under representations. This is although the principal issue here consists in the special advantage that is being taken of the association of the term with discursive propositions within an already formed language, which is not at all what is here in view. What is in view here has much more to do with the way in which meanings and language are originally formed.[12] There is no sense at all here reflected for the dynamic and processural character of the mediation that

---

[12] Verene reflects insufficient awareness of an extensive literature pertaining to Hegel's *spekulativem Satz* — for the most part in German, to be sure, that has accrued during the past couple of decades.
My discussion of Charles Hartshorne on Hegel on pp. 95ff (n. 29) is relevant here.

takes place in speculative propositions and judgments. Had the case been otherwise, rather than finding, in effect, a foundation for Hegel's Begriff in Cassirer's mytho-poetic consciousness, he might have been at least as inclined to find a foundation in Hegel for Cassirer.

Hegel's *spekulativer Satz*, which he sometimes refers to simply as the *philosophische Satz*, is the basic element of his dialectic. Before proposing that there is some type or strata of meaning that cannot be expressed in *spekulativen Sätzen* we should carefully consider that in his philosophy of subjective spirit he encounters no difficulty in employing this model in the explication of pure feelings. Furthermore its presence may be observed in the feelings themselves, if we follow Hegel's account with care, not, of course, as a method that is merely applied, but as an aspect of their immanent substance. What this has to teach us is that a feeling that is natively grasped as such is grasped in the form of a *speculativen Satz*. For Hegel, a feeling that is not grasped (*begriffen*, and this within the context of the Begriff, so that in it subject and substance — among other mediated correlatives constitutive of the occasion — as well are implicated) is of course not concretely actual.[13]

To be especially noted is that the German term, *spekulativer Satz* can refer either to propositions or to judgments immanent within knowledge. The sense of the latter would be especially difficult to convey by the use of the term "proposition." If justice is done to Hegel's doctrine of judgments, the unbridgeable antithesis between Hegel and Cassirer with respect to the issue at hand is rendered even more apparent. This is not at all to deny the power of mythological thinking, but to propose that, within a Hegelian type dialectic the serial ordering of which tends primarily to be determined by order of complexity, it belongs principally to the levels of art and religion and not to, or prior to, the stage of bare sense immediacy. If we acknowledge that *in actuality* or ultimately the meanings of all speculative propositions and judgments (within a given concrete whole) interpenetrate, each being concretely universal in all, we will in any case perceive a certain partiality in any liniarization simply because everything cannot be said at once.

I have proposed that the Cassirer/Verene account of image and metaphor is of a different type than that which may be found to be implicated within Hegel's *Phän*. I shall now approach this matter by reference to Verene's interpretation of the concluding sentence in

---

[13] Cf. SC, pp. 278-81, n. 25.

Hegel's Introduction to this *Work*. He places considerable weight especially upon the claim that consciousness will arrive at a point where "die Erscheinung dem Wesen gleich wird", where the appearance and the essence become *gleich* (17). "*Gleich*", he notes, means "the same, like, equal, equivalent, alike, similar, resembling, proportionate." Hegel, he notes, "does not say that they become identical, become one, merge into a unity, manifest a common principle, or exist through a common element." Rather, "they reach a stage in which they are the same, alike, proportionate" (17).

Among other things, Verene is concerned to point out the possibility of translating "gleich" otherwise than as "identical", as Baillie has it. Certainly this is to be granted. Some flexibility is allowable in the interpretation and translation of this term, which must be determined to some extent by the role the passage plays within the context of the *Work*. This seems not to make Baillie's rendition in this case to be necessarily false, however, especially when it is noted that within the same sentence Hegel presents us with the discriminated aspects being folded together (*zusammenfällt*) and considering the frequency with which Hegel's term "identity" ("*Identität*") turns up within systematically related contexts and how central a role the concept of identity plays within his conceptuality. It is well to bear in mind that it is identity in difference — i.e., identity in which also difference is preserved — that is ultimately here in view. It seems, moreover, that the verb "*zusammenfällt*" serves Hegel both within this context and elsewhere as an apt and lively image of this very relation.

It would appear that at the very least Verene errs in wishing to prove too much by what, if we accept his interpretation, is ***not*** said in this introductory statement — the thrust of his critique being to weaken what is being affirmed by Baillie and other interpreters — and by omitting reference to the many sources of evidence that might be cited to show that Hegel did indeed ultimately affirm an identity in difference not only in a dialectic conveniently labeled as such and not only as pertaining to appearance and its essence but to many other dialectical polarities as well. As though in this manner to underscore the concrete universality of this discrimination throughout his Begriff, Hegel indeed builds the affirmation of such an identity into his very concept of the speculative proposition (or judgment) — which he sometimes refers to simply as **the philosophical proposition (or judgment)**, thus implying that no other kind of proposition should rank as philosophical. Thus he writes, "Thus in the case of the philosophical judgment, the identity [*Identität*] of subject and predicate is not intended to destroy their distinction, as expressed in the form of propositions or judgments" (*Phän.*, 51; or *Phen.*, 120). In this connection it is interesting to note that Verene, in the passage above quoted from page 3 of his *Work* paraphrases rather than quotes this statement, and thus averts the use of the term "identity" (*Identität*).

Verene seems to be proposing by his interpretation of the concluding statement in the Introduction to the *Phän.* alone to have overridden the force of Hegel's concept of identity insofar as this concept finds expression within the *Work*. The net effect, where such a subversion to be permitted to stand, would be a loss of precision and rigor for dialectic and in a regrettable vagueness with regard to its formal properties. This comes to much the same as an earlier disposition on the part of John Findlay (whom Verene frequently cites) to trivialize the very concept of dialectic to the point that he relegated it to the status of a mere style of exposition. This entire program seems to me ultimately to lead, by a route that I cannot trace here, to a neutralizing domestication of it to the humblest sort of hypothetical reason put to the service of the hypothetico-deductive method, thus undercutting in a manner that is almost bound to be fatal the purchase upon concrete actuality to which Hegel can point us.

When we inquire what may lie behind Verene's attempt thus to undermine the role of Hegel's concept of identity the following explanation presents itself as a possibility. He appears to be considering the status of this concept with reference to things that present themselves as undeniably externally related rather than in terms of what Hegel construes to be concrete actuality *already* grasped as such. In other words, he is not seeking something analogous to what Hegel is talking about in concrete actuality as he himself actually grasps and knows it (as internally related) but in things, and in abstract ideas of things, that are undeniably externally related and thus of the sort that one can speculate about hypothetically. From this perspective the admission of a weak synonymy presents no problem for him, i.e., the kind of partial convergence — where imagery and metaphor do their work — of the polar aspects that Hegel is to view as mediated to identity in difference or as distinguished, while at the same time that he must withdraw from admitting this identity as something actually achieved.

Hegel having been a systematic philosopher of great skill and discipline, it would be the height of folly to suppose that an aspect of his conceptuality as crucial as the fact that his Begriff is grasped *a priori* could be left out of account without at least one other major additional error being introduced to in some way compensate for this omission. It is my impression that Verene's principal compensatory error consists in a denial of, or at least a marked diminishing of the force of, Hegel's concept of identity and the sense in which this identity is achieved in knowledge, following Hegel's account.[14]

To be appreciated here is that Verene is not prepared to admit a result or effect he cannot verify in the phenomenology of his own self-consciousness. In the case before us this permits the strong conjecture that he is "domesticating" Hegel's account to the shadow land of hypothetical thinking, where we theorize and prepare possibilities for possible concretization, rather than seeing it as pertaining principally to already mediated concrete actuality, grasped as such — the native land of truth to which the *Phän.* was supposed to guide us. For Hegel, concrete actuality grasped as such is already, or, as this comes to mean for a philosophical analysis-resynthesis, just was, this lived identity, grasped as such, which we now recollect as a gallery of disparate images and forms of the understanding that once constituted this unity. We should understand that this actuality presents itself *a priori*, and that we are not being asked to perceive it as a piecemeal occurrence so much as to acknowledge it as the subject-substance of an account of what has already happened, and which we now recollect as having happened in this way. On this account there is consciousness and a world is present for consciousness (and the plurality of things as externally related is **derivative** from this actuality). If we view matters in this way the difficulty that I suspect Verene wants to do away with vanishes.

That difficulty, I believe, consists in the belief that Hegel might be tempted to say with this concept that externally related things may somehow be rendered internally related, and thus actual, by some sort of magical imposition of a doctrine or of an intellectual exercise. This possibility Verene correctly rejects.[15] In this case it is a false problematic with which he is working, however, which results from a failure to perceive the full force and working out of the fact that Hegel's Begriff is grasped *a priori*, so that his absolute knowledge, far from being merely concocted out of ideas, is present *a priori* and prior to its philosophical explication as such. Concrete actuality grasped as such comes not at all as a mere concoction, if we follow

---

[14] Verene's weakening of the sense of the identity that is actualized would seem to imply a commensurate weakening of the actual force of Hegel's crucial concept of negation, even though I have no objection to raise with respect to his account of this concept (see pp. 20, 22, and 57).

[15] Indeed no serious thinker has ever, to my knowledge, affirmed this naive a form of idealism, although the fact that it has often enough been rejected by non-idealists might be taken to imply otherwise.

Hegel's account, but upon arising into consciousness out of a night of nothing, as it were, it is simply present. The "night" to which I make reference may from a temporal perspective seem very short or non-existent. What is essential to affirm if we are to preserve the integrity of Hegel's Begriff within the context of a plurality of passing occasions is that concrete actuality, grasped as such, is in every occasion a new creation (repleat with its own history as actual within the present within it), not to be accounted for as an effect of hypothetically construed antecedents that we might, by virtue of living in a technological theory-oriented cultural epoch, be tempted to regard as adequate to it.[16]

That one cannot move between these two types of accounts casually, i.e., apart from according adequate recognition to the radical difference between them, is ultimately because self-consciousness and its truth arise full-blown out of **nothing actual,** with the result that hypothetical speculation about causal antecedents — always implicated with futuristic thinking — must be of an entirely different genre from concretely actual speculation — which is actuality-constitutive — and of relations within concrete actuality grasped as such. In rendering an account of the latter we must go to the phenomena themselves which by analysis-resynthesis after the fact we are assisted to apprehend and to recollect as having constituted, in their togetherness, the lived occasion, self-consciousness and its truth.

This is not to propose that all of our play with images and metaphors takes place exclusively within the realm of hypothetical thinking, i.e., in the preparation, with forethought, of possibilities for possible concretization within a new occasion. Images and metaphors often take their origin in body dispositions and activities, in dream-work, and in the mytho-poetic consciousness, a finding that empirical investigations in their own way tend to corroborate. Any of these as they are grasped within the context of some lived occasion may certainly qualify as concrete, as indeed may anything at all that is so grasped. Even so, it is properly humbling to acknowledge that, whatever of the various sorts of concrete presentations given *a priori* may count as background, most of our play with images and metaphors *that we can be aware of as such* is bound up with hypothetical thinking. Insofar as this is the case such play presupposes and seeks out its bearings in concrete actuality, grasped as such. This

---

[16] I am here concerned with maintaining the integrity of Hegel's Begriff construed pluralistically, and this within the framework of a temporal alternation of actual and hypothetical perspectives. See p. 37 or, for a fuller treatment, SC, pp. 439-44 and 462-77.

is in a sense somewhat parallel to the fact that any language science that investigates phenomena of this type presupposes first philosophy as the discipline that has as its specific task the systematically complete explication by analysis-*re*synthesis of this concrete actuality.[17]

Having proposed that our play with images and metaphors *that we can be aware of as such* is principally in connection with hypothetical thinking, I must hasten to add that the proofstone of the success of such play must finally be in the lived concreteness to the *a priori* grasp of which it seems to lead. I say "seems to lead", because extreme caution is called for here if we are not to lose sight of the *a priori* character of concrete actuality grasped as such through neglecting the night out of which it emerges, a night that hypothetical thinking about antecedents must never be permitted to seem to eliminate. This is the night of creation, which to presume to displace by hypothetical constructions would involve us in the kind of intellectual hybris that supposes that mere ideas that we come to may be concretely actual apart from negation and mediation. The point of caution that I am urging is particularly in place owing to the fact that I am being more explicit than was Hegel in construing his Begriff with reference to each of a plurality of occasions, this being the most conspicuous mark of a temporal perspective. This is a disposition that Verene appears to share.

Insofar as these criticisms reflect a standpoint that accords a necessary role to hypothetical thinking in the preparation of possibilities for actualization, it reflects a problematic that has moved some way beyond Hegel. It seems to me that this was in place, here at the last, to enable me to point a direction that I believe must be taken if we are to find a proper context for the role of image and metaphor that is consistent also with those central aspects of Hegel's conceptuality that I have found not to be regarded seriously enough in Verene's account. Hegel's use of image and metaphor in the *Phän.* is impressive — a fact that Verene's account can assist us to see more clearly. Even so, I find this *Work* to provide even less of an account of the use of either than the author seems to believe he can make

---

[17] I have elsewhere proposed that the discrimination here indicated marks what I regard as the natural boundary between first philosophy and the theory of science (*Wissenschaftstheorie*), which carried on with a proper cognizance of first philosophy, is properly construed second philosophy. See pp. 40ff.

My intention is not, e.g., to deny that a creative writer may, whether implicitly or explicitly, perform the role of a first philosopher, or to whatever extent his training and genius may qualify him. The arbitration of a potential jurisdictional dispute over work rules is not a consideration here. I merely wish to call attention to a discrimination in the subject itself that I believe should not be overlooked by anyone concerned.

out. To be noted is that he virtually concedes that what he says by way of interpretation of Hegel's use of metaphor is being read into and not out of the *Phän.* Thus, in a passage previously quoted, he refers to "the view of metaphor that I am *applying* to Hegel's procedure..." (65, ital. added).

It can hardly be surprising that Hegel himself has nothing to say under this heading, when one considers that his method as it stands is ill suited for this task, which indeed cannot even be gotten under way in what he regarded as philosophical (speculative) propositions. It is *not* as though the *Phän.* were a report of images being made or, as Verene supposes, effecting their sway. What it reports has shown itself to be already present in concrete actuality known as such. It is in the realm of possibilities that identities may be either merely presupposed or merely contemplated as possibilities, but within which they are never rendered constitutive of concrete actuality. It is here that metaphors principally do their work, and it is here, as a consequence, that linguistic and other types of images may be formed and subject to reformation. Hegel is principally concerned with what has been concretely actualized in firm identities (for which he had no need whatever to apologize). His is primarily a success story, interested to report only such images as are integral, through mediation (mediation, that is, *to identity in difference or as discriminated*), with the actuality to the constitution of which they have contributed. We should not level Hegelian dialectic down to metaphor,[18] e.g., by softening the force of the concept of identity.

---

[18] Verene writes, "Hegel uses the tropes of metaphor and irony to characterize various states in the *Phän.* and as a weapon to attack opposite positions and states of mind. The whole table of contents looked at from this perspective is a table of metaphors." (22)
It seems to me that we cannot confuse dialectic with metaphor except by first weakening the sense of certain aspects of Hegel's conception; in Verene's formulation it is principally the sense of the concept of identity that is directly weakened.
Also Carl C. Vaught, whom Verene cites in closely related matters, closely associates metaphor with Hegel's dialectical *Aufhebung,* as when he writes,

> For an earlier stage of reflection to be experienced, or to be *aufgehoben,* is for it to be taken up, moved beyond, and preserved in some degree of tension within a later stage of reflection. But this is precisely what occurs in the construction of a metaphor. In metaphorical discourse, the ordinary meaning of a concept is taken up, conjoined with a different, sometimes even contradictory meaning, and held in tension with it to comprise a larger metaphorical unity. This is to say, metaphors differ from literal expressions in much the same way that ordinary conception of experience differs from Hegel's richer, more dialectical conception. In both cases, the sheer opposition between two terms is made more fluid, so that the first term is taken up, conjoined with the second, and held together with it to form a richer, more complex unity. (*The Quest for Wholeness* (Albany: SUNY Press, 1982), pp. 176f)

In his emphasis within this context upon fluidity and tension and in glossing over or overlooking the hard (negation and) identity in which for Hegel this has issued "before", in

Rather, we should extend Hegelian conceptuality to embrace also an account of the preparation of possibilities for possible actualization within which images and metaphors do their work. We can do this by first having a firm hold upon what there is to image and to represent. I shall unpack the preceding two statements just a bit in the paragraph that follows.

I understand the speculative proposition (and judgment) to consist, and this necessarily, in a negation and a mediation to identity, and to be radically particular in the identity that it mediates,[19] and I understand Hegel's *Phän.* to consist most essentially in a succession

a manner of speaking, we have consciousness and knowledge of which to render an account — this giving point to the entire phenomenological analysis-resynthesis — Vaught seems to me to be not far from Verene's position. Having stated the matter thus, I hasten to add that there is a certain artificiality in making reference at all to anything proposed as being "before" within this context, since strictly speaking, there is nothing that can present itself "before" concrete actuality grasped *a priori* as such. Such a usage can point to nothing more than a fiction, and this of a sort that belongs to a garden variety of hypothetical thinking and not to a phenomenological account pursuing Hegel's basic model. Strictly speaking such an account cannot concern itself with metaphor at all, except, at most, *in a strictly metaphorical sense*, i.e., from the perspective from which it has yielded up literal knowledge and is "no longer" (in a manner of speaking) metaphor in a commonly accepted sense of the term.

Here we confront an issue that I cannot properly follow up within the present context, which the remark to follow will at best serve only roughly to suggest. This pertains to the possibility that the essential form of a metaphor lying immanent within the concrete actuality that is the lived occasion may through anamnesis enter awareness as an aspect of the *Wirkungsgeschichte* (history as actual within the present) of an epoch of lived occasions. By way of telling a story that might perhaps be made to seem likely, let us suppose that this form has been inherited with cumulative reinforcement throughout a series of occasions that have passed. If we then allow such a possibility as I have proposed, this form, except for consisting in purely internal relations, will at least approximate being a mirror image of the metaphor itself. If so, then it will be actual only as an accent within an identity (being mediated) that is inclusive also of that which is known. Alternatively, the situation may be portrayed as follows: a metaphor from this actual perspective is grasped as the literal truth it has "yielded", this being within the context of its *wirkungsgeschichtliche* becoming within an occasion of the type that it serves. It is by virtue of this mediation that the representation of metaphor as an interaction of externally related aspects is possible. The mediation to which I have referred, being *a priori,* is ultimately to be seen to be prior to the latter, which, being a derivative abstraction, is its shadow image.

We are thus presented with the possibility of understanding a metaphor and the literal truth that it yields in a particular occasion each as being an accent within an identity inclusive of both, rather than merely as an abstract potential. Notwithstanding this possibility, I have continued to construe the term as referring initially to a pure potential in order to keep faith with its acquired meaning in ordinary language, which serves a worthwhile function, even while calling attention to the possibility of regarding it from a concretely actual perspective — i.e., a perspective from within an occasion of the type that it serves, which is of special significance for first philosophy. See Essay XII immediately following. For further remarks on Vaught's treatment of metaphor in relation to dialectic, see notes within SC on pp. 93, 112, 225, and 301.

[19] See SC, Book I, "The *Spekulative Satz*: The Unifying Rhythm of Spekulative Thought" (pp. 75-123).

of such propositions and judgments. By its very character a metaphor does not affirm such an identity, but is rather a play of polarities that precisely do not yield an identity, even an identity in difference. This being the case, it is not strange that Verene, in proposing to view the table of contents of this *Work* as a table of metaphors (22), should have felt constrained, in his effort to render this program plausible, to weaken the identity being affirmed in Hegel's dialectic. In doing so, he tends, in effect, to render the entire *Phän.* a mere exercise in hypothetical thinking. I am proposing that we should let phenomenological method remain what it most essentially is in Hegel's *Phän.*, namely, a system of speculative propositions and judgments — although we should acknowledge forthrightly that the members of this series are embedded from first to last in a matrix of conventional language that supports, and is essential to, the conveyance of their meaning, a fact which Hegel did not sufficiently acknowledge. We should then proceed to supplement the type of account suggested by the *Phän.* by an account of hypothetical reason preparing possibilities for actualization, within which process the play of image and metaphor can be shown to have its proper part. This is a task to which even Hegel's account of the dialectic of art seems to me not to be adequate, at least insofar as it is construed to consist most essentially in speculative propositions.[20] The way to solve this problem is not by diluting dialectic to its shadow existence in hypothetical thinking, but to supplement it at the point at which it cannot be rendered adequate.

[20] If we consider, e.g., Hegel's account of metaphor, image, and simile within his *Ästhetik* (vol. I, pp. 516-39), dialectical form is so inconspicuous and recessive an aspect as to cause the casual reader who has not been properly introduced to Hegel's method to construe this to be an ordinary descriptive narrative. This is because the movement throughout this series is so gradual that only when it is regarded in its entirety can one perceive that a philosophical proposition is here effecting a mediation of accents (sense and image) to constitute an identity inclusive of both. Apart from this shift one would be left without a sense of the dynamic of the literary forms of which an account is being given, because the achieved identity toward which they move would be presented as prior because *a priori*, i.e., in what for Hegel is its ultimately true light. If one has just previously been reading his *Phän.* or one of the logic texts, this shift is indeed so notable that grounds are provided for suspecting that philosophical (or speculative) propositions in Hegel's sense are not to be regarded as the essence of this particular exposition, which seems to have a far more direct relevance for the preparation of possibilities for actualization than could be the case if they were. The procedure that Hegel actually practices within this context thus appears to lend indirect support to my contention that a different type of account is required of our preparation of possibilities for actualization than is possible by an appeal to philosophical propositions and judgments as he conceives them. I have thus approached from a different perspective a notion adumbrated in Essay III, pp. 59-65, more properly introduced in Essay II, §6 (pp. 40ff), and subsequently accorded somewhat further development in SC, esp. pp. 224-26, 229-32, 451-56, and 471-77 and in Essay IV, esp. §7 (p. 66).
Where our interest is in a plurality of occasions conceived along the lines of Hegel's

It is because a report on the realm of hypothetical thinking cannot even be gotten under way in philosophical (speculative) propositions as Hegel uses this term that we can no longer speak of "the" philosophical (speculative) proposition, meaning the **concretely** (because it is grasped *a priori*) speculative proposition and judgment, as Hegel confidently did, as though this were the only kind of proposition that can now have right in philosophy. Hypothetical speculative propositions, for better and worse, must also be admitted to status within the discipline, apart from the employment of which we should be unable to prepare possibilities for possible actualization at all. Once we have our philosophical bearings in concrete actuality grasped as such, we are qualified to pursue this totally different type of account apart from losing sight of what we are doing and not doing.

I indicated at the outset that Verene's *Work* here under discussion might most appropriately be regarded as a constructive synthesis of Hegel's *Phän.* with certain other streams of thought, this way of regarding it being also not too far from his declared intention. The foregoing remarks — directed principally toward distinguishing the result from certain insistant dispositions of Hegel which seem to me to be deserving of more consideration than Verene accords them, should not be construed as a full-scale evaluation of Verene's position, the direction of which I find reason to appreciate in its own right. I especially appreciate his having reflected something of the spirit of Hegel's concept of concrete universality within a context in which Cassirer's sense for mytho-poetic consciousness also comes in prominently. Apart from such attempts to assimilate, by various strategies, the impact of the work of Hegel, the literature of philosophy would be poorer than it is. In this case, there is perhaps more to be gained, however, from the author's illumination of the literary side, and of the literary-historical background of Hegel's first major work. Finally, in his attempt to treat the use of image and metaphor in Hegel's *Phän.*, Verene has opened a theme that, precisely because its proper treatment requires a context that takes us decisively beyond Hegel — as he seems to be aware — is deserving of more attention from a Hegelian perspective than it has received. Verene's

---

Begriff, the need to reconcile the slowness with which the dialectical progression within Hegel's account of metaphor, image, and simile is unfolded with the supposed centrality of his concept of a philosophical proposition (and judgment) confronts us with an additional problem. This consists in the difficulty one may sometimes find in perceiving all of the stages of this progression as present within symbols found to be constitutive of a given occasion, each of which stages might with plausibility be regarded as necessary to the achievement of the hard negation and identity required to account for the absolute knowledge, grasped *a priori* as such, within that occasion.

treatment, although it will certainly not pass unproblematically as Hegelian, can nonetheless serve to show us that there is a need here that should not go unfulfilled.

XII

HYPOTHETICAL AND ACTUAL PERSPECTIVES ON METAPHOR FROM A HEGELIAN POINT OF VIEW*

Preface

In this essay I shall be developing a case for the claim, made by Donald Davidson, that a metaphor means "what the words in their most literal interpretation mean, and nothing more".[1] Since in doing so I shall be rejecting Davidson's view that the imaginative employment of words and sentences to which metaphor appeals depends entirely on the ordinary meanings of those words and hence on the ordinary meanings of the sentences,[2] I shall not claim on this account to be favoring his overall position on metaphor more than some others that I shall mention. It may well appear at first that what I am affirming in Davidson's position is not consistent with what I am denying. Yet there is consistency here, because I appeal to the context of the lived occasion for the normative meaning of terms and propositions, which context is understood as being shaped and

---

* In this essay I make focal and give systematic unity to a theme that emerges fragmentarily throughout the length of my SC, setting this within the context of some other recent and contemporary discussions of metaphor.

I wish to thank Giacomo Rinaldi and W. Welten, S. J. for providing me with very different types of criticism of one or more earlier forms of this paper. Father Welten assisted me in the completion especially of the Appendix, in which I relate the position taken on metaphor to the *analogia entis* of St. Thomas Acquinas. These assists notwithstanding, I must bear full responsibility for the final form of the paper.

[1] Donald Davidson, *Inquiries into Truth and Interpretation* (Oxford: Clarendon Press, 1984), "What Metaphors Mean", p. 245.

[2] Davidson, "What Metaphors Mean", p. 247.

partially constituted by the imaginative use of terms derived *from a priorly formed conventional language*, these terms being subject to alteration by being embedded within a new context. This is commensurate with my contention that conventional terms, in being rendered constitutive of, and being embedded within, a lived occasion become "the servants of the occasion",[3] and thus authentically expressive of its concreteness. This follows from the concrete universality that we have good reason for attributing to any aspect of a concretely actual occasion throughout its spatio-temporal extension.

Davidson's case for affirming that the imaginative employment of words and sentences depends entirely upon ordinary meanings hinges crucially upon his contention that metaphor involves an extension of use, which he is assuming can be conceived as not entering into the determination of meaning.[4] We could agree, I suppose, that meaning is determinative of use. It is my view that use may also effect an input into meaning. Thus when I broaden the usage of the term "mouth" by applying it to the opening of a river that is emptying into the ocean, this is almost automatically understood to contribute to a migration of its meaning. From this it follows that, although the discrimination of meaning and use is a useful one, it is not to be regarded as absolute, seeing that each, regarded concretely, ultimately contributes to and flows into the other.

The shift of meaning and of use that is involved in metaphor seems not to be unique to the metaphorical situation, although this situation may serve to call our attention to it in a special way. I shall view this shift as ontologically and dialectically[5] founded in the

---

[3] See Essay IX, §13 (pp. 177f).

[4] In explaining his disagreement with Max Black, Paul Henle, Nelson Goodman, Monroe Beardsley and others in their accounts of what metaphor accomplishes, Donald Davidson writes, "My disagreement is with the explanation of how metaphor works its wonders. To anticipate: I depend on the distinction between what words mean and what they are used to do. I think metaphor belongs exclusively to the domain of use. It is something brought off by the imaginative employment of words and sentences and depends entirely on ordinary meanings of those words and hence on the ordinary meanings of the sentences they comprise." "What Metaphors Mean", p. 247.

[5] The term "dialectically" in this context is intended to refer to the *Logos* in its processural dimension, hence to *becoming* in a manner parallel to that in which ontology refers to *being*. The phrase might read, "I shall view this shift as ontologically and processeologically..." were the latter term less awkward than it is. Indeed it is precisely the working out of, and the significance for the understanding of metaphor within the ontological and dialectical commitment that is here in view that I am interested to assess.

As pertaining to the ontological status of dialectic, whereby it is not only a method to be externally applied, but internal to actuality, as well, see, e.g., Essay I, pp. 9f, Essay II, pp. 33-37, and Essay IX, pp. 175f.

uniqueness of the process of contextual determination of every concretely lived occasion.

Max Black develops a case for classifying metaphors as instances of substitution, composition, or interaction,[6] the latter being the only type that are of philosophical interest. Insofar as interaction is involved within what I have just referred to as the contextual determination of a lived occasion, this typology fits in rather well with the present conception. This is although the present standpoint, by presupposing that no two occasions can be completely or in all respects identical, treats interaction between the dual subjects of a metaphor or — where allowance is made for the complex character of these subjects — between each and its surrounding context, as well as a built-in accompaniment of any metaphor whatever, however trivial a role this interaction may play in the particular case. This has the force of leaving us ontologically committed to an interaction going on in metaphor — the aspect that Black finds to be of philosophcial interest — whether or not this proves to be sufficiently marked in the particular case to be casually or initially perceptible.

Following the lead thus suggested, I tend in this essay to construe interaction as a principal characteristic of metaphor, along with what Philip Wheelwright describes as tensive language, which I understand to be a more explicitly dynamic term that can cover much the same ground. In Wheelwright's usage this is language that strives toward adequacy, as opposed to signs and words of practical intent or of mere habit, and he finds metaphor to be the element of tensive language that serves best to reveal its nature.[7] It will be clear that neither interaction nor the tensive character of metaphor may be regarded as defining characteristics of metaphor, seeing that neither can serve to set it off sharply from its context if this be construed to be ordinary language. This might be worked up into an argument for construing metaphor as broadly as ordinary language. This is a direction toward which I tend — which, incidentally, seems reason enough for following Wheelwright's disposition to play down "the grammarians' familiar distinctions between metaphor and simile"[8] —, but which I prefer merely to suggest rather than to render thematic or to labor within the present context.

---

[6] Max Black, *Models and Metaphors. Studies in Language and Philosophy* (Ithaca and London: Cornell University Press, 1962), "Metaphor", p. 45.

[7] Philip Wheelwright, *Metaphor and Reality* (Bloomington and London: Indiana University Press, 1962), pp. 46 and 70.

[8] *M and R*, p. 71.

An actual occasion, following the present account, is an organism, inclusive of all that is concretely actual, including its own (conscious) subject within it. I need not elaborate very much upon this concept within the present essay in view of the fact that I may presuppose the first three essays within this *Collection* and, hopefully, some acquaintance with the two essays immediately preceding, as well. What is here of special interest is that interaction of a sort that is *imaged* as taking place *between* two or more such occasions belongs to a hypothetical perspective, i.e., as though two occasions, each inclusive of all that is actual, were actually possible. Such a perspective can, of course, never be rendered actual. What may perhaps — to tell a story that might perhaps be made to seem likely — lend itself to actualization is a synthesis or mediation accruing from an interaction such as might thus be presented within the unity and concrete facticity of a new occasion. That this, as an aspect of a merely external account, can be no more than a likely story is because the concrete actuality that I grasp *a priori* as such can have no *actual* antecedents, but, at most, merely *hypothetical and posited* ones, seeing that again here we are within the realm of externally related things — the world of know-nothings and no-bodys. Metaphors that involve the interaction between two or more occasions are then at home within a hypothetical perspective, if this metaphorical usage does not strain overmuch the term "home".

The term "metaphor" is perspectival, belonging to the perspective of representational, and hence hypothetical, thinking.[8a] From the integrity of an actual perspective it belongs to the world of possibilities and of seeming. A metaphor grasped in terms of its literal truth for the occasion, so to speak, remains such *only in a metaphorical sense*. It becomes the truth that is the whole of the occasion, which is normally accompanied by a mere recollection of what it "was" (now viewed as such from a hypothetical perspective). A blank check has been filled in. However creative a form the representation of such possibilities may have taken, the creation that actually accrued in concretely actual fact is the measure of successes and failures. Seeing that what presents itself as concretely actual within the lived occasion grasped *a priori* as such constitutes the literal truth of the occasion, we thus find relief from the spectrum of an endless chain of ordinary languages construed as a potentially endless chain

---

[8a] D. Lynn Holt writes, "...if no verbal statement can be the adequate expression of a proposition, then all language is, in a sense, metaphorical". ("Metaphors as Imaginative Propositions", *Process Studies*, vol. 12, no. 4 (Winter, 1982), p. 253.) If by "language" we are to mean conventional language, also for the present standpoint all such language is metaphorical.

of metaphor on metaphor. But this is not the entire account. I turn now to a more detailed and systematically more adequate development of the standpoint thus suggested.

Part I

The following §§, will provide a focus for dialogues with other positions in the notes and in Parts II and III to follow.

§1   My concern is with concretely actual occasions. A concretely actual occasion I understand as necessarily having a conscious participating subject as well as objectivities present for this subject as its substance.

§2   The substance-subject of a concretely actual occasion are in their being-becoming mutually determinative each of the other. Indeed the relation is what constitutes each what it is. Moreover, they are known each as an accent within an identity inclusive of both, this being an identity that is being mediated (process and result being aspects of a unitary duration).[9]

§3   This mediation is of the type that is characterizable as *spek. Sätze* (speculative propositions or judgments, depending upon the context), the subject and predicate of any one of which are each accents within an identity inclusive of both.

§4   Substance and subject being mediated to identity may alternatively be construed as the **discrimination** substance-subject being determined, within which each aspect emerges as an accent within the identity thus affirmed.

---

[9] I am here paraphrasing Hegel's explication of his speculative or philosophical proposition (or sometimes judgment/ *spekulativen Satz*)

C. K. Ogden and I. A. Richards in *The Meaning of Meaning* (London: Routledge & Kegan Paul, 1923), have their appeal to "scientific objectivity" take the following form:

> We should develop our theory of signs from observations of other people, and only admit evidence drawn from introspection when we know how to appraise it. The adoption of the other method, on the grounds that all our knowledge of others is inferred from knowledge of our own states, can only lead to the *impasse* of solipsism from which modern speculation has yet to recoil. Those who allow beyond question that there are people like themselves also interpreting signs and open to study should not find it difficult to admit that their observation of the behavior of others may provide at least a framework within which their own introspection, that special and deceptive case, may be fitted. That this is the practice of all the sciences need hardly be pointed out. (pp. 19f)

If we should grant that the method thus sketched in might be in conformity with that practiced by the particular sciences, the present standpoint is that it can in no case be that of a first philosophy pursuing a maximally scientific course. This is assuming that a first

§5 The discrimination of subject and substance is a complex discrimination, containing other discriminations — each being alternatively construable as contrasting aspects — within it. Also these other discriminations are being mediated to identity.

§6 Indeed it is not even proposed that any object as such nor any philosophy, if it is to be plausible, must be pursued not only with the aim of achieving precision in its account, but completeness, or at least adequacy, as well. (In the present undertaking, this means rendering an account "retrospectively" — i.e., by secondary reflection, of the being-determined of *all* of the discriminations found to be *explicitly* constitutive of the occasion, regarded as typical of some relevant epoch that is under analysis-resynthesis.)

That Ogden and Richards are presupposing subjectivity and consciousness is clear, if this fact is underplayed and at times only implicit within their account. If this presupposition may be allowable for at least some of the particular sciences and perhaps for any one of them so long as it is pursued with some certain plausible (if perhaps restricted) purposes in view, the present standpoint is that for philosophy it cannot remain a mere presupposition, but must be taken systematically into account.

Consider another issue. Ogden and Richards assume here that there is only one alternative method to the one proposed — i.e., "*the* other method" (ital. added) — this being introspection. This method they (perhaps correctly) inform us can only lead to the *Impasse* of solipsism. If it is not made clear within this context whether philosophy within the Hegelian tradition is considered to qualify as "modern speculation", the general tenor of a later allusion to Hegel (p. 29) might lead one to suppose that this uninformed an allegation might be in the back of their minds. Having drawn from Hegel the idea that I can know neither exclusively subjective nor exclusively objective meanings, but each (within a particular occasion of experience construed after the fashion of Hegel's Begriff) as an accent within a mediation of both to identity, I cannot view this as a criticism that can apply to the present reconstruction. Moreover, I find it difficult to imagine a form of Hegelianism for which the method of introspection would not be as strongly disallowed as the theory of objective knowledge espoused by Ogden and Richards. Certainly these are two extremes that Hegelians typically must view as ever being resolved (and which philosophy ought to report as being resolved) through mediation.

When I refer to the internal perspective as the actual one, it is internality to the Hegelian Begriff — here the living occasion — that is in view. This has nothing whatever to do with a proposal that we can somehow peer into a subject, as such or somehow be purely — i.e., merely — subjective. What is merely subjective, following the present conception, cannot even be actual, seeing that being actual is being in relation with other beings, which is ultimately to be in a relation of becoming, relations (insofar as they are actual) being ultimately one or another form of mediation. On this account, if anyone should venture to conceive of his subjectivity as an object of introspection, this would have to be as a mere abstraction. This has the force that subjectivity can never as such — i.e., as introspected — be grasped within the context of the Begriff in its in-and-for-itself completeness of self-determination. Persons who resist reference to anything as actual, as do Ogden and Richards (p. 82), having isolated themselves within a world of abstract possibilities, may, I suppose, find this a puzzling distinction. For most of us, nevertheless, it appears to come quite naturally, and this apart from any special associations with a disease of the sort that these authors find metaphysics to be.

I should add that internality to the occasion does not cut me off from other human participants in the occasion of which I am the subject. That knowledge yielded by mediation does not in the least lead to solipsism is rendered even clearer if we observe that there is an intersubjectivity involved in the development and cumulative constitution (through recollection) of my own consciousness, even apart from other subjects, recognized as such, whom I may encounter within the present occasion.

subject as such — i.e., either in abstraction from the other — has actuality status. Rather, what is actual in the case of this or any other discrimination is *the being mediated* of the polar aspects. The aspects viewed as abstracted from this process are mere potentials. Thus a natural correlate of the process principle that I have just stated is that the creation that takes place in mediation is *out of nothing actual*.

§7 A mediation phenomenon is internal to the subject and the predicate, respectively, of the *spek. Satz* being mediated. Seeing that it is knowable only from a perspective internal to a living occasion, it can be properly described only from this perspective. The philosophical account of such an actual perspective may of course survive to stand outside of the occasion to *re*present this privileged perspective to persons who may have never assumed it. It is then conceded to be representative *in this particular and restricted sense*, which is to be strictly distinguished from a representation of a hypothetical perspective, i.e., a representation of a representation. The anticipation, of course, is that the reader of an account of such a privileged perspective will be able to identify mediations of the same generic types within occasions that he or she knows as actually living.

§8 From an actual perspective, the perspective of mediation as it is being concretely lived, the actuality is grasped for what is (becoming) in whatever grade of explicitness this presents itself.[9a] This grasping, which is an integral aspect of the being-becoming of the occasion, is what dialectical logic proposes to delineate. This grasping is knowledge in its native self-evidence. To demonstrate this

---

[9a] H. K. Wells has observed that "the relation between contradictory opposites, for Hegel and for Heraclitus, is internal", and that this differentiates his position from that of Whitehead, for whom process, on the one hand, and eternal objects (and, indeed, objects as such), on the other, remain externally related. (*Process and Unreality*, p. 184). Thus for Hegel,

> there is no necessity for a *deus ex machina*, for a thing is the conflict of opposites inherent in it, and through the conflict there is a gradual development to the point at which the one abolishes the other, and the thing, the opposition of which is the thing, transforms itself into something else, namely, a new opposition — and so the process has its own internal principles of motion, and is unending. Here is a concept of identity, without permanence, without the eternal unchanging. Heraclitus and Hegel then conceive of identity as found within the process and in terms of process. (*Process and Unreality*, p. 184).

Hegel's doctrine of internal relations has been taken over into the philosophy of concreteness, but whereas he sometimes, at least, construed discriminations as passing away or dissolving into the absolute, I have been unable to observe such a dissolution. There is only the perishing of the occasion, inferred from its self-evidence and our experience of change from one occasion to another. This perishing is associated with a transformation of discri-

proposal, however, would be as absurd as it would be superfluous. Of this we merely seek an *explanation* for purposes of which we turn to the original tensive[10] data, i.e., the constitutive mediations replayed in secondary reflection in their concrete particularity in such a way that each discrimination, in turn, may be rendered explicit within a now actual occasion belonging to the same homogeneous epoch as the occasion with which the investigation began.

§9 Human beings have the capacity not only to grasp what is — the becoming of the occasion that is actual — but to envision possibilities which, if actualized, would constitute change from one occasion to another. The development of this capacity is importantly linked to the capacity to manipulate abstractions *as such*, hence to the development of conventional languages. The prototype of hypothetical thinking, however, appears to be the envisionment of a plurality of actual occasions (each inclusive of all that is actual) being related to one another externally. We thus envision development occurring as the mind's eye moves from one to another in the series. Seeing that anything we can know must be actual and not merely potential, and this within the occasion that is now in the actuality of its becoming, such a plurality of occasions must of course be entirely hypothetical.

§10 The mediation of a concrete discrimination — e.g., that of substance and subject — is to be understood for what it is only from an internal (actual) perspective. In such a mediation the accents are actual only as being mediated. The creation that is here taking place, being *ex nihilo,* is out of nothing actual. From a hypothetical

---

minations, which as constitutive of the occasion were concrete, into abstract ones. Another difference from the Hegel of Wells' account consists in our systematic emphasis upon the prior status of the process by which opposition transforms itself into something else, namely new opposition, even while admitting that this process frequently becomes initially explicit to consciousness only through the analysis-resynthesis of occasions in secondary reflection after the fact. Once faced, the effect of this "after the fact" status of the rendering explicit of the process in linear language is softened by the discovery of the close approximation of this process to that which is discoverable within the lived passage of the presently grasped occasion. This shift of perspectives is within the philosophy of concreteness the counterpart to that climactic episode in Hegel's *Phän.* in which the Begriff, which up to this point had remained merely and object of external reflection, enters into consciousness, i.e., becomes constitutive of, and identical with, the consciousness which in previous phases of the account had merely entertained it (p. 205, n. 4). Thus the account becomes adequate to concrete actuality, grasped *a priori* as such. To be noted is that, although also within the present account, concrete actuality is indeed grasped *a priori* as such, an analysis-resynthesis of an occasion after the fact is in principle less than fully adequate to the uniqueness of a subsequent occasion as it is presently grasped.

[10] The term "tensive" is adapted from Philip Wheelwright's usage. See *M and R,* p. 40 and Part III following.

perspective it may be considered to be ***out of potentials,*** i.e., the subjective-objective data[11] inherited from a previous occasion, but this can be no more than a likely story about what may have conditioned the concrete actuality that is grasped *a priori* as such, quite apart from the aid of such a hypothesis. The two accounts are of totally different types, and neither can be clearly conceived if permitted to be confused with the other. They may be viewed as compatible and even coordinated, but they cannot be rendered interdependent aspects of a single mode of explanation. Also, in view of the consideration that we have no reason to believe that the conceptuality of one of these modes of explanation is translatable into that of the other, it is safest to regard them as explaining almost totally different things.

§11 For this reason, for purposes of a parallel (if only in part overlapping) account of this process from an external perspective I have for most purposes preferred to refer to a process of concrescence (the term being drawn from Whitehead) rather than to a mediating process. In such an account, rather than determining concrete identities by discriminating them, and then proceding to represent this process in its concreteness, one presupposes such a system of discriminations, i.e., a conventional language.

§12 In such an account the objects of reference are for the most part externally related, bearing with them only such internal relations as accidentally cling to them owing to past associations. The archetypes of the external relation that are normative are here hypothetically maintained to obtain between members of a plurality of actual occasions each of which is supposed to contain all that is actual within it, which relations, of course, could not even in principle be actual.

§13 Metaphor would belong most fundamentally to an account of dialectical mediation of subject and substance from an external perspective, were such an account possible. That such an account is not possible is owing to the fact that, insofar as it pertains principally (the qualification being noted in §§17-21) to external relations, it is an account of likenesses adumbrated and ventured, to be strictly distinguished from identities actually achieved. The achievements of metaphors, in other words, are appropriately qualified by such terms as "more or less". The relations of identity that constitute concrete actuality do not admit of this sort of qualification.

---

[11] For my case that immortality is subjective as well as objective, see Essay III, esp. pp. 57-65, and SC, pp. 256 and 356.

§14   The very concept of metaphor makes sense, however, only if there is a contrasting normatively literal aspect of the situation. With reference to linguistic metaphor, I have developed the concept of concrete language to fill this need. In the interest of achieving focus, I shall restrict my discussion to metaphorical and literal *language*.

§15   Conventional, hence representative language, merely by being such, is more or less metaphorical. Presentational — or concrete — language, I propose to be normatively literal. It is literal, this is to say, even if the form of words employed, regarded as belonging to a conventional language, might be considered metaphorical.

§16   What presents itself in authentically presentational language is, at least implicitly, the entirety of the occasion, in some grade of emphasis, truth being contextual.[12] The characteristic of an actual occasion, whereby every part is implicated within the whole and the whole within every part, I refer to as the concrete universality equally of both whole and part. With an utterance in concrete language is implicated the entirety of the occasion, either explicitly or implicitly, within which it occurs.[13]

---

[12] I. A. Richards, in *The Philosophy of Rhetoric* (New York: Oxford University Press, 1965), writes, "The traditional Usage Doctrine...treated language on the bad analogy of a mosaic, and conceived composition and interpretation as though they were a putting together or taking apart of pieces with a fixed shape and color, whereas, in fact, the interinanimation of the meanings of words is at least as great as in any other mode of mental performance" (p. 69). A bit further along he notes, "The view that meanings belong to words in their own right — and more sophisticated views which have the same effect — are a branch of sorcery, a relic of the magical theory of names" (p. 91).

From the present standpoint Richards correctly observed that the analogy of a mosaic is less than apt in the portrayal of language, but he appears to have been over-zealous in his effort to root out the form of sorcery that he alleges. Meanings do indeed belong to the words that constitute the concrete language that may be uttered within any occasion whatever. This is in every sense a feature of the normal course of events in which in a single word the integral meaning of the entirety of the occasion (within which that word is concretely universal) is present. Spookiness gets introduced into the situation where meanings thus belonging to words in concrete language are permitted, upon the perishing of the occasion, to pass unguardedly into *language use* — thus implying their universalization to all occasions, at least within a certain epoch. It is then that they may become mere stones in a mosaic, the context of the occasion the meaning of which they presented as concrete language being no longer present. This is with the result that they come to convey no more than a caricature of their original concrete meaning, whatever rituals may be played out to recapture the scene and thus compensate for their loss of presentational power.

There are doubtless concrete meanings that prove to be worthy of universalization as abstractions and of the support of myth and ritual in their representation within new occasions. In this case the respective myth and ritual may form a part of the structure of expectations of the subject, to which he or she appeals in the preparation of possibilities for possible concretization. The test of such then becomes whether they lend themselves periodically to proximate reconcrescence of the sort that renders them mere servants of the lived occasion. Myth and ritual that sustain this test are much more nurtured by such select

§17 Some have proposed that we often make a metaphor to murder it, i.e., to render it an aspect of conventional usage. Understood as an explanation of the evolution of usages, the proposal has a certain truth, but this should not blind us to the fact that in the orders both of being-becoming and of knowing, concrete actuality grasped as such is prior to derivative abstractions and the metaphors in which we play with derivative abstractions. There can be nothing more rabidly anti-scientific than to claim the opposite, nor can any form of intellectual hybris be more pernicious.

Once this priority is clearly understood, it will be seen that the more fundamental explanation of the direction of development of a conventional language is provided by an account of the concrete language (which, with the occasion within which it is uttered, is given *a priori*) from which it is derived, rather than by explaining one

---

occasions than are these occasions nurtured by them.

Where there is authentic historical consciousness, what, from a hypothetical perspective may have been called myth and ritual (as acted-out myth) are actualized in such a manner as to be describable from an actual perspective as *Heilsgeschichte* rendered actual within the lived occasion. *Heilsgeschichte* is that aspect or dimention of *Wirkungsgeschichte* which the spiritual individual shares most explicitly with other members of his spiritual community. It is that larger scheme that introduces order and intelligibility into his total history and development and that his concrete particularity fills out and completes as it actualizes (and vice versa). Thus myth and ritual on the one hand, and *Heilsgeschichte*, on the other, stand to one another in a manner parallel to that in which metaphor stands related to the concrete literal truth yielded by it in a particular occasion. In both cases alike the first term(s) represent(s) abstract potentiality and the second the concrete actualization of that which was potential; and in both cases alike a shift from one to the other term entails a shift from a hypothetical to an actual perspective or vice versa.

[13] Paul Ricoeur has with consummate skill and ingenuity drawn from Aristotle's *Poetics* something very close to the concrete universality as a functional and organic relation of part — in this case a metaphor — and whole in terms of which I have been characterizing the lived occasion. In this connection he notes that metaphor is only one of the parts ($\mu\epsilon\rho\dot{\eta}$) of diction ($\lambda\dot{\epsilon}\xi\iota\varsigma$), and that as such it belongs to a family of language procedures for departing from common usages. The unity of $\lambda\dot{\epsilon}\xi\iota\varsigma$ is found to consist in its function in poetry. It is, moreover, a part of tragedy, regarded as the paradigm of the poetic work; and tragedy within the *Poetics* represents the level of the literary work as a whole. The sense of the tragedy is owing to the fable or plot ($\mu\hat{\upsilon}\theta o\varsigma$, *mythos*) which must have unity and coherence and make of the action that is represented something complete. Ricoeur goes on to note that *if* metaphor is related to the "sense" of tragedy by means of its *mythos*, it is related to the "reference" of tragedy, thanks to its general aim which Aristotle calls *Mimesis* ($\mu\dot{\iota}\mu\eta\sigma\iota\varsigma$/ p. 108). From this he shortly moves on to characterize the *power* of metaphor as proceeding from its connection with the work, first with other procedures of diction, secondly with the "fable" — the immanent sense of the work —, and thirdly with the intentionality of the work as a whole. Even as the mtaphor is thus seen to exert its force throughout the whole, this power relation is seen to have been for Aristotle reciprocal, in that the whole also exerts its force upon the metaphor as a part. "If it is true that the poem creates a world, it requires a language which preserves and expresses its creative power in specific contexts" (p. 109). He then concludes, "Link together the *poiesis* of the *poem* and metaphor as an emergent meaning, then you will make sense of both at the same time; poetry and metaphor."

conventional language as though it were immediately derived from another *ad infinitum*.

§18 Concrete actuality being grasped *a priori* as such has the force that its constitutive *spek. Sätze* are grasped as actually being mediated to identity. This identity that is being achieved is unqualified; apart from which there would be no grasp of identities nor any identities to be grasped: the self-evidence of the occasion is such that it cannot even in principle be called into question during the life (duration) of the occasion.[14] Creation out of nothing seems to me to be a fact of life which to propose to qualify by any mere theory is to commit a category mistake. All of this holds for an actual perspective, i.e., a perspective from within an occasion that includes all that is actual within it, including its own self-conscious subject.

---

[14] I have already called attention to Carl G. Vaught's close association of metaphor and Hegelian dialectic (pp. 221f, n. 18). This parallel could not have been drawn, or at least not in the manner in which he draws it, apart from Vaught's having overlooked the fact that Hegel's Begriff is grasped *a priori* and the closely related consideration, which is just here my special concern, that *the identity being actualized in Hegelian mediation is unqualified*. It seems to me that we cannot confuse dialectic with metaphor except by first weakening the sense of certain aspects of Hegel's conception. I earlier noted that also in Verene's formulation, which I discussed in the preceding essay, it is principally the sense of the concept of identity that is softened, so that it can resemble the vaguely suggested or partially achieved identity of different meanings suggested by metaphors. As a consequence, the parallel that Verene draws is not between dialectic and metaphor, as he supposes, but between the shadow image of Hegelian dialectic in ordinary language and metaphor. What he has presented to us as Hegel's dialectic is not so much an account of reason's constitution of concrete actuality in its becoming as a kind of "domestication" of this dialectic to everyday hypothetical thinking. The latter must presuppose the actuality that is thus being passed over in the account, a procedure that is curiously at odds with that advocated by Hegel.

Also William Desmond, in *Art and the Absolute: A Study of Hegel.s Aesthetics* (Albany: SUNY Press, 1986) acknowledges that he is pursuing the lead of Vaught and Verene (see pp. 221f, n. 18) in the construal of the relationship between dialectic and metaphor, where he proposes, "Part of the power of Hegelian concepts derives from their metaphorical and analogical underpinnings" (pp. 16 and 173, n. 4). This is even though within his interpretation, owing to the fact that he is aware that all that is found to be constitutive of Hegel's truth which is the whole, including the aesthetic dimension, has *already* been actualized when its explication is undertaken, this seems to make for a tension. I must now render these matters more specific.

With regard to the statement just quoted, it is to be noted that within Desmond's most helpful explanation of how Hegel goes beyond the copy theory of art (see chap. I, "Art, imitation, and Creation", which I consider an especially helpful contribution, esp. p. 12), his proposal seems to me in no way to prove misleading; here the notion of an aspect within the occasion that is a mere copy, which is *aufgehoben*, serves him well. Where the view of metaphor as underpinning dialectic seems to lead him awry is within certain contexts — some of which I will shortly point out — in which it becomes clear that he permits himself to construe this aspect to be somehow prior to the truth which is the whole of the occasion. This occurs when the *aufgehobene* aspect is construed as in a temporal succession — as though within Hegel's "spirit in its external form in time" (*Phän.*, p. 558; or *Phen.*,

p. 800) — and then made to seem to be prior to the whole to the constitution of which it is maintained to contribute. This quite common way of making Hegel fantastic (and, it seems to me, ultimately impossible) is arrived at by overlooking what I believe we are not to be mistaken in referring to as the all-at-once character of concrete actuality grasped as such and of the knowing consciousness (see *Phän.*, p. 563 on the transition of the Begriff into consciousness, concerning which I shall shortly have more to say), within which all aspects being concretely universal throughout the whole, no one could properly be referred to as prior to the others, much less as having a favored status as underpinning the others, and then substituting for this whole a collectivity of temporalized aspects.

I wish now to quote three passages that may suffice to document the fact that Desmond is generally aware of the following two closely related aspects of Hegel's Begriff: (1) It is grasped *a priori*, i.e., as "already" having been actualized. (2) It tells us nothing about a future that lies beyond what is actualized in the occasion.

> The dialectical character of Hegel's philosophy is turned to comprehend the process of becoming in what has become, in the *Erinnerung* that comprehends the rationality in the becoming of what now is not in clairvoyance with respect to what is yet to become. (p. 160)

Indeed, as Desmond is careful to note, "The future...is always problematical in Hegel's thought" (p. 105). Again within the context of a discussion of deconstructionism he addresses himself again to the fact that Hegel's dialectic pertains to a Begriff that is grasped *a priori* and prior to its subsequent analysis.

> As a strategy of criticism, deconstruction has difficulty in making intelligible the possibility of this original synthesis. As a critical practice, it rouses the suspicion that this original synthesis is simply dissolved. Dialectic, by contrast, allows the strain toward dissolution in every synthesis, but the given experience of the synthesis indicates that contraries are *already* contained within this original unity. The art work itself is *already* a dialectical whole, *already* a unity of opposites within itself, regardless of how we subsequently analyse and take apart its constituent elements. (pp. 97f, italics added)

If one takes seriously desmond's careful explanation that the art work is already a dialectical whole, it will be difficult to avoid the conclusion that this same whole is grasped also by representational thought and ultimately by conceptual thought, following Hegel's account. Desmond seems to be at least assuming as much, even though he may be avoiding involvement with Hegel's absolute knowing within this *Work*. It is in the manner that I have just suggested that we arrive at such a wholeness and unity of reason as is *already* actualized as the Begriff enters into consciousness (*Phän.*, p. 563), and out of which, as it breaks asunder into its constitutive categories of the understanding, its constituent moments may be retrospectively analyzed. It may be noted that on this understanding we have no reason to regard Hegel's Begriff as being merely or ultimately a construction of hypothetical speculation, and hence no reason to weigh whether or not he has somehow demonstrated the unity of reason. What one in a flight of hybris on behalf of theoretical reason might have proposed to be somehow demonstrable is present as self-consciousness and world-present-for-self–consciousness *already* full-blown and self-evident. This unity needs only to be explicated in terms of its constitutive discriminations to be rendered available to our common understanding and ultimately to our common reason (this being, within the present reconstruction, within some occasion belonging to the same homogeneous epoch as the typical occasion with which the investigation began).

I have already shown that Desmond much of the time reflects an awareness that Hegel's truth which is the whole has *already* been actualized *prior to* its exposition being undertaken. Despite this fact, however, again and again in his account of what Hegel is doing he falls short of being consistent with what should be seen to be implied in this conviction. Thus he writes, "Where the art work gives sensuous, imaginative expression to such concreteness, the philosophical concept *tries* to be its reflective conceptual counterpart" (p. 23). I submit that Hegel's truth which is the whole is most fundamentally something that has been successfully accomplished by reason and never merely attempted, even though an occasion constituting a valet and his world may not exhibit its conceptual content with an explicitness equal to that of an occasion constituting a wide-awake philosopher and his world. If a given occasion is conscious, this suffices, nonetheless, to show it to be a unified whole, and not merely something attempted. If one wishes to question Hegel's *manner of representing* what has *already* been actualized, the representation may perhaps be brought into question. That which it represents, however, seems not in the implied manner to be at our disposal.

Again, where he raises the question as to "whether in actual experience there are occasions which right from the beginning wed universality and particularity" (p. 29), Desmond again betrays some sort of lapse with regard to the necessity that is implicated with a Hegelian Begriff that is *already* concrete actuality grasped as such before the Owl of Minerva takes its flight. This has to do with the fact that if universality and particularity are necessary constituents of Hegel's Begriff they have this status as *already* mediated − i.e., as his principle of concrete universality − and not owing to a deliberation on the part of hypothetical reason operating after the fact of the occasion under discussion but owing to the very character of being and thought of which they are constitutive.

Among the other instances that I might cite in which Desmond reflects what I can only view as a want of consistency with the status of Hegel's truth which is the whole as *already* having been grasped *a priori*, is his inability to perceive that (absolute) knowledge, following Hegel's account, requires completion and hence closure of an actual occasion. Desmond invests considerable ingenuity in the softening of this conclusion (nor do I wish to propose that all that he thus has in view is wrong-headed!), e.g., as when he writes:

> The sense of an end that art may offer us...need not force us into any spurious "closure" of history....The "open" wholeness of the art work need not be identical with "totalitarian closure". The story is not finished in this closed sense. But this need not entail the denial of any possibility of the sense of an end: the end "opens" our precisely because what its wholeness makes manifest is the sense of the presence of infinite inexhaustibility. On this point it is much less misleading to speak of the art work as a "whole" rather than a "totality", in that the latter concept more easile lends itself to wrong connotations of "totalitarian closure". "Wholeness" is a conception that can be freed of such restricitng connotations (p. 75; cf. also p. 99)

With regard to his reference to the possibility of being forced to an erroneous "closure" of history I should have been pleased to assume especially on the basis of the quotation from pp. 160 and 105 in the above that the term "history" in Hegel's usage can never, following Desmond's interpretation, refer to anything beyond what is concretized within the occasion that is actual. In chap. IV, "Art, History, and the Question of an End", however, Desmond is from first to last reflecting a futuristic orientation that appears to me to be incompatible with this properly circumspect conclusion. The reader who is caught up in a quandary of this sort might well consult Reiner K. Maurer, *Hegel und das Ende der Geschichte* (Freiburg/Munich: Alber Verlag, 1980[2]). If Hegel's system is ultimately exclusively constituted of internal relations − and it seems to me that methodological considerations prevented him from significant deviation from this principle, well enough established in Hegel scholarship − this can only be found inconsistent or to have its basis in a standpoint that is alien to that of Hegel, which it seems to me Desmond does not intend.

Moving on to the principle theme in the above quoted passage, one must feel a certain sympathy with what Desmond is seeking to achieve by his searching, if perhaps needlessly labored, plea for an "open" wholeness in Hegel. Hegel has indeed left us with a problem here, the solution of which requires a certain ingenuity. This is even though its solution cannot in my opinion be achieved at the price of compromising the definiteness of the closure that is implicated with Hegel's Begriff as the whole that it is upon entering into, and thus constituting, consciousness (and the world present for consciousness) as Desmond, in effect, proposes. It was this consideration, in combination with Hegel's apparently consistent refusal to enter upon a path of hypothetical speculation such as might have provided him with the possibility of rendering an account of a plurality of actual occasions, each self-evident in its temporal moment, that principally motivated my proposal of the theory

§19 From this perspective, if there is an awareness of a metaphorical aspect, this will be secondary to the literal meaning that this aspect may be regarded as having "yielded" to the concrete particularity of the occasion, and it will present itself as an aspect of the historical depth of the occasion conditioning this "yield". By historical depth within this context I make reference to history as actual — and as actually known — within the present occasion, i.e., *Wirkungsgeschichte*. *Wirkungsgeschichte* is prior to any *re*presentation of events as somehow existing in the (temporal) past, which in any case can be no more than its shadow image.

§20 Much of the historical depth of an occasion is not explicit to its subject from the perspective of the occasion as it is lived, but only through this being worked out in detail through an analysis-resynthesis in secondary reflection after the concrete fact, i.e., upon the perishing of the occasion. This is to say, such an analysis-resynthesis may yield retrospective *recollections*, from a hypothetical perspective, of historical depth, so that it is often found plausible to believe they were *implicitly* present as conditioning aspects of the lived occasion. The warranty for this belief may present itself within a subsequent occasion within the same, or a proximate, homogeneous

---

of the perishing of an actual occasion. My intent was that this theory might serve as a likely story to assist us to account for continuity (and change) apart from compromising the unqualified closure that Hegel correctly saw to be necessary to an account of absolute knowledge.

The foregoing criticisms notwithstanding, I commend Desmond's *Work* to the reader, especially for going quite far toward setting in relief Hegel's understanding of the necessary role of the aesthetic consciousness and of the art work in the constitution of concrete actuality, and this with a sensitive awareness of certain of those Greek antecedents that counted importantly in Hegel's thinking. This is even though I regret that he did not carry through with greater consistency in some matters that seem to me to be implicated with his clear sense that Hegel does not involve himself in any fundamental way in prognosticating any future that lies beyond what *already* has been actualized, and therefore has neither left us with a need to resolve what has sometimes been represented as "the problem of the end of history" nor has he burdened us with any farsighted judgments pertaining to the future of art.

The contrary conclusion, so far as I am able to judge, has been drawn where interpreters have mistakenly substituted Hegel's representation of his Begriff "in its external form in time" for his concretely actual Begriff and then — perhaps only half consciously — construed the "before" and "after" that they found to be applicable to these abstractions as being implicated with causal relations within the framework of theoretical speculation on the basis of the hypothetico-deductive method. Only in this way am I able to account for their having come to imagine that they find in Hegel a basis for an adventuresome projection of a distant and not yet actualized future. It is in part to avert this type of misinterpretation that I have proposed the perishing of an actual occasion as the decisive line of separation between the perspectives, respectively, of actual speculation and of hypothetical speculation. On the present reading, nothing could represent a more decisively confusing, and indeed undoing, departure from Hegelian principles than the error I have reviewed.

epoch of occasions, as the recollected content presents itself in the form of explicit aspects of the lived occasion that is grasped *a priori* in its native self-evidence. In this way insight into the conditioning antecedents of the occasion may be cumulative without compromising the occasion's native self-evidence by confusing it with mere theory and shadow imagery.

§21 Given that every occasion is a new creation and that predispositions and forms of becoming that are "inherited" from occasions that have passed are shaped by the occasion as a whole within which they are successively imbedded, strictly speaking and as a matter of principle no "recollected" metaphor can possibly be precisely that which was actual in an occasion previous to that occasion in which it is "recollected" as having been constitutive.

§22 On this account, and because the "recollection" of a metaphor as such is at least for the most part and initially *a posteriori* to the grasping of the lived occasion from an internal (actual) perspective, it seems quite appropriate to regard the concept of metaphor as an abstract potential as normative, even though the concept of metaphor as concretely actual is more fundamental and probably must be grasped before we can adequately understand the abstract potential for what it functionally is.

§23 Metaphor represents the tensive character of a discrimination of the sort that is mediated to identity within concrete actuality, except that, insofar as it is functioning within the sphere of representational thought, the identity is not, or at least not yet, achieved, and the discrimination, if it may be adumbrated, is not free of vagueness and ambiguity. Rather, the identity and the discrimination are merely pointed to — often in a playful mood — as something that might be ventured, or at least approached.

§24 There is a basic parallelism of structure to be observed between the two realms: that of concrete actuality as grasped *a priori* from an actual perspective, on the one hand, and the world as represented in hypothetical thinking, i.e., the world of seeming and of theory, on the other. These both exhibit dialectical form; in the one it is actual and in the other we may discern a residual shadow image of this actuality.

§25 Within concrete actuality, dialectical form is actual as being concretely mediated with the content to which it pertains. Its shadow or after-image is to be observed in the world of possibilities, e.g., in dialectic as dialogue, and as the opposition of such externally related things, and even persons, as constitute polarities, and which are represented as possibilities for being mediated in one or another way.

§26 Metaphors present us with such possibilities. They could not serve in this way if the possibilities they represent had already presented themselves as concretely achieved identities, i.e., as aspects of the concrete facticity of things. What is actual is thus, within this process perspective, "no longer" potential.[15] It must perish to qualify as possibilities, must give up its citizenship in what is in order to be made a subject-object of hope or of faith with respect to what might be. To have matters otherwise would be to relinquish Hegelian self-evidence (which is self-evident) and to retire to the ranks of those who have learned somehow to be happiest when, at least officially, the can have no concretely specific idea of what they are talking about.

With the foregoing as background, I turn to the further elucidation of the position proposed, now within the context of dialogues with the positions of Owen Barfield and Philip Wheelwright, each in turn, in Parts II and III following.

Part II

Owen Barfield in *Poetic Diction: A Study of Meaning*[16] in his own way lays hold upon these two levels that I have been discussing as he goes about explaining what the poet does. Thus, in addressing the question "What is a true metaphor?", he calls our attention to a passage that Shelley quotes from Bacon's *Advancement of Learning*: "Neither are these only similitudes, as men of narrow observation may conceive them to be, but the same footsteps of nature, treading or printing upon several subjects of matters" (Barfield, 86). These "footsteps" he finds to be the answer he is seeking.

> It is these "footsteps of nature" whose noise we hear alike in primitive language and in the finest metaphors of poets. Men do not *invent* those mysterious relations between separate external objects, and become objects and feelings or ideas, which it is the function of poetry to reveal.

---

[15] This is to affirm that initiative may originate at the secondary level, i.e., in hypothetical thinking. This, then, is initiative that does not, to use Barfield's term, merely follow in "the footsteps of nature" (see Part III following), but rather takes the lead. Being an aspect of the truth that is the whole of the occasion that is actual and being efficacious throughout this whole in its all at once (and all-or-nothing) becoming, it may serve as a perfect illustration of the principle of concrete universality.

[16] New York: McGraw-Hill, 1964³.

> These relations exist independently, not indeed of Thought, but of any individual thinker.[17]

Whether they find their echo in primitive language or in the metaphors of poets later on, we in some way are brought to hear them.

> The language of primitive men reports them as direct perceptual experience. The speaker has observed a unity, and is not therefore himself conscious of *relation*. But we, in the development of consciousness, have lost the power to see this one as one. Our sophistication, like Odin's, has cost us an eye; and now it is the language of poets, in so far as they create true metaphors, which must *restore* this unity conceptually, after it has been lost from perception.[18]

Thus relations that were previously not apprehended are in a sense "forgotten" because they were in some way "seen", he goes on to note. The imagination now sees them again. In this vein Barfield develops the idea of two opposing principles or forces. There is the force by which single meanings tend to split up into separate and often isolated concepts. We may call this non-poetic, so long as we note that to appreciate poetry, as such, it is as important as the other. Then there is the principle that we find given to us at the start as the nature of language itself at its birth, the principle of living unity. It observes the unity of things whereas the other principle marks their differences. The one marks what things are not, the other what they are. This leads him to conclude that what was self-evident, and therefore *not conceptually presented,* can *now* be reached only by an effort of the individual mind. The true poetic metaphor is the fruit of such effort.

It was principally Hegel who reconceived conceptual thought not only in such a way that it was not excluded from this primary level (with which also for him negation is primarily associated) but in such a way that this is discovered to be its primary locus. Abstractions derivative from this concrete actuality — the truth which is the whole of consciousness and the world present for, and determinative of, consciousness — are conceptual at most in a derivative sense. This important advance was made possible through the discovery that this primary level is grasped from within (Essay II), the subject being included within the concrete actuality that is grasped (throughout which it is a concretely universal aspect). Further — and this distinguishes his position and the present reconstruction sharply from that of Barfield — it is grasped *as discriminated,* the process of

---

[17] *Poetic Diction,* p. 86.

[18] *Poetic Diction,* pp. 86f. See also p. 88.

discrimination being integral to the grasping. Having previously given an account of this grasping from within by reference to Hegel's single most important methodological principle, his *spekulativem Satz* (speculative proposition or judgment, depending upon the context), I shall not enter into this matter in any detail here. By his discovery that the locus of conceptual thought is concrete actuality itself, grasped *a priori* as such, Hegel, appropriately interpreted, provides us with a natural context for construing "language itself at its birth", to use Barfield's term. This is via the concept of concrete language that I have previously introduced. A concrete linguistic utterance, being self-evident (Hegel's self-certainty of a presuppositionless reason lies in the background [CHSS] — to the subject of the lived occasion and perhaps to others participating in it (Essay IX) — has the force that, as in the case of every other aspect of the occasion, being concretely universal throughout its space-time extension, it is expressive of the occasion in its entirely. Seeing that an actual occasion includes all that is actual within it, it is thus not merely an expression of a human individual, but creation speaking for itself.

I shall now note, on the basis of the context above quoted and paraphrased from Barfield's *Poetic Diction,* how the standpoint that I am advancing finds significant, if sometimes qualified, confirmation at several specific points in his account.

(1) We may safely say that for Barfield a unity of *internal* relations is given at the primary level, which *internal* relations give rise to a more or less parallel complex of relations at the secondary level, except that these latter are *external or contingently mixed.* Thus we have, in effect, a system of external (or contingently mixed) relations derived from a system of internal relations.[18a]

[18a] An anonymous critic has proposed in a critique of Giacomo Rinaldi, "Hegel Updated: Gentile and Christensen on Self-conscious Individuality and Process", which the author thoughtfully shared with me, that there is a terminological and conceptual confusion reflected in my references to "internal relations", as, for example, in references to the I or self as "a completed system of internal relations". The allegation is that "there is no evidence of awareness" on my part "that a given relation may be "internal" (=constitutive) with respect to *one* relatum but "external" (=non-constitutive) with respect to an *other* relatum or *other* relata". "This key distinction was introduced by Whitehead", my critic goes on to note, "who held that the subject-object relation is constitutive with respect to the (present) *subject* but non-constitutive with respect to (either past or timeless) *objects.*" "Lacking such a distinction", my critic remarks, "the talk about 'internal relations' remains vague and unhelpful."

For the case that some of my readers may feel that this criticism of my concept of internal relations has cogency, I will reply to it here. I first call attention to the fact that my critic, in his reference to the possibility that the case might be different for a present subject as over against a past subject, seems to have committed himself to a discussion of relations *between* a plurality of occasions. This is not quite certain, but seeing that any effort to judge whether his critique can apply to my formulation would need to be clear on this point, the safest assumption seems to be that he is. Proceeding on this assumption then, it is proper to call attention to the fact that there can be no *actual* relations *between* a series of occasions regarded as in a temporal succession, each of which (prior to its being temporalized and thus relativized, through perishing, i.e., while it is yet actual) contains all that is actual within it. This being the case, there can only be hypothetical relations here, and his discussion then pertains strictly to the realm of hypothetical thinking. Where I make reference to an actual occasion, however, this being to a sytem of exclusively internal relations, I am not referring to relations between occasions, to which only his argument pertains. At least on this reading then, his criticism does not address itself to my position. In order not to overlook any possible interpretation of his point in the face of his ambiguity with respect to the crucial issue, however, consider now the case that my critic should have in view a presentation of myself as I once was, now made actual as an aspect of the *Wirkungsgeschichte* within the present occasion, within which I am also presented in my present form as "a completed system of internal relations". The case would then be very different, indeed, but there would be nothing of the sort of what he calls "non-constitutive" relations to be discussed. Thus his point also in this case would be lost. Incidentally, my critic's "non-constitutive" relations have something of the look of a species of what I call possibilities. In the actualization of an actual occasion, following my account, all of the possibilities that are actualizable are actualized, so that no possibilities as such are residual.

The fact that a relation may be internal with respect to one relatum but external with respect to another one or more such certainly proves an important consideration in the realm of hypothetical thinking, which my critic would seem to have made his *exclusive* concern. It would then be very relevant in the analysis of a conventional language. No doubt it is possible in this realm, within which everything is contingent, to perceive infinitely varied and complex arrangements with respect to the internality and externality of relations. For an illustration we need not turn to set theory; this sort of circumstance is illustrated every time I experimentally recast the outline of an essay, regrouping its component aspects. *All of this, however, is totally unrelated to the consideration that in achieved actuality as it is grasped a priori all relations are internal.* It is this system of internal relations to which Hegel is principally giving exposition. In my own formulation the concrete facticity of what is grasped before the perishing of the occasion consists precisely in this. The process perspective may facilitate our movement between the two perspectives here involved, which it seems to me we have no reason for judging to be finally irreconcilable. That my critic's point about internal-external relations can stem from a process perspective is because it is being assumed, with Whitehead, that "objectification is abstraction", which seems to me to introduce worlds of seeming, and as a consequence, confusion — the whole spectrum of a type of realism that I find it difficult to view as being any longer tenable for a first philosophy, if it ever really was, seeing that by this route we seem to have forever cut ourselves off from the possibility that we might know what we are talking about or might have to talk about — i.e., something that is knowable, something other than mere theory.

The contingency of a situation I understand to consist in that some of its constitutive relations are external even while some may be (contingently) internal and that it in principle admits of manipulation. It seems to me that I indeed grasp *a priori* in its self-evidence the concrete givenness of a lived occasion as a determinate being, or more precisely, as a being-determinate being, i.e., as being in its becoming (process and result being yet integral), there is no contingency in the situation. This is so long as it is the living occasion prior to its perishing that is being considered. I am able to see no way in which the argument about relations being internal in some respect (or with respect to some relatum) and external in others can be made to count here. Indeed, I find the discrimination between internal and external (or contingently mixed) relations to be at once so incisive and so decisive that I have made it the basis of my theory of temporal alternation between the actual and the hypothetical perspectives, the accounts of which I insist must be kept separate in order to avert a type of needless confusion that has frequently accompanied the interpretation of the Hegelian system. This follows from the fact that the actual perspective is retrospective —

(2) For Barfield, the speaker of primitive language has observed a unity. For the present position the speaker of a concrete linguistic utterance, which might occur within any lived occasion, has observed a *discriminated* unity, i.e., a unity *in discrimination or difference,* neither unity nor difference being actual except in their mutual determination each of the other. Consistent with point "1" above, the grasping of this unity in difference takes place within the lived occasion, and not merely (or principally) upon abstraction (from a hypothetical perspective upon it) following its perishing.

(3) It is evident here as elsewhere within Barfield's *Poetic Diction* that he regards metaphor as effective within the secondary level only. Also for the present perspective, metaphor, so long as we are guided by ordinary usages of the term, belongs to the sphere of the abstract and representative. At least for most purposes of literary criticism, the matter should probably be left at this. Where we are concerned to provide an account of a metaphor as actual, however, and not merely as potential, we will have no choice but to invoke the actual (internal) perspective from which it is viewed primarily with regard to the literal truth that it yields and that is contextually shaped within the content of a particular occasion. In this case, as well, we are aware of that function of the metaphor that we would from a hypothetical perspective have called an abstract potential. This is with the important difference that this will now be an historical (*wirkungsgeschichtliche*) background for the yield of literal content of the metaphor as this is imbedded within the present occasion. Insofar as this background — the process of becoming of the occasion

---

the Owl of Minerva flies at dusk — while hypothetical reason, which may enter upon the scene in secondary roles, is perspectival and futuristic. By passing over this theme lightly, if at all, my critic apparently failed to understand my position in relation to his criticism, and was content to judge me in terms of how far I fell short of being in agreement with Whitehead and a now somewhat outdated representation of Hegel by George L. Kline to which I had already accorded detailed attention. In this connection, compare the most recent version of Kline's "Concept and Concrescence: An Essay in Hegelian-Whiteheadian Ontology", George R. Lucas, Jr. (Ed.), *Hegel and Whitehead* with the substantially different mimeographed article bearing this title to which I accorded emphasis in CHSS and in SC, pp. 4-6, n. 2, because it seemed to represent his most recent work in this vein that was in the public domain at the time and because he had personally invited my commentary.

My reply to the criticism noted is based upon the assumption that it was tendered with some sort of philosophical seriousness and is not merely some sort of coded message — a kind of turn-bull — intended for persons with specialized skills in career diplomacy. For some my remarks may have given rise to the question as to how I may be assured that there are such systems of purely internal relations, as I affirm a lived occasion to be. It is to be at once conceded that no demonstration whatever, whether mathematical or otherwise, can here obtain, if by demonstration we mean a conclusion derived by manipulations performed within a system of fixed abstract ideas. The only "verification" for the non-contingency of the lived occasion is to live one such, and this apart from and as prior to its analysis or hypothetical speculation about it.

— is the becoming explicit of a disposition or engram immanent to the concrete actuality that is the lived occasion as it presents itself to its subject, who is internal to the occasion, it will of course be actual and not a mere potential. A metaphor that has become effective, if not as a lure for meaning, then as a lure for feeling, in the constitution of an actual occasion may, however, first come to be explicit in the analysis-resynthesis of the occasion after the concrete fact that it was, and hence recollected as an abstract potential, the literal truth it "yielded" (if we may tell a likely story) having priorly presented itself self-evidently during the life of the occasion.

(4) It is also evident here as elsewhere within Barfield's *Work* under consideration that the imagination performs its role within the secondary level alone. It is here that the imagination can see again things that were one time seen. There is no appeal here to a primary imagination, such as Wheelwright draws from Kant and Coleridge, that has left footprints to be followed, as it were, by the secondary imagination.[19] "The imagination" serves Barfield as a general term for the selective and discriminating integration of elements of abstract data into what I should prefer to call the structure of expectations[20] of the subject of the occasion. Within the position that I am herein proposing, this is analogous to a parallel integrative process at the primary level, which, however, I prefer to refer to by this name only when it is being considered from a hypothetical (external) perspective, where one benefits from the economy effected by not undertaking a concretely specific, discrimination by discrimination, analysis-resynthesis of the relevant occasion. In a concretely specific account of an actual occasion regarded as typical of a relevant epoch, mediation is the dynamical term that assumes the greater part of this burden. This is commensurate with the fact that on Hegelian principles the truth that is the whole is grasped as a discriminated identity or, more precisely (at least in my reconception), as *being* discriminated. The imagination as a general term is in fact most at home within a theoretical (and derivative) "perspective about" the concretely actual. Indeed for some purposes it proves not to be misleading to conceive of it as a faculty of theoretical reason going about its business of preparing possibilities for possible actualization. On its practical and dynamical side it is, nonetheless, the unity of the dynamical negation/mediation functions belonging to the primary level; i.e., viewed in this latter way, it is itself no mere

---

[19] *The Burning Fountain*, pp. 32f.

[20] See SC, pp. 439-44, 451-56, and 471-77.

representation but a presentation and hence actual.

To observe how this works out within the sphere of interpersonal relations, consider the following case. When I read the letter of a friend, in my effort to understand him my imagination clothes his words, so to speak, in the concreteness of my own lived occasion, to which all of my memories of, and associations with, him contribute in a major way. To make a long story short, it is thus that I am able to construe him as analogous to myself as subject, i.e., as another "I". This is with the result that the concretely lived meaning that his words take on for me is far richer than the signs belonging to a conventional language that serves to evoke this meaning. What we are here presented with is in my view construable as a case of primary imagination, even though we may well prefer, in a given instance, to treat the phenomenon in question by reference to its particular constitutive mediations and the terms involved, rather than merely in terms of generalities. Especially if the analysis is to be seriously philosophical, meanings will thus be traced through their constitutive mediations.

To understand the words of another apart from thus imaginatively clothing them in the concreteness of my own lived occasion — an essential condition for communicating with another person, thus rendered recognizable to me as such — is to understand them merely and at best with respect to accepted conventional referential meanings. Even if assisted by a high grade of logic chopping, so that precision within an abstract system of one sort or another is achievable, this precision may fall short of that achieved by an empathetic clothing of the same terms within the concrete particularity of my lived occasion. In any case, however, it will not be precision within the context of *my* lived meaning. Assuming that this concrete particularity is within the context of a single occasion, its carrying over from one occasion to another can be anticipated only within a homogeneous epoch, of which I am — successively from occasion to occasion through inheritance — the subject, and then only to a limited degree. On this account even a conventional language that is proximately derivative from the lived occasion under consideration will not long retain the full precision that the terms possessed within the lived occasion.

The foregoing case might alternatively be accounted for by an appeal to secondary imagination rather than to primary imagination in the following way. In this case I imaginatively bring into focus a structure of expectations evoked by the words of my friend which are then supposed (through inheritance) to condition the concrescence of a subsequent occasion, grasped *a priori* as such, in which his words appear clothed in concreteness.

The latter account may likely appear to be the more adequate one if I do not read very well or for some other reason need time to work up a proper construal of my friend's words. It also affords the advantage of presenting the situation so that concrete actualitie's character of being **prior** by virtue of being grasped *a priori* as such is less easily permitted to drop out of view by a conflation of actual with hypothetical speculation. The former account, however, offers the advantage of accounting for the fact that I am often hardly aware of grasping the words in my friend's letter as merely conventional signs: what I seem "immediately" to read, rather, are his words clothed in concreteness, and this within the "flow" of my own consciousness through a series of my own lived occasions. This "flow" following the present account is to be understood as the integral connectedness of a series of events and occasions presenting themselves as *Wirkungsgechichte* within the occasion being presently lived. It does not, however do away with the need for the hypothesis of the perishing of the lived occasion as a necessary companion piece to its self-evidence as the fully actualized and completed system that it presents itself as being.

I come now to some points where somewhat more marked differences from Barfield's account are to be noted, starting with his statement about the unity of primitive language, concerning which I noted that the present standpoint involves a **discriminated** unity or a unity *in difference.*

(1) The internal relations that we may safely say belong, for Barfield, to the unity of the primary level exist independently even though they cannot be maintained to exist in thought. Rather, they are said to exist in the individual thinker. Although I do not find him as explicit as one might wish, he seems to have in view that they exist immanently and at least relatively undiscriminated in the individual thinker. "The speaker has observed a unity", we are told, apart from being conscious of a relation.

From the present perspective, this is not possible. seeing that unity and relation are grasped only as integral aspects of a complex mediation that may also be viewed as a complex discrimination.[21] If the primary level is to be characterized as simple unity, then it cannot be self-evident, as Barfield wishes to maintain, seeing that it can only be

---

[21] See SC, e.g., pp. 94, 95, 98f, 221, and Essay IX, §24, p. 184.

self-evident from a perspective that is also discriminated, and this for thought, which Barfield insists in viewing as external to it.

That one of the constitutive discriminations of this complex mediation is being-thought has the force that being and thought are each accents within an identity (being mediated) that is inclusive of both. This discrimination may be grasped wholistically from either side, as it were (if only as discriminated), i.e., either as thought or as being.

(2) For Barfield the primary level is not only not thought. In addition, it is not conceptual. Attention is called to this in view of the fact that the perspective that I am advancing permits the construal of being as not merely, or narrowly, mental, and yet as being mediated it is conceptually grasped and in this sense conceptual and a necessary aspect of what is conceptual.[22] For the present standpoint, the primary level of mediated discriminations is certainly not less conceptual than the secondary level. Conceptual thought is coextensive with awareness and the actuality that is grasped *a priori* as such at the primary level, so long as there is consciousness. From this standpoint contents of hypothetical thinking, having only the status of abstractions, are conceptual only in a secondary and derivative sense. This secondary and derivative sense is by virtue of the self-evidence of consciousness and its world of (for the occasion) settled concrete fact, that ordinary people, in common with almost all Englishmen, tend to presuppose apart from entering upon a proper philosophical investigation of this hallowed ground. A standard taboo to which appeal is frequently made to halt such inquiry is that this would involve an appeal to "the method of introspection" (see note 9, paragraphs 3f) — as though it were being proposed that one could somehow peer into a subject as such — which is quite as far from the Hegelian truth of the matter as its opposite number, the theory of objective knowledge, subjectivity and objectivity being alike actual only as they are being mediated.

(3) As I noted at the outset, Barfield appears to be acknowledging a difference between the two levels, the primary level consisting in internal relations and the secondary level consisting in external relations. But he leaves the relations that he insistently attributes to the primary level impossible to make out except by appeal to the secondary level. It could therefore not be self-evident in the Hegelian sense to which I have appealed, seeing that, requiring something outside of itself to render justified, or even clear, what is being

---

[22] For some remarks on Hegel's concept of conceptual thought, see Essay III, n. 13*b*, the first three paragraphs and the passage within the text to which these are attached.

claimed for it, it is not self-contained.

From the present perspective, the fact that the primary level consists in internal relations and the secondary level in external relations, together with the fact that what is internally related is concretely actual and what is externally related, being dead, is only potential, is *all*(!) that distinguishes them, at least until the relations at the secondary level undergo a reformation of content through the preparation of new possibilities for possible actualization.

(4) For Barfield, at the primitive level we discern what things are not and at the secondary level we discern what they are. From the present perspective we do not know what things are not apart from knowing what they are and we do not know what they are apart from knowing what they are not, these being each accents within an identity — a unifying rhythm — inclusive of both. The self-evidence that Barfield quite properly attributes to the primary level could in fact characterize it only if it included the dynamic of the negative, i.e., the negation of being. This may be affirmatively expressed, as the mediation of being and non-being. If Barfield has in view something like this mediation, on his account it would have to take place between the two levels, rather than within the primary level. On this account the latter does not possess the self-sufficiency commensurate with the claim that it is self-evident. It is quite definitely not construable as Hegel's truth which is the whole.

Barfield recorded some important insights, some of which are traceable, to the German romantics, at a time when Ogden and Richards' *The Meaning of Meaning* was going through more editions than many thoughtful philosophers today would consider to have been really needed, but these insights are now deserving of a philosophically more adequate context than he could have provided them in his own time without becoming less effective than he has been. An age that seized upon Ogden and Richards' *Work* with such savage eagerness could hardly have been ready for the development of the two levels doctrine that I am proposing, which addresses a readership with interests that range as far beyond poetic diction as does the import of Barfield's now classical *Work*.

(5) For Barfield primitive language is characteristic of a bygone era and of poetry. For the present standpoint something at least vaguely resembling what he means by primitive language is at least implicit, and may be explicit, within a living occasion as concrete language. This need not, however, lend itself to being characterized as poetry. Forthright truth-telling is much nearer to being the generic hallmark of concrete language than is poetic diction.

(6) Barfield makes reference to "before-unapprehended" relation-

ships that are in a sense forgotten relationships. "For thought they were never yet apprehended, they were at one time seen. And imagination can see them again."

For the present perspective a relation once seen at the primary level is also a relation once (discriminated and) apprehended at the primary level. The imagination can see and apprehend such a relation in a modified way and within a newly shaped context at the secondary level. This transformation may in particular instances carry the force that something that is said to be "recollected" is only more or less what was previously apprehended. Moreover, the imagination at the secondary level may work up raw material that, except for having contributed to the dynamic of the primary level, was merely implicit (it did not contribute explicit discriminations)[23] and in this sense "previously unapprehended". Such natural dispositions or engrams may be said to be "recollected" in a manner that is reminiscent of Plato.

Part III

Philip Wheelwright in *The Burning Fountain* writes as follows:

> Particularly since Kant's doctrine of "imagination" (*Einbildungskraft*) began to affect informed critical opinion it has become more and more generally accepted that the human imagination is neither that mere decay of sensation which Hobbes had supposed it to be nor an irresponsible commentator upon a world already given, but an original contribution to the very nature of the world.[24]

He credits Coleridge with the renewal of Kant's doctrine that the mind — "that primordial, preconscious enterprise of comparison and selective recognition" — largely constitutes the world that it knows.

> The outreaching of the mind, in that primordial, preconscious enterprise of comparison and selective recognition, is what Kant calls the Transcendental Unity of Apperception, and Coleridge the Primary Ima-

---

[23] As I noted in SC:

> From an actual perspective — a perspective from within some actual occasion — the number of discriminations rendered explicit adds nothing to the degree of concreteness, which is unqualified. This is assuming that such discriminations (and their discriminated terms) as are considered to be minimally constitutive of self-consciousness as such, that is, 'concrete' universals, are rendered more or less (at least in some shadowy sense) explicit. (p. 241; see also SC, pp. 194f and Essay IX, §§31-33 entire, pp. 185f, from §33 of which I now quote:)

> Sub-discriminations that do not arise to consciousness, such, e.g., as arise beyond the horizon of the occasion, **normally** contribute dynamically, i.e., they selectively contribute emphases *to* (or, as the case may be, *through*) discriminations that do, thus contributing qualitatively and quantitatively to their specific characters.

gination. What Coleridge calls the Secondary Imagination — the more concrete activity of imagining that is employed in the poetic art — is a continuation and reflection of that "living power and prime agent of all human perception" which is the Primary Imagination. This conceptual layout gives Coleridge a theoretical criterion for distinguishing genuine poetry from artificial. The imagination that generates and guides an authentic poem, although Secondary by definition, maintains a living unity with the Primary; it is "a repetition in the finite mind of the eternal act of creation in the infinite I AM."[24]

Insofar as Wheelwright's reference to a "preconscious enterprise" is construed as an explanation, within the framework of the hypothetico-deductive method, of something yet prior to concrete actuality grasped *a priori* as such, this must lie outside of the perview of what is herein being advanced as an actual perspective. Also to be noted is that it seems perverse to regard "the Secondary Imagination" as more concrete than primary imagination. This latter is a criticism which would likely occur to anyone drawing upon Hegel, rather than Kant, for the fundamental underlying insight that there is an order of actuality that is primary and that is priorly laid hold upon and an order that is secondary and derivative. If these qualifications are kept in view and if we focus upon these levels — I shall be saying something about the imagination shortly —, Wheelwright in the passage quoted reflects a standpoint that lends itself to being viewed as complementary to that which I am advancing. Unfortunately, in the remainder of the *Work* from which I have quoted, he does not follow through consistently with the insight here set forth, but conspicuously overlooks, and indeed implies the denial of, the very subjectively informed knowledge of the world of which the human subject is here affirmed to be the producer and constituent, settling for a futuristically oriented quest for a warranted certainty of the sort that might satisfy the aspirations of an American pragmatist. Thus he writes,

> Mind is by nature a meddler, and there are no self-evident criteria by which to discriminate its insights from its commentaries. Still, the quest for certainty persists. The history of philosophy, save for sceptical interludes, is a record of men's shifting intellectual stratagems by which to secure some firm line of demarcation between truth and error.[25]

Wheelwright thus settles for a doctrine of knowledge as warranted belief rather than a doctrine of knowledge as carrying its warranty within itself prior to abstraction. I am able to perceive no way of

---

[24] *The Burning Fountain*, pp. 32f.

[25] *The Burning Fountain*, p. 56.

reconciling this position with that reflected in the passage first quoted, within which he draws upon Kant and Coleridge.

This impression of confusion can be confirmed if we turn to explicit remarks by Wheelwright about Hegel on p. 134 of the same *Work*. These evidence that he had no idea that the two levels doctrine is implicated within Hegel's thought if we only take account of the fact that his Begriff is always grasped *a priori* as actual and is always subjected to philosophical explication only after the fact, seeing that the Owl of Minerva flies only at dusk. His remarks tend rather to lead one to suppose that Hegel was merely another pre-critical ruminator operating in a grand way within the framework of the hypothetico-deductive method.

For the present perspective, the imagination is construed differently than in the longer quotation from *The Burning Fountain* with which I opened this Part. Here it is most naturally construed as an already formed faculty that is **employed**, hence it pertains principally to the constitution of the hypothetical perspective and to secondary reflection, i.e., to the reconstruction of concrete actuality after the fall, and to the structure of possibilities in anticipation of future concrescences. If it proves useful to make reference to the imagination as being at work in the primary constitution of concrete actuality, this will follow the direction that I have indicated in my critique of Barfield.[26]

I turn now to Wheelwright's crucial distinction between what he called steno-language and tensive language. He referred as follows to meaning that can be shared in exactly the same way by all persons using the same language or group of intertranslatable languages as *steno-meanings*.[27]

> Briefly there are two ways in which steno-language, or closed language, language consisting of static terms, may arise: by habit and by prescription. Language becomes closed and static by habit when the imagination fails, so that the same words are repeated without examination or critical integrity. Such language has lost its vitality.... Language that is closed... by default may be indefinitely susceptible of ambiguities; and such ambiguities, unlike the tensive ambiguities..., serve no good purpose. When language is closed by stipulation, on the other hand, as is done in scientific and logical usage, the aim is to get rid of ambiguity as far as possible and to establish semantic precision combined with sharability by all "normal observers", or, in the case of technical matters, all "qualified observers".[28]

---

[26] Consider Part II, point 4 under the "qualified confirmations" that I find in Barfield's *Poetic Diction*, (pp. 248f), together with the case study that follows this discussion.

[27] *M and R*, pp. 33.

Wheelwright goes on to note that in the case of any closed language that we can contrive, "there will always be a need, so long as human imagination remains alive, to explore and develop the resources of open language"[29] Thus he is led to his concept of tensive language. "[L]anguage that strives toward adequacy — as opposed to signs and words of practical intent or of mere habit — is characteristically tensive to some degree and in some manner or other."[30] This is irrespective of whether the language is made up of gestures, drawings, or of words, idioms, and syntax. Thus thought "in a significant degree" is possible only with language, and language, whether we are inclined to acknowledge this or not, requires metaphoric activity. Particular symbols, such as the cross or the flag, or the Divine Father, may be outworn or found to be superfluous. An outright rejection of all symbols would nonetheless, in the final analysis, be tantamount to a rejection of language and thought as such.[31] At length he finds metaphor to be the element of tensive language that serves best to reveal its nature.[32] Although he begins his account of tensive language by contrasting it with steno-language, in the final analysis he perceives almost all language as necessarily involved with the tensive element.

In all of this there is adumbrated the claim that all language is ultimately based upon tensive language. In the present perspective, this claim, in addition to being accorded more prominence, is radicalized to take account of the fact that the discriminations that constitute a steno-language, not less than those that constitute tensive language, are mediated anew within each passing occasion. The designation "steno-language" might well be called upon to serve less to indicate elements of a language that are absolutely unchanging than to affirm (as a likely story) that the forms of the mediations constitutive of the discriminations of which this language consists are inherited from one occasion by another to repeat themselves with only negligible variation throughout the lengthy series constituting the epoch of occasions that is of interest. What Wheelwright means by tensive language where he contrasts it with steno-language

---

[28] *M and R*, pp. 37f.

[29] *M and R*, p. 40.

[30] *M and R*, pp. 46f.

[31] *M and R*, p. 128.

[32] *M and R*, p. 70.

within the present context becomes, then, language the forms of mediation of the constitutive discriminations of which are inherited[33] less than essentially intact and are subject to more appreciable variation from occasion to occasion.

Thus if we view what takes place at the primary level, assisted now by an analysis-resynthesis of the occasion in secondary reflection after its perishing, we find that all language is equally tensive, and this tensive character is something that it shares with actuality as such, throughout all of its variant forms. "Strife is the common condition", Heraclitus observed, "and if strife were to vanish among gods and men, then their very existence would cease." As an Hegelian, I have found it natural, since I was prompted to this by Paul Kuntz, also to refer to this as the mediating rhythm of speculative thought — thought being understood to pervade all of actuality. In concrete language this tensive character of the primary level is to a greater extent explicit, along with everything else that is explicitly present within the occasion as a whole, than in the case of what is represented in abstract language. In the case of abstract language, this aspect, moreover, in addition to being less explicit, or totally inexplicit, is subject to being confused with the certain degree of vagueness that is intrinsic to hypothetical thinking of every sort, from simple story telling to philosophical generalization to scientific theorizing, and which, indeed, has a positive role to play here. Additionally to be noted is that, owing to the concrete universality of every discrimination explicitly constitutive of the occasion within every other, concrete language presents the entirety of the occasion — i.e., the entirety of the occasion as it is explicitly grasped (see Essay IX, Part II) — to those who are privileged to it from an internal (actual) perspective.[34] The language of hypothetical thinking, being that of the abstract understanding going about its proper business of preparing possibilities for possible actualization, by way of contrast, is oriented toward a representation of oft manipulated fragments and shadows of the actuality that concrete language presents holistically.

In connection with his basic characterization of language, Wheelwright in *Metaphor and Reality* writes:

> [T]he traditional Cartesian dualism of mind vs. matter, or in its later forms subjective vs. objective...has begun to yield in many quarters to a threefold thought-structure, in which subject, object, and linguistic medium play irreducible and inter-causative roles in the formation of what, for want of a better name, we may call reality. The older epistemological

---

[33] SC, pp. 260, 294, 368f, 379, and 389f.

[34] See esp. Essay IX, Part II (pp. 183-87).

dyad is becoming replaced, in much contemporary philosophy, by an epistemological triad. Letting S stand for the knowing subject, L for the language (in the broadest possible sense) by which S undertakes synbolic expression, and O for the meant or sought-for object, then the basic structure of any situation, so far as human beings can be aware of it or inquire about it, might be schematically represented thus:[35]

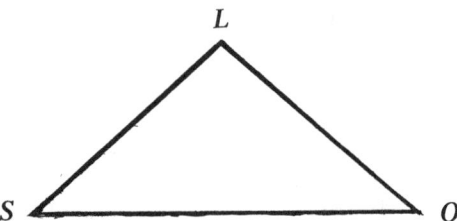

Wheelwright's presentation of the triadic relation of these three aspects seems not to be mistaken so long as we are considering them from a hypothetical perspective. His mistake is in proposing that this is adequate to the basic structure of any situation, so far as human beings can be aware of it. Within an actual perspective, I am proposing that concrete language occupies the middle position, this being a mediation of the S and O, to name only one of the contrasts (within a complex contrast) that is prominently involved.

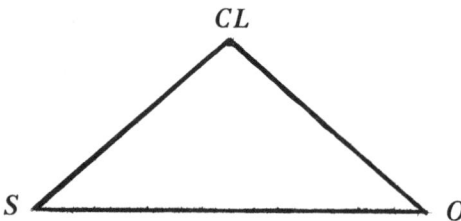

It is important to observe that these two perspectives are not only compatible, but, so long as each is respected for what it is and not permitted to usurp the place of the other, complementary, as well. The actual perspective is the perspective of the lived occasion, viewed from within in its process of being mediated. The hypothetical perspective is the perspective taken up upon the abstractions derivative from this lived occasion considered after the fact that it was.

I wish to consider Wheelwright's position at two additional points. The first pertains to his observation:

> From the cumulative evidence of ancient literary remains a general negative conclusion can be accepted as true without serious dispute: Namely,

---

[35] *M and R*, pp. 26f.

that early man, unlike ourselves, did not dichotomize this world into a law-abiding physical universe on the one hand and a confused overflow of subjective ideas on the other. Nature and self, reality and fancy, for him were radically interpenetrative and coalescent.[36]

From the present perspective the task we face is not that of undoing a dichotomy but of observing this dichotomy to be co-present with unity as *discriminated* totality within every actual perspective.

The additional point that I wish to bring up Wheelwright makes as follows:

> Reality is ultimately problematical, not contingently so: for to grasp and formulate it, even as a set of questions, is to fragmentize it. There is always, in any inquiry, something more than meets the eye, even the inner eye; the permanent possibility of extending one's imaginative awareness has no limits. A person of intellectual sensitivity is plagued by the sense of a perpetual Something More beyond anything that is actually known or conceived.[37]

If on the present view reality appears not to be ultimately or unmanageably problematical, this is because it may be observed to set itself apart from the contingent, and thus from that "something more beyond anything that is known or conceived" to which the imagination points us at the level of secondary reflection, where possibilities are prepared for possible actualization. That the world of possibilities and of seeming is of unlimited complexity should by now be well known. It seems to me that the ontological/processeological enterprise becomes one the execution of which lies within our reach if we can only keep from having our attention diverted to all manner of possible worlds and devote our full attention to world and self as mutually interpenetrated within an occasion of the type that is now actual. Even if I should seem overly optimistic in this matter, the proposal not to burden such an inquiry with possibilities not concretely actualized must appeal to anyone who seriously considers the matter.

---

[36] *M and R*, p. 134.

[37] *M and R*, p. 172.

Appendix:

METAPHOR AND THE *ANALOGIA ENTIS* OF ST. THOMAS AQUINAS

For the purposes of the foregoing formulation not only is the distinction between metaphor and simile, but also that between metaphor and analogy less than fundamental. This is so long as we employ the term "analogy" in its ordinary non-technical usage. If we take account of the quite special sense of the term that is in view by St. Thomas Aquinas in his doctrine of the *analogia entis*, e.g., the case is strikingly different. This difference, which is illustrated most readily by reference to Thomas' doctrine of God, may count crucially where we undertake to assign to significant and relatively stable terms, within (abstract) conventional languages, stations within a given hierarchy of discriminations and terms within a type of lived occasion within which they are subject to being reconcretized and within which a relation of concrete universality and mutual determination of all in all obtains.[38]

On Thomas's account man cannot directly intuit God's essence, but can only represent Him ***analogically*** as first cause — i.e., ultimately as "being-in-act" (*esse*, sometimes *ipsum esse*, Thomas' most proximate counterpart to what I, following Whitehead, have sometimes been referring to as the process principle[39]) — seeing that a

---

[38] The assigning of "stations" to which I refer is not intended to support or suggest a conflation of concrete and of abstract language or in any way to minimize the strategic importance of this crucial discrimination. In view is the conception of an abstract language that is sufficiently proximate to concrete language to render it ***relatively*** precise for purposes of a general account of the concrete actuality of a selected epoch of occasions in conventional language. This is to be accomplished by making the ultimate appeal of this conventional language to be concrete language and the logic of concrete language — i.e., dialectical logic — rather than predicate logic, the logic of abstractions. I hope to accord further treatment to this theme in a paper that I am now calling "Concrete Universality and Abstract Analogy".

For an introduction to the relevance of analogy to the exposition of different orders of being, see, e.g., Arno Anzenbacher, *Analogie und Systemgeschichte* (Vienna/Munich: R. Oldenbourg, 1978), pp. 9-27, esp. pp. 12ff.

Appendix: Metaphor and the *analogia entis* of St. Thomas

cause contains no less perfection than its effect. Thus, as Gilson notes, for Thomas "we...know with certitude that when a thing has a positive perfection, God is that positive perfection. But we also know that this positive perfection is God only as the effect is its cause, that is, according to a necessarily deficient mode of being."[40]

---

[39] Etienne Gilson, in *The Christian Philosophy of St. Thomas Aquinas*, insists that *ens* is and can only be ultimate in so far as it refers to the act-of-being: *"ens* signifies *habens esse"* (London: Victor Gollancz Lec., 1961), p. 40. He continues:

> Why does our understanding naturally desert the plane of the act of existing to go down again to that of essence? It is because the human understanding moves about easily in the realm of abstract concepts, and because we have an abstract concept for essence but not for the act of existing.

Two operations of the understanding are thus distinguished in St. Thomas, the first being that which Aristotle calls the intellection of simple objects (*intelligentia indivisibilium*). This consists in apprehending essence as something indivisible. The second combines essences among themselves or separates them, thus forming propositions. This second operation, St. Thomas calls *compositio*, both of these operations concern the real, but they "do not penetrate it equally far". Continuing on p. 40, Gilson notes:

> Intellection reaches the essence which the definition formulates. The judgment reaches the very act-of-being: *Prima operatio respicit quidditatem rei, secunda respicit esse epsius.* When we speak of the being of any being (*ens*), we are speaking of something having an act-of-being (*habens esse*). What comes first in the understanding is therefore the essential being; it is not yet the act whereby it is, or exists.

If we follow this lead, it is clear that the idea of process is in some way contained within *esse*, and it seems at least not absurd to suppose that there might be something analogous to a mediation (in the Hegelian sense of this term) of essence and existence here implicated.

[40] Gilson, *Thomas Aquinas*, pp. 106f.

Dorothy Emmet, in *The Nature of Metaphysical Thinking* (London: MacMillan, 1966), undertakes to develop the view that metaphysics is an analogical way of thinking. This is to say, "it takes concepts drawn from some form of experience or some relation within experience, and extends them either so as to say something about the nature of 'reality', or so as to suggest a possible mode of co-ordinating other experiences of different types from that from which the concept was originally derived" (p. 5). Her effort is of interest here because her approach to the issue reflects important Whiteheadian influence and can therefore assist us to see the type of analogical thinking that can be at home within Whitehead's conceptuality. This is at the same time that she finds a context for a critique of the *Analogia Entis* of St. Thomas, to which she devotes esp. chap. 8 (see also p. 14).

The great metaphysical systems of the past she finds to have been analogical in the sense mentioned.

> They start out from an idea drawn from some form of intellectual or spiritual experience which for some reason is judged to be especially significant or important, and then extend this idea so as to achieve some wider co-ordination in terms of it.
> A metaphysical analogy might express a relation to an object in part experienced and in part not experienced, describing it in concepts drawn from intra-experiential relations. In this case it would be necessary to understand "transcendent" not as meaning "beyond" or "outside" any possible experience....[but] for that which is "other" than our minds – "being" or "existence" apart from our interpretations. But this would not preclude our interpretations from arising within some situations in which we are related to that which is "other" than our minds. (p. 13)

A key to Emmet's position doubtless consists in her contention that the existence of a relation cannot be established by analogical argument, "but if there are independent grounds for asserting it, it can be described analogically" (p. 180). If her position is on this account to be distinguished from that of Thomas, she cites that philosopher's appeal to necessary being with approval.

> Thomism maintains that the sufficient reason for the existence of contingent things is to be sought by reference not to a system of laws or logical grounds (which would be ideas), but to a necessary **Being**. For law and logical grounds are essences, statements of possibilities; and the first premise of Thomism, as of Aristotelianism, is that no world can be derived merely from possibilities; actuality is prior, so that if anything exists, something must necessarily exist. (p. 172)

The problem with her conception of metaphysics, I shall be proposing, is that she is not consistent in pursuing the lead thus suggested. Before proceding further, however, I wish for purposes of comparison to substitute the term "first philosophy" for "metaphysics, which is not appropriately applicable to the analysis-resynthesis of concrete actuality on the Hegelian model that I am advancing, which I wish to maintain to be adequate to an account of the self-evidence of the occasion apart from an appeal to hypothetical speculation so long as we do not require the theory of "my own death" as a point of entrance into a (temporal) perspective upon *a plurality* of such occasions.

With reference to the statements above quoted, it is clear that Emmet intends to make her appeal to immanent being and to avoid an appeal to a *transcendent* being as an explanatory principle. It is equally clear that she intends to make the point of reference for the analogical thinking she recommends to the actual world and not merely to possibiliies. Her principal problem seems to be with respect to this latter intention, which I see as consisting in a failure to move from a phenomenologically given concrete actuality that stands both fully discriminated and theory-free (cf. Essay IV, §2) and that can therefore serve as a source and ground for the experimental projection of analogical relations and this apart from our invoking a principle of selectivity that might lead to bias. In this connection it is to be noted that, as in the case of Whitehead, she attempts to operate within the context of a "realist" ontology, which she quite naturally sets in opposition to positions that she shows to be mistaken, most of which she labels "idealism". Unaware that the ideal and the real have ever already been mediated in what we grasp *a priori* as concrete actuality, so that what we need is a purely phenomenological account of this and other mediations – not to be confused with data infiltrated by theory, whether realistic or idealistic – as Hegel has most especially assisted us to understand, she proceeds as though the realism/idealism controversy needed even at this date to be sustained and renewed on a basis that it seems to me should no longer be considered necessary or even tenable.

Being in want of the method of such an account, she must *select* relations out of the medium of hypohtesis-infiltrated thinking. In this selection procedure Whitehead's concept of importance quite understandably takes on a crucial role. Thus she writes, very much in the spirit of Whitehead, "If the judgment from which such an ideal derives has been happy in achieving some intuitive grasp of what is really *significant* in the thought of the time, the metaphysical 'model' will commend itself to civilized thought as self-evident" (p. 215, ital. added). From the standpoint of the present formulation this adventure with ideas – which, as she seems to perceive, can lead to arbitrariness – should have been found totally unnecessary.

Emmet relevantly cites Whitehead at another point that is strategic, also for the present standpoint, when she writes,

> [I]f we look on evolution as a study not of the procession of forms, but of the forms of process (to use a phrase of Professor Whitehead's), we cannot look on the relation of the process to an absolute Being as consisting of the actualization within the process of fixed possibilities, already existing formally as archetypes in absolute Being (p. 186)

In this connection, the present standpoint is that the creation that is an actual occasion is not, *at least so far as we can know*, born out of priorly fixed possibilities; and, from a

Appendix: Metaphor and the *analogia entis* of St. Thomas 263

That Hegel had no place for the Thomistic doctrine of analogy will be clear to anyone who has paid attention to his defense of Aristotle against the appropriations from him by the scholastic tradition and to his blanket denunciation of this tradition in its entirety. See Hegel's *Werke*, e.g., Vol. 19, *Vorlesungen über die Geschichte der Philosophie II*, (Stuttgart: Suhrkamp, 1971), 542-50, 587-600, and Giacomo Rinaldi, in *Ragione e realtà. Profilo di critica della metafisica dell'essere*.[41] When Rinaldi points out that the Thomistic theory is "rendered unavoidable by the presupposition of the absolute transcendence of...God...to the human act of knowing, and consequently by the radical dualism between the alleged to-be-absolute 'Truth-in-itself' and the inadequate 'truth-for-ourselves'",[42] he is reflecting a position that is not atypical of Hegelians. Here analogical reasoning, he goes on to note, consists in the attribution to a subject of a predicate that it is not experienced as having, by virtue of what is taken to be a 'similarity' between such a subject and another subject in which the predicate at issue is directly perceived. As Rinaldi notes, in the case in which I see a not yet explored island

---

temporal perspective, at least, there is reason enough for regarding every occasion as a new birth of freedom. A doctrine of divine providence may reasonably form an aspect of my structure of expectations, it is true; but although this commits us to a principle of order it need not commit us to some particular order fixed for all eternity. (If the latter were to be maintained, this would be upon grounds not self-evident within the lived occasion.)

I find Emmet's undertaking suggestive at a number of points for purposes of helping us to explain how we prepare possibilities for possible concretization. From the present standpoint, this is not, however, the principal task of philosophy. Moreover, pursued by itself and apart from necessary reference to its in any case more central tasks of rendering an analysis-resynthesis of concrete actuality as it is grasped *a priori* as such in occasions that are typical of the cultural epoch that is of interest, it seems to me that it is not properly construable as a task of philosophy at all, but of *Wissenschaftstheorie*. First philosophy, as I wish to maintain, has as its most central task the explication not of mere possibilities but of concretely lived actuality in its totality, including not merely those features that are for us in a given period counted as sufficiently important so that we select them out for special attention and in so doing accord to them the status of being especially adequate to represent actuality. Although Emmet intends otherwise, the actuality to which she points as a source for deriving analogies to be applied to our conception of actuality are themselves infiltrated by theory. This seems seriously to limit the effectiviness of the approach that she is advocating, especially if we are to require of philosophy serious work of a sort that is not merely to duplicate that of the impressionistic artist.

The question will be asked by some readers whether there is not at least implicit within the teachings of St. Thomas a phenomenology that might at least in some degree render superfluous my appeal to Hegel. If so, following the present view, this would need to be systematically developed as such and shown to be capable to standing on its own, i.e., of autonomously providing the elements of a theory-free basis for hypothetical speculation.

[41] Chap. II, "God", par. 5, "Critique" (Milan: Marzorati Editore, in publication). See also "L'atto logico-etico come principio della filosofia", *Studi filosofici*, Napoli: Bibliopolis, 1982-83, pp. 306ff.

[42] Rinaldi, chap. II, par. 5.

and conjecture that it will have certain forms of life on it owing to the fact that islands in the region that I have explored have been found to have these forms of life, we have every right to believe that analogical reason has cogency. This cogency cannot carry over to the case in which the subject to which the predicate is to pertain is a transcendent entity, Rinaldi argues, which in principle can never become the object of any direct experience. He shortly concludes, also on the basis of the consideration that quantitatively *more* perfection is to be attributed to the divine-transcendent one than may characterize the human-immanent *analogatum,* that the theory of analogy, rather than rendering possible a however imperfect knowledge of the essence of God, appears to be wholly unfit for such a task.

I do not find Rinaldi's objection adequate to its intent, principally because there are important nuances of Thomas' argument that are left out of consideration. Thus, although the example of an island is a typical piece of hypothetical reasoning, it does not involve an appeal to the concept of a cause, much less to one of a first cause. To be borne in mind is that the concept of God as prime mover and as first cause counted crucially for Thomas, but that he found himself unable to intuit the Divine Essence either univocally or equivocally commensurate with this representation, on which account he acknowledged the need to appeal to analogy.

That the exceptional status of the Thomistic sense of analogy can take on a special significance within the form of Hegelianism herein being advanced is owing to the introduction of a role for hypothetical reason in the preparation of possibilities for actualization pursuant of a method quite different than that which Hegel quite properly found appropriate to the analysis-resynthesis of concrete actuality, that can nonetheless complement the latter — in alternating temporal moments — along with the self-evidence of the lived occasion to which it gives exposition. Thus the doctrine may be found far less alien than Hegel could very well have found it to be, by opening up the possibility of providing an account of hypothetical reasoning preparing possibilities for actualization that appeals explicitly to the hypothesis of such a Being as Thomas had in view — whose essence cannot be directly intuited — as its ground. Thus (to tell a likely story) an input is effected into the idea of perfection and fulfillment ($\tau\acute{\epsilon}\lambda o\varsigma$) that in some shape or form is actualized within a subsequently lived occasion. What is then concretized is a set of compossibles that could lend themselves to commensurability with this end, itself subject to modification within the process of concrescence. The idea of perfection thus concretely grasped, along

Appendix: Metaphor and the *analogia entis* of St. Thomas

with the occasion in its entirety at its climax and closure, will necessarily have an ontological status that also more orthodox Hegelians may recognize as being not merely analogical, and which will serve as the standard for any (however deficient) ***representation*** of a Being, which, viewed from a perspective subsequent to the perishing of the occasion under discussion, is viewed as transcending it. I turn now to outline the position.

1) Concrete actuality grasped *a priori* as such being absolute, at least for the subject of the occasion, we may know what it is to attribute the same or a like absoluteness to the being and knowledge of God. He is thus conceived as the form and power of the occasion that I live.[43]

> ***First Remark:*** It is well to be reminded here that self-consciousness, as such, is socially conditioned (Essay IX). Beyond this, it is both shaped and crucially motivated by the religious community in its historical depth, and is thus not merely an attainment attributable to the individual alone. Within the present context, the point is crucial to an account of the individual's capacity to receive historically conditioned revelation apart from rendering him guilty, on this account, of intellectual hybris.

> ***Second Remark:*** The statement does not suffice to make God other than myself as the subject of a lived occasion. What it implicitly affirms, indeed, is that the attribution of absoluteness to His being and knowledge will ***not*** provide a basis for construing Him to be other than myself. Such a Basis must then be found elsewhere.

2) On this view, God's transcendence consists in His being, as the subject-object of my faith, also in like manner the form and power of all of the occasions other than the occasion that I am living. He is thus represented as the primordial mediator, not merely of occasions that I know, but of other occasions, as well, these being from a hypothetical perspective understood to constitute the human community, also in its historical depth. He is understood as exercising this role of mediation apart from my attributing to Him any greater completeness or perfection than I can come to perceive as being ***implicit,*** and in some degree explicit, in occasions that I successively grasp and from which I derive such ideas as I may natively (apart from special philosophical reflection) have of completeness and perfection. The word in the preceding statement that is here to be emphasized is "implicit", which is to be importantly qualified and

---

[43] References to God by the use of the masculine pronoun "He", "His", "Himself", etc. are to be viewed as abbreviations for "Her-Him", "Hers-His", "Herself-Himself", etc., these hyphenated terms being understood to name discriminations, each of the contrasting aspects of which is an accent within an identity being mediated within occasions within which this discrimination is constitutive.

specified, especially by the first, fourth, sixth, seventh, ninth, and eleventh remarks following. Allowance being made for these remarks, what makes God a subject-object of my faith, rather than of knowledge, is the attribution to him of the form and power of a like completeness and perfection in all actual occasions that are or ever will be. To be noted is that our appeal at this point is to an ordinary garden variety of analogical thinking such as I have discussed in the preceding paper.

> *First Remark:* The account to this point has been from a hypothetical perspective in order to accord priority to the issue of metaphor and analogy that is under discussion. This is to say, it is a theory and not a partial representation of concrete fact. On this account it must now be qualified in an absolutely crucial way by noting that *the distinction that I have drawn between the actual and the hypothetical perspectives is present and actual only from the hypothetical perspective, this being subsequent to the perishing of the occasion.* The polarity that is here involved, being one of alternates that occur in temporal succession only (and not in actual [space-]time) and thus not one that is mediated to constitute a discrimination, never shows up within the system of internal relations that constitute the *Wirkungsgeschichte* of a lived occasion. (It is thus in principle not knowable, although it can be represented in thought.) *Because the distinction between the actual and the hypothetical perspective is present only for the hypothetical perspective I can affirm that the prior actual perspective was not cut off from the infinite, i.e., from Divine Transcendence, prior to its completion, i.e., prior to its being grasped a priori and its perishing.*[44] This is to say, it is not cut off from the Divine Transcendence "until" the terminus of its process of determination through negation and mediation.[45] Within this process the infinite, insofar as it is not mediated through the self-determination of the occasion, is relegated to the status of a false infinite (*schlechte Unendlichkeit*). This is at the point at which the occasion climaxes in concrete actuality in and for itself — its freedom and end having been fully fulfilled and achieved just prior to its perishing. This way of putting the matter is only provisionally adequate, however, and

---

[44] Ultimately what is immediately subsequent to the perishing of the occasion may be understood as taking place within the early phases of concrescence of a successor occasion viewed from a hypothetical perspective, but this need not concern us greatly here.

[45] To be absolute is to continence no vacuum of determinateness. From an actual perspective, God's transcendence is a transcending *possibility* "until" the occasion is completely determined, at which point He is "fully actual" for the subject of the occasion. This is to say, He has achieved all that He is able to achieve within the occasion, given the limitations set by his previous creation, including those of the subject of the occasion. Subsequent to the perishing of the occasion, He is from a hypothetical perspective *construed* to be actual, but can no longer be *concretely* actual. The force of this latter assertion is that only as considered for His actual role within a successor occasion can He be considered "again" as *concretely* actual. This way of putting the matter makes for methodological cleanness by properly acknowledging the limits of theoretical reason. Since I do not propose that occasions are separated by temporal space, however, its practical import is commensurably limited. It permits us to consider theoretical reason in abstraction, i.e., without regard for the fact that it takes place within some actual occasion if it takes place at all.

must now be qualified: The time-space epoch of an actual occasion, being indivisible, and all of the constitutive aspects of the occasion being concretely universal throughout this time-space, strictly speaking, there can be no before and after (in the temporal sense of these terms) within this process. The perishing of the occasion marks the point of entrance of its subject into a hypothetical perspective, for which the lived occasion that was is a memory and hypothetical speculation proceeds apart from being so closely restricted to what *is* that fantasy cannot enter in.

Second Remark: The discrimination of the actual and the hypothetical perspectives is in the final analysis the discrimination of the occasion that is vividly recollected as having just previously been present, on the one hand, and the images themselves in which this recollection is represented, on the other, the latter being regarded — if we may be permitted a likely story — as an integral aspect of the concrescence of the occasion that is its immediate successor. The verification as actual of the actual perspective that is reconstituted by secondary reflection out of its constitutive discriminations to match the vivid recollection of what just previously was, is then, in the final analysis, within the lived occasion that is its immediate successor and that has a proximate content. This discrimination is reinforced if attention is called to the radically diverse methods by which each is approached, these being the methods advocated by Hegel and Whitehead, respectively. More specifically, with reference to Hegel I have in view what I have described as the phenomenological analysis-resynthesis of concrete actuality after the fact; and, with reference to Whitehead, his method of generalization, which may be observed to operate within the framework of the hypothetico-deductive method.[46]

---

[46] This may be as fitting a place as any to take note of an issue raised by Emmet in relation to Thomas as this pertains to the distinction that I have drawn between the actual and the hypothetical perspectives. In *The Nature of Metaphysical Thinking*, she writes:

> The expression "First Cause" should not be taken to mean the first term in a temporal causal sequence, but the ground on which the whole series depends. So the question before the Cosmological Argument is whether the sequence of contingent beings can only be explained rationally with reference to a necessary being on which the sequence depends. This relation...cannot be described as a proper *instance* of a causal relation. The term "First Cause" can therefore only be used analogically. (p. 173)

A few pages later she writes, "It may be said that the expressions **uncaused** cause, **unmoved** mover are a recognition that the word "cause" is only used of the "First Cause" analogically" (p. 182). If her case is well taken that a relation here obtains that lends itself to being thought of as analogical, and that also Thomas seems to accord recognition to this, this seems not, as she supposes, to settle the issue as to which, if either, type of "causality" is to be regarded as the more fundamental one, and which is to be regarded as deriving its sense from this. I, in any case, do not find it intuitively obvious at the level of *Verstand* that contingent causal relations should be regarded as the point of reference for talking about prime motion and "First Cause" — which I understand to be variant ways of referring to creation — rather than reversing the order of priority. And if we shift over to *Vernunft* — i.e., actual, hence teleological, reason in its inclusiveness within the lived occasion — seeing that within this sphere the truth is the whole and seeing that the whole and part (including *Verstand*, both as a whole and in its discriminated particulars) are without qualification concretely universal throughout one another, **there can be no *actual* priority** but only an

Third Remark: Faith being actual, the dynamic of faith is operative only within concrete actuality. A constituent of the hypothetical perspective is the memory of what was the lived occasion. The memory of the faith that was dynamic within the occasion that was, i.e., its afterglow, as it were, takes principally the form of some degree of theoretical belief or disbelief. Belief pertains to probability judgments within the sphere of hypothetical thinking, and is a shadow image of faith. Possibilities for actualization within a new occasion in which, from a hypothetical perspective, belief is vested are ***real*** possibilities. Faith as actual within the lived occasion has the actualization of real possibilities as its challenge and task. Faith, as in the case of every other respect that may be constitutive of the lived occasion, is necessary to, and concretely universal throughout, the occasion.[47]

---

order of presentation that makes good heuristic sense when approached with an interest in a plausibly formulated abstract language in view. Recognizing this limitation, it seems to make more sense to say that creation is imaged in causal relations — which as we most commonly view them in abstraction are contingent — than to say that causal relations are imaged in creation. For heuristic purposes only, then, a kind of priority is accorded to creation. Pursuing this lead, if we now shift over from the context of concrete language to that of abstract languages for purposes of establishing "stations" for the latter that are intended to approximate to the precision of concrete language, we will be inclined to regard the concept of creation as prior to that of contingent cause, and this while at the same time recognizing that also our abstract concept of creation is no more than a representation or image making about the creation that was actual in the lived occasion now just past. Creation being an all-or-nothing occurrence within the whole, within which also discriminated, and hence discrete, causal relations have their original concretely universal role to play, there is no priority to be assigned here that may properly be designated as actual. What we seek is merely an order that supports the need of our understanding from a temporal perspective that members of a community participating in a common temporal epoch approximately share.

The preferential status that Emmet accords to contingent cause and effect relations over ***uncaused*** cause and ***unmoved*** mover presuppose a "realistic" ontology and perhaps in addition an according of special recognition to the fact that our first deliberate reflections upon causality tend to be in connection with problem solving rendered necessary by an ***interruption*** of an ***expected*** flow of events. (Cf., Josef König, *Das Problem der Gesetzlichkeit*, ed. by Jurgius-Gesellschaft der wissenschaften in Hamburg [Hamburg: Meiner Verlag, 1949], vol. I, pp. 25-120, see esp. pp. 28f). It is to be acknowledged that an empiricist will likely be disposed to regard learning order as determining the issue, and it is only fair to remind the reader that, in making the all-or-nothing character of Hegel's truth that is the whole as embodied in every concretely lived occasion the relevant point of reference, I am moving from a quite different standpoint. On this account the relative antiquity of the portions of learning that — to tell a likely story — we inherit from occasion to occasion does not count here as a crucial issue.

[47] What I wish to note here pertains to this and several remarks following, including numbers six, eight, and ten. In note 40 above, the sixth paragraph, I noted Emmet's contention that the existence of a relation cannot be ***established*** by analogical argument, but that if there are grounds for asserting it, it can be ***described*** by analogy. Within the present formulation the grounds for asserting the doctrine of transcendence are at least principly given in ***actual*** reason. This leaves us with a situation in which the burden that Thomas seems to be placing upon the argument from analogy is commensurably lightened. This is with the result that the argument need not necessarily prove misleading so long as we are careful to label it a formula of hypothetical reason (which of itself need not, it seems to me, represent a marked departure from Thomas). This being the case, to the extent that we

Fourth Remark: Let it be assumed here that the occasion that I am living contains as *Wirkungsgeschichte* within it both inherited "natural dispositions", on the one hand, and the "memory" of occasions that I have lived in the past since the birth of my own individual consciousness, on the other. The form and the power of these occasions may then be construed as in some way and degree explicit aspects of the occasion that I am presently living. God, however, in addition to being maintained to consist in the form and power of occasions that I have lived, these being in Him **fully discriminated and fully explicit,** consists in the form and power of occasions constitutive of the community within which I live (including its historical depth), together with its inclusive environment — i.e., as causal past —, as well. These are occasions in which I have been no more than a partial (and sometimes only very remote) participant, many of which I will have taken no explicit account at all.

Fifth Remark: To the Divine Transcendence are thus attributed what I have sometimes called sub-discriminations (the name being initially attached to an order of dialectical exposition after the fact, but which is used to designate, as well, an approximate order of emphasis within the priorly lived occasion) constitutive of my lived occasion that are not explicit to me as such, but which make themselves felt by contributing to the dynamic of other discriminations. I have previously explained that, given that certain discriminations necessary to all occasions are present, a want of explicitness in sub-discriminations does not rob an occasion of its wholeness and self-evidence, but merely effects its degree of specificity of discriminations within the whole that it in any case presents itself as being. (See Essay VIII, Part II, esp. §§31-33.)

Sixth Remark: The completeness and perfection that I attribute to God — even to God as transcendent, who is the subject-object of my faith — is present in the lived occasion that I grasp *a priori*. This is irrespective of the degree to which His presence is explicit. His presence is more explicit in some grades of being-becoming than in others. Thus, e.g., it is more explicit in actual occasions than in events, which in my usage are hypothetically (maintained to be) actual only (so that they are not at all explicit), and it is more explicit within some actual occasions than within others, as, for example, select occasions within a cultural epoch enriched by a momentary insight or revelation, perhaps, or in part, historically borne.

Seventh Remark: The function of revelation is to render God's implicit being and character explicit. Whether, and in what sort of instance, His being and character may ever be made fully explicit through revelation poses an issue that cannot be considered here, except to suggest that this would not characterize an occasion the subject of which would be merely human. A complete revelation of God could in any case never survive what from a hypothetical perspective presents itself as the perishing of the occasion. Death thus presents itself as a barrier of limitation, even if one that faith will be found capable of overcoming.

---

can place confidence in an account of concreteness attaining to the theoretical possibility of being rendered theory-free, we shall have less reason than might otherwise be the case to recoil from this outside extreme of hypothetical reason.

Eighth Remark: To attempt to characterize or convey a revelation in advance of the fact is to state a belief, convey a conventional meaning or sense of significance. In the case of an actual revelation — i.e., a revelation that is actually grasped —, however, the language within which it presents itself, far from being merely conventional language bent to a task, is concrete language — creation speaking for itself — from which conventional languages are ever derivative. It is indeed *presentational* language, the very language of the grasping.

Ninth Remark: Revelation renders explicit the λόγος *(Logos)* of creation that was implicit. A particular occasion being a new creation, the input of real possibilities into it may be determinative of what is implicit within it.

Tenth Remark: A representation of the completeness and transcendence of God should be based upon His self-disclosure insofar as this is, or can be rendered, explicit within a lived occasion. As a representation it is "after the fact", however, and on this account merely an analogue of that being-becoming (analogous to the being-in-act of St. Thomas Aquinas) which the subject of a concretely actual occasion with some degree of explicitness grasps *a priori* as such. Its deficiency on this account is the greater owing to the fact that the climax of the occasion in achieved coherence is but the prelude to perishing, in which an idea of perfection concretely realized in openness to Transcendence is cut off and rendered relative to "what might have been", which in hypothetical thinking now tends to dominate the imaging of Transcendent Being. To this extent the subject of the occasion has his attention diverted from the memory of what just previously was and, in addition, devotes less effort to the rendering explicit to consciousness (in successor occasions) of the as yet merely implicit side of the achieved ideal through recollection (*Er-innerung*).

The situation might otherwise be stated as follows: From the hypothetical perspective posterior to the perishing of the occasion, concrete actuality with its openness to Transcendence with the perishing of the occasion is relativized to become a memory of Divine Immanence that was. This is at the same time that the role of imaging transcendence tends to be passed to the imaging and representation in hypothetical thinking of what might have been but is not. Each of these modes of representation being in its own way deficient, the attempt to construe God's completeness and transcendence otherwise than as the subject-object of (actual) faith is likely to be dominated less by my comprehension of concrete actuality, grasped *a priori* as such, or by the desire and the means for rendering this grasp more fully explicit (e.g., through historically borne revelation) than by hypothetical thinking, i.e., ratiocination, which is secondary to this grasp. What results is a flight from concreteness. In this regard it is relevant to observe that ratiocination is appropriate to the preparation of possibilities for actualization but utterly unsuited to tell me whether or not anything at all is actual or true. It is not apparent that God, who, at least as considered with respect to his transcendent "side", is pure actuality, can have a need for such a device, even though this befits the rank of man, *insofar as he is a temporally existing being*. (Man is not exclusively a temporally existing being; he also *makes* (is a co-creator with God of) *time*[-space].)

Eleventh Remark: As for Hegel, it is in the Son, i.e., in the God-man and

Appendix: Metaphor and the *analogia entis* of St. Thomas

as His reconciliation with the Father as the Holy Spirit within the Church, that God becomes fully actual. "Gott ist Gott nur, indem er als Gott gewußt wird; das Gewußtwerden ist sein Sichwissen und 'sein Sichwissen ist...sein Selbstbewußtsein im Menschen'."[48] This is to say, God is actual only in His eternal activity of "othering" Himself in the world. This is in the person of the Son, the eternal λόγος. It is thus that in the fullness of the temporal process He ultimately attains to self-consciousness and to concrete actuality *in man*. The rendering explicit of His actuality to consciousness, in which it is ever implicit, is the religious quest the fulfillment of which — wherever and whenever this occurs — is the hallmark of the God-man.

All of nature being immanent within any lived occasion, the foregoing statement is not to be understood as denying that the Son, as Divine λόγος, is immanent in nature, or to imply the attribution to the God-man of the character of an unending, or in principle irreconcilable, strife between a natural and a spiritual order. Neither does it rule out the possibility of nature existing as a hypothetical entity — God being implicit in it — apart from our knowledge. It may properly be understood to suggest that it is only in entering into what finite beings know as a state of consciousness that God can make his presence — also his presence in nature — explicit.

What is not, or at least not explicitly, the case for Hegel, and what can have far reaching ramifications with respect to the possibility of a dialogue between the Thomistic and the Hegelian traditions, is that, viewed from a temporal perspective, the occasion perishes, an effect of which is that God's presence in the occasion that was is rendered relative to a God now imaged merely as potential and in terms of potentials.

Twelfth Remark: The dynamic Godhead consists in the eternal self-othering of the Father in the world in the person of the Son, and in the reconciliation of His "other-being" with Himself as the Holy Spirit within the Church. This dynamic may be specified further as *Heilsgeschichte,* which in Christianity refers to the history of healing and wholeness of the individual person through participation in the death, passion, and resurrection of the Christ and in the fellowship of the faithful, independent of racial, social, or political affiliations. The contribution of the notion to the kingdom of God does not depend upon the numbers of the elect or upon their *specific* social accomplishments or failures.[49]

---

[48] *Enzy.*, §564. For relevant reflections consult Richard Kroner, *Von Kant bis Hegel* (Tübingen: J. C. B. Mohr, 1961), vol. II, pp. 523, 410, and 414f.
That God is actual only in His eternal activity of "othering" Himself in the world is an affirmation of "natural reason" which a faith affirmation may, of course, override or transcend. Even so, the point may well pose a difficulty to many Thomists.

[49] Cf. Karl Löwith, *Weltgeschichte und Heilsgeschehen* (Stuttgart: Kohlhammer, 1979⁷), pp. 178f and 106f.
The term "specific" in the above may be crucial for discriminating my position from that of Löwith. God can be actual, and thus make Himself explicit to us, only in his self-othering in the world and subsequent reconciliation with this his other-being. In other words, he is actual only in (original) mediation, or in what a Whiteheadian would call concrescence. As Richard Kroner has remarked concerning Hegel, " Das Versöhnungswort, welches das Wissen spricht, kommt nicht aus dem einseitig gefaßten 'Intellekte', aus einem dem praktischen entgegengesetzten theoretischen Bewußtsein, sondern aus dem konkreten Geist, der sich als konkreten in jenem Wissen begreift".

Within the present formulation *Heilsgeschichte* principally and directly determines the concrete aim, order, and emphases of occurrences which we may designate history as actual within the present, the lived occasion's *Wirkungsgeschichte*, which includes all that is actual within it. A likely story being permitted, some aspects of the same progression of occurrences, as well as some of the dispositions that are present within a given lived occasion, will normally be expected to be carried over to its successor occasions in the temporal process through inheritance. Such a story is to account for continuity and progression, and thus for the possibility of perceiving in temporal history a shadow image of the dialectic that is *Wirkungsgeschichte*.

To render an account of a succession of occasions as externally related, each of which consists in a complete *Wirkungsgeschichte*, is to render an account of temporal history. Temporal history is arrived at by abstracting aspects out of the *Wirkungsgeschichte* of the occasion that has just been lived and imaging these as a series of interconnected happenings now past. It belongs to the realm of abstract possibility, out of which theoretical reason works up expectations that may prove ripe for actualization in successor occasions.

An account of temporal history, as in the case of an account of *Wirkungsgeschichte*, may be of varying ranges of comprehensiviness. A dialectical account of history tends to record only what, with respect to a given aim, present themselves as "progressions". Where the reference is to temporal history a plurality of aims may make themselves felt, each being derivative from the particularity of a lived occasion. Also because "regressions" may in this way occur, we lack a basis for judging that a progression that is intrinsic and necessary to the *Wirkungsgeschichte* constitutive of a given or typical lived occasion will necessarily carry over into temporal history. Temporal history, then, being contingent, exhibits only as much teleology and progression as we find there. Even so, such teleology and progression as we do find is traceable to the *Wirkungsgeschichte* of the lived occasion or occasions from which it is ultimately derived by abstraction, and to their determining *heilsgeschichtlichen* core.

Given that a dialectical account normally reports only progressions, a less comprehensive account of temporal history will normally report more progression in a given period than a more comprehensive one. In the case of this type of account it is thus easier to find purpose and progression in one's personal or family life[50] or in the life of one's immediate community than in universal history. Personal identity may be meaningfully extended only to a social community that is sufficiently intimate so that participation in purposive progression proves possible.

---

[50] Goethe, in *Leiden des jungen Werther*, "Am 22 Mai" writes:

Well is it...with those who can label their rag-gathering employments, or perhaps their passions, with pompous titles, and represent them to mankind as gigantic undertakings for its walfare and salvation. Happy the man who can live in such wise! But he who, in his humility, observes where all this issues, who sees *how featly any small thriving citizen can trim his patch of garden into a Paradise*, and with what unbroken heart even the unhappy crawl along under his burden, and all are alike ardent to see the light of this sun but one minute longer; — yes, he is silent, and he too forms his world out of himself, and he too is happy because he is a man. And then, hemmed-in as he is, he ever keeps in his heart the sweet feeling of freedom, and that this dungeon

Given that the impulse to seek out purpose and progression in temporal history, as well as the form of the same that is found there, are rooted in the *Wirkungsgeschichte* of the lived occasion of which this temporal history is a shadow image, it is to be anticipated that anything as grand as a schema of universal history will be projected somewhat differently by different individuals. This difference will be most notable where the individuals concerned speak out of different cultural traditions. What is crucial for the philosophy of concreteness is that respect for differences of this sort, which follows from taking radical particularity into account in a way that Hegel did not, in no way effects a weakening of the claim being made for the necessity of the *Wirkungsgeschichte* of a living occasion or for the self-evidence of the occasion as it is lived.

3) The concept of God that I entertain from a hypothetical perspective subsequent to the perishing of an occasion, is on the present account of a piece with all other representative thinking. This is to say, it is ever in some degree analogical or metaphorical. This is, on the one hand, because, viewed from this perspective, the being and power of God is never totally explicit within a single occasion constitutive of a merely human subject and the world present for that subject being mediated, and, on the other, because the reaching beyond the achieved ideal that is actual faith does not survive the perishing of the occasion. In the hypothetical perspective analogical thinking assumes a compensatory role by representing that which from this perspective is not concretely grasped or graspable as possible, *including what was grasped only as implicit.* This is also in anticipation of the creation of a new occasion, for which possibilities are thus imaged and worked up. Analogy, then, also in something like the Thomistic sense belongs to the very language of representation that here pertains. What presents itself is the form and power of being that (as an integral aspect of its being what it dynamically is) is *a priori* grasped as such. Insofar as God is only implicit within the lived occasion, viewed from the hypothetical perspective subsequent to its perishing, this is felt as a privation of being, with reference to which God as he was explicitly grasped is now relativized. Insofar as there remains some degree of privation of being, we may thus conclude with St. Thomas that the Divine Essence is not intuited, but can only be represented through the *analogia entis.* This is to appeal to Thomas' quite special sense of analogy. But this must be further specified.

From an actual perspective — i.e., from a perspective within the

---

can be left when he likes. (The translation is taken from Thomas Carlyle, "Goethe", in *Critical and Miscellaneous Essays,* in six volumes [London: Chapman and Hall, 1869], vol. 1, p. 257, ital. added.)

lived occasion — God is indeed intuited as the idea of perfection that is effective in the actualization or concretion of the occasion and that, to whatever extent and degree it is found compossible with the real potentialities present, is therein concretized. What is not intuited in any occasion the subject of which is merely human and merely temporally oriented, is what St. Thomas referred to as His Divine Essence, where this would be construed as implying that He were fully explicit. The analogical representation of this Divine Essence by theoretical reason — i.e., as original motion and as first cause, and as embodying at least such perfections as we perceive in creatures as His effects — may play a decisive role in the preparation of possibilities for concrescence. The preceding two statements seem especially strategic in the forming of a bridge between the Thomistic tradition and that form of the Hegelian tradition that I am advancing.

As for Hegel, it is in the God-man — in the Son — and in His reconciliation with the Father in the person of the Holy Spirit in the Church that God becomes fully actual. The rendering explicit of this His actuality to consciousness is the religious quest that is perhaps never finally achieved, except perhaps in the exemplar of this faith, and then in a mediation that is actualized only after the abandonment of the quest by the anguished cry to the Father, "Why have you forsaken me?", signifying the ultimate alienation (*Entzweiung*). This becoming fully actual doubtless embraces what it most essentially means to be a person even though its achievement may for a temporal being be merely "occasional" in its duration.

It may have occurred to a thoughtful and sufficiently informed reader that the foregoing formulation suggests the possibility of assigning a role to the Thomistic doctrine of analogy within a conceptuality within which also the ontological "argument" can play a decisive role.[51] Although the point is one concerning which there is an

---

[51] St. Anselm's "argument", which is presented in his *Proslogium* in various forms, may be summarized as follows: "I have an idea of a Being than which none greater can be conceived. The idea of a Being that exists is greater than the idea of a Being that does not exist. Therefore God exists." Interpreters have sometimes proposed that what we have here is less an argument than a kind of faith commitment, in the Spirit of Anselm's declaration in chap. 1, "I do not seek to understand that I may believe, but I believe in order to understand."

Within the present context I am presupposing that St. Anselm's argument (along with its for our purposes most relevant descendents) is most fundamentally not an argument at all, and that it lends itself to being an aspect of a phenomenological account of actual faith in pursuit of understanding within the context of an inclusive actual reason. (Thus it must in principle be expressible in the concrete particularity of its presence within a lived occasion in *spek. Sätzen.* following the Hegelian model.) Continued on the page following.

adequate basis for contention, my own present associations lead me to view the first as functioning primarily within theoretical reason and the second primarily within actual reason. This is not, however, to overlook the consideration that any argument, path, or "way" of theoretical reason, to have validity, must reflect some discernable character in concrete actuality. When due consideration is taken of the fact that these two principal aspects of reason — which are approached by the completely different methods advocated by Hegel and Whitehead, respectively — become distinguishable as such only retrospectively, from the perspective of the perished occasion, as alternative ways of representing the occasion that was, the anticipation of what may seem to promise to be a useful bridge between Thomas and a kind of Hegelianism that has no need to shrink from affirming absolute knowledge in Hegel's sense will be made out. This is the case even though this is within a context in which, upon the perishing of the occasion, this knowledge is relativized retrospectively by a grade of Being that from this perspective is found to transcend it.

The foregoing account may well be read as implying a special status for a Thomistic model of theoretical reason preparing possibilities for experience. Indeed, it seems to me that the very extreme of theoretical reason positing a concept of God whose essence cannot be directly intuited, but which we can represent analogically, is complemented by being understood as one pole of an alternating temporal succession, concrete actuality grasped *a priori* as such in what I have described as the Hegelian sense being its alternate pole. If I am correct in this, the complement may well be mutual. Certainly there are issues here that could not be settled in so brief a projection. Nor would I at this point consider it proper to close out the possibility of conceiving the Divine Transcendence in terms of the role of hypo-

---

An argument, considered as such, will where relevant be a function of theoretical reason. Because it operates within a system of abstract ideas, however, it can never be an aspect or function of concretely actual reason. (Concretely actual reason, being *a priori*, does not come to us as the conclusion of an argument or with any antecedents that we may know as such.) That the indicated exception is made in the case of the ontological "argument" is not intended to suggest that other arguments for the existence of God (or about anything whatsoever) might not reflect shadow images of actual reason within the cultural epoch within which they are appealed to with some degree of adequacy. It simply means that, considered *as arguments* and thus as having merely representative ideas as their direct and primary reference, that they have no status within concrete actuality. Regarded as paths or "ways" of reason, however, a role within actual reason, as well, may be in view. The ontological "argument" in my usage normally refers to an idea of perfection concretely realized — or, perhaps better within some contexts, concretely realizing itself — this being the intelligible aim of the occasion.

thetical reason in a theology that, e.g., in the manner of Karl Barth, finds its basis in the concreteness of revelation as witnessed to in the Biblical account, and on this account, at least to a commensurable degree, escapes the need for analogical thinking in the Thomistic sense here considered. The present context is hardly the place to attempt to take up the complex issues that lie here. My principal intent here has in any case been the less ambitious one of showing a possible compatibility and even a complementarity between what I have proposed as the solution to the issue of the status of metaphor, on the one hand, and the Thomistic concept of analogy, on the other, notions that Hegel did not assist us to see as compatible and which up to now, so far as I know, we have on the whole been given little reason for finding compatible.

XIII

CULTURAL RELATIVITY
AS AN ASPECT OF ABSOLUTE TRUTH:
A NEO-HEGELIAN/WHITEHEADIAN CONSTRUAL
OF THE RELATIONSHIP BETWEEN SOCIETY AND TRUTH

1. The Problem

The president of Senegal, presently under the rule of a socialist government, recently said that the socialist regimes of Western Europe in their reception of the teachings of Marx and Lenin had had to work out a "third option" and that even this would not do for Africa. He then remarked that countries such as his own would need to work out still another — a fourth — option.[1] He appeared to be giving expression to two conclusions: (1) that there is something of positive value in the Marxist/Leninist doctrine with regard to historical development that we cannot afford to ignore, and (2) that the political and economic planning and development of peoples must be with due regard to their life styles and to continuity with their historical and cultural background.

I shall not presume to propose such a fourth option for the reception of Marx/Lenin. What I have undertaken is a modification of the methodological basis of first philosophy whereby something like the Hegelian-Marxist type of dialectic is made more viable by rendering the historical determinism that has been associated with it softer, broader (with reference to Marx, at least as he is generally understood), and amenable to a more adequate account of cultural particularity. To the extent that the modification may be found acceptable, it can contribute a basis for working out not only a fourth but any number of variant receptions of Marxist doctrine.

---

[1] The remarks were made on a television film on the European tourist industry in Africa, carried by Austrian National Radio Corporation (ÖRF) on March 8, 1981.

In *Kapital,* Chap. 25, Marx writes,

> Political economy confuses two very different sorts of private property, the one based upon **the labor of the producer himself,** the other upon the exploitation of the labor of strangers. It is forgotten that the latter not only stands in direct contradiction to the former, but also follows only upon its demise.
>
> In western Europe, the homeland of political economy, the process of original accumulation is more or less completed. Capitalism has here either directly taken over the entire national production or, where the relation is as yet less developed, at least controls indirectly the various still existing, degenerating social levels belonging to the outmoded way of production. The louder the facts cry out against its ideology, political economy applies the idea of right and ownership of the precapitalistic world to this completed world of capital with that much more anxious officiousness and unctuosity.
>
> It is otherwise in the **colonies.** There the capitalistic regime clashes everywhere with the producers who, as owners of their own conditions of labor, thereby enrich themselves rather than the capitalists. The Contradiction of these two diametrically opposed economic systems operates here practically by warfare. Where the capitalist is backed up by the power of the motherland, he endeavors to clear away such ways of production and appropriation as are based upon the labor of the producer himself, if possible by force.[2]

The above passage reflects the presupposition generally in evidence throughout Marx's Works that cultures develop by stages and that various political economies, although they may represent different stages of development must tend strongly to follow the same general pattern of development. On his account this is not owing merely to a scientific method that is in principle deterministic. His determinism is rather supposed to be intrinsic to the actuality under consideration. In this respect he is thoroughly Hegelian. This may be seen from the consideration that Hegel's logical idea is not merely an internally immediate form of actuality, but one that externalizes itself in nature. The following passage reflects the Hegelian background against which Marx worked in several ways that will pertain throughout this paper.

> The idea exists as concrete, as a unity of discriminations... essentially not as intuition but as discrimination in itself and with this development it in itself enters into being and into externality in the element of thought; and thus pure philosophy appears in thought as an existent advancing in time. This element of thought is itself abstract, however, the activity of a single

---

[2] Karl Marx, *Ökonomische Schriften* (Darmstadt: Wissenschaftliche Buchgesellschaft, 1962), Vol. 1, *Das Kapital. Kritik der politischen Ökonomie,* ed. by Hans-Joachim Lieber and Benedikt Kautsky, pp. 928f. Here and following, unless otherwise indicated, the translations in this paper are my own.

1. The Problem

consciousness. Spirit exists not only as single, finite consciousness, nonetheless, but as in itself universal, as concrete. This concrete universality, however, comprises all of the developed ways and sides in which it is and becomes its own object corresponding to the Idea. Thus its thinking by which it grasps itself is at the same time an advance that does not pass through the thought of the *individuum* to present itself merely as a single consciousness but universal Spirit presenting itself in the kingdom of its forms in the history of the world. In this development what thereby takes place is that a form, a state of the Idea, arises to the consciousness of a people, so that this people and this time expresses this form only, within which it constructs its universe and works out its situation, the higher stage to follow, however, emerging hundreds of years later in another people.[3]

The problem, stated with reference to Hegel, consists in that he seems often to be maintaining a historical determinism of such a character that any nation or peoples construed within the scope of universal history must have passed through, or have yet to pass through, precisely the same dialectical and developmental phases as those by which the nation states within Germanic culture are maintained to have been historically constituted and to be currently constiuted. Even in the case in which a regarding of the European and Western culture here in view as dialectically the most inclusive one, and in this sense as the model of cultural maturity, were not to be found to pose a problem, the position raises serious issues with regard to the status of, and respect for, cultures within predominantly "pre-industrial" cultures. So long as we follow Hegel in construing all instances of concrete actuality alike as constituted by precisely the same dialectical stages, it remains impossible to render an account of differences between either individuals or cultures upon any other basis than a difference with regard to which phases of the single dialectical path have been rendered explicit and which are as yet only implicit. It is small wonder, then, that he so often depreciated the importance of particular and individual differences, as for example in his reference to "mere sports of nature",[4] even though his having done so stands in strange contrast with his having made free spiri-

---

[3] Georg Wilhelm Friedrich Hegel, *Einleitung in die Geschichte der Philosophie* (hereafter *Einleit.*), pp. 37f.

[4] "Wir können die Natur in der Mannigfaltigkeit ihrer Gattungen und Arten, und der unendlichen Verschiedenheit ihrer Gestaltungen bewundern, denn die Bewunderung ist ohne Begriff, und ihr Gegenstand ist das Vernunftlose. Der Natur, weil sie das Außersichsein des Begriffes ist, ist es freigegeben, in dieser Verschiedenheit sich zu ergehen, wie der Geist, ob er gleich den Begriff in der Gestalt des Begriffes hat, auch auf's Vorstellen sich entläßt, und in einer unendlichen Mannigfaltigkeit desselben sich herumtreibt. Die vielfachen Naturgattungen oder Arten müssen für nichts Höheres geachtet werden, als die willkürlichen Einfälle des Geistes in seinen Vorstellungen." *Logik,* II, pp. 247f.

tual individuality [together with the world present for (and discriminated from) the free spiritual individual] the highest achievement of his dialectic and of concrete actuality, which is dialectical through and through. His not having taken individual differences into account, insofar as such escape the net of his dialectical method, moreover, proves irreconcilable with his concept of concrete universality, insofar as this notion rests upon our being in a position to display truth that is the whole *as in every part and aspect essential and as containing nothing merely accidental or contingent.*

When we look to Marx the general pattern in this respect is similar, although the focus is much more upon the economic and social implications found in Hegel's dialectic of Lordship and Bondage: It is throughout argued or assumed that the pattern of the development of capital and the means of production, the exploitation of labor by capital, the formation of the bourgeoisie as a class, and the ultimate and inevitable class revolution, once discovered, is one through which every developing culture is supposed to pass. Pursuing this view, each culture is portrayed as some stage of a march more or less in lock-step toward the prophesied revolution. To overlook the possibility that the peculiarities of a particular people and culture may affect its historical development uniquely in ways that might affect this possible outcome seems to require credulity. Moreover, at least some of us are inclined to believe that it ought to be possible, by taking sufficient thought, to alleviate the potential causes of such a revolution before they are fully developed as causes. Indeed were we not persuaded of this, we might not philosophize.

I am not interested to deny that by a sufficiently detailed and generous interpretation the problem can be rendered more manageable than it might at first appear to be. Nonetheless, it seems hardly to be entirely done away with apart from some fundamental alterations of the Hegelian conceptuality. It ought to be somehow made possible to report only such patterns of development as are actually found to repeat themselves, apart from being methodologically bound to find a once given form of development of the logical idea unfolding itself to constitute history. In pursuing this aim we can safely dispense with predictions about the future — a specialty of Marx for which no precident can be found in Hegel,[4a] and which would appear to have resulted from a conflation of methods.

[4a] So far as I have been able to observe, the occasions on which Hegel makes reference to the future are to be found not within philosophical (or speculative) propositions but within introductions, notes, and other occasional and informal remarks about what he regarded as philosophical exposition proper. This follows as a matter of principle from the fact that predictions of the future fall outside of what can be said in propositions of this type, which

1. The Problem

An intrinsic limitation of a dialectical history following the Hegelian model consists in that it can take account of dialectical *progressions* only. This is to say, times in which no dialectical progression is exhibited will be blank times,[5] and in this sense, for purposes of the account, unhistorical. I do not propose to alter this characteristic, but, by providing for the possibility of rendering an account of a concretely actual occasion that exposes its uniqueness in relation to other such occasions, to radically alter its impact. The principle that applies here is that insofar as an account of the development of a succession of occasions is sufficiently fine-grained and short, it will exhibit correspondingly more progression. The following stipulation, together with two principal innovations — one drawn from, and one inspired by, Whitehead, to be introduced in the §§ following — will render this principle amenable to taking more adequate account of concretely particular differences between both individuals and events than did either Hegel or Marx. A particular history may normally be made either broad or narrow in compass, ranging all the way from universal history to the history of a particular community through a brief period. At the lower end of the scale, it will serve the purposes of the present account to extend the range of possibilities to a sequence of events within a human life cycle, as well.[6] A short history or one with a narrow range will generally exhibit more dialectical detail (a greater number of sub-moments, or discriminations) in the account of a given occurrence than will a longer history or one with a wider range. This renders it in principle possible, for example, to provide a detailed dialectical account of the development of a particular human individual despite the fact that (also on Hegelian principles, as I would maintain) this must be a recapitulation of stages that have already been mediated within the cultural history within which the individual was born, and on this account would not merit attention in that history. What will be shown to be more important, it renders possible at least in principle the provision of an *exhaustive* dialectical account of an actual occasion of experience. This possibility, even though some practical difficulties may be encountered in the execution and even if its complete execution may only be ap-

---

involve an account of the grasping, as discriminated, of a settled past and in the way in which it is (or was) discriminated. See SC, Book I, chap. 1.

[5] "The History of the World is not a theatre of happiness. Periods of happiness are blank pages in it, for they are periods of harmony — periods when the antithesis is in abeyance." Hegel, *Phil. of Hist.*, pp. 26f.

[6] This facilitates my reference to "history as actual within the present" within an actual occasion. See §5 and SC, pp. 477-86.

proximated, is strategic for the philosophical method implicated with the understanding of absolute truth which I wish to render tenable.

The concept of absolute truth herein proposed is modeled upon Hegel's absolute knowledge, with two principal differences the introduction of which, I wish to maintain, render this notion tenable. This concept will be unfolded — also with regard to cultural relativity — under three sub-heads, titles of successive sections to follow, each suggested by a key statement taken from the passage from Hegel's *Einleitung in die Geschichte der Philosophie*, earlier cited.

2. Concrete Actuality as Constituted by Discriminations

"The idea exists as concrete, as a unity of discriminations... discrimination in itself." Hegel's position that concrete actuality is constituted of discriminations is most readily understood with reference to his concept of the speculative proposition or judgment (*spek. Satz*),[7] sometimes referred to as the philosophical proposition or judgment, seeing that every phase of his dialectic is constituted by such a proposition, the first and second moments of each being the subject and predicate, respectively.

The subject and predicate of a *spek. Satz* are not of the habitual or ordinary sort, already formed and ready to be set together and connected by a copula. Rather, they form one another, i.e., are mediated. Consider the proposition, "This table is round."[8] To understand this as a *spek. Satz*, bracket out all other tables from consideration and all other instances of round. "Table" thus referred to has its entire meaning with reference to "round" thus referred to, and vice versa, and all meanings external to this relation are set aside. As in the case of the logical correlatives "husband" and "wife", each is definable only with reference to the other. The S and P of a *spek. Satz*, in the course of their being mediated each becomes an accent within an identity inclusive of both. This is a discriminated identity[9] (although Hegel sometimes inconsistently writes as though the discrimination passes away, thereby posing a problem). It is

---

[7] *Phän.*, pp. 45-54, esp. 49-53.

[8] I can do no better than use an example proposed by Josef Simon. See the quotation on p. 6 above.

[9] Hegel, *Phän.*, p. 51. Hegel seems not uniformly consistent in regard to this being a *discriminated* identity. Even the passage referred to, at the close, casts doubt upon his position in this regard by the statement: "...daß aber das Prädikat die Substanz ausdrückt und das Subjekt selbst ins Allgemeine fällt, *ist die Einheit, worin jener Akzent verklingt*" (emphasis added).

2. Concrete Actuality and Discriminations

the relation between the discriminated aspect — in other words the discrimination — that is actual, and each aspect may alternatively lend its name to this relation. The discrimination is not abstractable from the aspects discriminated.[10] Hence the discriminated (each or both) *are* the discrimination and vice versa.

The above statement must once be qualified, first by noting that *it is not so much the discrimination as an achieved result that is actual as the process of being discriminated along with its result, the latter being not yet abstracted from its process of becoming.* Secondly, it should be noted that a *spek. Satz* need not be conscious; it may be a judgment *constitutive of* experience (and of actuality) and hence transcendental.

As an alternative to transcendental *spek. Sätzen*, we may, following Whitehead, define experience so broadly that it includes prehension as well as self-conscious comprehension (where the latter is attained this is for him from the perspective of a successor occasion), and let unconscious experience in the form of contrasts [formed by decisions (W), which we might now call judgments] displace transcendental judgments as providing the conditions for the possibility of conscious experience. The important thing for present purposes is that the process of concrescence be explicated by *spek. Sätzen*, seeing that to date no alternative means would seem to have been found for providing an account of an actual occasion from an internal (actual) perspective.[11] On this head it is to be noted that neither Hegelian categorial conditions to account for the possibility and actuality nor Whiteheadian contrasts ought properly to be construed to function merely hypothetically. Hence it will not do to cast the latter in the language of external, contingent relations, as does Whitehead.

Various kinds of identities have or contain sub-identities, as, for example, "this table" has legs, each of which may in turn be constituted by discriminations that are mediated by *spek. Sätzen*. "This table", moreover, is a sub-identity within more inclusive identities,

---

[10] This characteristic of discriminations, intrinsic to concrete universality, is referred to specifically in §4. Whitehead's contrasts are likewise non-abstractable; see PR, p. 228.

[11] The nearest parallel in Whitehead to Hegel's *spek. Satz* is his contrast. Hegel's *spek. Satz* and Whitehead's contrast are both alike rendered fully actual within the process of concrescence, with the result that they have no unexpended potency, no residual "lure for feeling" at the conclusion.

For Whitehead affirmation-negation is the most important contrast (PR, p. 24). In fundamental import, this could come to much the same as Hegel's having made the *spek. Satz*, and with this the principle of negation, his central methodological principle. As a matter of fact, however, Whitehead accords to negation not only less systematic exposition but also less emphasis than does Hegel. See Essay II and SC, pp. 419-22.

such as room, community, state, nation, desire, person, intention, ought, right, etc., the ultimate inclusiveness being exhibited by that identity constituted by a self-conscious subject and the world (or universe) present for that subject, each being accents within this identity, the latter being inclusive of both. This most inclusive identity may be designated an actual occasion (Whitehead)[12] and its contrasting aspects constitute the "highest" discrimination, i.e., the discrimination inclusive of all others.

There may be other tables than "this table" in some sense included within the occasion. Some may stand in view, or on the periphery of my vision. Certainly many are present in the form of history as actual within the present and in the form of possibilities for future actualization. (Such will belong especially to the earlier phases of concrescence.)[13] Hence it is possible meaningfully to employ the universal concept and term "table" with reference to the content of a single occasion, i.e., *concretely*. This usage is to be strictly distinguished from reference to the abstract universal "table," in which the reference is to tables within a plurality of occasions. Talk of a plurality of occasions is always hypothetical in character, seeing that evidently no one has ever found himself (or herself) situated outside of that some one actual occasion 'presently' (within the context of temporality) constitutive of him (or her) and of the world present *for* him (or her.) This necessarily follows from the fact that an actual occasion contains within it all that from its perspective is actual, in some grade of emphasis.

The mediation of a discrimination, viewed as a process, has a beginning and an end. It begins with immediacy and ends with the mediated (discriminated) aspects, i.e., the "settled" subject and predicate of some *spek. Satz*. It is the process only that is actual, however; the mediated aspects, when abstracted from the living process of becoming, are merely residual, i.e., static data.[14] If the idea

---

[12] This term is adapted from Whitehead's usage. My actual occasion, by contrast with Whitehead's, includes within itself its own self-conscious subject. Rather than the occasion being distanced from its understanding, interpreting subject by reflection, reflection is one of its constitutive contrasts. (Indeed, the term reflection may with a certain plausibility be broadened to be nearly synonymous with contrast.) Absolute truth is then possible by virtue of the subject's privileged position within the occasion. Knowledge does not first arise as abstract (and relativized) following upon the perishing of the occasion.

[13] See figures 1-3, p. 199.

[14] In PR, p. 29, Whitehead writes: "In the philosophy of organism it is not 'substance' which is permanent, but 'form.' Forms suffer changing relations; actual entities 'perpetually perish' subjectively, but are immortal objectively. Actuality in perishing acquires objectivity, while it loses subjective immediacy." To be noted is that objectification takes place

2. Concrete Actuality and Discriminations 285

of the "perishing" of an actual occasion is not, or at least not explicitly, traceable to Hegel,[15] it can serve to rescue his absolute knowledge from what from a temporal standpoint might be described as an absurd old age.

Against this background, as a provisional heuristic device shortly to be qualified, I propose the following (abstract) definition of absolute truth. The absolute truth is the whole of that some one actual occasion at any given temporal instant present in and for a self-conscious individual, which whole contains all of the discriminations needful for its explication. This must be qualified just here by noting that at any given temporal instant — no matter how thin — either the occasion in its self-evidence is present as the consciousness of its subject (and world) or, in case it has perished, its hypothetically entertained data are apprehended by the subject of the subsequent occasion.[16] The truth that is the whole is thus a climactic, episodic, all-or-nothing affair. And its alternate is derivative and hypothetical, analogous to the fading image on the retina of the eye after it has been exposed to a flash of light. Death is the ever shifting dividing line between the true and the hypothetical.

That the concrete discriminations given in an occasion are adequate to its explication has the import that the occasion requires nothing outside of itself to be what it is, and that it is in this sense absolute.

By absolute truth I mean the force of self-evidence with which what we at once perceive, conceive, and intend presents itself, these three terms being merely intended to suggest (1) that when one undertakes to render an account of an actual occasion there is no stopping point short of a consideration of the entirety of its constitutive discriminations[17] and (2) that there is no experience and no feeling that is not in principle expressible as a discrimination in process of

---

within the occasion, rather than, as for Whitehead, merely accompanying abstraction. For Whitehead, "objectification is abstraction" (PR, p. 101).

[15] See pp. 12ff above, including n. 19.

[16] In the reconstruction here in progress, the self-creation of an actual occasion takes place in *actual* time, i.e., its own time. This is to be distinguished from temporality, clock time, which pertains to the relations between occasions, something derived and hypothetical in character. The supposition that the future will resemble the past in respect to its temporal scheme is thus a part of the conception of nature as a permanent possibility of experience out of which real possibilities for concrescence are selected. (See p. 145, n. 14, 3rd par.) Thus what Hegel often means by time (as e.g., in *Phän.*, p. 558 or *Phen.*, p. 800) from the standpoint being explicated falls on the side of temporality.

[17] This judgment is to be understood as qualified by p. 69, n. 19.

being mediated, i.e., as a *spek. Satz*, or as a combination of *spek. Sätzen*. What is self-evident needs no bolstering, of course, least of all by a philosophical demonstration, which would be as presumptuous as it would be absurd. It is the fact with which we begin, which invites explication from the person who is ready to submit him- or herself to the required discipline.

We can derive from Hegel's dialectic a sense of the variety and types of discriminations constitutive of concretely actual occasions. Abstractly considered, these are generic discriminations only, that is to say, merely types. Absolute truth can never be arrived at by a combination of such generic discriminations into a whole. Such an artificially constituted occasion (such as we arrive at by reading Hegel's *Phen.*, or by the analysis and synthesizing of the discriminations constitutive of an occasion) at least until it shall have been approximately concretized, might perhaps be potential for concrescence, or partially so, but not actual. In the natural order of knowledge as well as of being, **fact is prior to theory**, as every farmer knows instinctively. An actual occasion that presents itself with the self-evidence native to it may be regarded (during its pulse of life) as a complete fact.[18]

3. The Process of Concrescence

"Spirit exists not only as single, finite consciousness... but as itself universal, as concrete.... its thinking by which it grasps itself is at the same time an advance fulfilled by the developed actuality in its entirety..." It is the second of the two statements that I shall enlarge upon here. Knowledge on Hegel's account does not begin with intuition but with actuality fullblown, as the whole discriminated or, what comes to the same, the unity and wholeness of discriminations. In the place of an intuition of a self — just here mind (spirit) as thinking — void of all actuality and possessed only of a few innate ideas, as for Descartes, the subjective or ideal side of an actual occasion is enriched by content from the objective pole[19] throughout the course of their mediation, and vice versa. This is with the conse-

---

[18] Whitehead on several occasions refers to his actual occasion as a "complete fact", once at least with specific reference to Plato's Sophist, 248E. For this reference see pp.23f, inc. n. 1.

[19] Due to the fact that objectification is held to occur within an actual occasion, rather than, as on Whitehead's account, following its perishing, we can properly refer to an objective pole of the occasion rather than restricting our reference to its physical pole, as does Whitehead.

3. The Process of Concrescence

quence that the self-concept is determined by and possessed of the same material and objective content as is the world, and knows itself only as possessed of this content and as at once discriminated from, yet identical with, its world, subject and substance being in this sense identical, even as distinguished. Knowledge and the actuality known constitute one of the contrasts, or discriminations, that, generically construed, is constitutive of every actual occasion, and that may thus be said to be abstractly universal to all occasions. To express this most un-Whiteheadian notion by the use of Whitehead's term, reflecflection is *a contrast,* or perhaps we should rather say that *reflection,* now more broadly construed, *is the contrast,* for then we shall be left with the idea of thought mirroring actuality at all levels of its concrescence. This will be well and good if we do not conclude that this mirroring is the only function of thought, which is also involved in selectivity and decision.

The concretion of many discriminations, at least initially, takes the historical form of a struggle lived through to a resolution of conflict by which each side is found to be essential to the other and to the identity thus discriminated. Hegel's Lordship and Bondage, just here regarded as a discrimination actualized within the life space of a human individual (let us say, in working through the authority crisis of puberty) will be suggestive of the existential stress that this may involve. In the case of this particular discrimination, the effects of its lived-out resolution may be inherited, at least through such subsequent occasions as are constitutive of the life span of the individual.

That the dialectic of Lordship and Bondage is an inherently social phenomenon and as such likely to be conditioned by the cultural setting within which it occurs will be obvious, seeing that it involves a life and death struggle of two human beings and seeing that for the bondsman this struggle issues in the birth of a free self-consciousness. Many discriminations are inherently social that might appear at first not to be. Thus, for example, space-time, considered in its concreteness, is social in character. This is seeing that we are treating of spaces and times in respect to the contents of *nature* and *history* respectively,[20] each of which, considered concretely, is an accent within an identity inclusive of both: There is no nature or aspect of nature that is not at least implicitly historical process, which is inherently social, even as there is no history that does not include the history of

---

[20] "History in general is...the development of Spirit in *Time,* as Nature is the development of the Idea in *Space.*" Hegel, *Phil. of Hist.,* p. 72. Also see p. 183, §22.

a natural order in space.²¹

It will be clear from the foregoing that the concrete particularity of a cultural heritage can contribute, and contribute discriminations, to the unity and wholeness of discriminations that constitutes an actual occasion. This is not, however, to overlook the fact that the physicist has his more abstract (or less richly inclusive) space-time concept, which doubtless becomes concretized or partially concretized as space-time discriminations in at least some contemporary actual occasions, and this without in any manner insinuating his hypothetico-deductive method into first philosophy, the suitability of which is restricted to the shadow land of theories, i.e., to the preparation of possibilities for concretization.

Whatever space-time discriminations, or combination, is concretized within a given actual occasion, the space-time system actualized within the occasion is uniform and universal in scope throughout the occasion, i.e., throughout the universe. This is with the result that each occasion creates its own time and space, so that we can with plausibility say with Heidegger, *"Es zeitigt sich"*, and *"Es räumt sich ein"*.

Can a discrimination constitutive of a theory that is not true be concretized? A theory that contains no truth cannot be concretized. But excluding this extreme case, theories come in all degrees of truth. If a theory establishes some connections of data in the process of the concrescence of an actual occasion, it contains some (however meager) truth and may indeed be the best available at the time. If a theory functions as a "lure for feeling", to employ Whitehead's term, it has some truth; this is to say, the relations to the formation of which it contributes in the completed occasion, as essential aspects of absolute truth, will have absolute status. Thus the relative truth or falsehood of theories can never in any way relativize absolute truth, which is the ***being-mediated of what is, i.e., what is being concretized***.²²

---

²¹ On dialectical principles, it is history that is here the more inclusive category and social in character.

²² Moreover, the whole of an actual occasion being implicated in its every part (whole and part being each accents within an identity inclusive of both), strictly speaking, there can be no particular generic discrimination, no matter how carefully specified in accordance with the definitions of terms supposed to be required for the hypotheses of some particular science, that upon being concretized does not take on the character of the occasion in its entirety. Generic discriminations derived by abstraction from culturally determined absolute truth may be expected to reflect their source. These two circumstances tend to indicate that there is no such thing as a neutral standard of objectivity that stands free of cultural determination and of culturally determined value systems, and that no abstract science, however precise, is capable to representing actuality with precision.

3. The Process of Concrescence

When an actual occasion has yielded to analysis-synthesis, discrimination by discrimination, the dialectician's task is done. In the matter of truth, it is of the utmost importance both to recognize when one has it and when one has given an account of it, and not to wander through the earth in search of the kind of certainty that was present at the outset or that has been achieved, if perhaps disguised by a poor upbringing, an alienating type of education, or the felt need to disemble. Above all, it is in no need of being projected upon a future, as in the case of a theory.[22a] Once this is recognized, the data of a past occasion can quite properly contribute to hypothetical thinking awaiting possible concrescence, apart from our supposing that the dialectical method, as in the case of the hypothetico-deductive method, somehow requires this for its justification. I say "awaiting possible concrescence". Although, once an occasion is actual, its subject (or any other of its constituent aspects) may properly be construed as its cause (see §14 following), prior to this the synthesis of life that it is lies beyond the capacity of the subject alone to determine. Creation cannot be rushed by declaring an aspiration or a conjecture to be constitutive of actuality before the fact.

[22a] In notes within SC I have devoted what some may be inclined to regard as an excessive amount of attention to what might be called "future mongering" Hegel scholarship. As I reflect further on this, to me weird, aberration, I have found ever more reason to believe it to be very often traceable to a relatively innocent source. This consists in a tendency, when we note that for Hegel the dialectical categories that constitute the knowing consciousness are ultimately found to be identical with their historical unfoldment, to then dismiss the former from further consideration and proceed to characterize his position exclusively in terms of the latter. This tendency is rendered understandable, on the one hand, by the originality and impact of his concept of historical unfoldment, and on the other, by the fact that the organization of the caregories as a linear series serves as a simplification device that renders them more readily understood than is a representation of them in their integral all-at-onceness as constitutive of the knowing consciousness. Even so, it is unwarranted, and it proves pernicious on several accounts, one of these being that the conception of a linear temporal series tempts us to construe this series as continuing into a future extending beyond that which has been rendered concrete. Such a future is, of course, beyond anything to which a dialectical account of the type of Hegel's could possibly pertain, seeing that the Owl of Minerva takes flight only at dusk. It can thus lead to the substitution of hypothetical speculation for Hegel's concrete speculation — what I have sometimes referred to as "the arch anti-Hegelian fallacy" (SC, pp. 64, 92, 101, 209, 436) — and to a host of related errors and muddles in Hegel interpretation to complement this one.

The tendency to which I refer is quite common. It is to be observed in the background, at least, of the manner in which John Smith construes Hegel to have seen religion to be *aufgehoben* by philosophy: "Religion must stop short of Philosophy and that is Hegel's ultimate conclusion; it is not in any way qualified by the consideration that the content of both is the same" ("The Meaning of Religious Experience in Hegel and Whitehead", in George R. Lucas, Jr. (Ed.), *Hegel and Whitehead*.... Following, Smith finds a corrective in Whitehead: "...there is no hint in Whitehead's treatment that religion is a limited or inferior form of some other kind of truth that in the end surpasses it, nor is it seen as a phase among others in a more encompassing process of development" (p. 298). The reference in the last statement is clearly to an external and temporal historical development — to what Hegel in his first major *Work* regarded as spirit in its external form in time (*Phän.*, p. 558; or *Phen.*, p. 800). It is by virtue of this that Smith is able to view Hegel and Whitehead as having addressed the issue with which he is concerned on much the same level. Hegel's Begriff — concrete actuality grasped as such (the truth that is the whole of absolute knowing) — is quite definitely constituted exclusively of internal relations, however, and in a serious encounter between the two philosophers with respect to the issue with which Smith is concerned, one should surely wish to see an account being taken of Hegel's conception of concrete actuality (grasped as such) and not merely of (externally related) representations of that actuality. In doing so, one would in some manner encounter what I have been referring to as the internal (actual) perspective.

It is with the first of the two quotations immediately preceding that I shall now be concerned. Here the "stopping short" of the religious consciousness that Smith has in view is clearly being construed as within Hegel's order of historical unfoldment *and not within the unity of the knowing consciousness* — i.e., self and world being grasped (and not merely represented) in (and for) itself as concrete actuality. The difference is more than a subtle one, in that where Hegel's Begriff is understood in terms of the knowing consciousness, what rhe religious dimension of the unity of reason represents in the symbols of religion are conceptually grasped and this grasping is the lived actuality to which religious symbols have made their necessary contribution. Assuming that for Hegel the truth is indeed the whole, and that we should take him at his word where he finds that all of the categories that are constitutive of this whole are counted essential to it, apart from this grasp religious symbols would be as blind as bare sense perceptions. That religious symbols are grasped (*begriffen*) is indispensible to the knowing consciousness (and world present for this consciousness), and this means nothing less than that *apart from this grasp there would be no consciousness*.

It would be difficult, indeed, to explain how a philosophical basis for pluralistic personalism could ever have been found in Hegel had he been understood on the basis of an account which, in the manner that I have noted, passes over the unity of the knowing consciousness. Furthermore, this is to pass over his absolute knowledge. If the truth of Hegel is the whole of Hegel, as I suggested in the Preface, this is surely too conspicuous an omission for us to retain much hope that this would leave much remaining of Hegel worthy of salvaging. Unless it should turn out to be the case that life begins with theory, from the present standpoint, Whitehead's metaphysics as it stands is not a viable option as a first philosophy. What such a theory needs is to be given a foundation in concrete fact, as it is actually grasped as such. In leveling Hegel toward Whitehead, Smith has given up too much; we are left with less than a basis for the development of a viable philosophy of concrete fact.

The reader may raise the objection that what I mean by grasping in the foregoing is not distinctly philosophical. This is true. The standpoint I propose is that the categories that for Hegel constitute knowledge for the philosopher are not different than those that constitute the knowledge of others. Indeed, where knowledge is concrete actuality grasped *a priori* as such, the case could not be otherwise. The difference consists in that for the philosopher the categories are all supposed to have been rendered explicit. On this reading of Hegel, where Smith refers to a "stopping short" of the religious consciousness, what he should mean is that *an account that does nto get further* fails to account for (inherently knowing) consciousness within which religious representations and symbols are contained as *aufgehobene* aspects of what presents (and not merely *re*presents!) itself as concrete fact, i.e., concrete actuality grasped *a priori* as such.

The position of which I am critical has had representation from early on, doubtless in part because it finds sympathetic reverberations in the futuristic thinking of Marx and his followers. Nonetheless, it is untrue to Hegel's more fundamental intentions. That it should be corrected, however, is not least because, where serious first philosophy is being pursued and not merely a propagandistic platform for social action, the position that I have sketched in offers an option that is more promising and that results in an over-all simplification of our understanding of Hegel that should be welcomed.

It seems to me that it is only where there is forgetfulness of Kant's unity of reason, con-

3. The Process of Concrescence

Consider two concretely actual occasions, each constitutive of an individual and the world present for this individual, the two individuals differing widely in range of understanding and intellectual endowment. Let the highly endowed individual be "a" and the less highly endowed "b". In the interest of simplicity, let us stipulate that "a" and "b" share the same cultural background and are participating in some common activity within proximity of one another. The ideational content of the two occasions may be compared by a comparison of their constitutive discriminations. Although the occa-

---

sisting in a theoretical and a practical faculty, which was so prominently reflected within the intellectual atmosphere within which Hegel worked and with the further development of which he has with irrefutable right been associated, that the issue I am here treating can arise.

In my reconception of method for first philosophy, I have introduced a concept that, among other things, can serve as a safeguard against what I regard as Smith's less than adequate way of regarding Hegel's ranking of the philosophical consciousness as higher than the religious consciousness. This is the concept of *Wirkungsgeschichte* — history as actual within the present occasion. Unlike Hegel's order of historical unfoldment, which is an external order of temporally related aspects, *Wirkungsgeschichte* in my usage is a necessary aspect of the lived occasion or, better, the lived occsion in its entirety considered with respect to its historical depth. Being grasped *a priori* as such from an internal (actual) perspective, moreover, *it is this prior to the derivative abstractions that constitute its historical unfoldment after the fact.* As in the case of the concept of inheritance from the causal past, the concept of temporality does service within the context of an account of the preparation of possibilities for possible actualization. Temporal relations are thus not accorded ontological status but merely constitute an aspect of what is at best a likely story.

This aspect of my reconstruction permits me to be in substantial agreement with Hegel for having construed the Begriff as a historical unfoldment, i.e., the Begriff *in time*, even though in my usage time is not be confused with the temporality that Hegel clearly has in view in the pasaage in the *Phän.*, p. 558 to which I made reference in the foregoing. In my own account time is always actual and it may, indeed, refer to concrete actuality grasped as such. It is thus strictly distinguished from temporality, which always refers to relations within the realm of possibilities. Considered with respect to the becoming of being that is lived time, the latter are merely derivative abstractions — residuals of the perished occasion.

I suspect that Hegel may be making reference to time as actual when he writes, "History in general is...the development of Spirit in *Time,* as Nature is the development of the Idea in **Space**. (*The Philosophy of History*, Sibree trans., p. 72), as when he sometimes refers to the Begriff *as* time. If so, he appears not to have been consistent in his usages, or at least not to have developed his position adequately with respect to the issue thus suggested, which becomes focal in my reconception.

Nathan Rosenstreich, in "Rorty's Interpretation of Hegel" (*Review of Metaphysics*, Vol. XXXIX, No. 2 (Dec. 1985), §5, interprets the position of time within Hegel's system in a way that I believe can achieve much the same as I am intent upon achieving more economically by developing the discrimination of time and temporality that I have proposed. This is within the context within which he writes,

> The historization of the spirit and thus of philosophy is...only one element of Hegel's system; that element itself cannot be detached from the total exposition of the relationship between activity, i.e., philosophical activity, or activities in art or religion, activities seen not as an expression but as a manifestation. The manifestation is partial but that which is manifest or manifested is total. (p. 329)

sion constitutive of individual "a" will be more highly discriminated, both occasions alike will exhibit absolute truth. It might be supposed that the occasion constitutive of "a" might somehow be more theoretical in character. This could be true with respect to its earlier phases, but not of the occasion viewed from the perspective of full concrescence and with regard to its final phase. At full concrescence, seeing that all potentiality has spent itself into the hard coin of actuality, no theoretical component remains. Each of the occasions, in its end phase, is constituted of a unity and wholeness of discriminations, and each exhibits the character of absolute truth. The difference consists in what discriminations, generically viewed, are concretized, and in precisely how they are concretized, i.e., the form and content they exhibit in the particular concretion.

The differences between "a" and "b" may be viewed primarily as a difference in capacities to assimilate their (largely shared) causal past and to derive from it "real potentiality"[23] for concretization. If this kind of difference can be detected in individuals sharing the same culture, it will be abundantly clear that the concrete particularity of one culture that distinguishes it from another can fundamentally determine what individuals find in it by way of real potentiality of self and world that can affect the totality of discriminations concretized as absolute truth.

The social dimension of a discrimination, generically viewed, implies the need to make allowance for great variety in its concrescences. If it is to be conceded that, where the organic character of nature has been overlooked, the value-freedom that has been attributed to the natural sciences has tended to be exaggerated and construed simplistically, these sciences nonetheless have to do with a subject matter that, within limits, is by comparison more or less reliably uniform.

Whitehead, despite the fact that his concept of an actual occasion is dominated by physical models, appears to have had in view something very much like infinitely varied actual occasions. This might go far toward explaining why he did not undertake concretely to specify the contrasts (his term was discriminations) within his more inclusive actual occasion — more inclusive by virtue of including its own understanding, interpreting (and indeed reasoning) subject. This was essential to his attempt at showing an actual occasion to be presuppositionless by virtue of containing within itself all of the discriminations needful for its explication. This program, which I hold to be in

---

[23] PR, pp. 23, 65f.

3. The Process of Concrescence 293

principle achieveable with respect to selected occasions, certain qualifications being held in view, even while admitting that the execution of this ideal may face some difficulties of a practical nature, failed in Hegel's hands. This failure was largely on two accounts. On the one hand, there was wanting a clear-cut concept of the mortality of an actual occasion as a necessary complement to its absoluteness within the framework of an organic concept of nature and spirit. On the other hand, there was a want of a way of taking into consideration the differences between individuals and occasions whereby these would not be set aside in an account in which the concrete universality of *all* constitutive aspects of absolute knowledge requires that there be no accidents or unessential aspects of content.

In the § to follow I shall propose a typology of discriminations construed with respect to their range of abstract universality which will readily accommodate this infinite variability apart from compromising in the least the possibility of rendering an exhaustive analysis-synthesis, discrimination by discrimination, of an actual occasion, required to justify presuppositionlessness, or the self-evident character of absolute truth.

I wish now to call attention to a discrimination constitutive of *some* concretely actual occasions. To ameliorate the shock with which what I have now to say may well be greeted, let me begin with a question. If we assume that everything at all that is actual takes place within some actual occasion (while it is yet living), then must we not assume that human speech takes place within such? If this must be conceded, perhaps the hearer will at least have the patience to hear me out when I propose that discriminations constitutive of an actual occasion may be mediated in authentic (non-dissembling) human speech. This is not to suggest that an actual occasion can be entirely spoken forth in linear speech before it has perished. Given the limitation of the medium — which, so far as it reaches, is one with the message — some of its constitutive discriminations will obviously need to be inferred indirectly, and where there is an understanding relationship with the speaker, others will be more or less safely presupposed. I return, nonetheless, to extend my original proposal: some one discrimination constitutive of some one actual occasion may be mediated in human speech, others following through a series of inheriting successor occasions, until a hearer shall very nearly have before him at one time and within a single context the discriminations constitutive of one occasion representative of the series. In an ideal case he will grasp this one occasion with the clarity and completeness of discrimination with which the speaker grasped (as change)[24] successive occasions in the series.

Seeing that concrete language — which is spoken in *spek. Sätzen* — is inherently social in character, discriminating as such at the level of self-consciousness is social in character.[25]

Concrete language is speaking authentically, in which (1) the use of priorly determined social conventions, where such are appealed to, is incidental to the primary fact that subjects and predicates are being *concretely determined* and bear the concrete mediations of the occasion, which is a new creation; and (2) in which they are at once spoken with the whole self (as an accent within the whole occasion), and thus express contextually the integrity of the world present for the subject of the occasion. Understood in this manner, concrete language and the world present for the subject are each accents within an identity that is concrete actuality, inclusive of both. It seems not misleading, so far as the statement reaches, to say that actuality bodies itself forth in concrete language. Or, as an ancient Hermetic teaching has it, *"In the beginning was the Word."*

4. Concrete Universality and Particularity

"Concrete universality... comprises all of the developed ways and sides in which it is and becomes its own corresponding to the idea." Every part and aspect of the occasion has its distinctive function with respect to the whole and its every part, and the whole in turn is implicated within every part or aspect. Thus every part or aspect is concretely universal throughout the whole and the whole is concretely universal throughout every part.

If these characteristics are extended to the construal of an actual occasion as a "complete fact", then it may be said that every sub-fact has its distinctive function with respect to the complete fact and that the latter is implicated in every sub-fact. A sub-fact is equally absolute so long as it is construed as integral with the context of relations that constitutes it what it is.

Consider the distinction between concrete and generic discriminations in the light of this notion. Let space (nature)–time (history) exemplify the latter. Then the space-time discrimination that (along with a plurality of other discriminations) is concretized within the actual occasion present to me when I turn right is a different space-time discrimination than is concretized within the actual occasion present to me when I turn left. Even if distinguished by no other dif-

---

[24] *"Death is a theory*...what I concretely know is merely *change."* See p. 145, n. 14 and the two paragraphs in the text preceding.

[25] See Essay IX.

ference — suppose that the left side of the room is a mirror image of the right side — the two occasions would on this account be different occasions, owing to the fact that the second follows the first and, to use Whitehead's term, inherits from one more.[26]

We see here illustrated that there are no non-essential aspects of absolute truth, seeing that the alteration of the manner in which even a single discrimination is concretized effects an alteration of the entire occasion of which it is a constituent, which may be reflected in a difference — however slight — of a good many discriminations.[27] This renders it a mere tautology to say that cultural particularity is an essential aspect of absolute truth.

Now it seems highly probable that the discrimination space-time, generically construed, is abstractly universal to all occasions. It is difficult to conceive an occasion apart from special and temporal relations.[28] The above illustration renders plausible, I think, that even such a discrimination affords the possibility of taking account of cultural particularity. This is not to suppose that the difference between the scene right and the scene left is of any great cultural moment.

The illustration was selected primarily to show that we face no practical limit in distinguishing specific concretized space-times. But if we now consider the relation of less proximate concretized space-times, in which widely different historical concretions are presented, it will be seen that keeping the distinction (borrowed from Whitehead)[29] between concrete and generic discriminations (his term is "contrast") clearly in mind can afford the possibility of taking account of more in the way of cultural particularity within a dialectical account than otherwise would be possible. The point will be seen the more plainly if the all-encompassing character of the dialectical triad constituted by the logical idea, nature, and absolute spirit (or history) within Hegel's system is taken into account, within which

---

[26] The second, in other words, has a different history as actual within the present.

[27] The disposition of the "same" discrimination, generically considered, to undergo alterations within successive occasions is understood to import a certain relativity in what we regard hypothetically as the laws of nature and history. I have elsewhere referred to this phenomenon as "the settlement effect" (*die Einbettungswirkung*"). See Essay VII, §3 (pp. 129-38),

[28] Strictly speaking, a judgment in this matter must remain a hypothesis, seeing that it pertains in the final analysis to relations between actual occasions, and no one has ever *actually* taken up a vantage point outside of that some one occasion constitutive of him and the world present for him at a given instant (which contains within itself all that from its perspective is actual) to certify such relations.

[29] For Whitehead's use of "generic contrasts," see PR, pp. 266, 229ff, 276.

history (concrete time) emerges as an all-inclusive category.[30]

The import of this I think should be that sub-triads (or discriminations) of the primary triad constitute its further specification. An increment of specifying discriminations does not, or at least does not necessarily, call attention to content that was previously simply overlooked or not present. Nonetheless, detail of discrimination of itself adds a certain richness to the account of concreteness that dialectic is supposed to yield.

When one considers the plurality of sub-categories and several levels of subsumption of such within history, however, the move invites a yet more fundamental one with respect to the objective in view. This is to allow for differences also in the generic discriminations that might be concretized as sub-categories.

I believe that there are several possible approaches to rendering plausible the proposal that all actual occasions are *not* constituted by precisely the same discriminations, generically construed. Discriminations come to be discovered that were not known previously to exist, and sometimes they are worked out and come into use and, so far as we are able to judge, come into being as well. **Discriminating persons,** frequently artists, often call our first attention to such as are discovered. For the justification of my position at this point, I appeal only to an argument from decent modesty, namely, that it would be going beyond the evidence to suppose, as Hegel would seem to have supposed, that all discriminations constitutive of concrete actuality are alike constitutive of it in every actual occasion, differences between such being explained solely upon the basis of which discriminations are explicit and which are yet only implicit. The position I advocate is to take account of discriminations *as we encounter them,* rendering judgments respecting their range of abstract universality throughout the plurality of actual occasions accordingly, as best we can. Then if experience and closer investigation should direct this, we can always move from any position that follows from this to one more nearly approaching that of Hegel. Fortunately, this is an area in which, if we take reasonable caution not to affirm too much, a mistake can be of no great moment and is readily corrected. This, as well, argues for the position I am advocating. The important thing is that the investigator **be open** to the full variety and particularity of discriminations constitutive of the type of actual occasion he is investigating, to render maximally possible the realization of the ideal that his analysis-synthesis shall be

---

[30] For a clarification of the import of "all inclusive" in this usage, consult Hegel's note on *Aufhebung* at the conclusion of Chap. I of his *Logic.*

complete with respect to discriminations that present themselves.

These considerations in view, the fourfold typology of discriminations considered with respect to their range of abstract universality throughout the plurality of actual occasions that I have already set forth within several contexts[31] provides for the possibility of reflecting the uniqueness of any actual occasion also by reference to its constitutive discriminations.

Only insofar as the ideal of an analysis-synthesis of an actual occasion is found somewhere nearly approachable through the abstract *re*construction of an actual occasion typical of some relevant epoch is it possible definitely to replay for the understanding, as it were, the specific functions of the various constituent discriminations and discriminated aspects of an actual occasion throughout the entirety of the occasion, so as systematically to perceive their concrete universality. The possibility of a vigorously executed first philosophy seems to rests upon our being carried far enough along in the execution of this ideal so as to see concretized the *idea* of such a program, thus rendering it regulative. So long as a dialectical account is permitted to pass over specific details of difference in the manner in which Hegel openly did, it cannot hope to achieve the precision requisite to this task. This is owing to the consideration that the very notion of concrete universality rules out the possibility of attributing any accidental or non-essential characteristics or aspects to an actual occasion. There is at this point a deep and telling inconsistency in his work in this regard. One may read the system and, owing to its systematic character, remain not quite cognizant of this fact. But one cannot have a sense for the variety of living cultures following this model and remain unaware of the difficulty. This is a difficulty which Marx, with all of his concern to avoid ideology, failed adequately to perceive and avoid.

5. First Philosophy and the Particular Sciences

My intention in the foregoing has been to show absolute truth to be amenable and complementary to cultural particularity and cultural relativity. Implicated with this intention has been a relativizing of theoretical knowledge by rendering it subordinate to absolute truth, i.e., the complete fact and its sub-facts. Within this formulation all knowledge cast in the language of relations between actual occasions must necessarily be theoretical, and subject to prediction and future

---

[31] See Essay I, §3, par. 1 (p. 9f); Essay II, §5 (pp. 39f); Essay III, §2 (pp. 47f); and in SC, pp. 219f, 224, 237, 388, 421, 463f, 466, 474, and 477f.

verification persuant of the hypothetico-deductive method. This is in the final analysis derived knowledge, in the sense that it is worked up on the basis of abstractions derived from data of perished occasions. What passes for theoretical "knowledge" may in some degree contribute to the concretization of absolute knowledge in the manner suggested in §3, apart from a theory in its entirety being concretized. For the most part it remains, notwithstanding, in the shadow land of the more or less probable, and of the vaguely true and perhaps vaguely untrue, to be combined and recombined with other theories contributing to that construct called "nature as a permanent possibility of experience", which, however hypothetical, can nonetheless, as potential, have a kind of existence of its own so long as no ontological status is claimed for it and so long as the terminology associated with it is made amenable to generic discriminations that are concretized within actual occasions.

With the foregoing methodological statement is thus implicated a clearcut distinction between the role of first philosophy in going about the demanding work of explicating relevant types of concretely actual occasions, the complete fact and its sub-facts, discrimination by discrimination, on the one hand, and that of the particular sciences and of the theory of science (*Wissenschaftstheorie*) in developing theories derived by reconstruction of the abstract data left by perished occasions and justifying these theories by the hypothetico-deductive method (necessarily involving the prognostication of the future as one aspect), on the other. So long as this distinction is observed, along with its implicated division of labor, a dialectical exposition will not prognosticate the future, although it may report, among other things, prognostications that have been made and the manner and degree to which these have been fulfilled in concrete fact. The way is thus opened for dialectic as such to be open not merely to a fourth way of receiving Marx-Engels (requested by the President of Senegal) but to any number of ways. This is because insofar as philosophy is to involve itself with the prediction of the future, this will be a role for second philosophy, and it is the business of the particular sciences, primarily sociology, economics, and political science, as I should suppose, guided by the course of self-consciousness as such in the relevant culture, to lead the way. This leading should be by a method that is aware of concreteness and of the fact that these sciences operate most properly with abstractions, completely free of dialectical dogma projected upon the future. Marx of course overstepped this line, or was more or less oblivious to it and, except for feeling a need for philosophical justification for his historical-economic determinism, remained primarily on

5. First Philosophy and the Particular Sciences   299

the side of the particular sciences.

To understand this division of labor is to understand how first philosophy can approach the ideal of being theory-free and stand more or less sharply distinguished from all disciplines concerned primarily with theory.

The prognostication of the future that is a proper part of the particular sciences, if it takes place at all, must take place within actual occasions, seeing that on the present account nothing at all takes place outside of such. It seems therefore well to indicate in closing how this can be commensurable and distinguishable from the anticipation of the future that gets itself concretized within the same occasion.

To be noted is that an actual occasion contains history as actual (*Wirkungsgeschichte*) — as the record of its causal past selectively valued and appropriated — within itself. By virtue of having this actual past within itself it can project a future that is in some degree commensurate, i.e., that fulfills the past as it receives it. Let the three figures following — each, read from left to right, represents a phase of the process of concrescence — be taken as suggestive of the manner and degree in which that future is actualized. The first figure indicates a commensurability of "past" in the special sense of history as actual within the present (not to be confused with memory, which postulates the past *as past,* i.e., as something that was, in occasions

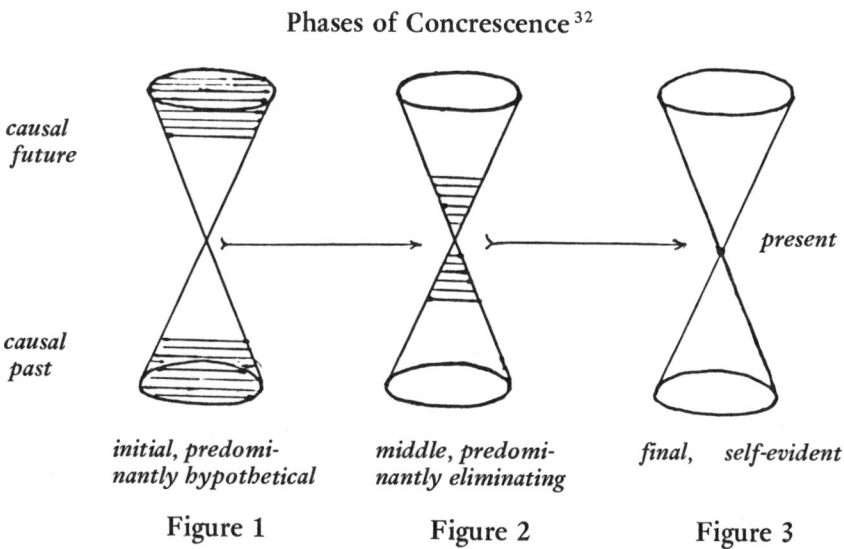

Phases of Concrescence [32]

causal future

causal past

present

initial, predominantly hypothetical

middle, predominantly eliminating

final, self-evident

Figure 1   **Figure 2**   **Figure 3**

that have perished) and "future" in the special sense of a projection of the fulfillment of possibilities intrinsic to this "past". Figure 2 shows past and anticipated fulfillment rendered less remote with respect to time differential and also more nearly commensurate through mediation (Hegel and — if rarely — Whitehead) or positive and negative prehension (Whitehead) with respect to content. Figure 3 shows the point of full concrescence achieved, a point into which past and future have been condensed, which lies beyond temporality and is construable only in actual time or, to express the matter more concretely, only in the space-time system of the occasion itself.

This being the case, all hypothetical thinking, including the disciplined prognostication of the future on the part of the particular sciences, must take place within the early phases of concrescence and not, or not appreciably, in the final phase. In other words, where theory contributes to the concrescence of an actual occasion, it is gradually eliminated throughout the course of concrescence and totally absent from the unity and wholeness of discriminations that contstitutes the fact and its sub-facts at full concrescence.[33] Nonetheless, as an aspect of the determining interior of the occasion, it is _remembered_.

---

[32] What are shown here as "Phases of Concrescence" is an adaptation from my "The Throb of Existence" figure from SC, Figure 5, p. 483.

[33] So long as we are rendering a report of the process from an internal perspective, i.e., in *spek. Sätzen,* these earlier phases will necessarily be construed as constituted by sub-triads of later phases and finally of the final phase, it is true. Even so, the distinction I have drawn stands up, because the enhancement of detail implicated with the increment of discriminations gained by the recognition of this principle of inclusion does not add to the content. This pertains to discriminations over and above such as are minimally required to constitute self-consciousness, an essential attribute of a *concretely* actual, as opposed to a merely *hypothetically* actual, occasion, which I refer to as an event.

That the earlier phases may be construed as sub-triads of later phases is rendered consistent with negative prehension by virtue of the fact that contrasts undergo alteration throughout the process, an upshot of which is that, strictly speaking, the discriminations yielded by an analysis-synthesis of an actual occasion that is directed toward exhibiting the basis of its self-evidence as a completed and closed system are all constitutive of the final phase of concrescence (the culmination of the process whereby external relations are rendered internal), in which alterations resultant from negative prehension have been effected.

See p. 309, n. 1.

XIV

THE WHOLE THAT IS THE CONTEXT OF MEANING*

I suppose there is no proposition concerning which it would be easier to win a consensus than one affirming that meaning is contextual in character: it comes in wholes. It is when we characterize the sort of whole to which we should appeal that problems, and with these the ontological predispositions that divide us, make their appearance.

An inquiry into the meaning of life or the meaning of history, if we regard these categories as inclusive, must appeal to a whole of commensurate inclusiveness. Even if it is the meaning of a particular action or event that is of interest, this is to be found or made manifest within an inclusive context. To paraphrase one of the more familiar utterances of Hegel, "The truth of meaning is the whole."

By a selective appropriation of Hegel's concept of "the whole" supplemented by some aspects of Whitehead's philosophy of nature and, more particularly, of his concept of an actual occasion, I shall propose in outline a concept of "the whole" as a context for meaning. In addition to effectively meeting the criticism by Feuerbach and Marx to the effect that Hegel does not do justice to nature, the concept I shall propose is intended to reflect something of Whitehead's assimilation of the Einsteinian revolution in modern physics, as well as Whitehead's own contribution to relativity theory. In this way the formulation is intended to go somewhat beyond what Hegel, Feuerbach, or Marx might be expected to have anticipated.

A recent discussion of Marx's reception and further development

---

* This paper was initially invited by Janusz Kuczyński for a volume to be devoted to the theme, *The Meaning of Life — The Meaning of History*, that was to be published under the sponsorship of the Polish academy of Science with support from UNESCO. The appearance of the volume having been long delayed, I have requested permission for it to appear here.
I wish to thank Arnór Hannibalsson for a detailed and thoughtful criticism of a late version of it, that assisted me to gain clarity at a few points.

of Feuerbach's critique of Hegel by Andrew N. Woznicki provides the immediate context for my reference to this critique. What has especially interested me is the manner in which Woznicki finds Marx to anticipate the integration of the social reality of man with nature which, correctly understood, must be integral with human nature.

> "Natural science will in time incorporate into itself the science of man, just as the science of man will incorporate into itself natural science: there will be one science."[1] In a word, for Marx "The *social* reality of man, and *human* natural science, or the **natural science of man**, are identical terms."[2]

The whole that I propose as the context of meaning resembles that of Hegel in several ways that I will now list. My way of stating some of these points is in anticipation of what I shall be drawing from Whitehead.

1) "The whole" is concretely actual and inclusive of all that is concretely actual. It is thus in principle unlimited — hence absolute — it being impossible for it to be rendered relative to anything outside of itself.

2) What is to be emphasized in the conception of this whole is not, however, its inclusion of all spacial-temporal relations that might hypothetically be supposed to be actual, but that it is a wholeness of concrete discriminations, including, to be sure, that of (concrete) space-time.

ASIDE: I must here avert the somewhat complex issue concerning "how much" of "the physical universe" may be concretized within the whole that is the context of meaning, to concern myself with what is sufficiently proximate within such a whole to contribute discriminations to it, grasped as such, i.e., grasped as mediating processes.

3) The concrete actuality of this whole consists in that within it substance and subject (in the sense of a self-conscious subject) are one, each forming an accent within an identity of meaning inclusive of both.[3] Thus to speak of a subject-independent actuality within

---

[1] *Karl Marx/Frederich Engels Collected Works,* New York, International Publishers, 1975; "Economic and Philosophic Manuscripts of 1844", III, p. 304.

[2] *Ibid.,* p. 35. Cf. also "The German Ideology", V. p. 35. The quote in its entirety is from Andrew N. Woznicki, "Marx on Religious Alienation", in, *Dialectics and Humanism,* 1981, No. 1, pp. 64f.

[3] The subject and predicate of a speculative (or philosophical) proposition on Hegel's account are each accents within an identity — in the present context the whole of meaning — inclusive of both. In this connection, the following statement needs to be considered within its context:

this frame of reference would be to refer to something hypothetical or possible — perhaps to what the empiricists have often referred to as "nature as a permanent possibility of experience" — that can have no status in actuality. Thus the (contextual) meaning of my life and the meaning of the world present for me at a given place and time, e.g., as nature and history,[4] are not ultimately separate things or beings — although they may be provisionally conceived so for purposes that might be served by abstraction — but inextricably intertwined.[5] Each is what it is only in relation to the other, even as space and time are actual only in relation, i.e., as they are being discriminated (within the context of other discriminations constitutive of the occasion$_h$), as space-time.

4) My reference in the above and following to *"the* whole" is warranted by the consideration that it is in principle not possible that a human individual — by which expression I mean a self-conscious subject within a concrete actuality inclusive of all that is actual — should *in actuality* take up a perspective outside of that whole. This is not intended to deny that we may with justification hypothesize the existence of a plurality of such wholes, as there have been a plurality of historical occasions, each containing a self-conscious subject in some way and degree actualizing freedom. It is rather to prepare the way for drawing a sharp line of distinction between what is concretely, and what (as abstract) is merely hypothetically, actual.

ASIDE: I shall subsequently refer to such wholes, viewed from a hypothetical (as distinct from a privileged, internal) perspective as a plurality, as "concretely actual occasions$_h$" or for short, "actual occasions$_h$", or simply, "occasions$_h$". Since the term "actual occasion" is Whitehead's, I have appended an "$_h$" to indicate that, insofar as the singular case is concerned, in all principal respects it is a Hegelianized actual occasion that I have in view.

An occasion$_h$ as viewed hypothetically, i.e., as one *among a plurality of such,*

"Die Form des Satzes ist die Erscheinung des bestimmten Sinnes oder der Akzent, der seine Erfüllung unterscheidet; daß aber das Prädikat die Substanz ausdrückt und das Subjekt selbst ins Allgemeine fällt, ist die *Einheit,* worin jener Akzent verklingt." G. W. F. Hegel, *Phänomenologie des Geistes,* Hoffmeister Edition, Hamburg: Meiner, 1952, p. 51.

In my appropriation of this insight, which I take to have absolutely central importance with respect to Hegel's conception and practice of dialectic, by according consistent emphasis to the *process* of mediation as the subject and predicate of a *concrete* proposition (whether immanent in nature or explicitly expressed), the discrimination between the two is preserved within their identity rather than being done away with, as though every accent (and every discrimination) were to vanish.

[4] "History in general is therefore the development of Spirit in *Time* as Nature is the development of the Idea in *Space."* Hegel, *Phil. of Hist.,* p. 72.

[5] As Gert Hummel aptly puts it, "We ourselves are always the world too." In: "Recognition — Reality — Meaning", *Dialectics and Humanism,* 1981, No. 2, p. 75.

shares with Whitehead's actual occasion the characteristic of being a purely hypothetical entity. This is to say, what can be "known" of an actual occasion from this perspective is something derived, an element of abstract thought, following upon the perishing of the occasion, the "knower" being the subject of a successor occasion. This is even though a singular occasion$_h$ shares the character of self-evidence (self-certainty, i.e., concrete actuality speaking for itself) attributable to Hegel's absolute whole, inclusive of all that is actual and known with certainty from an internal (actual) perspective. A plurality of occasions$_h$ cannot as such be concretized, but only as a single occasion$_h$.[6]

5) Concrete actuality is a *process* of the mediation of opposites, ontologically determined as such within, or as, the process, that culminates in the identity referred to under point 3.

6) Thus dialectic is not merely a method of exposition — a mere stage play *about* the world — but actuality itself in conscrescence, an identity of being and thought, even as the two are being discriminated.[7]

---

[6] I maintain this distinction between the hypothetical and actual perspectives to be crucial, also for understanding Hegel, who by his procedure in the explication of such matters has posed an impass for his readers. This is in part because he always moves from the abstract toward the concrete in his dialectical expositions, even while recognizing the priority of concreteness, i.e., that *nothing* is prior to the whole that is the context of meaning, even in the case in which this whole presents itself as relatively undetermined, its constitutive discriminations being for the most part merely implicit.

It will be noted that Whitehead's metaphysics — which I have sometimes portrayed as a more or less inflated theory of science (see Essay III, pp. 60f) — has most to offer in the area of theory and least original to say in the area of the phenomenological analysis of concrete actuality, with which Hegel more or less exclusively occupied himself. Thus, the doctrine of the perishing of an actual occasion, as in the case of his concept of the inheritance of data from one occasion to another, belongs to the picture language of theoretical constructs that, at least as such, can never be concretized. This is simply to repeat in other words the truism that I can never experience my own death, either following an occasion$_h$'s peaking in self-certainty — which (following a suggestion from Whitehead) might be very roughly estimated in conventional temporal terms as occurring at an average rate of ca. twenty times per second — or as the termination of the series (or "society") of such constitutive of my life span. Nor can I experience my own birth, except perhaps in some way and degree that lies deep within the illumination in self-certainty in which an occasion$_h$ climaxes, largely hidden from view. That I cannot experience my own birth or death accounts for the fact that I am in want of a direct awareness of discontinuity between occasions$_h$ successively peaking in self-certainty, and that what I experience is rather a "flow of consciousness" and a world in a more or less steady state of *change*.

For further developments of this theme, see Essay V, in which I criticize the Peircean form of pragmatism as being less a philosophy than a theory of the particular sciences.

[7] I find Gert Hummel's statement that "...deep down past, present and future merge into one" (op. cit., p. 75) of interest. Within the present perspective past and future spend themselves into the present of an actual occasion$_h$ as it progresses toward full conscrescence. This is not, however, as though the present as such might be concretely grasped except as an aspect, i.e., within the context of, the occasion$_h$, i.e., most "proximately", if we consider the matter with regard to dialectically proximate categories, within the context of past and future converging, as it were, through mediation, to become the actualized present. What is

7) This process may be considered with respect to subject and substance — its most fundamental and inclusive constitutive discrimination — alone, in mediation, or as a plurality of constitutive discriminations. which may most readily be conceived as complexly contained within this one.

8) A dialectical *exposition* of concrete actuality takes place "after the concrete — that is wholistic — fact", that is, after the self-certainty of reason *of which it is a report or reconstruction.* ("The Owl of Minerva flies only at night".) This is although a kind of retracing of the mediations that contribute to the unity and wholeness of the occasion$_h$ through a second reflection, to account for its character as self-certain, is in principle possible.

ASIDE: Insofar as such a retracing of discriminations constitutive of an occasion$_h$ can have a bearing upon the character of self-consciousness, this must be through a cumulative effect upon occasions$_h$ that "inherit" and reconcretize the abstract data of occasions$_h$ that have perished, which thereby undergo change through being rendered actual within new wholes.[8]

9) A dialectical account of an actual occasion is an account of all of the discriminations needful for the explanation of its self-containedness and its resulting self-certainty, otherwise explainable by the circumstance that it stands presuppositionless, needing no conceptuality outside of itself to render it explicit or to explicate it.

ASIDE: How detailed such an account must be will depend upon the totality of constitutive discriminations that present themselves as self-evident.

10) A discrimination is not abstractable from its discriminated aspects, which is to say that, considered out of context and in abstraction from the unity and wholeness of the occasion, its concreteness is lost and it becomes merely generic and a piece of common language. Thus it ceases to have a concretely universal role

---

concretely grasped is the process of becoming of this discrimination (as one member within the context of a unity and wholeness of discriminations, including, most assuredly, the discrimination space-time). This notion renders it unnecessary to appeal to such equivocating notions as that of a "spacious present". On the present view such a "spacious present" becomes a stage on the way of the mediation of the past and future prior to full concrescence, upon the attainment of which they are fully mediated to form a present that has lost its spaciousness and that, regarded in itself and apart from its process of becoming, is a mere abstraction.

[8] The retracing of the mediations that contribute to the unity and wholeness of an occasion$_h$ referred to under point 8 is possible because the same identical discrimination may first be known as a lived process of concrescence and subsequently as an abstract and hence hypothetical entity. That the identity of a discrimination survives the perishing of the occasion$_h$ that is first grasped as living is the single (but I believe quite strong) thread upon which hangs the possibility of the pursuit of first philosophy as a science.

throughout the occasion and becomes a merely abstract universal, i.e., something derivative, of possible use in telling *a story about* actuality, but not a concrete actuality speaking for itself.

I shall not here attempt to justify these points as, excepting the asides, attributable to Hegel, although I believe that, given sufficient space, a reasonably good case might be made out for each of them, if perhaps not always one that would unambiguously prevail against contending interpretations.

To render point 10 above clear and consistent I must appeal to Whitehead's concept of the perishing of an actual occasion, which he derived by analogy to the brief duration of an electro-magnetic event formed within a field of forces. Also an actual occasion$_h$, upon peaking in self-certainty, perishes, to provide abstract data for concrescence within successor occasions$_h$. Self-certainty pertains here to the entirety of the occasion$_h$, i.e., its process of concrescence, and not merely to its climactic result, which considered alone would be an abstraction.

In this way the Hegelian absolute, in the concrescence of which nature and history as accents in identity within the substance of the self-conscious subject are created anew — as is the subject itself — by virtue of its mortality cannot become overbearing by being made to seem to outlive its concreteness. In addition, the introduction of the notion of perishing from Whitehead renders it possible both to say that I am historically determined and at the same time to account for nature here and now as a necessary aspect of each and every historical determination as a concrescence of freedom. In addition, nature as concrete is seen as "historical" through and through and thus as intrinsically evolutionary in character, consistent with Hegel's (pre-Darwinian!) conclusion at the end of the *Phän.*, where the freedom of the subject passes over into nature. In this respect, as well, we seem to have been brought very near to a position consistent with Hegel's dictum that "History…is the development of Spirit in ***Time*** as Nature is the development of the Idea in ***Space***" apart from speaking of the two as separate entities, as though purely temporal relations could be real apart from being at the same time spatial, or purely spatial relations apart from being also time determined, a view that both Feuerbach and Marx at times seem mistakenly (if indirectly) to be attributing to Hegel. This might well have contributed to a tendency to conclude over-hastily that Hegel, in the *Aufhebung* of Nature, simply ceased to have regard for it. This interpretation, although deeply untrue to Hegel, lends itself readily to propagation, seeing that it can appeal to one of the ordinary meanings of "*auf-*

heben" and related terms.

The hope for, and the possibility of, a scientific first philosophy for the explication of what I propose as the whole that is the context of meaning seems to rest upon two basic assumptions which, when they are explicated with sufficient care, appear to lend themselves to being found self-evident. The first is that the truth is the whole — more specifically, that it is a concrete actual unity and wholeness of discriminations constitutive of an actual occasion$_h$ that includes within itself all that is actual, including history as actual within the present, i.e., *Wirkungsgeschichte.* The second is that dialectical mediations as the basic substrate of our experience and of being itself (in its becoming, and as an accent within an identity of being and becoming) may be directly perceived, conceived, and "intended". Of such lived (*erlebte*) discriminations as this and not-this, quality-quantity, self-other, form-content, lordship-bondage, and numberless others, many of which are less suitable for generic treatment, are constituted the very stuff of our beings-becomings. Such mediations are often uttered in authentically concrete statements that are simply true for the person who is fully present and in some way and degree "privileged" to the occasion within which they are uttered and of which they are constitutive.

I have previously portrayed the thus characterized whole that is the context of meaning as a throb of creation.[9] This follows from the concluion that actuality is process and, as such, has a beginning and an end. Meaning on this view is inherently concrete, a creation of the occasion$_h$. Nonetheless, it may "grow" from one occasion$_h$ to another, and is especially prone to do so within compatible "societies". Here we come upon a theme into which I cannot now enter, except to say that from the perspective here being portrayed the notion of such "societies" can be rendered more meaningful than I find possible on the basis of Whitehead's account, by virtue of being based upon the concept of an actual occasion$_h$ that has been conceptualized philosophically, i.e., been subjected to a *concretely specific — constitutive discrimination by constitutive discrimination* — analysis (and resynthesis) to render more fully explicit *for the abstract understanding* its capacity to speak for itself. More than this, the theory is expressed in a conceptuality proximate to the living occasions in which it was priorly concretized, having been prepared for this role by the analysis-synthesis (not of theories but) of discriminations proximate to the place of their birth and perishing.

---

[9] See TCMM.

308   Chap. XIV, The Whole that is the Context of Meaning

Creativity seems to lay claim to being the principal generic characteristic of meaning,[10] to be portrayed within a suitable proximity to particular occasions found to be "types" of relatively stable societies of occasions, making due allowance for creative novelty.[11]

---

[10] Janus Kuczyński writes "Creation — the supreme form of praxis and understanding — creates beings through constituting new senses and subsequently through their embodiment and realization" ("The Meaning/Sense of the Word...", *Dialectics and Humanism*, 1980, No. 1, p. 175). This might also be affirmed within the present frame of reference, along with Kuczyński's proposal that "Sense is above all a relational character", (p. 175) which he then goes on to portray as "a humanistic and rationalistic superstructure" (p. 177). I seem to differ most notably with Kuczyński where he finds meaning to be prior to language, construed in the following way:

"Language deforms man's contact with reality and the contents of linguistic expressions can and should remind of this fundamental contact. It is precisely for this reason that we shall demonstrate the fact that sense refers to deeper strata of being, hidden under the cover of everyday life: to creational praxis, essences of things, rules of development or finally, to the essence of beings and the essence of life as well as of universal history." (p. 170)

From the perspective herein proposed, it seems necessary *also* to make reference to a kind of primal language that speaks the truth with authority, at least within the context of a given fleeting occasion$_h$ or society of similar occasions$_h$. This I wish to maintain to be a proper and allowable fruit of RAtP. Kuczyński is perhaps not so very far from this position when he writes, "at the beginning was the word" (p. 170). I think that I may have hit upon a way of according meaning to this utterance that is more closely bound up with "authentic" language use than is possible on the basis of his account.

[11] See pp. 66ff. For a consideration of the idealistic dimension of the reconstruction of the concept of concreteness herein adumbrated, see Essay II.

XV

ON THE MODERATION OF SCEPTICISM
FIRST PHILOSOPHY AND THE PARTICULAR SCIENCES

1. Introduction

It is my intention in this essay to propose a strategy whereby the force of the ontological scepticism that haunts the present time may be moderated through a rehabilitation of the concept of absolute truth. Notwithstanding the presence among us of insistent Hegelians, the concept has been in difficulty for most professional philosophers at least since the enlightenment.[1] (This is supposing that something akin to this notion can be traced back to antiquity.) This fact stands in ludicrous contrast to the proliferation of knowledge in the 20th century — an I think unwarranted if understandable circumstance owing to a confusion of the methods appropriate, on the one hand, to the particular sciences and to the theories of the sciences and, on the other, to first philosophy. Accordingly, following the model provided by the former, it is today most frequently supposed that all truth ought to be regarded as relative, or that, strictly speaking, we have a right to refer to nothing more than opinion.

I shall be arguing that a theory of truth as relational implies a system of relations (1) which it ought to be possible to refer to as a whole, (2) which, as a whole, is absolute, and within which each part or aspect, considered in respect to its relations to all of the other parts or aspects, is also absolute, and (3) which is graspable, is in fact grasped, or, still better, it is *self-grasping*, as absolute, in some non-trivial sense. This absoluteness, and the fact that a certain wholeness of relations is grasped in, and as, self-consciousness, is evidenced by the self-certain character of consciousness, as such.

In making this broad claim I am of course not venturing beyond

---

[1] For a useful overview of modern scepticism, see Robert M. Lawson, "Mechanistic-Materialism and the Gesesis of Modern Scepticism". *Kinesis*, Fall, 1969.

Hegel's concept of concrete universality. What needs to be taken account of, following this understanding, however, is (1) that the system culminates in truth as a coherence of the whole, rather than merely being something that statically *is*. In other words, truth is something which, with actuality itself, *comes into* being. This is at least if we are portraying the situation from a temporal perspective. If we assume a native disposition to experience something as here and now true, this may give rise to a question as to how this truth can stand related to some future truth. This is especially in view of the circumstance that (2) a completed truth system would appear to contain no place for further development and, in this sense, no freedom. (3) These two considerations, regarded together, seem to require that the truth which is the whole be attributed a climactic, episodic character: such "occasions" of truth succeed one another in order, each arising, developing, and, upon being fully actualized (concretized), perishing. The intent is not to rule out the possibility of there being enduring, and possibly even eternal, truth, but to focus upon the here and now, not, however, in such a way as to exclude the past *as actual within the present.*

The treatment will of necessity be sketchy, so that it may well seem to give rise to more questions than it answers. I may hope, nonetheless, to convey the sense of a strategy that seems promising, and the importance of the objective of which will warrant the consideration of the reader.

2. Concretely Actual Occasions

Three characteristics of such successive wholes as those to which I have made reference, each of which, from the perspective of its time and place, is the truth which is the whole, cause me, in reminiscence of Whitehead, to designate them concretely actual occasions. To be noted parenthetically is that Whitehead's concept of an actual occasion was modeled upon the physical concept of an electro-magnetic event, and was proposed as a way of taking account both of general and special relativity in physical theory. (1) The first of the characteristics of these wholes is their process character: they are not so much actualized coherent wholes as wholes *in the course of being at once concretely actualized and rendered coherent.* (2) The second is that, upon achieving full concreteness, the throb of existence which is an actual occasion perishes; in other words, coherence once achieved is not sustained: by perishing, the absoluteness of the truth is saved from an absurd and inflated old age. (3) The third is that their process of concrescence is one in which opposites are mediated to become contrasts, the difference between polarities and contrasts consisting in that the relation between contrasts is intrinsic to their character, whereas in the case of opposites, it is only their being externally related that is yet rendered explicit. With an eye to Hegel, I shall prefer to refer to a contrast as discriminated elements and aspects, and to the discrimination which concretely defines this relation; the most basic principle, however, is the same.

My concretely actual occasion is most markedly distinguished from Whitehead's by three considerations: (1) The unity and wholeness of contrasts which constitute it (which I shall now refer to as discriminations) are explicitly maintained to be adequate to its explication, ultimately, to its character of being *self-explicating*. This characteristic of an actual occasion was referred to by Hegel as its presuppositionlessness, or affirmatively, as the self-certainty of reason. I refer to it as its self-evidence. Thus an actual occasion is self-evident owing to the consideration that it can be explicated by the exclusive use of discriminations, and terms concretely determined with reference to discriminations, intrinsic to istelf. (2) A particularly crucial discrimination with respect to this function of the concretely actual by virtue of which it is self-explicating, and one which it seems necessary to attribute to all concretely (and not merely hypothetically) actual occasions, is that between an understanding, interpreting subject and the world as present for this subject. Seeing that a discrimination is obviously not abstractable from its discriminated aspects apart from losing its character of being concrete, this means that both the subject and the world as present for the subject are internal to the occasion. Were its self-conscious subject not internal to an actual occasion, it could not possibly be self-evident, as indeed some occasion or other ever presents itself as being. (3) The understanding, interpreting subject being internal to an occasion, it will not seem strange that the occasion can in principle be made to yield to a phenomenological analysis-synthesis of its constitutive discriminations. The approach to this may be designated transcendental phenomenology, following to a significant degree Hegel's phenomenological method, but specifying this at points at which he would seem to have been less than fully explicit, in part because he was without a fully explicit concept of the perishing of an actual occasion, which on the present approach is considered to be an absolutely essential companion piece to his concept of presuppositionlessness.[2] It is at this point that I am in this paper embarking upon a

---

[2] This is to say, perishing is an essential companion piece to the concept of self-evidence *viewed within a hypothetical perspective*.

Perishing, as such, can on principle never be concretized. The only persons who will

necessary aspect of the strategy above reviewed (with the aim of the present treatment in view) which I have not previously treated in satisfactory detail; but I must first make brief reference to Hegel's philosophical proposition.

3. The Philosophical Proposition

Hegel's exposition of a concretely actual occasion is by a series of philosophical propositions (*Sätze,* which may be translated either proposition or judgment, depending upon the context.) The subject and predicate of a philosophical proposition, (in and) following upon their mediation, are accents within an identity inclusive of both. This identity, in other words, is a discriminated identity. It is achieved by "speculation", this being speculation that is inherent to the self-constitution of actuality, not to be confused with some

---

contest this are such as claim to have the capacity to experience their own death, and for present purposes I shall regard such as an exception. What I wish to affirm, then, is not that perishing is essential to self-evidence, as such, but merely that it seems to be a necessary companion piece to the *understanding* of the concept of self-evidence *viewed as an explanatory theory.* To maintain that it is essential to self-evidence as such would imply that the theory could never lend itself to being self-evident, i.e., to being concretized, which I wish heartily to deny. The upshot is that my Hegelian account of self-evidence, apart from appealing to an explicit concept of perishing, can, at least in principle, stand theory-free. The difficulty with such an account, however, is that it can appear incredible *to the understanding;* i.e., *despite the certainty of what it affirms, the understanding is left behind.* It is *the understanding* to which the theory of perishing lends an assist, even while self-evidence itself, i.e., self-evidence to *and as* reason (in its comprehensive character, i.e., as the self-comprehending of the living occasion) does not await this adjunct.

Once grasped, the concept of absolute knowledge poses less of a problem for a Hegelian than the *conveyance* of this notion, at first through such poor categories of the understanding as may lie at hand, to someone who has not undertaken the labor of secondary reflection. Typically a dialogue must *begin* with *the understanding* of one discrete sentence following another, each of which requires supplementary presuppositions. Ordinarily it approaches concreteness, in which the presuppositions have been transformed into explicit contextual meanings, only gradually and by stages, the ideal of concreteness being one in which a single utterance and finally a single word (or gesture) conveys the entirety of the shared occasion. See p. 16, n. 24.

It is being presupposed here that space-time is actual within, and only within, the lived occasion. As inclusive of all of the discriminations needful for its explication, an actual occasion is of course inclusive of space-time, and with this, of all spacial and temporal relations that are actual. I would remind the reader that the background out of which I have developed this notion, significantly enough, is what I refer to as the phenomenological dimension of Hegel's *System.* Hegel's *Phänomenologie des Geistes* is with respect to this issue strategically variant, in that here he has spirit appearing in time just so long as it does not grasp its pure Begriff. (See *Phän.*, p. 558 and the Preface to the present *Collection,* n. 3. In other words, in Hegel's *System* there is a basis for saying that time is concretely lived, i.e., as space-(nature)–time(history), which I believe to be closer to his matured intent and to the truth of occasions that I have lived, and it is this direction upon which I have been building. Also, see p. 145, n. 14, and p. 288.

3. The Philosophical Proposition 313

external sort of rumination or speculation in a "pre-critical"[3] sense. Any particular concretely actual identity is of course multiply discriminated, requiring a substantial number of philosophical propositions, each containing a subject and predicate mediated to an identity of meaning, to render its constitutive discriminations explicit. Hegel's system, oriented as it is toward the exposition of such more inclusive identities as include their understanding, interpreting subjects, here called concretely actual occasions, shorn of all commentary, consists of approximately 165 philosophical propositions, each at once the dialectical exposition of a discrimination and a specification of the discriminated aspects. Thus, for example, this/not-this, quality/quantity, space (as nature)/time (as history), and subject/substance are discriminations and each of the paired members is specified by the process of discrimination. Concrete actuality as well as thought is constituted, following Hegel's account, of discriminations determined as such by philosophical propositions (or judgments). Thus, following his account, dialectic is finally immanent within nature and history, and not merely within thought. Parenthetically, it may be noted that Whitehead later seems to emulate this disposition when he construes contrasts to be constitutive of actuality, quite aside from the consideration of whether they have arisen to explicit consciousness.

4. The Fact and What is After the Fact

A principal premise of this method employed in the analysis-synthesis of discriminations constitutive of an actual occasion is that when I synthesize the meanings of contrasting aspects of actuality in such a way as to exhibit their structure, this same fundamental structure may be presumed to be constitutive of these "same" (when generically considered) discriminations, as they function as constitutive of the concrete identities the self-evidence of which, or the presupposing of which, provided the existential basis for this exercise.

If Hegel reflected an awareness of the point here at issue in his generally precise expositions of method, he would seem not to have accorded it appropriate recognition. It is a point which follows from taking with complete seriousness, and indeed rendering norma-

---

[3] No reference to actual (historical) time [see p. 145, n. 14 (in context)] is here intended, the force of which is that allowance is made that also in the ancient world there were philosophers who were not, or not merely, pre-critical. Even so, the terms pre-critical and critical seem to me useful to suggest the drawing of a line between pre-historical and historical philosophy in something like the manner implicated in Hegel's use of the term "historical consciousness".

tive for purposes of interpretation, his pronouncements to the effect that the highest achievement of the dialectic is concreteness, and his having made the dialectic of spiritual individuality the final phase of a cumulative exposition.

For the statement at issue to be fully intelligible, it should be observed that any deliberately pursued analysis or synthesis of one or more discriminations presupposes certain concrete identities of fact or at least of meaning which present themselves with a self-evidence appropriate to their type. No one places everything in radical doubt at one time. When I entertain certain conceptions hypothetically, I either grasp some facts or other concretely or hold ideas of such before the mind which I presuppose unproblematically.

It would be a mistake to propose that discriminations constitutive of concretely evident facts can as such be under analysis at the same time that they are self-evidently given. This is although the two may be contiguous. That discriminations constitutive of concretely actual facts cannot as such be under analysis at the same time that they are self-evidently given is due to the fact that in its analysis a discrimination is abstracted, seeing that it is precisely what is concrete — a unity and integral wholeness of discriminations, which, when the occasion is subject to an analysis-synthesis, proves adequate to its explication — that is self-evident. This is to say, a concrete fact is self-evident, and the abstraction of a discrimination is after the fact. Now the abstraction may be so proximate to the fact that it follows as to allow of no doubt that its data were constitutive of the fact. This does not, however, alter the circumstance that under analysis it is no longer concrete but abstract. This is even more emphatically the case where the discriminated aspects of an abstracted discrimination are abstracted from one another, thus to constitute the terms of our ordinary language and aspects of things to which these terms are held to refer.

This is of course not to say that discriminations are not known in their integral unity — as though self-evidence awaited an analysis-synthesis or a "scientific" attitude or some sort, seeing that this kind of knowing is precisely in what self-evidence consists. Indeed, a particular discrimination may figure as a sufficiently prominent aspect of a given occasion that it is discernable in context, apart from abstraction. A fact being precisely a discriminated identity and known precisely as discriminated, it would be a mistake to suppose that it could be grasped apart from knowing or presupposing its particular constitutive discriminations.

Neither is the consideration that under analysis a discrimination is

4. The Fact and What is After the Fact 315

no longer concrete intended to suggest that the mediation process by which discriminations are constituted may not be felt or perceived. This is a point which should be sufficiently covered by noting that it is the mediation process which is actual,[4] the result of this process partaking of this actuality only while it is yet integral with it, and prior to being separated off from it by abstraction.

Before according further consideration to the founding mediations of thought and of actuality, however, I must give attention to the second (external) reflection[5] by which, through the analysis-synthesis of particular discriminations, the means is found for according a precise linear account of the concretely actual suited to the limitations of the understanding, which concretely actual we normally know as reason itself in its all-at-onceness, in the facticity of which it is constitutive and with which it is in fact identical. Such a linear account permits a concern for details which noramlly tend to pass unaccentuated or to be merely presupposed (filled in by the imagination) in the grasping of the concrete in its all-at-onceness.

5. After the Fact Reinactment

A word of caution is here in order: the concretely actual is not merely immediate, although it may at first be thought to be so when contrasted with its abstracted results. Rather, it is actual *only as being mediated*. Its analysis-synthesis after the fact is a *reminiscence* and a *reinactment* of this *being mediated*. First, by analysis we arrive at the contrasted elements or aspects in their discreteness which lie behind, or better, within, every synthesized meaning. Then we retraverse the synthesis in abstraction. In this way, we arrive at categorial conditions to account for the possibility of the concretely actual, the fact and its sub-facts.

Every concretely actual occasion, viewed as a single identity and as a fact, also contains sub-identities and sub-facts, each of which is likewise constituted by discriminations and performs a necessary and unique role within the occasion, determining it to be the occasion that it is. In other words each sub-identity and sub-fact is concretely universal in its function throughout the occasion regarded in its entirety. Each sub-fact, and not merely the identity which is the occa-

---

[4] Here in view is an analogue to Whitehead's perception in the mode of causal efficacy; this can be a "pure mode", however (to use his term), only as abstracted from the identities of which it is an aspect. See pp. 54f.

[5] Refer to pp. 175f: §7, esp. nn. 7 and 7a.

sion as a whole, is thus contextually specified, i.e., the truth of the whole, and hence absolute, in its season. Fact and sub-fact alike, moreover, are multiply discriminated. Such a concept of a concrete fact is commensurate with the confidence we are natively disposed to place in facts.

If Hegel's statements to the effect that the final result of the dialectic is concrete actuality are taken at their face value, an account of the relation between dialectic immanent within concrete actuality and dialectic as philosophically practiced something like that contained within the foregoing seems required. This is not to suggest that he pursued the direction to which this leads. To this I add two additional remarks.

6. Some Related Considerations

Dialectic as a philosophical discipline is guided in its recapitulation of the process of mediation which lies intrinsic to the fact by the feeling or perception of the latter. Indeed a process of recollection is at work here, the final result of which is a mediation of what is internal to the fact and the externality of the recapitulation. This process of recollection indeed qualifies the transcendental character of categorial conditions to account for the possibility of the fact. This qualification, however, does not render the notion of this transcendental character superfluous, but, rather, places it within the framework of a dialectic within which it is contained as a moment, *this being a moment, however, which is sublated within every occasion and within every concrete fact and sub-fact.*

A matter which has complicated the understanding of the foregoing considerations is bound up with one of Hegel's great innovations. To state this in language most suitable to the present context, this is his attempt to understand the discriminations constitutive of his rendition of Schelling's identity *also* as unfolding themselves in series to constitute history. The word *"also"* in the preceding sentence is absolutely crucial, seeing that this historical turn should not be understood as an abandonment of the notion that the knowing consciousness that is a here and now actuality at a given point in history is constituted by less than the full complement of discriminations present in their all-at-onceness as constitutive of concrete actuality. This is although some of these discriminations at a given point in the developmental process that is history may as yet be only implicit.

If the foregoing account is to be rendered commensurable with some essential aspects of this notion of historical unfoldment, it seems necessary to specify that a discrimination, generically viewed (i.e., viewed as a *type* with respect to its role within a plurality of actual occasions), before it can be successively constitutive of concrete identities which I grasp as such, must in some sense have been lived through historically. What is here in view may readily be exemplified by reference to Hegel's discrimination of Lordship and Bondage, although I suspect it may pertain equally in the case of discriminations which arise for us less "dramatically". The Bondsman achieves the higher self-directed consciousness of the Lord through negation, i.e., anxiety in the face of death. Subsequent to this the discrimination will be constitutive of every occasion within the life cycle of the individual who has undergone this *Erlebnis,* in a manner analogous to Whitehead's account of the data resulting from one occasion that has perished being inherited by another. Although living through the mediation of a discrimination, whereby it for the first time becomes constitutive of facticity for a given individual, undeniably involves its arising to self-consciousness accentuated as something freshly discovered, this does not imply that it is to be necessarily recapitulated in each and every analysis-synthesis for the understanding. Something *roughly* similar to Hegel's distinction between ordinary and philosophical consciousness is here in view.

7. The Variance of Occasions

In appearing much of the time to suppose that all occasions are constituted by precisely the same totality of discriminations and by not having sufficiently observed the distinction between concrete and generic discriminations, Hegel would seem to have gone beyond the evidence and departed from the strictness of his critical methodology and indeed to have erred. Caution suggests that allowance should be made for the following three possibilities, for which he would appear not to have allowed: There would seem to be no reason for ruling out the possibility (1) that the discriminations constitutive of different occasions might not be precisely the same, (2) that a discrimination, once actualized, does not necessarily remain actual; or, in language more suitable to the present context, is not necessarily reconcretized in every subsequent occasion, or (3) that novel discriminations arise.[6] These possibilities may be admitted apart from undermining in the least the basic methodological principles that, with

---

[6] For my fourfold typology of discriminations, viewed with regard to their range of abstract universality see esp. pp. 296f, 47f, 23f, 9f; or SC, pp. 419-22.

respect to any given occasion, the concretely actual contains all of the discriminations needful for its explication and that the discriminations constitutive of an actual occasion are in principle available to analysis-synthesis in philosophical propositions. To be noted is that no limit is placed upon the number of discriminations which may be constitutive of a given occasion or the range of (abstract) universality a given discrimination may be found to have throughout any given series (or epoch) of occasions. Nor does the possibility of explicating the self-evidence of an occasion any less rest with the possibility of rendering an exhaustive account of its constitutive discriminations,[7] any one of which plays an essential role in the occasion to the constitution of which it contributes.

The variety of discriminations accorded dialectical exposition within Hegel's system — many of which, generically regarded, more or less adequately approximate discriminations being concretized today — provides a fair idea as to the type of undertaking here in view. The according of a place to discriminations to which (abstract) universality throughout the plurality of occasions cannot be attributed, to novel discriminations, and the proposal that the number of discriminations which may be found to be constitutive of a particular occasion cannot be determined in advance of its analysis-synthesis, all seem to distinguish the resulting position from that of Hegel, who failed to work out fully the pluralistic dimension of his thought implicated with the understanding of individuality as the highest achievement of his dialectic.

8. Ideal Execution and Practice

Three considerations are to be noted which qualify the ideal rigor with which the analysis-synthesis of an actual occasion can be pursued. (1) A practical result of the briefness of duration of a single occasion — a consideration of which Hegel was certainly not entirely unaware, but which goes relatively undeveloped within his conceptuality — is that what is subject to analysis-synthesis is an occasion taken to be *typical* of some relevant epoch of occasions, such as a cultural epoch, the epoch constituted by the life-cycle of a human individual within a given culture from birth to death, or the epoch constituted by a particular act. (2) There is an intrinsic difficulty associated with the analysis-synthesis of a novel discrimination, in which art can play a crucial role. (3) Yet another consideration con-

---

[7] For further considerations of the problematic of an "exhaustive" account, see p. 69, n. 19 and p. 300, n. 32 in their respective contexts.

sists in that the results of an analysis-synthesis of an actual occasion must of necessity be reported in language abstracted from occasions which have perished — which may be only more or less adequate to the presently actual —, a language which may add to efficiency of expression at the cost of the ideal precision intrinsic to concrete language. By concrete language I mean language which arises to consciousness as facts speaking for themselves. This is language which is an accent within an identity of language and actuality, this discrimination being one of those constitutive of a concretely actual fact. With regard to this language it may as truly be said, "in the beginning was the word" as "in the beginning was actuality, i.e., the fact and its sub-facts". Concrete language may alternatively be viewed as actuality bodying forth.

If these considerations point to a limit respecting the possibility of in practice carrying through an ideally complete analysis-synthesis of the discriminations constitutive of an actual occasion, at least in some cases, the idea and the ideal of such an undertaking, in principle possible and approximated in practice (sometimes, I am persuaded, in the case of occasions in which there is no dissemblance, very closely approximated), are not on this account obscured from view.

9. Generic and Concrete Discriminations

The emphasis upon the difference between occasions construed in the foregoing with respect to their constitutive discriminations points toward the centrality of the distinction between concrete and generic discriminations. This is most readily illustrated by reference to the discrimination space-time. If I turn my head from left to right there can be no question but that the concrete spatio-temporal relations constitutive of the second concrete occasion, in which the view to the right figures, will be different than those constitutive of the first, in which the view to the left figures. (This is assuming that the visual modality of perception is dominant.) The discrimination, as concrete, is in both cases unabstractable from the discriminated aspects (in the relation between which it consists) as well as from other discriminations constitutive of the respective occasion. Yet the two occasions may alike be characterized as being constituted by the discrimination space-time, generically construed, i.e., in terms of its abstractly universal characteristics. In other words, they may be characterized in terms of the same general *type* of discrimination.

There are certainly a goodly number of discriminations which, generically considered, are, so far as we may judge, abstractly universal to all occasions. Hegel called our attention to many of these, and thought some to be universal which may well not be. Such probably constitute the minimal conditions to account for the possibility of experience and actuality, this statement being qualified, however, by two considerations. (1) In the case of every single occasion, the categories which function transcendentally to bring it about are as such sublated in its concretization. (2) Where discriminations additional to these are constitutive of an occasion, these will be equally essential to the concrete universality of the occasion and its sub-aspects and sub-facts.

10. Generalizations and Hypothetical Thinking

The analysis-synthesis of concreteness stands as distinguished from hypothetical thinking by virtue of avoiding generalizations construed as pertaining within more than the 'one'[8] occasion that may at any point in temporal succession be actual. Whitehead's metaphysics is a search for ultimate generalizations. Insofar as the reference is to generalizations with respect to the plurality of actual occasions, and not merely to generalizations within the occasion presently actual for a given individual, this is the last thing a first philosophy ought to aim to be. To generalize with respect to the plurality of actual occasions is inevitably to speak hypothetically, seeing that no one has ever taken up a position outside of that some one concretely actual occasion which at a given instant is constitutive of himself and his world, as discriminated aspects. This is seeing that every occasion includes within it all that from its perspective is actual.

11. The Inside and Outside Perspectives

Theories are expressed in the language of the relations **between** actual occasions, an entirely hypothetical perspective. The inside (actual) perspective is necessarily that from which the explication of concrete actuality is alone possible. To construe the matter otherwise would be to confuse the roles of first philosophy in its explication of concreteness in philosophical propositions with that of one or more of the particular sciences (and with the theory of science), which are most centrally concerned with the construction of theories on the basis of selected types of abstractions from concrete facts, and which must be content to presuppose the latter in their changing

---

[8] Following my intended usage, "one" with reference to the occasion that is actual, by virtue of setting this occasion off from others imports a hypothetical perspective. The use of single quotes is to indicate that my usage is metaphorical.

characters. Otherwise stated, the various particular sciences proceed on the basis of certain assumptions about concrete facts and operate with abstractions from them, which are subsumed under hypotheses and theories. For this purpose an external (hypothetical) perspective serves them well. Theoreticians of various sciences are likewise preoccupied with theories, with the analysis and comparison of them with an eye to seeing what they import. Here as well an external perspective is right and necessary. To first philosophy, however, falls the quite different task of rendering an explication of concrete facts and the characters of particular concrete facts, which these and other sciences presuppose, and this requires an internal perspective, apart from which there is no going beyond theory to what is being concretized as present fact. When the attempt is made to undertake this latter task from an external (hypothetical) perspective, the result, so clearly illustrated by Whitehead in his metaphysics, is neither fish nor fowl but a more or less inflated theory of science (*Wissenschaftstheorie*) that fulfills the requirement of methodological rigor appropriate to neither mode of inquiry. Its results, taken as they stand and unaided by reinterpretation, must finally be relegated to the limbo of pre-critical rumination and to the shadow-land of theory, seeing that they can have no more stability than the particular theories that are selected for inflation into metaphysical generalizations.

12. Abstractly Universal Discriminations

It may be argued, of course, that the concrete facts for the explication of which first philosophy is responsible vary, as well, and that in a process world the analysis of one fact complex does not suffice to present us with the essence of another, on which account a similarly pervasive relativity obtains here. Up to a point all of this is true, and this is a very important truth, on which account we are reminded that the explication of concreteness is in principle a never-ending task, the fact that it comes in discrete wholes notwithstanding. An important characteristic of facticity, however, sets a certain relevant limit to the poignancy of the criticism. Certain discriminations, generically considered, appear to be (abstractly) universal throughout all actual occasions, and additional ones as well appear to be universal at least within the present cosmic epoch. With reference to the first group, we seem unable, for example, to conceive of a single fact not constituted by space/time, quality/quantity, form/content, structure/function, individual/community, and subject/object. And there are many more discriminations which are at least relatively stable, in the sense that they tend to be concretized anew within each actual occasion.

If there are eternal truths, an issue upon which I shall not here enter, these must, following the present account, be ultimately traceable to discriminations, viewed as forms of becoming, which prove to be (abstractly) universal to all actual occasions.

13. Solipsism

That the internal perspective of an actual occasion creates itself through intercourse with an external world (which, however, is no less internal to it than the subject), is what secures its abstract universality for other subjects (the concrete worlds of two proximate subjects can have much in common), even though, strictly speaking, it is concretely universal only for one (for surely, e.g., the space-time constitutive of the subject and its world of one occasion are not that of any other) and for only its brief temporal moment of existence at that. But space-time is not unique in its relativity and in the fact that its character as concrete and as generic is ever to be distinguished.

It might be correctly construed from the foregoing that the solipsistic predicament is on this view never completely overcome. Indeed, strictly speaking, the differences between particular individuals constituted within different occasions rests in part upon this very fact. Its overcoming is most clearly approached in authentic speaking, in which the conventional character of language gives way to its concreteness, i.e., contrasting subjects and predicates being mediated in the act of speaking, and in relations between two persons in which knowing has means which most decisively exceed the limits of ordinary words, as in the intimacy of affection and love. It is in such circumstances, perhaps, that words which may have been merely conventional most readily lend themselves to becoming live with meaning and concrete: *flesh, and spirit as well.*

14. History as Actual within the Present

Reference was made in the above to the actual and hypothetical perspectives, the inside and the outside perspectives "upon" actual occasions. Only insofar as past occasions are actual within the present occasion are they concretely, and not merely hypothetically, actual at all. That they are rendered actual within present occasions as actual history, however, is an absolutely essential aspect of the knowledge of facts in their concreteness. Indeed, apart from their historical depth, concrete facts could not maintain the authority over us which they in fact do. I mention this extremely important consideration, which I have treated elsewhere, only in passing, although it in some way qualifies much that I have said.[9]

15. Abstraction in Philosophy and in the Particular Sciences

It is the inside perspective from which the analysis-synthesis of discriminations must ultimately be begun and terminated, discrimination by discrimination, omitting none, a matter which Hegel for the most part understood very well. The analysis-synthesis of an occasion necessarily involves abstraction, as has been noted; this operation, however, is within the early phases of concrescence of occasions subsequent to the one under investigation. Abstraction undertaken in the course of providing an analysis-synthesis of concreteness falls within the province of the methodology of first philosophy. So long as the abstractive process is ultimately viewed from the perspective of the occasion at full concrescence, as indeed it must be if it is a part of the analysis-synthesis of discriminations which recapitulate the fact or facts they follow, such abstraction does not involve a breach of critical principles germane to this discipline.

In ordinary living and in the particular sciences alike abstraction is to be understood as a preparation of possibilities for concrescence, or possible concrescences. So long as the concretely actual is not denied by being surreptitiously displaced by abstractions, and so long as a sharp line of distinction can be drawn between the concretely actual, or fact and sub-fact (the later in context), on the one hand, and what is merely hypothetical, or theory, on the other, such theorizing on the basis of abstractions need not be misleading. This is although it goes beyond the strictures of critical principles appropriate to first philosophy in the execution of its role in the exposition of the concretely actual.

It will be obvious in the light of the foregoing that the belief, common among philosophers today, that there are no theory-free facts is from an actual perspective untenable. The notion that no fact can have been conditioned by a theory is equally untenable. But once a fact has become such, or is such in its becoming, whether its becoming was conditioned by a theory or not, it is theory-free.

This statement is justified by the consideration that in the process of concrescence of an actual occasion, which process is itself *the actual,* something occurs: what was potential, also sometimes what

---

[9] See Essay III; and SC, II, chap. VIII (pp. 309-48).

was potential that takes the form of theory, is rendered actual.

16. The Continuity of Consciousness and World

If the self-evidence of occasions appears to require that concrete actuality be understood to be episodic and climactic in character, it may be felt necessary to explain the continuity of consciousness and world, neither of which appears to pass momentarily into and out of existence. The reply to this need is surprisingly simple: by hypothetical thinking preparing new possibilities for concretion and possible concretion. To state the matter in more broadly neutral metaphysical terms, the discrimination between internal and external relations, generically considered, appears also to be one of the discriminations constitutive of every concretely actual occasion. That each is an accent within an identity inclusive of both has the import that the discriminated aspects are mediated within every occasion. Otherwise stated, *every occasion is an internalization of external relations and in this sense a many becoming a one.*[9a] Stated in this theoretical manner, what is here involved seems very close to Whitehead's formula-

---

[9a] This is of course no more than a likely story. How, indeed, could it possibly be more, having been told from a hypothetical perspective? From an actual perspective, concrete actuality is grasped *a priori* and it would amount to a confusion of categories if, having said this, we were to propose within the same account to shift over to hypothetico-deductive reasoning and propose to speak of something being yet prior to, and a cause of, this. From this it is clear that the most we can hope for in relating the two accounts is that, when each is understood in terms of its own genius and integrity, they may be found to be generally compatible. Accounts of these two types can be integrated into a single comprehensive account only by each being developed principally in terms of its own integrity and only secondarily with reference to the other.

In this connection one might at first glance be inclined to applaud Jan Van der Veken's plea for what he calls an "open and humble form of Hegelianism" that is also in line with "some very mild but authoritative interpretation of Hegel", were it not for his somehow seeing fit to construe Whitehead's thought as its fulfillment. This is in "A Plea for an Open, Humble Hegelianism", in George R. Lucas (Ed.), *Hegel and Whitehead...*, p. 109. Especially if one approaches the Hegel-Whitehead relation presupposing a Hegelian absolute inflated with wild pretensions for hypothetical reason, this may suggest a mind-set that is in some way "appropriately" compensatory. Confronted with such an issue as I have just raised, however, it becomes apparent that Van der Veken's proposal, which has the force of leveling Hegel to Whitehead, does not show up well. If such a plea is to be more than a diplomatic platitude, we should need to be shown that such a mild interpretation of Hegel as would be called for would not reduce his attempt to account for absolute knowledge as a completed fact of life to be explained to a kind of hypothetical reason that fell short of its overly adventuresome aim. Van der Veken's discussion leaves us with the impression that he would reduce Hegel's reason to a form inadequate to grasp the concrete actuality (that it has itself formed) to leave us with a hypothesis free-floating above whatever might be, to which one might give or withhold ascent, as in the case of Whitehead's reason. If so, could this be the authentic interpretation, and if it were, would there be any actual standard of truth to which to appeal, or any way of pointing to such a standard, even in principle?

tions, allowance being made for the pre-critical character of his thought, symbolized by the fact that he attempted to exclude the understanding, interpreting subject from his actual occasion, which he nonetheless construed to be a complete fact, on the one hand, and by his failure to perceive the possibility of rendering a concretely specific account of the concretely actual, discrimination by discrimination, omitting none, or, in Hegel's language, rendering an account of thought (which also turned out to be equally an account of actuality) in its own native form, on the other.

But there is more to be said in regard to just how, within technological and theory-oriented cultures, the factual and hypothetical blend and overlap in such a way as even to permit us to lose sight of the fleeting, spasmodic character of self-evident truth, which on the face of it seems to lend itself to being made obvious enough. It would seem clear in any case that if we are to accord first priority to giving an account of self-evidence, which, at least within a temporal perspective, seems to require perishing as its companion piece,[10] we shall be forced to conclude that it is through interests and expectations of both a pre-conscious and a conscious sort in the service of the possible and the hypothetical that we bridge these moments of absolute truth, in which the possible and the hypothetical have spent themselves for the hard coin of concrete actuality.

17. Concluding Reflections

Although there is much more to be said on this head, the foregoing may suffice to suggest a point of view that the present day crisis of philosophical confidence calls for nothing so decisively as for a large dose of serious first philosophy, of a sort that does not apologetically ape the particular sciences, as has so often, and with such tragic consequences (as are today to be seen on every hand), occurred, but which finds and executes its own role with responsible rigor. All in all, nothing would be quite so salutary in its total impact as fifty years of philosophy carried out without much regard to the results of the particular sciences, except for observing what discriminations their practitioners are employing. At the end of such a time, it might be common knowledge that and why Plato, for example, unaided by the developments of modern science, somehow managed to be and to remain so 'strangely' relevant as he is today.

The execution of the role required of first philosophy could con-

---

[10] This is not, of course, to propose that perishing (my own death) can be a part of a phenomenology, which would be absurd. See n. 2 above.

tribute toward the alleviation of the alienation from self and fellowman which characterizes cultures oriented too exclusively toward the natural sciences and technology, an alienation to which the theory of science posing as first philosophy has often contributed. Two features of the approach adumbrated in the foregoing are in this connection especially to be noted.

(1) Concrete actuality is in the nature of the case human and personal. This does not of course prevent us from hypothetically maintaining that there are occasions not comprehended within the occasion which constitutes me and my world and which is now actual. It simply calls attention to the fact that, seeing that this occasion includes within itself all that from its perspective is actual, and seeing that to take up a perspective external to it, e.g., to consider relations between two or more occasions, is to take up a hypothetical perspective, such can only be hypothetically actual.[11]

(2) Discriminations constitutive of life and the life sciences count as substantially in the constitution of an actual occasion (within which there are no accidents) and its sub-facts, as do discriminations constitutive of the "inorganic" sphere and of the physical sciences. Thus the myth that concrete facts are or may be purely physical is exposed for what it is, and all causes set aside which could possibly result in the continuance of the hegemony of discriminations constitutive of the physical sciences, which have tended to dominate western thought since the 17the century.

A parallel statement might be made respecting discriminations constitutive of ethical and political aspects of our existence and of political science and sociology, seeing that such count as essentially in the constitution of contemporary actual occasions as do such as render particular service with respect to physical existence or the realm of life.

If the structure of the self-certainty with which we natively experience concrete facts can be laid bare through the analysis-synthesis of their constitutive discriminations, as I have maintained, what results is a foundation in fact, and in the character of facts, for the particular sciences. By the adoption of the point of view — written into the very character of the philosophical proposition, also as normally spoken forth every day of our lives, although I should hesitate to say that it is ordinary — that self-evidence is an episodic phenomenon of a complex sort climaxing in the coherence of its data, I have intended

---

[11] An 'occasion' that is only hypothetically actual I designate an "event" by virtue of its non-inclusion of an understanding, interpreting subject. See, e.g., p. 145, n. 15.

to establish the manner appropriate to the pursuit of this result, sought from Kant's time to the present, upon fundamentally new, and I believe substantially less problematical, ground. If the particular sciences can be based upon nothing but fact, as I suspect we must finally discover to be the case, it seems high time for serious philosophers to construe facts in a way that is commensurate with the role they play and with the trust that we can, do, and indeed must of necessity invest in them, i.e., as absolute, each within its temporal setting. This construal is the most central aspect of the strategy that I have pursued.

USAGES

Doubled Square Brackets: Comments or adaptations introduced into quoted material by the author, except for the case of changing a lower case letter to a higher case letter or vice versa, are placed within doubled square brackets. Where a lower case letter is changed to a higher case letter or vice versa, single square brackets suffice.

Scope Indicators: A page reference may follow a phrase, a sentence, or a group of sentences (the latter usually constituting a paragraph) being quoted or paraphrased. Where the reference pertains only to the phrase or sentence it immediately follows, this is indicated by the placement of the normal punctuation mark — usually a comma or a period — following the parenthesis.

> Whitehead's simple declaration, "Objectification is abstraction" (p. 67), reflects his philosophy of science more adequately than it does his metaphysical orientation. [Not: "...abstraction," (p. 67)]
>
> Hegel writes: "What philosophy begins with must be either mediated or immediate, and it is easy to show that it can neither be the one nor the other; thus either way of beginning is refuted" (p. 67). [Not: "...refuted." p. 67)]

Where the page reference serves to document more than one sentence, it stands free of punctuation. In this case the paragraphing or some other stylistic device serves to co-determine the scope.

INDEX OF TERMS

A few references are to contexts that exhibit something of the meaning of a term rather than to its explicit use or mention. The concern has been more to indicate significant usages and approximate analogues than to be exhaustive. Hyphenated correlatives refer to discriminations construed in a Hegelian manner, and these may be thought of as embodying or exemplifying Whiteheadian contrasts, as well. Where plausible, simple terms are listed under such correlatives. If a term is not located at once, the reader is advised to seek it out under an assumed correlative. No references are made to the Preface.

Except on occasion for purposes of indicating a definition, a relevant discrimination, or one or more illustrative usages, the following terms have not been listed because their meanings are omnipresent, either explicitly or implicitly, in some cases in more than one usage, on almost every page: actual event, actual entity, actual occasion, *a priori*, *a posteriori*, Begriff, concreteness, the concrete, concrete actuality, concrescence, correlative synthesis, mediation, negation, method, polarity, post-Kantian, process, phenomenology, reason (*Vernunft*), self-consciousness, speculation (except for a distinction), self-evidence, and *spekulativer Satz*.

(the) Absolute, absolute: 3, 11, 15, 29, 33f, 50, 58f, 89, 101f, 120, 124, 168, 172, 224, 265, 281f, 285, 290, 297, 302, 309, 312.
abductive inference (Peirce): 106f, 109; concrete universality and abduction, 109-13.
abstraction: 17, 28, 43, 49, 86, 89f, 112f, 159f, 166, 258, 323; method of, 159f.
actual history (history as actual within the present): 3, 15, 44, 194, 247f, 250, 272f, 281, 291, 299, 307, 322f; See also "nature-history" and "nature-spiritual self-consciousness".
actual perspective: see "perspective".
alienation (estrangement): 274, 326.
analytic-synthetic (analysis-resynthesis): 2f, 10, 16ff, 60, 62, 67ff, 80, 90, 105f, 185ff, 221f, 232, 234, 248, 263, 267, 289, 296f, 307, 311f, 311-14, 318f, 323, 326.
art: 41, 69, 90, 96, 215, 238-41, 253-59, 263, 318.
being-becoming: 32, 57f, 172, 182, 228, 231, 233, 246, 269, 270, 283, 307; being-in-act (Thomas): 260, 270; becoming: 18, 131. See also "being-nothing", "being-thought", and "ontology".
being-nothing: 118f. See also "ontology", "being-becoming", and "being-thought".
being-thought: 304. See also "being-becoming", "being-nothing", and "ontology".
biological: 65, 123f, 131.
causal past: 131, 179, 180f, 269, 292, 299.
causal efficacy: 51, 53, 54, 55, 56, 156.
certainty (*Selbstgewißheit*): see "pre-

suppositionlessness", "theory-concrete fact", and "perspectives, actual".
change: see "permanence-change".
coherence (exemplary): 1, 16, 27, 43, 56, 73, 127, 310.
concept, concentual (df.): 61-64, 251.
concrete actuality, grasped as such (df.): 7, 290.
concretely universal, concrete universality: 4, 7, 8, 9, 11, 29, 32, 38f, 41, 109-13, 120, 131, 151, 173ff, 195f, 206, 209f, 228, 236, 237, 245, 257, 267, 278ff, 284, 297, 305f, 309f, 315f.
consciousness (Whitehead's df.): 56, 78, 91, 137, 282.
contingency: 140, 181f.
contrast: 2, 24f, 28-33, 35, 42, 45, 50, 352, 54f, 60, 65, 79, 86f, 94, 191f, 287, 310-13; affirmation-negation: 191; complex: 28, 29, 191; concrete: 54; contrast and discrimination: 29, 30, 87, 135f; generic: 29, 36, 38f, 52-54, 58, 295: multiple: 29. 51. 87; typology of generic contrasts: 39f, 47f.
correlativity: 142f.
correspondence: 16, 127.
corrigibility: 31f, 33.
creation, creativity: 15, 149, 155, 160, 165f, 169f, 176, 220, 267f, 270, 273, 289, 308; creative event: 167; creative novelty: 308; creative interchange: 155, 158, 159, 167ff. See also: "language, concrete", inc. "facts that speak for themselves".
creation out of nothing: 41, 219, 233, 238.
creation speaking for itself. See "language, concrete".
critical principles: 25, 35, 50, 59, 65, 101f, 141.
death: see "perishing".
descriptive generalization. See "ultimate generalization (metaphysical generalization)".
dialectic: 304f; dialectical circle, 13f. See also "dialectical and conventional logic", and "proposition, speculative".
dialectical logic and conventional logic: 26, 96f.
discriminations: 1f, 9, 15f, 19, 46f, 50, 52, 59, 76f, 87, 102, 105, 111, 126, 174f, 183-87, 192, 233f, 244f, 247, 250, 257, 259, 260, 267, 269, 278f, 282-86, 299f, 307, 310f, 314-23; complex: 184 (§24); concrete: 67f, 186f, 233f, 305, 319, 322; generic: 67f, 186f, 307, 316-19, 322.
duration: 18.
dynamic: see "energy", etc.
electro-magnegic event: 57, 65, 171, 190, 310.
emergence (Popper): 151, 150f.
emphasis: 184-87, 191, 269.
empiricism: 198f, 213.
energy (dynamic, power, appetition, potency): 11, 46, 90, 178, 186f, 192, 205, 212, 214f, 223, 229, 248, 253, 265f, 269, 273. See also "causal efficacy", "feeling", and "lure for feeling".
epoch: 10f, 40, 67, 146, 249, 267, 281, 318.
error: 28, 31, 33, 43, 54, 105, 112f, 177, 254.
eternal objects: 29, 38f, 42f, 59f, 88.
eternal truths: 322.
evaluation: 128, 130.
event (author's usage): 326f.
evolution: 123; evolutionary stages (Popper): 125, 128.
fact. See "theory-concrete fact".
faith: 266, 268, 269, 270.
(the) fall: 255.
feeling (*Gefühl*): 53, 61, 69, 73, 85f, 116, 214f.
firstness, secondness, and thirdness

Index of Terms

(Peirce): 133, 116ff.
first philosophy – second philosophy: 15ff, 19ff, 40ff, 61.
form-content: 307; form, 24, 82, 92, 269, 273; subjective form: 84ff, 88f. See also "form-matter" and "subjective form".
form-matter: 59; form: 82; materialized thinking: 74. See also "form-content" and "subjective form".
freedom-determinism; freedom: 11f, 19, 43, 102, 262f, 280.
God-world: 29; God: 260-76; the God-man (the Son): 271; (the) God-complex: 57, 59, 125.
Hamlet: 38, 104, 107, 110.
Heilsgeschichte: 234, 271f.
here-now: 54.
historical consciousness: 94, 178f.
history as actual within the present: see, "actual history".
(the) Hohensalzburg: 145.
Holy Spirit: 29, 271, 274.
"home": 230.
horizon, perceptual, conceptual, and intentional: 11.
horizon of expectations (Popper): 130f; the author: 130, 136f.
hybrid proposition (Whitehead): 19.
hybris: 138, 220.
hypothetical-deductive method (or reasoning): 63, 80, 204, 210, 213, 217, 267, 258, 298, 324.
hypothetical structure of expectations. See "possibility" and "potential order".
ideal-real: 262.
identity-difference (diversity, discrimination), identity: 8, 31, 84, 187, 193, 198, 210, 216-19, 221f, 235, 238, 242, 302, 305, 310-13, 315; law of difference (identity and non-contradiction): 25ff.
image (*Bild*): 203, 204f, 209-11, 220f.
I-me: 137.

immediate, immediacy: 42.
immortality: 59; subjective: 59; objective: 13, 33; subjectively immortal aim: 33; subjective-objective: 33, 59.
imagination: 36, 132, 248, 249, 253f, 255, 315.
inborn (or organismic) knowledge (Popper): 130, 132, 313.
individual-social class, individual: 1f, 71f.
induction: 149.
inheritance: 3, 36, 55, 131, 135, 177, 179, 181, 185, 195, 242, 256, 287, 295.
in itself, for itself, in and for itself: 16.
intelligible aim: 275.
internal (actual) perspective. See "perspective".
introspection: 231ff, 251.
intersubjectivity: 195.
I-Thou: 180, 195.
judgment: 83ff; intuitive: 83ff, 88, 275.
knowledge: 4, 16, 84, 123-53, 155, 166, 176; as warranted belief: 254; realistic theory of: 123-53. See also "language, concrete".
language, concrete (literal, inc. "facts that speak for themselves"): 16, 17, 19, 33-37, 38, 54f, 134, 166, 177f, 180ff, 196, 209, 212, 236ff, 244f, 257, 258, 268 293f, 308, 319, 321f; "creation speaking for itself": 17, 40, 43, 60, 166, 176, 178ff, 197f; abstract (common, ordinary, habitual, hypothetical): 74, 96, 111, 137, 166, 193, 198f, 206, 212f, 230f, 236, 238, 249, 257, 260, 269f, 294, 305, 318f, 322; metaphorical: 190, 196ff, 201-76, 235f, 273; perfect: 138, 193, 195; authentic: 293, 308, 322; pretational: 111, 236, 248f, 270; tensive (Wheelwright): 234, 242, 255ff;

steno (Wheelwright): 255ff.
law of nature: 147f, 159, 179f.
levels of concretion. See "seriality".
logic: 26f, 73ff, 77.
lordship-bondage: 40, 287f, 307, 317.
lure for feeling: 19, 25, 51, 137, 248.
macroscopic occasions. See "microscopic occasion – macroscopic occasion".
mediation (df.): 18, 31, 77-80, 90, 95f, 118f, 128, 161f, 168, 192f, 199, 232f, 248, 250, 258, 273, 282-85, 310f, 313, 316f; God as mediator: 265.
memory: see "recollection".
mental pathology: 34, 54, 186.
metaphor: see "language, metaphorical".
microcosmic occasion–macroscopic occasion: 148.
mind-body interactionism: 149f.
mutation: 148.
mytho-poetic consciousness (Verene/Casirer): 14, 205-15, 224.
natural science: 302.
nature-history (reason): 183, 185, 287, 291, 306, 312, 313; nature: 172f, 169, 303, 317; history: 321f. See also "nature – historical self-consciousness".
nature – spiritual self-consciousness, nature: 72f, 303. See also "nature-history" and "particularity-plurity".
negativity, negation, negate: 46. See also "affirmation-negation".
novelty: 69.
object: see "subject-object".
objectification: 285.
one-many: 60, 324, many: 140.
ontology, ontological: 6, 519, 228, 259, 264f, 298; ontological principle: 274f. See also "being-becoming".
organism, organiscism: 25, 71f, 230; organic understanding (Popper): 133f.
part-whole: 71.
past-future: 299f.
perceptual-conceptual-intentional experience: 81, 186f, 191.
perception: 72, 109f, 148, 186f, 198; perceptual judgments (Peirce): 110.
perfect dictionary: 74.
perfection: 264ff, 269, 270.
perishing: 2, 3, 12ff, 17, 27, 35, 39f, 43, 48, 50, 59, 67, 103, 111, 144ff, 166, 171, 173f, 184f, 187, 190, 193, 246, 268f, 270, 271, 284f, 293, 304, 306, 310, 311, 325.
permanence – change; change: 14f, 144f, 172-74, 181f, 293, 304.
person: 195.
personal society: 194f.
perspective, actual (internal): 2f, 11, 56, 80f, 140f, 148, 150, 198, 232f, 234, 238, 257f, 290, 299f, 303f, 320ff; hypothetical (theoretical, external): 2f, 5, 16, 42, 61, 139ff, 146f, 148, 180-83, 230, 234, 235, 245ff, 258, 290, 299f, 304, 320ff.
philosophy of science (Whitehead): 72.
physical feeling – conceptual feeling: 25, 29, 53, 59, 61f.
(the) poet: 89f, 243-53, 254. See also "mytho-poetic consciousness".
polarity: 45f, 59, 60. See also "contrast" and "discrimination".
possibility (potentiality): 181, 246, 259, 271. See also "eternal objects" and "discriminations, genetic".
potential order (real possibility): 26.
pragmatism: 19, 37f, 103f, 115-22; critique of: 104-7, 254; pragmatic theory of truth: 16.
prehension: 24, 28, 53, 55, 59, 73, 82ff, 86, 88; positive: 83, 95, 136; negative: 19, 59, 84, 86, 135; mental (conceptual): 82; cognitive: 82f; prehending-*com*prehending: 86, 135,

136.
presentational immediacy (Whitehead): 54f, 56.
presuppositionless, presuppositionless philosophy: 2, 9, 47, 112, 120, 311.
presupposition, presupposed: 18f, 110, 179, 195.
privation of being: 273.
process, processual (sample usages): 25f, 43, 56, 64, 75f, 146, 192ff, 246, 286-94.
process phenomenology: 189-99.
proposition (exemplary): 30-33, 78f, 92, 105f; the speculative... (introduced: 32, 75ff, 78, 91; conformal: 31; conventional (ordinary, habitual, hypothetical): 52, 91f (see also "speculative philosophy, two types" and "language, concrete"); generic: 31,; hybrid: 31f, 51, 52, 87; philosophical: 52; propositions and judgments: 135, 174.
quality-quantity: 163, 307, 313, 321.
real potentiality: 292.
recollection: 13, 44, 112, 178ff, 202f, 242, 267, 270, 299, 316.
reductionism: 55, 65, 98, 150ff.
reflection: 35f; secondary: 41, 42.
relations: 4f, 28, 34, 38, 86, 92, 109, 111, 118, 121, 139f, 235, 245ff, 250ff, 311f, 324; internal: 38, 42, 92, 109, 121, 139f, 196, 233f, 235, 245ff, 251, 290, 294, 311f, 324; external: 38, 86, 92, 121, 139f, 196, 230, 235, 245ff, 251, 311, 324; external relations being rendered internal: 60f, 139f, 324f.
revelation: 269f, 271.
revolution: 280.
rhythm, unifying rhythm: 72, 74, 75, 257.
retrospective-prospective: 246f.
scholastic realism: 106.
second philosophy: 20f, 40, 61, 143f.

self-certainty: see "presuppositionlessness".
semiotic: 103, 111f, 120f.
sense impression, sense perception, sensed qualities: 253.
seriality, serial order: 10, 29, 80, 140, 184ff, 206-10.
(the) settlement effect: 132, 136, 147f, 179f, 186f.
shadow(s): 2, 42, 61, 144, 166, 212, 223, 242, 257, 275, 321.
society: 39f, 147f.
solipsism: 231, 322.
space-time: 8, 25, 53f, 183, 185, 192, 245, 266f, 267, 294, 295, 302, 305, 312, 313, 319, 321, 322.
spacious present: 305.
species universals: 39f, 48, 196, 284.
speculative philosophy, two types of: 19fff, 73f, 143f, 220, 263, 297-300, 323; Whitehead's spec. phil.: 72ff, 81,-85, 92-99, 30-33; Hegel's spec. phil.: 74-80, 312f, 32.
stream of consciousness: 14, 304.
(the) structure of expectations: 130, 248.
subjective aim: 141, 191f, 195.
subjective form: 82, 86f. See also "form-content" and "form-matter".
subject-predicate (language, proposition, judgment): 4, 25, 31-33, 75, 83, 192f, 231, 263, 303; subject: 31; logical subject: 29f; predicate: 31; logical predicate: 32f.
subjective pole – physical pole: 25 53.
subject-object: 54, 59, 76, 83f, 87, 89, 91, 105, 124, 141f, 254, 257f, 269, 270.
subject-superject: 50; superject: 50, 57, 58.
sublation (*Aufhebung*): 115, 118f, 124, 153, 165, 238, 306.
substance-attribute: 7, 75, 85.
subject-substance (or world present

for the subject): 65, 137, 141f, 162, 185, 192, 195, 231, 235, 258f, 273, 279f, 287, 302, 307, 309, 311, 313, 324f.
symbol (servant[s]) of the occasion): 177f.
symbolic reference: 54f. See "language, metaphoric" and "language, symbolic".
teleology: 267.
temporality: see "time-temporality".
theory – concrete fact: 59, 61, 104f, 126, 129-38, 142-47, 166f, 297f, 323f; theory, inc. the theory of science (*Wissenschaftstheorie*): 19f, 28, 36, 57, 59, 79f, 128f, 138f, 142ff, 299f, 313ff; complete fact: 18, 23f, 27, 49, 50, 59f, 120, 137, 167, 323f; theory-free fact: 43, 56, 105, 128, 142f, 194, 269, 294, 299f, 323.
theory-free facts: see "theory – concrete fact".
theoretical reason – practical reason: 158, 290f; theoretical reason: 297f.
theory of science (*Wissenschaftstheorie*): 2, 19, 40, 55, 64, 74, 128f, 137, 138ff, 147, 298f. See also "speculative philosophy, two types of".
this – not this: 307, 313.
throb of creation: 124, 310.
time-temporality, time: 270, 285, 291, 295f, 300f: temporality: 135, 238f, 270, 274, 285, 291, 300f, 325, 327; temporal history: 272f.
transcendental, transcendental deduction: 67f, 155ff.
transition: 53.
transport phenomena: 194.
truth: 1-3, 7, 15f, 43, 104, 142f, 161, 191, 196, 254, 285; 309-27; the truth (that) is the whole: 39, 81, 126, 161, 164ff, 168, 177, 191, 209, 248, 267, 268, 285, 301ff, 309, 310, 315f; truth as regulative idea (Popper): 127, 143; actuality-truth crests; 146.
ultimate (or metaphysical) generalization(s): 320, 321.
understanding (*Verstand*): 5, 38, 24, 203, 267f, 312.
unity-plurality: 250f.
universal, abstract: 65, 113, 305f, 319-21; typology of abstract universals: 9f, 39f, 47f, 284, 297. See also "concretely universal".
vacuous actuality: 64.
values of nature: 73.
verisimilitude (Popper): 134, 136.

INDEX OF NAMES

Achilles: 107
Allen, George: 45, 53
Anzenbacher, Arno: 260
Apel, K.-O.: 104
Aristotle: 149f, 155, 237
Ashmore, Jerome: 85f
Baillie, J. B.: 216
Barfield, Owen: 243-53, 255
Barth, Karl: 276
Beardsley, Monroe: 228
Bennett, John B.: 81
Berkeley, George: 82
Bergson, Henri: 37
Black, Max: 228f
Blanchette, Oliva: 180
Broyer, John: 164
Buber, Martin: 16, 36
Caesar, Julius: 81
Carnell, Edward John: 163
Carr, H. Wildon: *xxviii*
Cassirer, Ernst: 201, 205f, 207, 213, 215f
Christensen, Renate: *xxx*, 17, 60
Christian, William A.: 28, 82
Cobb, John: 90
Coleridge, Samuel Taylor: 248, 253ff
Carlyle, Thomas: 273
Davidson, Donald: 197, 227f
Descartes, René: 83, 150, 257, 286
Desmond, William: 238-41
Düsing, Klaus, 62, 63
Eccles, John C.: 123
Einstein, Albert: 301
Emmet, Dorothy: 261ff, 267ff
Engels, Frederich: 302
Felt, James: 35
Feuerbach, Ludwig: 301, 306
Findlay, John: 201
Ford, Lewis: 45, 53, 58
Freud, Sigmund: 95f
Gadamer, Hans-Georg: *xxv*
Galileo, Galilei: 159
Gentile, G.: *xxviif*
Gilson, Etienne: 261
Goethe, Johann Wolfgang: 272f

Goodman, Nelson: 228
Grassi, Ernesto: 201, 208, 209
Hamlet: 104
Harris, Errol E.: *xvff*, 199
Hartshorne, Charles: 89, 95ff, 97
Hausman, Carl R.: 197f
Heidegger, Martin: *xxv, xxix*, 90, 288
Heilbrunn, Gunther: 6, 76, 162
Heintel, Erich: 45, 60
Henle, Paul: 228
Heraclitus: 233
Hobbes, Thomas: 253
Holt, D. Lynn: 230
Horn, Joachim Christian: 95
Hummel, Gert: 304
Husserl, Edmund: *xxvi, xxviii*, 81, 159
Kant, Immanuel: *xx*, 79, 104, 156, 157f, 248, 253, 255, 290f, 325
Kaulbach, Friedrich: 152
Kessler, Gary: 158f, 167, 169
King, Martin Luther, Jr.: 65
Kline, Geroge L.: 45, 61f, 247
König, Josef: 268
Kroner, Richard: 271
Kuczyński, Janusz: 301, 308
Kuntz, Paul: 14, 257
Lango, John: 82
Lauer, Quentin: 76, 79
Lawson, Robert M.: 309
Leclerc, Ivor: 23f
Leddy, Thomas: 197
Leibniz, Gottfried W. F.: 183
Lobo, Jorge Luis: 52, 58
Löwith, Karl: 271
Lucas, George R.: *xv*, 4, 61, 62, 206, 247, 324
Marx, Karl: *xxii*, 277f, 280f, 290, 297, 301f, 306
Maurer, Reinhart Klemens: 240
McKeon, Richard: 125
Mill, John Stewart: 169
Miller, A. V.: 207
Mittelstrass, Jürgen: 150, 183
Nagl-Docekal, Herta: 45
Neville, Robert C.: 4f

Nobo, Jorge Luis: 50, 52f
Orden, C. K.: 231f
Oppenheim, Paul: 150
Peirce, Charles S.: *xi, xxi,* 101-114
Perry, Ralph Barton: 159
Plato: 23, 33, 149f, 155, 253, 325
Popper, Karl: *xi, xxii,* 95, 123-53
Prauss, Gerold: 56f
Putnam, Hilary: 150
Quine, Willard van Orman: 80
Rethy, Sonja: *xxx*
Richards, I. A.: 231f, 236f
Ricoeur, Paul: 237
Riedel, Manfred: 150
Rinaldi, Giacomo: *xiii, xxvii, xxviii,* 41, 227, 245ff, 263
Rorty, Richard: 291
Rosenstreich, Nathan: 291
Shelley, Percy Bysshe: 243f
Simon, Josef: 5f, 152, 162, 282
Smith, John: 289
Sullivan, William S.: 91
Sussman, Henry: 181
Taylor, Charles: *xvf*
Thomas of Aquinas: 260-76
Tarski, A.: 127
Usener, H.: 206
Van der Veken, Jan: 324
Vaught, Carl C.: 221f, 238
Verene, Donald Phillip: 201-25
Wallack, F. Bradford: 92
Wells, Harry Kohlsaat: 25ff, 64, 152
Welten, W. S. J.: 227
Wheelwright, Philip: 229, 243, 253-59
Wieman, Henry Nelson: *xi, xxi,* 155-70
Wiener, Philip P.: 183
Wolf-Gazo, Ernest: 62
Wordsworth, William: 95
Woznicki, Andrew N.: 302